CURRENCY AND EXCHANGE IN ANCIENT POMPEII

BULLETIN OF THE INSTITUTE OF CLASSICAL STUDIES SUPPLEMENT 116

DIRECTOR & GENERAL EDITOR: JOHN NORTH

DIRECTOR OF PUBLICATIONS: RICHARD SIMPSON

CURRENCY AND EXCHANGE IN ANCIENT POMPEII
COINS FROM THE AAPP EXCAVATIONS AT REGIO VI, INSULA 1

RICHARD HOBBS

INSTITUTE OF CLASSICAL STUDIES
SCHOOL OF ADVANCED STUDY
UNIVERSITY OF LONDON

2013

ISBN 978-1-905670-41-3

Designed and computer typeset at the Institute of Classical Studies.

Printed by Short Run Press Limited, Bittern Road, Exeter EX2 7LW.

for E.K. x

TABLE OF CONTENTS

ACKNOWLEDGEMENTS

I first worked with the Anglo-American Project in Pompeii in the summer of 2001, at the invitation of Drs Damian Robinson and Rick Jones, then of Bradford University. I continued returning to the site annually for parts of the excavation and post-excavation seasons to study the assemblage of coins detailed in this book. I would like to thank Rick and Damian for inviting me to collaborate and for their assistance over the years.

During my time in Pompeii, I crossed paths with many individuals who helped facilitate my work, generously shared their knowledge, or bought me bottles of Moretti (and/or all of the above): Barry Hobson, Diana Blumberg, Jaye McKenzie-Clark, David Griffiths, Robyn Veal, Eric Poehler, Amy Flint, Will Wooton, Giacomo Pardini, Albert Ribera, Briece Edwards, 'Bones' Jones, Pat Daniels, Astrid Schoonhoven, Jen Wehby, Arthur and Jennifer Stephens, Gary Forster and Mike Burns, as well as Hazel Woodhams and John Dore, both of whom are tragically no longer with us. Please forgive me if I've forgotten anyone else. I must single out Hilary Cool for all her support and advice, and for organising vast quantities of contextual data which would otherwise have been nigh on impossible to make sensible use of. Michael Anderson, Claire Weiss and Phil Murgatroyd have also been enormously helpful with regard to the site stratigraphy and I specifically thank them for their help with sections of this book that deal with this aspect of the study. I am grateful to Lindsey Smith for helping me organise the coins in the depository and make casts, and Jim Farrant for providing the illustrations of the local types in Chapter 2. In Pompeii and Naples, I would like to thank Dssa. Teresa Giove at the National Archaeological Museum, the staff at the Soprintendenza and particularly Giovanni and Giacomo (and their magic coffee) in the central repository.

I would like to single out two individuals who have been particularly influential on this work. Firstly, Sas Hemmi, without whom none of this would have been possible: Sas cleaned and conserved the coins from the AAPP excavations with great skill, under far-from ideal conditions, and I'm extremely grateful to her for turning grubby corroded pieces of metal into objects of meaning. Secondly Clive Stannard, who's given me a huge amount of help and advice since I first began to study this material – I must also thank Clive for suggesting I make casts and then showing me how.

I am indebted to Michael Crawford for his careful reading of various drafts of this book, his many suggestions for improvement (although all errors remain my own), and for checking my identifications of the Roman Republican material. Andrew Burnett, Amelia Dowler, Richard Abdy and Sam Moorhead in the BM helped me identify difficult material. Thanks to Jonathan Williams for encouraging me to publish with the ICS, to my colleague Ralph Jackson for reading and commenting on the text, and my editor Richard Simpson for his fantastic work knocking everything into shape.

Finally, the British Museum has offered unwavering support for my involvement in the project, allowing me study leave and providing funds for my seasons of fieldwork. I am grateful to the British Museum Research board for funding a trip to Naples and Pompeii in March 2009, and the Martin Price Memorial Fund, administered by the Royal Numismatic Society, for their generous support for a period of study in Naples and at the British School in Rome in March 2007.

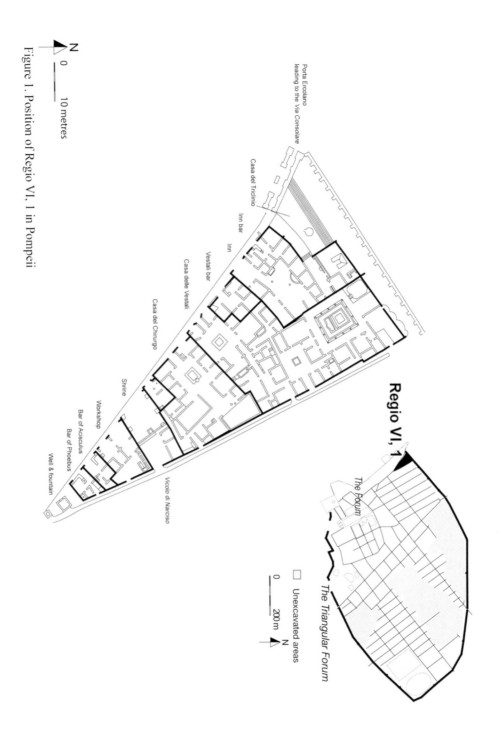

Figure 1. Position of Regio VI, 1 in Pompeii

N
0 — 10 metres

Porta Ercolano
leading to the Via Consolare

Casa del Triclinio

Inn bar

Inn

Vestali bar

Casa delle Vestali

Casa del Chirurgo

Shrine

Workshop

Bar of Acisculus

Bar of Phoebus

Vicolo di Narciso

Well & fountain

Regio VI, 1

The Forum

The Triangular Forum

Unexcavated areas

0 — 200 m

N

1 INTRODUCTION

This monograph catalogues and contextualises an assemblage of coins excavated at Pompeii, one of the most celebrated archaeological sites in the ancient world. Before the town was destroyed by the eruption of Vesuvius, in AD 79, probably during late summer,[1] the town had enjoyed a long and prosperous history as a Mediterranean port sited, as it was, at the mouth of the river Sarno in the Bay of Naples, and therefore strategically placed to exploit both inland riverine and pan-Mediterranean trade. The first evidence of nucleated settlement, which centres principally on the south-west of the town, dates back to at least the sixth century BC, although a few finds of earlier date allude to more ancient origins.[2] Of the public buildings still standing today however, only a few were built much before the third century BC, and it is this period which also provides the first solid evidence for the use of coin.

The Anglo-American Project in Pompeii (AAPP) was established in 1994 with the aim of excavating an entire block, Regio VI, Insula 1, a triangular-shaped plot in the extreme north-west of the town beside the Porta Ercolano, flanked by two converging streets, the Via Consolare and the Vicolo di Narciso (Figure 1). The excavations were completed in 2006, by which stage all the areas of the insula where it was possible to dig the underlying archaeological strata had been taken back to the natural ground surface[3].

---

[1] The generally accepted date of the eruption is 24th August AD 79, a date given by Pliny the Younger (*Letters*, 6.16). More recently it has been argued that the eruption occurred at a later date, possibly in September or even October. Cooley (2009) suggested that the eruption must have occurred after 8th September AD 79, because a *denarius* of Titus, found in the Casa del Bracciale d'Oro (VI, 17, 42) (see Giove (2003), 420) appeared to record his fifteenth Imperial triumph ('IMP XV'), known to have occurred on the 7th or 8th September. This is certainly incorrect, as recent examination of images of the coin by staff at the British Museum show that the crucial part of the inscription in fact reads 'IMP XIIII', meaning that the coin was struck *circa* July AD 79 (Richard Abdy pers. comm.). Others have argued that the high number of autumnal fruits also favours a later date: Borgognino and Stefani (2001-02), or even that a perceived paucity of coins abandoned *in situ* fits with a later date too: '… in the seasonal chronology of the various crops, the last three months of the year, if one compares them to the first half of the year, seem to be a slack period as regards payments and revenue': Andreau (2008), 217.

[2] *E.g.* Geertman (2007), Beard (2008), 26-37, with references. A discussion of the stratigraphic evidence for Archaic Pompeii is provided by Coarelli and Pesando (2011). See also Guzzo (2011, same volume).

[3] The insula was originally discovered in 1769, and the overlying volcanic debris was cleared over the course of the next few decades. During the eighteenth century most of the decorative elements were removed to what subsequently became the Museo Archeologico Nazionale di Napoli (hereafter Naples Museum). In 1943 parts of the block were badly damaged by an Allied bomb. Amedeo

Figure 2. Regio VI, 1 from the south. The Porta Ercolano is just visible top left, Vesuvius in the background.

From a numismatic perspective, the excavation strategy, one of detailed contextual recording, provided a unique opportunity to examine the currency in use in one specific part of the town, and a sizeable assemblage of 1,512 coins had been collected by the time the excavations were complete.[4] This represents one of the largest assemblages of coins from Pompeii recovered to date, and in archaeological terms is of exceptional value to understanding the everyday coinage of the ancient town.

Insula 1 in Regio VI at Pompeii was excavated between 1995 and 2006[5]. An open-area excavation strategy was adopted and conducted using hand-trowelling and sieving of all contexts using a fine mesh.[6] Most fills and occupation deposits were also floated to isolate environmental evidence. This strategy led to an extremely high retention of recoverable

Maiuri was the first archaeologist to excavate below the AD 79 levels in Regio VI, 1, principally to try to establish a date for the construction of the Casa del Chirurgo which Maiuri believed – erroneously – to be one of the earliest in the town: Maiuri (1930).

[4] For interim reports regarding the numismatic assemblage see Hobbs (2003; 2005; 2011; forthcoming).

[5] The project was directed by Drs Rick Jones and Damian Robinson, then of Bradford University, by field directors Briece Edwards and Michael Anderson, and involved trainee archaeology students and specialists from Europe, the USA and Australia.

[6] The standard size used was 1 cm.

artefacts, including the coins catalogued here. Crucially, almost every coin can be assigned to a specific archaeological context within the block, with the exception of only four unstratified coins.

In practical terms, the assemblage presents many problems for the numismatist. Most of the coins are in poor condition, the result of being buried in acidic volcanic soils (and sometimes additional corrosive elements such as the high levels of ammonia present in cess-pits which cause coin surfaces to bubble and crack). The fabrics used to make the coins often appear to have been poor, meaning that many coins have visibly deteriorated after recovery.[7] For these reasons, after cleaning and conservation work was completed a plaster cast was taken of each coin unless it was too badly corroded for this to be practical. Casting is not generally used in the field, but proved to be an extremely effective means to record the assemblage for future study and preservation.[8]

Coins were recovered from all the properties within the block and the two streets and walkways which run down either side (the main street, the Via Consolare, which runs north-westwards to the Porta Ercolano, and the narrower backstreet, the Vicolo di Narciso). A brief summary of the main features of the block is provided here.[9]

1.2. Regio VI, Insula 1: background (Figures 1 and 2)

The occupation of this area of the town can be traced to the late fourth century BC,[10] although the nature of this occupation – which probably contained many areas of open land – is difficult to characterise as it was largely obliterated by later development. By the second century BC the residential and commercial plots were laid out and the road network long established.[11] The first century BC onwards was the most intensive period of construction with space at a premium, which eventually led to the addition of upper floors to existing buildings during the first century AD.[12] The visible remains today largely represent the appearance of the insula at the time of the eruption in AD 79. At the north end of the block beside the town wall and to the south-east of the Porta Ercolano (Herculaneum gate) is an 'L' shaped inn, which was its primary function in the town's latest phase; in previous periods, it produced evidence for metal working and perhaps fish processing. To the south of this is the largest property in the block, also 'L' shaped, the Casa delle Vestali (House of the

---

[7] The coins are retained in the central archaeological repository beside the Forum at Pompeii. The storeroom is not a controlled environment and humidity levels fluctuate considerably over the course of the year.

[8] It is the intention that the casts will be housed in the longer term in the department of Coins and Medals at the British Museum.

[9] For more details see Jones (2008), with references.

[10] Jones and Robinson (2004), 109; Jones and Robinson (2007), 389-90.

[11] Jones and Robinson (2004), 112. The Via Consolare was established during the Archaic period at a similar time to the construction of the town wall and the Porta Ercolano; the Vicolo di Narciso in the fourth century BC: Robinson (pers. comm.).

[12] Jones and Robinson (2005), 706.

Vestal Virgins).[13] In its latest manifestation it was a double atrium property with a peristyle at the back and a large number of rooms and service areas, and had an upper floor. Incorporated into the corner of the house on the Via Consolare is a street side bar, which is likely to have been managed or leased by the owner of the Casa delle Vestali, given that it is to all intents and purposes part of the same house.[14]

Immediately to the south of the Casa delle Vestali is the only other identifiably private domestic property in the block: the Casa del Chirurgo (House of the Surgeon), with a single atrium.[15] Like the Casa delle Vestali this property also incorporated a retail unit in its southernmost corner facing on to the Via Consolare and also had an upstairs apartment. On its northern side it incorporated a possible workshop that produced some industrial residue of glass and metal-working, perhaps small-scale smelting, from the Augustan period to the mid first century AD, after which it was paved over with an *opus signinum* floor.[16] To the south of the Casa del Chirurgo is a roadside shrine, which, prior to about the mid first century AD, was used for industrial activities and possibly also commercial functions. To the south of the Shrine, as the insula narrows to its apex, there is an area of commercial activity characterised principally by metal working and, like other parts of the block in earlier phases, fish-processing.[17] Further south there are two adjacent bars, the bar of Acisculus and the bar of Phoebus.[18] Finally at the apex of the triangle there is a public well (covered by a small rectangular barrel-vaulted building) and a fountain, originally fed by the aqueduct until the water supply was interrupted by the earthquake of AD 62.

This brief description of Regio VI, 1 illustrates how the block encompassed within its footprint a whole range of social, religious and commercial activities. The Casa delle Vestali was one of the town's grandest private properties and was expanded and modified continuously right up to the time of the eruption; inside you could view exquisite wall paintings in most of its rooms and enjoy an ornamental water feature in the peristyle, fed by a large open air cistern (which served no other purpose than to keep the fountain

[13] The name has no scientific basis. It is derived from the mistaken belief that a wall painting in the house (now in the Naples Museum) depicted the Vestal Virgins, when in fact it shows Venus at her toilet. Guides from about 1820 onwards referred to it as the 'Casa delle Vestali', and the name stuck. See also Eschebach (1993).

[14] For a discussion of the commercial portfolio of the owners of the Casa delle Vestali see Robinson (2005).

[15] This house was named after a number of medical instruments found in the house in 1771: Bliquez (1994), 79-81. Whether the owner was a surgeon or not is never likely to be known; it may be that the owner of the medical instruments had taken refuge in the house, or was a guest when the eruption occurred, and abandoned the tools of his trade.

[16] Robinson (pers. comm.).

[17] This area was known previously and inaccurately as the 'Fabbrica del Sapone' ('the soap factory'), because the vats found on its northern-most wall were thought to have been used to make soap.

[18] For the inscriptions from which these names derive see *CIL* IV, 102 and 103.

operational).[19] The Casa del Chirurgo was much the same on not so lofty a scale, but was, nonetheless likely to have been the residence of a member of the town's successful elite.[20] It is evident that both private households sought to exploit their prime commercial position by giving some of their street-side space over to bars and workshops. The Shrine is an obvious example of the religious activity embedded in every aspect of ancient daily life. There were also a range of commercial activities taking place, not least the vending of foodstuffs and beverages in the bars, with the complementary facility of an inn with facilities for the stabling of pack animals and horses and an outside dining area (the 'Casa del Triclinio'). Demonstrable commercial activities may have included fish processing, glass and metalworking, although it is not certain what sorts of products were being manufactured. Non-coin finds include many kilograms of pottery which include imported amphorae and finewares from all across the Mediterranean, over 3,000 sherds of glass, over 500 objects of worked bone and ivory, almost 1,500 iron objects (not including a couple of thousand nails), about 1,000 objects made of copper-alloy and numerous artefacts of fired clay and worked stone.[21]

The block's location within the town is a clear indication as to why such a range of urban activities was taking place in Regio VI, 1, sited as it was in a prime spot for the receipt of visitors to the town through the Porta Ercolano and the last stopping point for those leaving the town via that gate. The insula even bears the battle scars of the town's long and eventful history: the town wall immediately to the north of the insula is pockmarked with stone ballista-balls from Sulla's attack on the town during his siege of 89 BC, and many stone balls and lead slingshot fired into the town were found during the AAPP excavations.[22] Some of the properties, particularly those closest to the town wall, were substantially damaged in the attack. The AD 62 earthquake also had a major effect beyond interrupting the water supply and probably provided an impetus for a final phase of space re-modelling and re-building, for example the addition of upper floors or modifications to supply and drainage of water.[23]

1.3. 'Live' coinage at Pompeii in AD 79

Over the centuries, from the time of the discovery of Pompeii by the workmen of Charles of Bourbon in 1738, many thousands of coins have been recovered from the town and many thousands more must still lie awaiting recovery.[24] One survey has gathered details

---

[19] Prior to this in the Augustan period to the mid first century AD there were three fountains: Jones and Robinson (2005).

[20] Anderson and Robinson (forthcoming).

[21] Baxter and Cool (2008); Cool (forthcoming).

[22] Jones and Robinson (2007); Burns (forthcoming). The block also bears more recent battle scars from the Second World War (see n. 3).

[23] Jones and Robinson (2005).

[24] Roughly one-third of the town has never been dug and still lies under some metres of volcanic debris, *i.e.* parts of Regio I, Regio III to V and Regio IX.

of 32,721 coins,[25] although the underlying data is not provided in detail, and indeed there is not as yet a comprehensive study of all known coin finds from the AD 79 levels.[26] It is important however to make a distinction between two very different categories of coin found at Pompeii, and other sites in the region also buried under the succession of pyroclastic flows and ash falls which engulfed parts of the Bay of Naples. The sudden eruption of the volcano led much of the population to abandon their businesses and homes and flee the area, and in the process, rapid decisions were made as to what to rescue in terms of personal possessions. Many chose portable valuables, such as jewellery, small items of silver tableware or tools of their trade (for instance medical instruments), and many – of course – chose coins. But there is ample evidence to suggest that the urgency of flight incumbent on the town's residents led many to make the stark choice to abandon their valuables, and in terms of coin, that meant both their savings – their 'stores of wealth', invariably in the form of gold and silver – and their everyday currency, their 'small change', invariably in the form of brass and bronze. The abandoned money provides a snapshot of the currency in use at the time of the eruption itself; I term this type of coin evidence 'live' coinage, for it was still an active part of the town's wealth storage and commercial activity. It would have continued to be used if the eruption had never occurred, until gradually falling out of use as it became obsolete, either withdrawn from circulation (officially or unofficially), to become superseded by later issues (by this stage in Pompeii's history, a tri-metallic Roman Imperial coinage system with a number of denominations).

The most evocative examples of 'live' coinage (which are numerous) are coins found on the failed fugitives, those fleeing individuals overcome by the eruption, or those who chose to stay and found themselves trapped in their properties. At Oplontis for instance, a skeleton of a man was found with two groups of coins on his person.[27] One group consisted of 176 *denarii,* mostly dating to the Roman Republican period, secreted in a wooden box; about half of these came from the period 50 to 1 BC (including 38 legionary *denarii*), and the rest earlier, with a single pre-200 BC coin.[28] This might surprise us, as it clearly suggests that old coins were retained by the AD 79 residents for some time after their date of issue, although an explanation is readily found: these were high purity silver coins with high intrinsic value, so it made economic sense to retain them, unless they were kept for reasons of sentimentality which would seem illogical. Clutched to his chest he also had 81 gold coins; in contrast to the mostly Republican *denarii* in the wooden box these coins could not have been more mint-fresh and up-to-date, for they were all gold

---

[25] Duncan-Jones (2003).

[26] 'As for a comprehensive study of all the coins, we do not seem to be much better off than we were half a century ago': Andreau (2008), 208. Comprehensive summaries of coins from different regions of Pompeii are however being published by the Instituto Italiano di Numismatica: see Cantilena (2008) (for Regio VI), Taliercio Mensitieri (2005) (for Regio X) and Giove (forthcoming) (for Regio I).

[27] Castiglione Morelli (2000; 2003).

[28] 102 coins were of Roman Republican date, and can be broken down as follows: pre-200 BC, 1 (0.6%) 200-151 BC, 5 (3.2%); 150-101 BC, 29 (18.4%); 100-51 BC, 26 (16.5%); 50-1 BC, 81 (51.3%) (including 38 legionary *denarii* of Mark Antony); undated/illegible, 16 (10.1%).

Figure 3. Wall painting from the Praedia di Giulia Felice.

aurei issued by the emperor Vespasian, who had only been dead for a couple of months when Vesuvius erupted, and whose coins have naturally been found at Pompeii in some abundance. Another example of 'live' coinage is a wooden box from the Casa del Menandro, which contained gold and silver jewellery, 118 pieces of silver plate and 46 coins comprising 13 gold *aurei* and 33 *denarii*. Unlike coins found on fleeing bodies however, no attempt seems to have been made to rescue the chest, which was probably being kept in safe storage whilst building works were being conducted at the property.[29]

Yet gold and silver was not the common currency of everyday life, despite the impression given by a wall painting in the Praedia di Giulia Felice (Regio II, 4, 3) which depicts a pile of gold and silver coins as if left lying around for all to see (Fig. 3). They were simply too valuable: the owner would have kept his or her gold and silver coins well protected, under lock and key, or perhaps in a jar secreted in an unobtrusive wall cavity, or even buried a set number of paces from a familiar tree in the surrounding countryside. Yet the same painting also shows a separate pile of copper coins; these, we can imagine, may have really been on open display, or at least were less likely to be kept in a secure location. This juxtaposition neatly illustrates that for everyday, run of the mill 'live' currency – the town's 'small change' – we have to look for different snapshots of AD 79 commercial life. Two examples come from premises on the via dell'Abbondanza, Pompeii's east-west arterial street. The first is the *thermopolium* ('hot food counter') of Asellina which was

---

[29] Painter (2001).

abandoned in something of a hurry, fortunately for us, and we would hope the owner, if it meant he succeeded in making his escape.[30] Included amongst the furniture, pottery lamps and various drinking paraphernalia such as glass cups and bronze storage vessels were what are likely to have been the bars' recent (perhaps daily) takings: 67 coins in total, mostly of Imperial date.[31] On the other side of the street at Regio I, 8, 8 (the bar of Lucius Vetudius Placidus), a much larger group of 1,385 coins were found, most of which were inside one of the large *dolia* set into the bar's counter.[32] Was this large sum the till float, used to provide change during an expected period of feverish activity, or the takings of the bar over the previous month, week, or even day?[33] This question is never likely to be answered, but whatever the reasons behind the amassing of this group, the coins provide an important snapshot of 'live' 'small change' in AD 79. The coins consist of mainly Imperial *asses* with some *dupondii, semisses* and *quadrantes,* some of which had been deliberately halved (Table 1 and see p. 57).

The contrast with the coins found with the Oplontis body could not be greater. The bar's 'till float' consists entirely of copper coins, to facilitate the bar's commercial activities, namely the vending of food and drink, rather than a 'store of wealth' for the owner (although in theory the owner could have converted all or parts of this sum into intrinsically valuable silver *denarii* or gold *aurei* if required). The profile of the coins is also rather different to that of the Oplontis victim: about half the coins are of Vespasian, Titus or Domitian, as one would expect, although it is interesting to note that some Republican copper coins (1.6%) were present in the assemblage, as were two 'foreign' imports. Clearly the thirst for small change meant that coins which we might expect to have fallen out of use a long time ago were still retained – not unlike, for instance, finding Edwardian pennies in a British high-street shop-till prior to decimalisation in 1970, or pennies of George IV still in circulation in the 1940s.[34]

Despite the discovery of this *in situ* 'live' coinage, we know surprisingly little about the practicalities of supply and usage of liquid currency. Pompeii is generally considered not to have struck its own coinage (although as we shall see, it has been argued that it may have struck imitative coins in the late second to early first centuries BC), and we know next to nothing about how foreign coins made it through the town gates, apart from the fact that they did so in abundance: the c. 33,000 coins catalogued in a recent survey have already been mentioned.[35] If the population of the town was somewhere in the region of

---

[30] Stefani and Vitale (2005).

[31] The assemblage consisted of 6 Imperial silver coins, 7 *sestertii*, 6 *dupondii*, 41 *asses*, 3 *quadrantes* and 4 coins of Roman Republican date.

[32] Castiello and Oliviero (1997), Table 1.

[33] Andreau (2008), 214, suggests that the sum is too large to be single day's takings, and that they rather represent 'more than a single day's work'.

[34] Crawford (pers. comm.).

[35] Duncan-Jones (2003).

	asses	semisses	trientes	quadrantes	sextantes	
Ptolemy II						1
Amestratus (Sicily)						1
Republican AE	14	1	5	1	1	22

	sestertii	dupondii	asses	quadrantes		
Augustus	1	1	18	3		23
Tiberius	3	0	185	0		188
Gaius	0	1	3	0		4
Agrippa	0	0	73	0		73
Tiberius or Gaius	0	0	2	0		2
Claudius	12	0	219	0		231
Nero	4	2	4	0		10
Julio-Claudian unc.	0	0	51	0		51
Galba	59	20	26	0		105
Vespasian	156	177	201	0		534
Titus	19	20	31	0		70
Domitian	0	1	48	0		49
Imperial uncertain	1	2	4	0		7
Imperial totals	*255*	*224*	*865*	*3*		*1347*
Illegible						14
					Overall total	*1385*

Table 1. 'Live' currency recovered from the bar of L. Vetudius Placidus (I, 8, 8) (after Castiello and Oliviero 1997).

12,500 around the time of the eruption[36] that would equate to 2.64 coins for every man, woman and child in the town. This may not sound a great deal, but these 33,000 coins are only the tip of the iceberg: many thousands of coins would have disappeared into private collections over the centuries of excavation and many still lie awaiting discovery. Cantilena was able to put together details of 3,329 coins from Regio VI alone.[37] In short the ubiquity of coinage is unequivocal and the economy of Pompeii was clearly heavily monetised by the time the eruption occurred.

1.3.1. Supplementary evidence for the use of 'live' coinage (Figure 4)

For the last few decades of the life of Pompeii, we also know a little more about the economic life of the town and the place of coin within it. In addition to the instances of 'live' coinage discussed above, which demonstrate that coins were important to the town's inhabitants as both 'stores of wealth' and facilitators of commercial transactions, there are also instances of graffiti, written documents, reliefs and wall paintings which illustrate different aspects of commercial life. Some make direct references to coin by giving prices for goods and services, usually in Imperial *asses*. These include the Casa dell'Hedone on the via degli Augustali, which had a bar attached to the front of the house (the bar is just around the corner from the infamous brothel). On the outside of this house the following graffito was discovered:

> Hedone says you can drink here for one *as,* if you give two, you will drink better; if you give four, you will drink Falernian.[38]

Falernian, according to Pliny the Elder, was one of the best local wines.[39] More comprehensive is a long list of products found in the atrium of Regio IX, 7, 24-5, which was connected via a door to a bar with a serving counter. The list records food either sold or bought. Numbers are given but not denominations, but they are probably *asses,* apart from instances when the symbol for *denarius* is used. There are references to 'bread 8', 'wine 1 *denarius*', as well as more unusual items, 'whitebait 2', 'leek 1, for a small plate 1', 'small sausage 1'.[40] The reason this list is not considered to be a price-list is that the items are listed under different days, *e.g.* '7 days before the Ides'. (And in any case if they were charging one silver *denarius* here for wine whilst Hedone was only charging an *as* they would have quickly found themselves short of customers). Nevertheless a clear connection with commercial transactions involving coin is evoked. There are other lists of products in rather incongruous locations: for instance in the Large Palaestra at Regio II, 7,

---

[36] The median point of an estimated population of between 10,000-15,000: Geertman (2007), 16, note 90.

[37] Cantilena (2008), 81, table 3.

[38] *CIL* IV 1679; Cooley and Cooley (2004), H12.

[39] Pliny, *Natural History* XIV, 8.

[40] *CIL* IV 5380; Cooley and Cooley (2004), HI5.

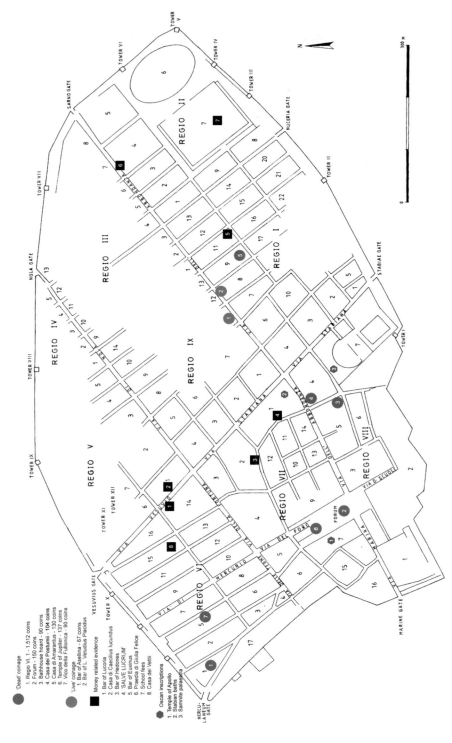

Figure 4. Locations of coin finds and other evidence of commercial activity in Pompeii mentioned in the text.

a list headed 'Pompeii' includes 'p[ound?] of lard 3 *asses*, wine 1 *as*, pork 4 *asses*'.[41] The list is believed to be a note of one individual's expenditure.

Money is also priced as a product in itself in a few instances of usury. Faustilla was one such money-lender and records of her transactions have been found at two different places in Pompeii.[42] At the Taberna di Lucoria (VI, 14, 28), a graffito records the lending of some modest sums and the interest to be paid:

> 8 February. Vettia, 20 *denarii:* interest 12 *asses*. 5 February from Faustilla, 15 *denarii:* interest 8 *asses*.[43]

In the two other instances of Faustilla's money-lending, which both appear on the wall of a *cubiculum* at I, 8, 13, goods were used as a deposit in case of default, *e.g.* '15 July. Earrings deposited with Faustilla. Per two *denarii* she took as interest one copper *as*.'[44] The modest sums are dwarfed by those of the Sulpicii family, which are in an entirely different league (discussed below, p. 14).

Advertisements for property to rent have also been discovered. One painted notice at Regio VI, 6, 1 states: 'To let from 1st July next in the Insula Arriana Polliana, now owned by Gnaeus Alleius Nigidius Maius; shops with upper rooms, quality apartments and houses. Lessees contact Primus, slave of Gnaeus Alleius Nigidius Maius.'[45] Unfortunately no prices are given, but rent was presumably paid periodically in coin.

Sometimes graffiti record payments for services rendered rather than goods. The sale of sex is evidenced in a number of places across the town, including bars: 'Felicla the slave 2 *asses*', 'Acria 4 *asses*, Epafra 10 *asses*, Firma 3 *asses*.'[46] Another example relates to schooling: on one of the columns in the Large Palaestra (Regio II, 7, column 18) a teacher writes: 'Whoever has paid me the fee for teaching, let him have what he seeks from the gods.'[47] It is accompanied by a list of boys who have paid their fees, for instance 'Agathe[m]er[us] 2 *a[sses]*.'[48]

In addition to money-lenders, Pompeii also had its share of bankers, although they did not fulfil all the functions of a bank which we are used to in the modern era but were more akin to middlemen in commercial exchanges and individuals with whom accounts could be held. The most famous banker in Pompeii was Caecilius Iucundus, who lived in a grand house on the via del Vesuvio (V, 1, 26) with a mosaic of a sleeping dog in the

---

[41] *CIL* IV 8561; Cooley and Cooley (2004), H17.

[42] The locations are quite a distance apart, so Faustilla presumably must have operated all across the town, unless there were two individuals of the same name.

[43] *CIL* IV 4528; Cooley and Cooley (2004), H39. Cooley and Cooley use the word 'usury' instead of 'interest' which is what is meant. See also Andreau (1974), 120.

[44] *CIL* IV 8203; Cooley and Cooley (2004), H41. See n. 43.

[45] *CIL* IV 138; Cooley and Cooley (2004), H50.

[46] Beard (2008), 232.

[47] *CIL* IV 8562; Cooley and Cooley (2004), H45.

[48] *CIL* IV 8565; Cooley and Cooley (2004), H46.

entrance passage.[49] 153 wax tablets were found in the property in 1875 and of those which can be deciphered, a large number of business transactions are recorded which date between AD 15[50] and January AD 62, just before the devastating earthquake.[51] How Iucundus made his living is summarised by Andreau: '[Iucundus] was an *argentarius* or *cofactor argentarius*…. At auctions he would pay the sellers the price of the objects sold and would extend credit to the buyers. When he paid the sums due to the sellers, they would give him receipts, which he would keep. The vast majority of the tablets discovered in his house are receipts of this type'.[52] One tablet is exceptional because it tells us exactly what Iucundus himself derived from the transaction:

> [During the consulship of Q. Volusius S]aturninus and [P. Cornelius Scipi]o (*i.e.* AD 56), on the 11 November.
> I, [name missing], slave of Umbricia Antiochis, [have written] that she has received 645 *sesterces* from L. Caecilius [Iucundus], for the auction [which was performed on her behalf], for the objects removed from a property sold earlier. Out of this sum [she has received] 200 *sesterces* [in cash], with valuation costs adding up to 20 *sesterces,* incidental expenses adding up to 13 *sesterces,* and the banker's fee of 51 *sesterces* having been deducted from the price; finally I received today the sum of 360 *sesterces.* Transacted at Pompeii.[53]

The tablets of Iucundus also record the highest sum known from the ancient world from an auction sale, 38,079 *sesterces* in January AD 55.[54] It seems unlikely that this huge sum was *physically* paid, or at least not entirely in coin.[55] Although credit notes, if they existed, have never been found, economic historians believe that large payments were normally documentary transactions.[56] Nevertheless reference to such a sum underlines that coinage was woven into the fabric of Pompeian commercial life in the first

---

[49] Andreau (1974; 1999; 2008).

[50] The earliest is of a relative, probably father or uncle, Lucius Caecilius Felix; Iucundus' own tablets start in AD 27.

[51] One theory has it that Iucundus died in the earthquake, which may explain why a relief (the only one from Pompeii) depicting this catastrophic event was found in his house: Beard (2008), 178. It should be noted that the first tablet can be dated to AD 15, the next to AD 27, the majority between AD 54 and 58 and the last to January AD 62: Jones (2006), 88.

[52] Andreau (1999), 35.

[53] *CIL* IV 3340.23; Cooley and Cooley (2004), H75. Andreau (1974), 326-27, Tablet 23. The figures are slightly out: the amount retained by Iucundus add up to 84 *sesterces* (20+13+51), meaning that the client should have received 561 *sesterces* (645-84), but in fact received 560 *sesterces* (360+200). Presumably Iucundus decided to round down the amount owed to a convenient figure.

[54] *CIL* IV 3340.10; Cooley and Cooley (2004), H73.

[55] Andreau (2008), 218, has affirmed that the verb 'numerare' which is sometimes used in the tablets means 'to pay in cash', *i.e.* with coins, so if this accepted then it appears that some transactions at least were in coin.

[56] Harris (2008b), 176; Andreau (2008), 219.

century AD, as is also clear from another set of tablets found about 600 metres south of the Porta Stabia in 1959.[57] Known as the tablets of Murecine or the Sulpicii archive, these documents concern the business dealings of the Sulpicii, a group of businessmen, all sons of freedmen, from the port at Puteoli (modern Pozzuoli), some 40 kilometres away. Why they were in storage at Pompeii is unclear, but like the Iucundus tablets they too concern various transactions and also end abruptly just before the earthquake of AD 62. Their activities are again summarised by Andreau:

> ... the Sulpicii undertook either to look after the documents belonging to their clients or business contacts, or to keep some of their debt-claims safe in a strongbox; or else they themselves acted as creditors in conjunction with others.[58]

Some tablets concern loans, which usually required material security; for instance one tablet concerns the loan of 10,000 *sestertii* with the guarantee on the loan in the form of 7,000 *modii* of wheat, whilst another required the deposition of 4,000 *modii* of chickpeas, flour and lentils.[59] What is less clear is to what extent the Sulpicii used coins in their transactions; in one instance they borrowed 94,000 *sesterces* from an Imperial slave by name of Phosphorus Elpidianus, but in a similar manner to the huge sums mentioned in the Iucundus tablets it is not clear if all or part of this constituted physical payment, and if it did presumably it would have been in higher denominations than bronze, or at the very least in a mixture of precious and non-precious coin and perhaps even bullion.

Other references to money and commerce are rather more prosaic. A conspicuous desire to *make* money is provided by the mosaic in the entrance to the Domus Sirici at VII, 1, 47: 'SALVE LVCRVM' ('Hail, profit.').[60] A similar sentiment is expressed in another house at Regio VI, 14: 'Profit, joy.'[61] There is also an interesting still life of money in the Praedia di Giulia Felice at Regio II, 4, 3 (Figure 3, discussed above, p. 7). The two heaps of coins and a cloth bag are accompanied by a depiction of a stack of wax diptychs and a stylus, possibly for accounting purposes. Is this a direct reference to the commercial activities of the estate owner, or was the owner someone who controlled, or was involved with, the production or distribution of coinage?

Which brings us finally to a frieze found in the Casa dei Vettii (Regio VI, 15), one of a series which shows Cupids engaged in a diverse range of manufacturing activities, from garland making to perfumery.[62] This particular frieze shows the Cupids working metal. Some of the work involves large objects, which includes, on the far left hand side of the frame for instance, a bronze bowl being worked on by a Cupid. Other pairs of Cupids are engaged in very small-scale work, which includes a pair hammering small pieces of metal

[57] Camodeca (1992); Andreau (1999), 71-79; Jones (2006).

[58] Andreau (1999), 73-74.

[59] Camodeca (1992), 181-84, TPSulp. 51; also discussed in Jones (2006), 92-94.

[60] *CIL* X, 874; Cooley and Cooley (2004), H36b.

[61] *CIL* X, 875; Cooley and Cooley (2004), H37.

[62] For background information on the Casa dei Vettii see: www.stoa.org/projects/ph/house?id=18. For the paintings themselves see Beard (2008), 126, with references.

on anvils; beside them is a table on which there is a double steelyard and a set of weights on a tiered stand. Another Cupid holds a *trutina*, a hand-held balance with two curved plates, and he is paired with a seated Cupid who holds out a hand as if expecting payment after the weighing has been completed. Is it conceivable that the Cupids are engaged in the manufacture and assaying of coins? The problem is that the smallest items in the frieze are impossible to make out. Small dots on a shelf below the steelyards might conceivably be coins, but may also be finger-rings or other small items of jewellery.[63] Nonetheless the possibility that this frieze depicts the production of coins (or at least blanks) or the assaying of coinage has been suggested; for example the image is used on the cover of the guide to the collections of the Medagliere in Naples Museum and captioned 'Amorini intenti a coniare monete e forgiare metalli preziosi' which makes it clear that the authors believe it shows coins being minted, although the scene is not discussed further in the text.[64]

1.4. 'Dead' coinage at pre-eruption Pompeii

These brief glimpses of commercial life and how they relate to 'live' coinage are undoubtedly intriguing, but they only relate to the last few decades of the life of the town, such that we can, for instance, be certain that when a glass of wine is priced at one *as*, it means an Imperial *as* of the types found in the abandoned bars, rather than a Republican *as* of the second century BC. But for the two or so centuries of coin use *prior* to the Roman Principate the evidence is rather more limited – although there are some inscriptions in Oscan which relate to commercial life and economic activities (see below).[65] One literary reference of particular interest dates to the early second century BC, and comes from 'On Agriculture' (XXII, 3), the only complete surviving work of Marcus Porcius Cato Censorius:

> A mill is bought near Suessa for 400 *sesterces* and fifty pounds of oil ... At Pompeii one is bought complete for 384 *sesterces*; freight 280 *sesterces*. It is better to assemble and adjust it on the ground, and this will cost 60 *sesterces*, making a total cost of 724 *sesterces*.

This is an important piece of written evidence, for it demonstrates that to a writer in the second century BC, Pompeii was seen as a town where it was not unusual for large-scale commercial transactions to take place. (It is interesting that at Suessa, mills could be purchased with a combination of coin and product, so payments in a combination of coin and kind were presumably common; we can reasonably infer that these types of arrangements also applied to Pompeii). However there is some debate as to the type of coin being referred to by Cato, for he can only mean a silver *sestertius* at this date, not the later bronze

---

[63] A recent study describes the Cupids simply as 'goldsmiths' without further elaboration: de Angelis (2011).

[64] Cantilena and Giove (2001), 71.

[65] Crawford (2011).

coin; Crawford suggests that Cato may have meant the *diobol*, which 'survived as a unit of reckoning in Campania in the second century and was in due course called the *sestertius*'.[66]

None of the Oscan inscriptions from Pompeii refer specifically to prices or coins, but a number do at least refer to the use of money. For example, an inscription on an altar found at the foot of a ramp up to the *pronaos* of the temple of Dionysus translates as:

> Mr. Atinius, son of Mr., aedile, from his own money.

The inscription has been dated to the last quarter of the third century BC.[67] The same name was found on a sundial on the floor of the Stabian baths, this time dated to the second half of the second century BC:

> Mr. Atinius, son of Mr., quaestor, from money from fines, by decision of the assembly, had (this) made.[68]

Part of the pavement at the entrance to the cella of the temple of Apollo has the inscribed border:

> O. Campanius, [son of ?], quaestor, [by decision] of the assembly, from the money of Apollo, had [the pavement] made.

The inscription has been dated to around 140 BC.[69]

An Oscan inscription found in the Samnite Palaestra (Regio VIII, 7, 29) translates as:

> In respect of the money which V. Adiranus, son of V., gave by will to the Pompeian *vereia*, from that money V. Vinicius, son of Mr., quaestor at Pompei, let the contract for this building to be constructed, by decision of the assembly, the same person passed (it) as completed.

This has been dated to after 123 BC.[70]

Aside from this one literary reference and these Oscan inscriptions, all other evidence for coin use in the third to first centuries BC has to derive from archaeological sources and numismatic study, although there is another inference to be made about the epigraphic sources which is quite intriguing. The earliest tablets of the banker Iucundus, which can be dated to AD 23, belonged to his father or uncle (see n. 51). This could imply a family tradition of dealing with large sums of money, as could the tablets that relate to the Sulpicii family (although they were based at Puteoli – see above). It was common in the past, as it is in many parts of the world today, for family businesses to be passed on through the generations. Therefore even though these documents can be firmly placed in the Imperial

---

[66] Crawford (1985), 346.

[67] Crawford (2011), Pompei 16 (vol. II, 642-43).

[68] Crawford (2011), Pompei 21 (vol. II, 650-51).

[69] Crawford (2011), Pompei 23 (vol. II, 653-55).

[70] Crawford (2011), Pompei 24 (vol. II, 656-58).

age, they do hint at a longer tradition. If this is the case, then the implication is that their predecessors were involved in using coin at precisely the period of which we know little.

Despite all these hints at a monetised economy in the third to second centuries BC, it is not known if the introduction of coinage at Pompeii was a deliberate decision taken by the town authorities or if coins began to circulate for reasons of convenience for certain types of exchange. As economic historians such as Andreau have outlined, we know that the services of *nummularii* and *argentarii* (both terms for assayers and money-changers) were in demand in the ancient world and there is no reason why Pompeii should be any exception, even if there is no direct evidence that they operated in the town (although we can hardly expect there to be traces in the archaeological record and there is no reason why they should be specifically mentioned in the epigraphic sources).[71] Money-changers converted high value gold and silver coins (and probably also bullion) into bronze, and charged a commission in order to make a living. But in turn – and this is perhaps the crucial point – town authorities could raise a levy on this commission, a tax which 'helps to explain why cities were so keen to mint money'.[72] Hollander concurs with this view: 'Coinage made transactions and accounting easier while minting coinage provided profits (through the emission of fiduciary bronze coins) and prestige (to those who controlled the designs)'.[73]

The problem with the idea that the authorities at Pompeii made a conscious decision to strike their own coinage during the late Oscan phase (second to first centuries BC) is that there is no direct evidence for this either in the form of any coins with a mint-mark, the use of any Oscan letters, or the discovery of the means to manufacture coins, for instance dies or coin moulds to make blanks. So how did coinage arrive? From the archaeological evidence it is known that from about the second century BC, and probably earlier, coins (mostly bronze) began to appear in Pompeii in relatively large quantities, although this is only by extrapolation from assemblages such as the one catalogued here – the scale is at present impossible to calculate. There are two possible scenarios for how this occurred. The first is that coins began appearing as a result of commercial links between other towns around the Mediterranean, and reached some kind of critical mass where they began to be seen as a standard means of making small-scale transactions. The second more controversial notion is that coins were deliberately imported *en masse*. Whatever the mechanism, and perhaps it was a mixture of the two, we know that although the coinage of Republican Rome is found in large quantities, it is other mints that seem to have provided the bulk of the monetary stock. In Pompeii's case, as indeed it seems from anecdotal evidence much of Campania (see p. 110), the principal mints from which coins derived were Massalia and Ebusus. Other foreign coins also arrived, but seemingly in far smaller numbers. When these external supplies could not meet demand, imitations of coins of these two places started to be produced, somewhere in the Campanian region, to judge from what we know of where these coins are found; Pompeii is a possible production site,

[71] Andreau (1999), 36.

[72] *Ibid.*, 37.

[73] Hollander (2008), 127.

and indeed it has been argued that this was the case,[74] but equally it could be another major town such as Capua, or perhaps Herculaneum, or even Neapolis – until a full-scale survey of all the evidence is conducted we can pin it down no more closely than Campania (or possibly beyond the modern region, perhaps southern Lazio or even Molise).

This is when we run into difficulties, because we have little idea of the practicalities. Who was responsible for striking coin? Who decided what to put on the dies and what denominations to produce? Where did the metal come from and where were coins struck? How were coins released into circulation? How were coins withdrawn from circulation and re-minted? Presuming it was possible to convert gold and silver coins (and possibly bullion) into bronze units and vice versa, but what were the rates of exchange? Where did money changing take place and how was it regulated? Were these locally struck imitations, which – as will become clear – are found in abundance in Pompeii, simply tolerated or officially sanctioned? Should we even think of them as imitations, or should we consider them 'official' issues?

These are just some of the questions that at present cannot be answered with any degree of confidence. For pre-Imperial Pompeii we also know nothing about prices of everyday goods (with the exception of mills (p. 15), and, as we have seen, this reference presents its own problems) and how these might have been subject to inflation and deflation depending on the shortage and surplus of tradable goods and liquidity of the coinage supply. We know nothing about the amount of coinage in supply and what happened if supplies fell short, although the fact that coins found at Pompeii are often very worn (the modern equivalent of this might be very worn banknotes in unstable economies where new supplies of money are wanting), and since Republican bronze coins, particularly *asses*, were sometimes deliberately cut into fractions, there is a strong suggestion that this was a real problem. From the view-point of the user, we have no idea which strata of society used coin, and what proportion of commercial activity relied on it; we have no idea if certain coins ('special purpose money') were struck for certain activities. We have no idea if the end users of coin understood the adopted iconography, the degree of selectivity for certain coin types, if certain coins were discarded as worthless and other types hoarded; we have no real sense of what proportion of the population had attained a high enough level of literacy to read inscriptions on coins. Then again, maybe this did not matter: was an object which was small, round and composed of metal enough to satisfy most?

One aspect of economic life in early Pompeii which is equally uncertain is the balance between coin exchange, barter and 'tab running'. Kinship and social links must have been of enormous importance in deciding which methods were used in exchanging goods and services. 'Neighbourly' transactions may well have been completed without coin, for instance a bronze worker whose workshop sat beside a bar (there is an example of this in Regio VI, 1) may have satisfied his hunger each day in exchange for ensuring that the bar owner always had utensils from which to pour his wine and iron fittings for his pack animals. And were foreign visitors treated differently to town residents when it came to exchanges in coin? Did owners of commercial premises overcharge newcomers, taking

---

[74] Stannard and Frey-Kupper (2008), 373, see n. 168.

advantage of their poor knowledge of the local currency? All these questions remain almost entirely unanswered.

Which brings us to the subject of 'dead' coinage. I use the term 'dead' coinage to define coins which had already fallen out of use when the eruption occurred, *i.e.* coins recovered from below the AD 79 destruction level. These are coins accidentally lost, deliberately discarded, or in some cases hoarded, buried, and never recovered, not because of the eruption but because of other circumstances, such as the unexpected death of the owner, or because they were a religious or votive dedication.[75] There is no way of knowing how many unprovenanced coins from early excavations at Pompeii fall into this category, but given that most early excavators contented themselves with reaching the latest visible street level and recovering material from the streets and premises, then the proportion is highly likely to be small.[76] One antiquarian group which is certainly pre-AD 79 is a purse hoard found in a sewer in the Republican baths at Regio VIII, 5, 36 (referred to from the point onwards as 'The Bathhouse hoard') but this is very much the exception to the rule (this assemblage is discussed more fully below, p. 66; a list is provided in Appendix 2).

This means that the only way we can hope to better understand how coinage was supplied and used in Pompeii is by delving into the archaeology to find the 'dead' coinage dating to the 250 or so years before the Imperial age. The assemblage from the AAPP excavations is important in this regard, because it is one of the few assemblages from Pompeii that is both well recorded and substantial in size. But what of the comparanda? In the Naples Museum there are around 15,000 coins from Pompeii.[77] It is likely that the vast majority of these are 'live' coins from the AD 79 levels, although there are some early types that are probably from earlier strata.[78]

Very few coins from early excavations in Pompeii can be re-assigned back to their specific places of origin. A survey of the coins recovered from Regio IX, for instance, provides a good example of the limitations of the numismatic evidence derived from early excavations.[79] The report established that between 1748 and 1864, coin finds from Pompeii were predictably numerous, but none are well provenanced; of the c. 2,000 coins removed from the site between 1879 and 1897 which made it as far as Naples Museum, associated information is devoid of detail. Between 1897 and 1971, 7,890 coins were recovered, and these at least have some supporting documentation regarding specific locations provided by the excavation notebooks. The study is able to trace 3,639 coins that come from Regio IX, but the vast majority of these were recovered from the AD 79 levels, which is clear from the

---

[75] The most likely circumstance would be the use of bronze coins as offerings to the gods.

[76] Only a tiny percentage of the town has been excavated below the AD 79 level: see n. 348.

[77] Cantilena and Giove (2001), 9.

[78] Stannard's examination of 1,300 bronze coins in Naples Museum established that the vast majority of the coins were of Roman Imperial date, which means that they probably came from the AD 79 destruction level. However he was able to isolate about 60 Ebusan coins presumably from pre-eruption contexts: Stannard (2005a), 122.

[79] Taliercio Mensitieri (2005).

balance of metals: 86 gold coins, 1,415 silver and 2,138 copper.[80] A few instances of earlier coins could be traced, for instance five coins (3 Ebusus and 2 Roman Republican) found in the atrium of the Casa di M. Sextilius (IX, 13, 1), but the information is no more detailed, and in any case could conceivably have derived from AD 79 levels too. Two coins thought to date to the third to first centuries BC, one of Paestum and one of an unspecified local mint, were found in the south-east corner of *cubiculum* 21.[81] Again, these may be candidates for coins from earlier strata, but there is no certainty of this. The study of the coinage of Regio IX thus demonstrates that what seems at first site a promisingly large dataset rapidly dwindles to a handful of coins of limited use for understanding early coin use in Pompeii.

The principal source of data on the 'dead' coinage of Pompeii therefore comes from more recent campaigns of excavation, all of which have sought to better understand the history of the town's development. Great strides have been made in characterising these coins, particularly in a series of papers published by Clive Stannard.[82] Stannard based his 2005 studies around the coins recovered from the British School at Rome excavations during 1995 to 1999 at the Casa di Amarantus, which recovered 183 identifiable coins. Other recent excavations include those of the Università degli Studi di Perugia (144 coins),[83] the German School excavations at the Casa dei Postumii (104 coins)[84] and Paul Arthur's Forum excavations in advance of electrical works (150 coins).[85] But in all these cases, the number of coins recovered is relatively small, which makes the assemblage of 1,512 coins from Regio VI, 1 highly unusual. How the AAPP compares with these other groups is discussed on p. 67.

---

[80] Excavations below the AD 79 levels very rarely produce gold and silver coins – the AAPP assemblage has no gold and only 30 silver coins and most of the latter are in any case plated.

[81] Taliercio Mensitieri (2005), 335.

[82] Stannard (1998; 2005a; 2005b).

[83] Ranucci (2008a; 2008b).

[84] Stannard (2005a), 124; Dickmann and Pirson (2005).

[85] Stannard (2005a); Arthur (1986).

2 COINS FROM THE EXCAVATIONS BY THE ANGLO-AMERICAN PROJECT IN POMPEII (AAPP)

2.1.1. Discoveries from previous campaigns of clearance and excavation

Previous discoveries, prior to the excavations by the AAPP, have been examined by Cantilena[86] whose results are summarised here. Regio VI, insula 1 was one of the first areas of the town to be excavated; after sporadic investigations from 1764, the main period of exploration took place in 1769-70 when the Via Consolare and the buildings immediately adjacent were uncovered.

The number of known coins found during the explorations of the seventeenth and eighteenth centuries number 240: 49 AR (48 *denarii* and 1 *didrachm* of Neapolis, with reverse showing Victory crowning a bull; probably HN 565, which dates to the second half of the fourth century BC) and 191 AE (24 of large module, 101 of medium module, 54 small and 12 uncertain). Out of these only four have more information; aside from the *didrachm*, the other three were bronze coins of Tiberius, Vespasian and Vespasian for Domitian.[87]

It seems that the Casa delle Vestali proved most productive, accounting for 119 of these coins (8 AR and 111 AE), spread over various rooms, with the exception of 22 coins (including 6 AR) found next to a skeleton in an area to the north of the peristyle.[88] As for the Casa del Chirurgo, no coins are recorded except for the Neapolitan *didrachm*. The three bars produced 30 coins: VI, 1, 2, 4 (the Inn Bar) four coins; VI, 1, 17, 17 (Bar of Acisculus), ten coins and VI, 1, 18, 18 (Bar of Phoebus) sixteen coins. Some smaller groups of coins were also found between the Porta Ercolano and the Porta Vesuvio.

2.1.2. The AAPP assemblage

An examination of the AAPP assemblage, with reference to these smaller comparable groups, allows us to address the following questions: what made up Pompeii's pre-AD 79 currency, and how did it change and develop over the course of Pompeii's long history? The coins from the AAPP excavations are summarised in Table 2 and their origins are shown in Figure 5.

It is clear from comparisons with other assemblages that the AAPP assemblage provides a respectable sample of the coinage in circulation in Pompeii between the early third century BC and the mid first century AD. It can be divided into two categories: imports and locally struck coins. These will be discussed in turn.

---

[86] Cantilena (2008).

[87] Cantilena (2008), 28-30 and 115-27.

[88] *Ibid.*, 117.

Source	No.	%	% Total (by group)	%Total (excluding illeg.)
Regional imports (Italy, excluding Rome)				
Neapolis (Campania)	8	0.5		
?Arpi (Apulia)	1	0.1		
?Canusium (Apulia)	1	0.1		
Paestum (Lucania)	10	0.7		
Thurii (Lucania)	3	0.2		
?Vibo Valentia (Bruttium)	1	0.1		
Rhegion (Bruttium)	7	0.5		
Katane (Sicilia)	2	0.1		
Leontinoi (Sicilia)	1	0.1		
Siracusa (Sicilia)	1	0.1		
Motya? Croton?	1	0.1	*Italy: 2.4*	3.0
'Foreign' imports (outside Italy)				
Epidamnos Dyrrachium (Illyria)	2	0.1		
Megara (Attica)	1	0.1		
Sicyon (Corinthia)	5	0.3		
Boeotia (uncertain mint)	2	0.1		
Samos (Asia)	2	0.1		
Volcae Arecomici (southern Gaul)	1	0.1		
Carmo (Hispania)	1	0.1		
Kese (Tarraco), Hispania	1	0.1		
Kese? Other Spanish?	2	0.1		
Hispano-Carthaginian	1	0.1		
Cyrene (Cyrenaica)	13	0.9		
Uncertain mint, Cyprus	5	0.3		
Jerusalem/Judaea (Palestine)	3	0.2		
Uncertain imports	7	0.5	*Non-Italian imports: 3.0*	3.9
Massalia, anomalous local, Ebusus				
Massalia and Campanian Massalia	287	19.0		24.2
Anomalous local types	15	1.0		1.3
Ebusus and Campanian Ebusus	386	25.5	*Massalia, Ebusus, Local: 45.5*	32.5
Rome				
Roman Republican	162	10.7		13.6
Roman Republican (cut fractions)	107	7.1	*Roman Republican: 17.8*	9.0
Octavian/Augustus (27 BC-AD 14)	71	4.7		
Tiberius (AD 14-37)	29	1.9		
Gaius (AD 37-41)	13	0.9		
Claudius (AD 41-54)	29	1.9		
Nero (AD 54-68)	4	0.3		
Vespasian	3	0.2	*Roman Imperial: 9.8*	12.5
Illegible	324	21.4		
Total	1512			
Total (excluding illegible)	1188			

Table 2. Origins of coins in the AAPP assemblage.

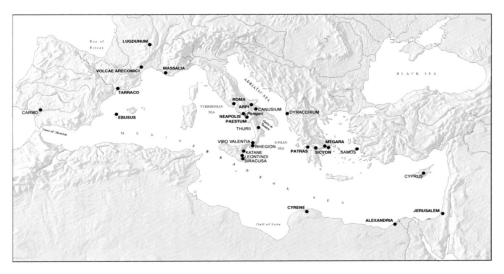

Figure 5. Origins of coins in the AAPP assemblage.

2.2. Imported regional and 'foreign' coins

Roughly 6% of the Regio VI, 1 assemblage consists of imported coins (excluding those originating from Rome, Ebusus and Massalia, which are discussed below). Already in 1950, Breglia raised the question of whether these coins were purely residual or whether they had remained in circulation, not for their intrinsic value, but because their acceptability had become locally embedded.[89] The imports form two groups: 'regional' and 'foreign' coins. 'Regional' equates to modern day Italy, for example coins from Neapolis (modern Naples), Bruttium (modern Calabria) and Leontinoi and Katane (Sicily), whilst 'foreign' means coins from outside modern Italy, such as Carmo in Spain to the west and Epidamnos/Dyrrachium (Thessaly), Megara, Samos, Jerusalem and Cyrene (modern Libya) to the east. Although few in number, they demonstrate clearly Pompeii's extensive links with other coastal towns across the entire Mediterranean.[90] These imports are the earliest coins in the AAPP assemblage, some dating to the third century BC: although coins struck in the fourth century BC have been found at Pompeii none are present in this group (although it should be noted that a fourth century coin of Neapolis was discovered in the Casa del Chirurgo; see p. 21).

What these 'foreign' coins were doing in Pompeii's currency pool is not known, but most ancient sites have produced a small number of coins from well beyond their immediate zone of influence so Pompeii is hardly atypical. It may be that on occasion these pieces made their way physically into an individual's possession via a direct commercial (or perhaps familial) relationship with the place in question. A hypothetical

---

[89] Breglia (1950).

[90] And indeed beyond, as evidenced by the discovery of an ivory statue of the Indian goddess Lakshmi: Beard (2008): 24.

example is a *garum* merchant venturing to Tarraco in Baetica to sell his produce and picking up a few coins whilst he was staying overnight in the town. On his return he slipped these coins into the circulation pool of Pompeii, either because they were an acceptable medium of exchange or because he passed them into another hand unnoticed, until the coins were accidentally lost or deliberately discarded because they were not 'legal tender'. However it functioned, the Mediterranean region should perhaps be viewed as a 'currency zone' in which bronze coins struck by a host of different places infiltrated 'closed' local currency systems, purely because there were hundreds of thousands of coins washing around the various Mediterranean entrepôts. The fact that these imports make up a small proportion (barely 3%) of our assemblage is perhaps testament to this. Further evidence for this comes from shipwrecks (see pp. 35-36).

The nature of this Mediterranean circulation pool in the pre-Christian age is beginning to become better understood, although a great deal more synthetic work needs to be conducted. Here are provided some observations on comparable material from Pompeii and a few other Mediterranean sites: not intended as an exhaustive survey, but to provide some indications of how common these finds are and to provide a base for further research. Stannard and Frey-Kupper have provided a useful summary of 'small change' circulating in southern Italy and Sicily, including a comparative table listing the number of different imported issues from locations in Pompeii: the Casa di Amarantus (I have also been able to consult a copy of Stannard's unpublished report, with appendices detailing material Stannard examined in Naples Museum from old excavations and the votive site at Gragnano), Minturnae (Stannard's own collection from the river Liri and other assemblages) and a small assemblage from Rome (a group of 122 coins from the Tiber).[91] Other sources include the studies of coins from Regio VI[92] and Regio X[93] and the reports on excavations at Pompeii in the series Rivista di Studi Pompeiani (ongoing). Other published assemblages are included, such as the catalogue of coins from Morgantina, Sicily[94] and the research conducted by Michel Py on the pre-Roman coinage of southern France.[95] In addition any stratigraphic evidence provided by the AAPP to date is included: this may help to provide others with evidence which may refine the dating of some of these issues, for it is often uncertain when precisely these coins were struck. Further discussion of the stratigraphic evidence is provided on pp. 68-81 (see also Appendix 1).

2.2.1. Regional imports (excluding Rome)

Neapolis (Campania) (1-8)

Amongst the earliest coins in the AAPP assemblage, all of which are very worn, are coins of Neapolis, which date to the third century BC (cats 1-8). Four types are represented: two

---

[91] Stannard and Frey Kupper (2008), Table 8.

[92] Cantilena (2008).

[93] Taliercio Mensitieri (2005).

[94] Buttrey (1989).

[95] Py (2006).

large denominations with a standing bull being crowned by a Victory and head of Apollo, a smaller module of similar type, and another smaller denomination with a tripod. Neapolis coins dominated the votive deposit excavated below the temple of Jupiter; in the excavation report, it is noted that two further were found in the Triangular Forum.[96] Elsewhere in Pompeii, Neapolis coins have also been excavated at the Casa di Amarantus (9 coins)[97], and there are also two coins in the Bathhouse hoard (Appendix 2, nos. BH1-2). Two examples have been found at Regio VI, 5, the Casa del Granduca Michele[98] and a further two from VI, 14, the Casa ad atrio,[99] found during campaigns of excavation by the Università degli Studi di Perugia and Istituto Orientale di Napoli. Also in Regio VI but in the neighbouring insula (2, 16-21), a single coin of Neapolis was found as part of a hoard of 15 coins in a small *lararium*,[100] but of an earlier type of the late fourth century BC, with head of Apollo and the head and forepart of a bull, no instances of which have been found in Regio VI, 1.[101] A further 10 Neapolis coins are listed as coming from the excavations in VI 2, VI 5, VII 15, VIII 4 and VIII 6 conducted between 2002 and 2007 by the Università degli Studi di Perugia.[102] They are the commonest type found in the Privati deposit (see also pp. 64-65), where at least 300 were recovered,[103] and they are also well represented at Minturnae, where they account for 197 out of a total of 1,649 coins, approximately 11%.[104] The high representation in the Privati deposit is most likely explained by the fact that the deposit is very early, from the end of the fourth to the early third century BC, when 'Neapolis was by far the dominant mint in Campania'.[105] I am not aware of any published studies of the distribution of Neapolitan bronze coins across the Mediterranean; Michel Py lists a single example from southern France (the same type as cats 2-3) from Vieille-Toulouse.[106]

Cat. 5 comes from one of the earliest deposits in the Casa del Chirurgo (277.088) dated to phase 3, first half of the second century BC, which is in keeping with the supposed production date of the late third century BC. Cat. 3 was found in a context (271.234) of phase 6 of the Inn, a post-Sullan destruction deposit, with the majority of the 29 coins in the same context being Massalia and Ebusus; another (cat. 2) is from Phase 7 of the Casa del Triclinio (270.036), so certainly residual.

---

[96] Maiuri (1942), 304-08.

[97] Stannard and Frey-Kupper (2008), 393, Table 8; Stannard (unpublished), nos. 31-39.

[98] Cantilena (2008), 41-42, 157 and 160.

[99] *Ibid.*, 66 and 264.

[100] The hoard was found in a small shrine formed of four crude limestone slabs under the sidewalk: Anniboletti (2005), 381.

[101] Ranucci (2008a); (2008b), Table 1, no. 8.

[102] Ranucci (2008b), Table 1, nos. 2, 5-6, 25, 59, 86-87, 124, 129.

[103] Cantilena (1997).

[104] Stannard and Frey-Kupper (2008), 393, Table 8.

[105] Stannard (2005a), 140.

[106] Py (2006), 703.

Arpi and Canusium, Apulia (cats 9-10)

There are only two coins from Apulia (modern Puglia) in the assemblage. One is from Arpi (cat. 9) although the identification is doubtful because the piece is very worn. One is also known from the Privati deposit, but no others are recorded by Stannard and Frey-Kupper from other sites within Pompeii itself, although a small number (8) are known from Minturnae.[107] The other coin (cat. 10) is from Canusium, but again as the coin is very worn the attribution is doubtful. No other examples are known from Pompeii or other comparable sites.[108]

The possible Arpi coin is from a context as yet unphased, but the possible Canusium coin is from a context (180.015) dated to Phase 5 of the Inn (pre-Sulla), although this still means it was discovered in a context well after its supposed production date of the late third century BC.

Paestum (Lucania) (cats 11-20)

Coins of Paestum are not commonly found at Pompeii, and there are only ten examples in the AAPP assemblage (cats 11-20). The Casa di Amarantus excavations also produced a single example.[109] There is another example of HN 1258 (cats 15-16) from excavations in Regio VI, 5 between 2003-04, the Vicolo della Fullonica;[110] another example of the type from excavations at the Casa di Arianna (Regio VII, 4), conducted by the University of Valencia, was shown to the author in 2010 (unpublished). Another Paestum *semis* (type not described) was found in the corner of *cubiculum* 21 in the Casa di M. Obellio Firmo (IX, 14, 2.4).[111] It has been suggested that imitative coins of Paestum and also Panormus (modern Palermo) may have been struck at Minturnae where they are more common.[112]

Of the pre-Imperial Paestum coins from the AAPP assemblage, one is an unusual type with swan noted previously by Crawford,[113] the others are the *dextrarum iunctio* type, which, it has been argued, were both official and imitative.[114]

Only one Paestum coin (cat. 11) is from a dated context (222.002) which comes from Phase 7 of the Inn (late Augustus to early Imperial).

---

[107] Stannard and Frey-Kupper (2008), 395, Table 8.

[108] *Ibid.*, 395.

[109] Stannard (unpublished), no. 44.

[110] Cantilena (2008), 159; Ranucci (2008b), 168, no. 43.

[111] Taliercio Mensitieri (2005), 336.

[112] Stannard and Frey-Kupper (2008). The AAPP assemblage does not produce a single Panormus coin: only one has been recorded from the Casa di Amarantus and a further example from Gragnano (*ibid.*). The authors consider cat. 13 to be an imitative coin, not struck at Paestum but copied elsewhere, they argue at a 'pseudomint' at Minturnae (*ibid.*). Stannard also notes other coins which are found in large numbers at Minturnae but not at Pompeii, for instance a type with Dionysus and panther, and various odd Italo-Baetican issues, for instance a man holding an *askos*: Stannard (2005a), 121, 140.

[113] Crawford (1973), no. 23/2a.

[114] Stannard and Frey-Kupper (2008), 355-58.

originating from elsewhere, in much the same way as with the use of poorly sorted clays in the production of 'imitative' local pottery.[178] A programme of analyses of the local bronze coinage has the potential to provide a better insight into this matter.[179]

On the other hand, perhaps Stazio was correct (see above p. 32) in suggesting that these coins are simply a factor of a particularly intense mercantile relationship between Pompeii (and other towns in central Italy), Massalia and Ebusus in the late second to first centuries BC, which meant that more coins from these places were introduced into Pompeii's circulation pool, skewing the archaeological record in their favour. After all, the vast-scale import of both Italic wine and Campanian ceramic wares into Gaul, often using Massalia as the point of entry, is well attested, coinciding with the period when the local coinage at Pompeii appears to massively increase.[180] At Rue du Souvenir, Lyon, for example, 14,000 amphora fragments (mostly Dressel 1), representing at least 761 vessels and almost certainly coming from the Bay of Naples were found dating to the late second century BC.[181] At Massalia itself, although small numbers of imported pottery types such as Megarian cups are known, assemblages of the late second century BC are dominated by Campanian wares.[182] Another obvious way to assess the scale of the trade comes from shipwrecks, which not only provide evidence of the bulk trading of goods but also provide hints that the merchants on board were carrying mixed bags of 'small change'. The Madrague de Giens wreck for instance is the largest classical wreck yet excavated; it sank with 6-7,000 wine amphorae, and had about 400 tons of cargo.[183] The Isla Pedrosa wreck, Spain, was carrying hundreds of black-slip vessels, Campanian A ware of the mid second century BC, as well as lava mill-stones from the Naples region; of great interest in this context a group of bronze coins was also salvaged from the same wreck, which surely belonged to a merchant, included six Massalia, a Rome and a Neapolis.[184] Another example is the wreck excavated off the coast at Cavalière, France, which included about 25 Dressel 1 amphorae, some Campanian black-slip ware and pottery of Spanish origin: 'twelve coins were [also] found, all bronze or lead; the three in the mast-step were illegible, but the other nine comprised five of Massalia, five of Numidia… and one of Carteia in southern Spain'.[185] Parker goes so far as to suggest that the vessel was lost in the last few years of the second century BC, and had 'visited North Africa (Punic

[178] McKenzie-Clark (2012).

[179] Such a programme of analysis constitutes part of Giacomo Pardini's current doctoral research at the University of Salerno.

[180] Tchernia (2009).

[181] *Ibid.*, 104.

[182] Goudineau (1983), 79-80; Tchernia (1983).

[183] Parker (1992), 249-50, no. 616; Tchernia *et al.* (1978). Only five coins were recovered during the salvage operation, only three of which could be identified; these were all Roman Republican silver *denarii*: *Ibid.*, 15-16.

[184] Parker (1992), 217-18, no. 520.

[185] Parker (1992), 133-34, no. 282.

amphoras and Numidian coins), Campania (pottery and wine-amphoras from Apulia and Campania)… she had called at Antibes (ballast) and perhaps Marseilles (coins).'[186] He also suggests that all the cargo could have been taken on at Marseilles.[187]

Parker's extensive survey – he lists 674 wrecks of the period 200 BC to 200 AD – does not suggest that coins were the product of trade in the pre-Imperial period, *i.e.* there is no conclusive support for Stannard and Frey-Kupper's theory, although there are examples of the wholesale transport of coins in the fourth century AD: examples include the wreck found at Mangub, Libya, which had 28,000 *nummi,* some dated to AD 306-12;[188] or the wreck from Meloria, Italy, 4,000 bronze coins of Constantine II, contained in a small amphora.[189] But the evidence for merchant seafarers taking on cargo in the Bay of Naples, then sailing up the coast as far as Massalia and on to the Balearic Islands and the coast of Spain is very sound. And although the number of coins recovered from pre-Imperial shipwrecks is small, the make-up of the coins that have been recovered is at the very least intriguing; of the few examples cited here, most include a mixture of bronze coins from different production sites around the Mediterranean. It is of course possible that merchants may have carried coins relevant to the different ports in which they stayed, in the same manner that a UK citizen might have a mixture of pounds and euros in a purse when they return from a trip to Europe and vice versa; but equally it may suggest that small bronze coins were acceptable literally in every port, regardless of their point of origin.

So at the present moment, the question of where exactly the Campanian Ebusus and Campanian Massalia were struck cannot be answered with certainty. If a mint was located in Pompeii we do not know where, as direct evidence for the striking of coin at Pompeii itself has never been formally identified, which is why 'Pompeii' is not listed in standard reference works such as *Historia Numorum* (HN) or *Sylloge Nummorum Graecorum* (SNG). Maybe in the future when the excavation of the rest of Pompeii is completed evidence of coin production might finally come to light. But at present no coin dies or clay moulds for the production of blanks have been found within the town's environs, although until recent times such evidence may have gone unrecognised and been discarded. It should also be clarified that the coins themselves do not bear a mint mark, unlike the coinage produced in neighbouring towns such as Neapolis, Paestum and Velia: the latter two sites were the only regional towns to use a mintmark in the late Republic[190] – maybe this was because these towns were Greek colonies and Pompeii was not. But the lack of a mint-mark obviously does not help the argument for Pompeii striking its own coins.

---

[186] *Ibid.*

[187] *Ibid.*

[188] Parker (1992), 258, no. 645: '20,000 folles, found in 1922-3, and a further 8,000, dated AD 306-12, found in an amphora in 1930, are thought to derive from a single shipwreck'.

[189] *Ibid.*, 275 (unnumbered).

[190] Stannard and Frey-Kupper (2008), 377-78.

In addition to the imports and imitations of Ebusus and Massalia there are also a handful of anomalous local issues (cats 370-84). The most distinctive of these 'anomalous' types have a bridled horse's head on one side. These coins are extremely important because they are not just highly localised (no examples have been found outside Pompeii) but crucially sometimes share dies with the Campanian Ebusus types, although not, as yet, types which imitate Massalia. This provides almost categorical proof that there was a mint site in the region that was striking all these types together. However it should be noted that these types make up less than 1% of the overall total (Table 2), so it appears they were struck in only limited numbers. These local anomalous issues are also discussed in more detail below.

The local coinage at Pompeii can be divided into three principal groups: a 'Massalian' group and an 'anomalous' group (with stylistic links with Roman prototypes) and an 'Ebusan' group. These groups are schematised in Figure 6 and discussed in turn below. (Figure 6 is based purely on stylistic evidence and the links between the different series, for example the sharing of dies between some of the anomalous local types and the Ebusus types. It should not be read as providing a chronology of when the different series were struck and when these coins circulated, discussed in Chapter 3.) The dating evidence for these local types is discussed separately (pp. 81-89).

2.3.1. Massalia and Campanian Massalia (Figure 6)

One of the largest groups of coins in the assemblage, making up almost 20% of the overall total, are imports from Massalia and local types which copy two Massalia prototypes.[191] The group is rather less varied than the Ebusus types (see below) with all the sub-types having a bust on one side (usually Apollo) and a butting bull on the other. Nevertheless the series is complex and apparently employed a number of dies.[192] Inscriptions are often difficult to read as most of the coins are worn and corroded, hence there are large numbers listed in the catalogue as Type 2 (unclassifiable) (cats 166-367); some of these may be imports from Massalia, some Campanian Massalia types; it is not possible to make a judgement without conducting a thorough die study which is beyond the scope of this book. The coins have however been arranged by diameter from the largest (15mm) to smallest (10mm) which may provide some indication as to which are imports and which are local imitations as the imports tend to be of larger module than the local types (see also pp. 52-53).

---

[191] Depeyrot (1999); Stannard (2005a); Py (2006); Stannard and Frey-Kupper (2008); Frey-Kupper and Stannard (2010).

[192] Stannard and Frey-Kupper (2008).

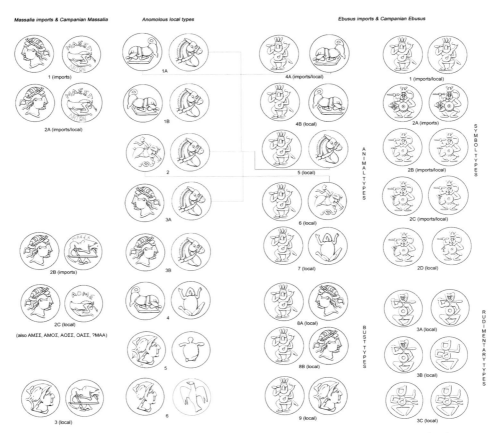

Figure 6. Massalia types, anomalous local types, and Ebusus types represented in the AAPP assemblage.

Type 1   Type 2A   Type 2B

Type 1: obv. head of Apollo facing left; rev. bull butting right, 'ΜΑΣΣΑ' above, 'ΛΙΗΤΩΝ' below exergual line.

This is an imported type which does not appear to have been copied locally; 'Apollo head left' examples are far less numerous than 'Apollo head right', with this assemblage producing only nine examples (cats 83-91). Py suggests a weight standard of 2.08g (with a weight distribution of 1.05 to 3.01g);[193] this is higher than the average weight of the examples in this assemblage (1.40g), but this is not surprising given the high degree of wear on the AAPP coins.

[193] Py (2006), 193-94.

Type 2A: obv. head of Apollo facing right; rev. bull butting right, 'ΜΑΣΣΑ' above, 'ΛΙΗΤΩΝ' below exergual line.

In the AAPP assemblage, 54 coins (cats 92-145) have been identified as having the prototype legend or traces of the legend visible above or above and below the butting bull. Some of these coins are likely to be imports – particularly those which are of a larger flan (14 to 16mm), but some are probably Campanian Massalia, *i.e.* local imitations; it is almost impossible to distinguish between the two types, because the series is so complex and the coins are badly worn and corroded. Further research, particularly a full die study, might lead to a better understanding of how to make a distinction. However it is clear from coin finds from archaeological sites in southern France[194] that this was an extremely large and complex series with a hugely variable quality of output: many of the coins catalogued by Py and Feugere are smaller than the expected standard, have poorly rendered iconography and epigraphy which in itself raises questions about official issues versus local imitations. Thus the difficulties of distinguishing between the types is not restricted to Pompeii.

Type 2B: obv. head of Apollo facing right; rev. bull butting right, above 'ΜΑΣΣΑ', below exergual line 'ΔΑ'.

Like type 2A, the type was copied locally[195] but it is virtually impossible to distinguish between imports and local imitations in the small number of examples in this assemblage because all are poorly preserved (cats 147-51); the lettering on the reverse below the exergue is doubtful in most cases.

Type 2C   Type 3

Type 2C: obv. head of Apollo facing right; rev. bull butting right, garbled legend above or below bull.

Type 2C covers a number of different examples of coins that have garbled inscriptions on the reverse above or below the bull. These include: ΑΜΣΣ (cats 152-53), ΑΜΟΣ (cat. 154), ΑΟΜΣ (cats 155-56), ΑΟΣΣ (cats 157-79), ΟΑΣΣ (with the sigmas reversed; cat. 160) and possibly ΜΑΑ (cats 161-62). Other variants include ΜΟΣΣ and theoretically examples with inscriptions in the exergue, although this is unproven because no examples with inscriptions below the exergual line have been identified in this assemblage.[196]

Type 2C are certainly local imitations: 'the types probably derive from originals with the short legend, ΜΑΣΣΑ, above the bull... the most probably models are PBM 45, 46, 47 and 48'.[197] Py (2006) and Feugere and Py have not published any examples of these

---

[194] Py (2006); Feugere and Py (2011).

[195] Stannard (forthcoming).

[196] Stannard (forthcoming). An example with 'ΑΟΥ' in the exergue has been published as a Campanian Massalia type: Frey-Kupper and Stannard (2010), 141, but this is in actuality a type from Avignon: Feugere and Py (2010), 181, no. AVI 2521 (Stannard pers. comm.).

[197] *Ibid.*

particular letter combinations in their surveys of coins from archaeological sites in southern France and it is highly likely that the few in French collections were probably acquired in the Naples region. An examination of 400 small Massaliot bronze coins in the Bibliothèque Nationale unearthed only four certain examples of these types, two of which were published by de la Tour as his numbers 2227 and 2242.[198] As Stannard has commented: 'Such anomalous-legend pieces have in the past been given to Celtic tribes in the hinterlands of Massalia; but their association in mass at Pompeii with Pseudo-Ebusan material, and the many die-links, all suggest that they are central Italian imitations, and that the relatively few pieces in French museums ... are, in fact, of central Italian origin'.[199]

Type 2C variant: obv. head of Apollo facing right; rev. bull butting right, no exergual line, below ?animal.

There are three coins (cats 163-65) that appear to be another local variant, although as these have not been identified in other assemblages[200] judgement at present needs to be reserved. The best preserved is cat. 165. The distinctive feature of these coins is a small, possibly zoomorphic, device below the bull, which is angled towards the hind legs. The type also lacks an exergual line which is another point of divergence from the rest of the series.

Type 3: obv. head of Mars right; rev. bull butting right, inscription above or below exergual line.

There are two variants of this Campanian type in the AAPP assemblage (cats 368-69). The first (cat. 368) shows a beardless head of Mars right on the obverse and a bull butting right on the reverse; below the exergual line are the letters 'ΔA'. The prototype for the obverse of this coin is probably *RRC* 25,[201] whilst the reverse is probably taken from Depeyrot (1999), nos. 47-9 (Massalia Type 2B in this assemblage – cats 147-51). The obverse of the second (cat. 369) shows instead a bearded Mars, and thus resembles *RRC* 44/2,[202] although (unlike Anomalous local type 5 – cat. 383) there is no value mark behind the bust. In any case, how this was used as prototype is unclear as it is an early gold piece; unless it had been retained until a later date, for example as an item of jewellery. The reverse apparently has the letters 'MA' above (the bottom of the coin is off flan meaning that any inscription which may have been below the bull is no longer discernible).

---

[198] La Tour (1892); Frey-Kupper and Stannard (2010), 136, fig 10.

[199] Stannard (2005a), 140.

[200] Stannard (pers. comm.)

[201] Stannard (forthcoming).

[202] Stannard (forthcoming).

2.3.2. Anomalous local types (Figure 6)

There are a few examples of coins in the assemblage (15 coins, cats 370-84) which are anomalous types not found elsewhere, which further strengthens the case for a mint somewhere in the vicinity of Pompeii or Pompeii itself. For some of these we can be certain these are local issues because they are die-linked with the Campanian Ebusan series; for others, they are considered to be local because they are found only at Pompeii and have stylistic links with both the Ebusan and Massalian types. The types have been discussed by Stannard.[203]

Some of these anomalous local types have been recognised in other excavated assemblages but are not represented in the AAPP assemblage. For instance this assemblage has not produced any examples of Stannard's group IV with 'small heads and borders of large pellets'.[204] A coin from the Bathhouse hoard[205] (but not represented in the AAPP assemblage) provides a stylistic link with types with either a head of Mars or a toad. A type with horse head on one side and a galloping horse on the other was found during the excavations by the Università degli Studi di Perugia,[206] and another during excavations by the Via Consolare Project (unpublished, identified by author). In addition there are some examples of types which are far more clear than in this assemblage where the coins tend to be very worn; for example in Naples Museum there is a very clear example of type 3B, with bust of Apollo right and horse's head, which is represented by two coins in the AAPP assemblage both of which are listed as 'probably this type' (cats 378-79).

Horse's head – Types 1A to 3b
The prototype for these types are probably early silver and bronze coins from Rome with a bridled horse-head;[207] this assemblage produced a single worn example of one of these coins (cat. 771). There are die-links with the Ebusus series and the sharing of dies with other types; *e.g.* anomalous local type 2, with leaping bull (cat. 373) shares this die with Campanian Ebusus type 6 (cat. 745), whilst the reverse of cat. 373, the horse's head side, is die-linked with Campanian Ebusus type 5 (cat. 743). Type 1B with bull butting right clearly relates, stylistically at least, to the Massalia and Campanian Massalia types, although I am not aware of any examples where traces of any legend above or below the butting bull can be seen. There is however an important die-link with Campanian Ebusus type 4A (bull butting left); cats 370 and 732 appear to share the same die.

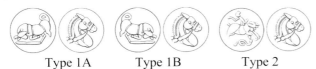

Type 1A   Type 1B   Type 2

Type 1A: obv. bull butting left; rev. horse head with bridle right.

---

[203] Stannard (2005b), 67-68.

[204] Stannard (2005b), 68-69.

[205] Stannard (2005a), Group IV, 1, no. 35; Appendix 2, cat. BH18.

[206] Ranucci (2008a), Figure 4, 1; Ranucci (2008b), Table 1, cat. 71 (Plate 1, no. 11).

[207] *e.g. RRC* 25/1 and 25/3; as noted by Stannard (2005a), 135 and note 50.

As first noted, this coin (cat. 370) is obverse die-linked to cat. 732. As far as I am aware this is the only example of the type known to date; Stannard does not list other examples of the type in his various papers.[208]

Type 1B: obv. bull butting right; rev. horse's head with bridle facing right.

One (cat. 371) is probably die-linked with type 2, which is in turn directly die-linked with Campanian Ebusus type 6 (see Figure 6). The only other example of this type I know of from Pompeii was found during excavations by the Via Consolare Project (unpublished, identified by author).

Type 2: obv. bull leaping right, snake below; rev. horse's head with bridle facing right.

This (cat. 373) is another type of which to the best of my knowledge this is the only example. It appears to show a bull leaping right with a snake below; there is a very distinctive die break which runs across the 'obverse'.[209] There is a direct die-link, both obverse and reverse, with Campanian Ebusus types 5 and 6 (cats 744-45), and also with anomalous local type 3A (cat. 377).

Type 3A   Type 3B

Type 3A: obv. bust of Apollo facing left; rev. horse's head with bridle facing right.

To the best of my knowledge these are the only four examples of this type (cats 374-77); none have been found elsewhere. The only parallel for the left-facing Apollo of the obverse is an imported Massalia type 1 (discussed above). The reverse is shared with both other local anomalous types and Campanian Ebusus type 5.

Type 3B: obv. bust of Apollo facing right; rev. horse's head with bridle facing right.

The best preserved example of this type is not from this assemblage but from a coin found in a cinerary urn in one of the tombs excavated outside the Porta Nocera, now preserved in Naples Museum; as Stannard comments: 'I hesitate to draw much significance from the fact that [this coin] was deliberately buried in a tomb, but it is a suggestion that the issue is Pompeiian'.[210] The four examples from these excavations (cats 374-77) both confirm the type and strengthen the case for local production.

[208] Stannard (2005a; 2005b; 2008).

[209] Frey-Kupper and Stannard (2010), 118, Figure 1 no. 7.

[210] Stannard (2005a), 128 (Table 6, no. 30), 135. The tomb is on the south-west side of Via delle Tombe, Porta Nocera, code OS 7: d'Ambrosio and de Caro (1983).

Anomalous toad, turtle and eagle types

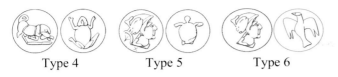

Type 4   Type 5   Type 6

Type 4: obv. bull butting right; rev. toad with front legs extended.

There is an inscription above the butting bull which could be construed as the remnants of 'ΜΑΣΣΑ', but as this is clearly not a Massalia type, it provides a useful link between the Campanian Ebusus type with toad (type 7) and the Campanian Massalia types (2B to 3). Bronze coins from Luceria and Venusia[211] have been suggested as possible candidate prototypes for the toad reverse.[212] Neither I nor Stannard are aware of any other examples of this type from Pompeii.

Type 5: obv. head of Mars right, behind anchor (value mark 60?), below 'X'; rev. turtle.

This type is represented by only this single example (cat. 383) for which no parallels have been found in any other assemblage, including the large group of material from the Liri.[213] The obverse copies a Roman 60-*as* gold piece, including the 60 value mark behind the bust (*RRC* 44/2); although it is unclear how such a relatively rare type survived in order to be copied (see also comments on Massalia Type 3, p. 40). The turtle appears on a silver issue of C. Vibius (*RRC* 449/5), but as this dates to 44 BC it would seem surprising if this was the prototype;[214] another suggestion are cast coins from Tuder.[215] The helmeted head is stylistically related to the Type 2 with toad, and also Campanian Massalia type 3 and Campanian Ebusus type 9, although no die-links have been found.

Type 6: obv. head of ?Minerva right; rev. eagle stg. facing.

This (cat. 384) is the only example of this type known.[216] The obverse shows a helmeted bust which is slighter than the types with heads of Mars, which is why the current attribution suggests the bust represents Minerva not Mars.

---

[211] *HN*, nos. 682 and 725.

[212] Stannard (forthcoming).

[213] Stannard (pers. comm.), I am grateful to Clive Stannard for suggesting that this coin is a local type.

[214] Unfortunately the coin was in a context currently undated: see p. 85.

[215] Stannard (forthcoming); *HN*, no. 39.

[216] Stannard (forthcoming). I am grateful to Clive Stannard for identifying this coin in the assemblage.

Figure 7. Two depictions of Bes: a sculpture in the Baracco Collection, Rome (left); a wall painting from the Temple of Isis at Pompeii.

2.3.3. Ebusus and Campanian Ebusus (Figure 6)

The prototypes for this series originate in Ebusus (modern Ibiza) in the Balearic Islands.[217] The majority of the coins are characterised by the figure of the Egyptian dwarf-god Bes on both obverse and reverse, although some types combine the figure of Bes with other motifs. Bes was a minor Egyptian deity popular across the Mediterranean and was depicted as a dwarf with a large head and a pot-belly, a depiction intended to inspire joy and drive away pain and sorrow. As Dasen notes, he was 'primarily a helpful deity concerned with the protection of the household', whose 'tutelary functions involve at least five spheres of human life: the protection of women and childbirth, of sleep, of warfare, of the dead, and the celebration of music, dancing and wine'.[218] Images of Bes in sculptural form or painting have been found across Pompeii, the best example a wall painting in the so-called *sacrarium* of the Temple of Isis, one of the first parts of Pompeii to be unearthed (Figure 7).[219]

The assemblage from the AAPP excavations includes both prototype ('canonical') Ebusan coins imported from Ebusus itself as well as local Campanian Ebusus imitations. Although there is no certainty as to how quickly the type was copied locally, it is indisputable that the type was copied in large numbers. Ebusus is represented by 386 examples, around a quarter of the whole AAPP assemblage, and around 80% appear to be

---

[217] Campo (1976; 1993); Stannard (2005a; 2005b).

[218] Dasen (1993), 67.

[219] d'Alessio (2009).

local imitations.[220] This correlates well with the proportions found in other excavations: for example of the 130 coins excavated by the British School at Rome in the Casa di Amarantus, 19.2% of these were Ebusan and Campanian Ebusan.[221] A recent survey has demonstrated that the type is widely found in Italy and Sicily, 'though never in such quantities as at Pompeii and Minturnae'.[222] 'Canonical' Ebusus have been found as far north as Cosa and Rome, and Campanian Ebusus (in addition to Pompeii and Minturnae) at Sarno, Mirabella Eclano (Campania) and Rocca d'Entella and Morgantina in Sicily.[223] Ebusan coins have also been found on sites in the vicinity of Massalia, but these are of a different style and may themselves be local copies.[224]

Stannard provides the most detailed surveys of Ebusus and Campanian Ebusus, drawing on the work of Campo.[225] Canonical coins struck on the island of Ebusus are full-figure Bes coins with the deity shown on both sides, with or without symbols in the field, or Bes combined with a standing or butting bull left or right. Stannard (2005a) divided the Campanian Ebusus types (*i.e.* the locally produced imitations) into a number of groups (Stannard refers to these types as 'pseudo-Ebusus'). Group I (2005a: Figure 5) consists of Bes combined with a butting bull; group II with horse's head (2005a: Figure 6); group III with bust right (2005a: Figure 6); group IV with a toad, either in combination with Bes or with a head of Mars (2005a: Figure 6). Group V are small units which return to the Bes/Bes full figure combination in conjunction with symbols in the field, some of which are present on the 'canonical' issues and others not (2005a: Figure 7). Group VI are 'rudimentary' Bes types, which are the most haphazard and schematic types in both appearance and metrology; Bes appears as a rudimentary stick figure on the obverse and reverse, sometimes with a slanting 'T' symbol in the right-hand field,[226] and in one instance with a standing figure with palm frond (a type not present in the AAPP assemblage). Group VI, 9 and 10, and group VII are additional rudimentary Bes types perceived to be 'half-units'.

Stannard's classification is the starting point for all study of the local Campanian Ebusus types. It is possible to track developments within the series such as the simplification of the Bes figure which has a logical bearing on the chronological arrangement of the series. Unlike the rigid structure of the Republican Roman monetary system based on fractions of a pound, it is more difficult to isolate denominations. (Although Stannard suggests that there were units and half-units, I did not find convincing evidence for this – see 'Metrology', p. 50).

[220] 78 coins are either definite Ebusus imports or probable Ebusus imports.

[221] Stannard (2005a), 121.

[222] Stannard and Frey-Kupper (2008), 370.

[223] *Ibid.*, Figure 4.

[224] *Ibid.*; Py (2006), 685-88; Feugere and Py (2011), 399.

[225] Stannard (2005a; 2005b; forthcoming).

[226] Campo (1976), group XVIII, 71.

For the purposes of this publication I have simplified Stannard's classification of the Ebusan material by dividing the material into three groups, each with two or three sub-types (Figure 6):

Types 1-3: a standing figure of Bes on **both** obverse and reverse.
Types 4-7: a standing figure of Bes on the obverse and an **animal** on the reverse.
Types 8-9: a standing figure of Bes on the obverse and a **bust** on the reverse.

In Figure 6 (p. 38) imported Ebusus and local Campanian Ebusus types are indicated in brackets below the relevant illustration (for example Ebusus type 2B with cornucopia can be both imports and local, type 7 with toad, local only).

<u>Types 1-3: Bes on both obverse and reverse (cats 385-728)</u>

There are 344 coins of this group in the assemblage, representing around 90% of the Ebusus/Campanian Ebusus coins, meaning that this group is by far the commonest.

Type 1   Type 2A   Type 2B   Type 2C   Type 2D

Type 1 'no symbol' (cats 385-410): a standing figure of Bes on both sides with his right arm raised. In his right hand he holds a hammer and in his left a serpent which extends out to the side;[227] on his head is a lotus flower. The figure of Bes is fully rendered and it is often possible to make out small details such as his cheeks, lips and eyes. The field is un-populated.

This is one of the earliest types in the series, as Bes is well defined and detailed, and the coins are usually larger and heavier (see discussion of 'Metrology', p. 50). Most of these coins are imports (cats 385-401) but some are probably local imitations (cats 402-10), as these are of smaller module and less well rendered.

Type 2 'symbol' (cats 411-45): the same as type 1 but there is a symbol in the field, which may appear on obverse and reverse or just one side. There are four clearly identifiable symbols and a few anomalous and debatable ones:

2A: a four-petalled lotus flower; there are no examples of local imitative types.
2B: a cornucopia; imports and local types.
2C: a caduceus; imports and local types.
2D: cornucopia on one side, dolphin on the other; local imitative type only.

---

[227] It should however be noted that equally, it may be that his left hand is also holding a shield over his body, for during the Ptolemaic period Bes is often transformed into a warrior: Dasen (1993), 29 (and see also Plate 11, 2, a terracotta figure with Bes holding both sword and shield). If this is the case, then the ring on these coins which is normally taken to represent Bes' pot-belly may in some cases represent a shield.

The caduceus type (2C) is the commonest (12 recognised examples), followed by the cornucopia (2B), (11 examples), followed by 2D (5) and 2A (2).

Unfortunately most coins in the assemblage are too worn to categorise, and it is not possible in every case even to distinguish between types 1 and 2; thus there are a large number of coins listed in the catalogue which have been lumped together as types 1 or 2 (cats 446-613). However a subjective assessment has been made of whether or not they are imports or Campanian Ebusus types in the notes for each catalogue entry; this is based on a judgement of the style and other factors such as diameter and weight. This group is listed by diameter and then weight.

Type 3 'rudimentary' (cats 614-728).[228] These bear a distinctively schematic, rather 'slap dash' figure in comparison to types 1 and 2, with Bes reduced to a simple stick figure. In extreme cases, the figure of the dwarf-god is so disjointed as to be almost unrecognisable (for example cat. 644). Metrology and comparison of average coin size suggests that these coins were struck later on in the series as does the contextual work conducted on the dating of the local series (see p. 87). Type 3 is a purely Campanian Ebusus coinage, with no examples found on Ebusus.[229]

The group can be divided into three sub-types:

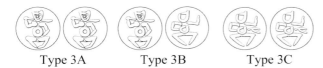

Type 3A   Type 3B   Type 3C

Type 3A (cats 614-624): Bes with right arm raised on both sides. Bes holds a hooked staff behind his head. These are the most closely related to types 1 and 2, and logic would dictate that these are probably the first of the 'rudimentary' types to be struck.

Type 3B (cats 625-36): Bes has right arm raised on one side and left on the other.

Type 3C (cats 637-699): Bes has his left arm raised on both sides; a slanted 'T' symbol is usually visible on the obverse and reverse to the left of the figure in the field. The meaning of this symbol is unclear: Stannard suggests that it is a corruption of the cornucopia seen on type 2B.[230] This is the largest sub-type of Ebusus group 3 (63 examples, as opposed to only 11 type A and 12 type B) and are probably the latest in the Bes/Bes series, but there may be considerable overlap between the groups. It seems highly likely that they resulted from dies being cut by copying the coins direct, thus reversing the position of Bes' raised arm.[231]

---

[228] Campo (1976), group XVIII, 71; Stannard (2005a), types VI and VII.

[229] Stannard (2005a), 120.

[230] Stannard (2005a), 137.

[231] *Ibid.*, 136, n. 58.

Group 2, types 4-7: Bes combined with an animal (cats 729-46)

This group runs parallel with Types 1 to 3 (Bes on both sides), but generally has a full figure of Bes rather than the 'rudimentary' figure, with the exception of Group 7 (Bes/toad). There are five sub-types within this group:

      Type 4A   Type 4B

Type 4A: obv. a full and detailed figure of Bes on obverse with right arm raised; rev. bull butting left on reverse.
Type 4B: obverse as 4A, reverse bull butting right.

Type 4A with bull butting left is found on Ebusus and other Spanish sites[232] and cats 729-31 are believed to be imports. By virtue of a smaller flan and lower average weight cats 732-34 on the other hand are considered to be local imitations and conform with Stannard's group I, 5.[233] One example in this assemblage possibly provides a link between this type and Type 2D with caduceus and dolphin, a purely Campanian Ebusus type, thus further demonstrating the case for large-scale local production (cat. 735).

Type 4B with bull butting right is present on Ebusus but only as a distinctive type on a small flan (*c.* 10mm) with sharp edges, no examples of which have been found in this assemblage.[234] Therefore the five examples in this assemblage of Type 4B (cats 736-41) are considered to be Campanian Ebusus coins.[235] In any case the style of the Bes figure is clearly different to that of imported examples; compare for instance cats 741 and 729.

There is a notable variant of the type (cat. 742) that might provide a link with the Massalia series, as there appears to be a legend above the bull, although this is unfortunately illegible. It should be noted that this coin is both obverse and reverse die-linked to a coin in Stannard's group I, 4 (2005a, no. 24) which came from excavations in the Forum.[236]

      Type 5   Type 6   Type 7

Type 5: obv. full and detailed figure of Bes on obverse with right arm raised; rev. horse's head with bridle facing right.

[232] Campo (1976), Group XII, 14-17.

[233] Campo (1976), Group XIV, no. 18; Stannard (2005a), Figure 5.

[234] Campo (1976), Group X, 13.

[235] As Campo (1976), Group XIV, no. 19 and Stannard (2005a), Group I, 1.

[236] Arthur (1986).

This type can be die-linked to both the type with butting bull and the type with head of Apollo (Anomalous local types 1A to 3B: see above). This is almost certainly an imitative central Italian issue, as no examples have been found on Ebusus. The horse's head 'probably copies the well-modelled bridled horse-head on early Roman pieces, rather than the flat unbridled Sardo-Carthaginian type, often found in Italy'.[237]

Type 6: obv. full and detailed figure of Bes on obverse with right arm raised; rev. bull leaping right, snake below.[238]

The AAPP assemblage has produced only one very worn example of the type (cat. 745), comparable with another example found in the river Liri.[239] The reverse is die-linked to Anomalous local type 2 where it is combined with a horse's head, which in turn is die linked to the Ebusus type 5, which further demonstrates the large degree of die sharing between the different series.

Type 7: obv. more schematic figure of Bes; rev. toad with pellet below.

There is only one example of this in the AAPP assemblage (cat. 746). Although the Bes figure is rather poorly rendered, it is not quite 'rudimentary' in style. Its closest parallel is a coin from the Bathhouse hoard (Appendix 2, cat. BH65)[240] although this is a smaller coin and appears to show Bes leaning on a staff. The toad also appears on Anomalous local type 4, but no die-links between these types have been noted.

Types 8 and 9: Bes combined with a bust (cats 747-61)

Type 8A   Type 8B   Type 9

Type 8A: obv. full and detailed figure of Bes with right arm raised; rev. laureate head of Apollo left.
Type 8B: obv. as 8A; rev. laureate head of Apollo right.

Both these varieties of Bes combined with a bust of Apollo can be linked stylistically with the anomalous horse's head type (Types 3A and 3B) and the Campanian Massalia series; Stannard speculates that type 8B (his Group II, 4) is a hybrid between Campanian

---

[237] Stannard (2005a), 135.

[238] The iconography of this coin is difficult to interpret. The leaping bull could be interpreted as a horse, and there is a curious extension to the animal's back, which is probably a die flaw as opposed to a rider (Stannard pers. comm.).

[239] Stannard (2005a), no. 18 (Liri 27.051). It should also be added that another type recorded by Stannard, with Bes on one side and standing figure with palm frond on the other is also not represented in the AAPP assemblage and thus seems to be an issue local to Minturnae: Stannard (2005a), 131, group VI, 8.

[240] Stannard (2005a), Group IV, 2, no. 36.

Massalia and Campanian Ebusus.[241] The style of the Apollo bust on the AAPP examples (cats 751-58) do not appear to be the same as that on the Campanian Massalia pieces, but only a full die study would establish if dies were shared. Both types 8A and 8B are not known on Ebusus itself, with the example published by Campo[242] coming from the Berlin cabinet, and likely to be of central Italian origin.[243] One example of Type 8B has a particularly distinctive type of bust (cat. 759).

Type 9: obv. bust of Mars right; rev. full and detailed figure of Bes on obverse with right arm raised.

The type (cats 762-63) can be linked stylistically, if not as yet through shared dies, with both the toad (Anomalous local type 5) and Massalia groups (Campanian Massalia type 3). The two coins in the AAPP assemblage (cats 762-63) are the only known examples.[244]

2.3.4. Metrology of the local coinage

Because the AAPP assemblage is so substantial, it offers the opportunity to study the metrology of the Massalia and Ebusus types (Table 3).[245] The point of this exercise was to establish if it is possible to discern a weight standard for the two key groups of local issues, particularly as Stannard suggested that there was a unit and half-unit of Ebusus.[246] The diameter of these groups is also considered below (p. 52).

The analysis shows that the Massalia types are almost invariably much lighter than the Ebusus types. Type 2A, on which the 'ΜΑΣΣΑ' legend is still visible and which is considered an import (although many are probably local copies) average slightly more than 1.4g, a whole gram lighter than the earliest Ebusus types; the rarer Type 1 with bust left is also roughly this weight. The average weight of all the more common type 2 Massalia coins is about 1.5g. This contrasts with the calculations made by Michel Py: for PBM types 39-40, these have an average weight of 2.17g; PBM types 48-8 around 1.96g.[247] So the Pompeii examples are around half a gram lighter, some of which is likely to be the result of circulation wear, but most of which is probably the result of local imitation.

There is a wide fluctuation in the weight of the different sub-types of Ebusus coin, but – assuming that the assumption is correct that the 'rudimentary' types do indeed follow the full-figure types – there seems to be a gradual decline in weight. Type 1, which

---

[241] Stannard (2005a), 135.

[242] Campo (1976), 125, Group XVI, no. 21.

[243] cf. Stannard (2005a), 135, note 52.

[244] Frey-Kupper and Stannard (2010), 118, figure 1 no. 21.

[245] Broken and partial coins were excluded from the weight calculations, as were coins which had not been weighed to anything greater than one decimal place. Sub-types represented by only a few examples were also excluded.

[246] Stannard (2005a), 135: 'Group II, 3 (no. 31) and II, 4 (no. 32), appear to be a unit and a half.'; *ibid.*, 139: 'In Group VII, I assemble further halves, of a variety of styles.'

[247] Py (2006), 215 and 234.

MASSALIA	Av. wt. (no. egs.)	Mean	ANOM. LOCAL	Av. wt. (no. egs.)	EBUSUS	Av. wt. (no. egs.)	Mean
Type 1, imports	1.40 (5)		Type 1B	1.54 (2)	Type 1, imports	2.67 (15)	
Type 2A, imports/local	1.41 (42)		Type 3A	2.80 (2)	Type 1, local	2.14 (6)	
Type 2B, imports/local	1.60 (2)	1.51			Type 2B, imports	2.83 (7)	2.42
Type 2C, local	1.49 (6)				Type 2C, imports	2.43 (5)	
Type 2C, local variant	1.55 (3)				Type 2C, local	2.05 (4)	
					Type 2D, local	1.50 (3)	
					Type 3A, local	1.94 (10)	
REPUBLICAN QUADRANS, c. 146-100 BC							1.91
					Type 3B, local	1.82 (9)	
AAPP	3.30 (2)				Type 3C, local	1.96 (49)	
British Museum	4.03 (97)				Type 4A, local	1.95 (3)	1.77
					Type 4B, local	1.58 (5)	
					Type 8B, local	1.80 (7)	

Table 3. Metrology of the Massalia, Ebusus and anomalous local issues. Figures for Republican *quadrantes* are provided for comparison.

includes imports and local copies, has an average weight of 2.67g for the imports and 2.14g for the locally produced. Type 2, with a symbol in the field, again tend to be of higher weight for the imports than the locally produced pieces. Taking all the full-figure types together (excluding type 2D, as these seem to be anomalous) gives an average of 2.42g. The 'rudimentary' types (3A to C), all of which are of local production, generally hover around 1.8-1.9g, so are roughly half a gram lighter than the types 1 and 2 coins with a full-figure of Bes; this marries well with their generally poor appearance. Their mean weight is 1.91g. The number of examples of the other categories (Bes/animal, Bes/bust) are rather low to be statistically reliable, but their metrology suggests that type 4 (Bes/butting bull) is rather lighter than the main Bes series as is the type with bust (1.77g and 1.80g respectively).

There are so few examples of the anomalous local types it is difficult to gain more than an impression of the intended weights. However it can be noted that the types with butting bull (Type 1) correlate well with the Massalia types, averaging around 1.5g; but rather contradictory to this are the types with head of Apollo, which appear to be heavier, more akin to the Ebusus series, normally over 2g in weight, in one case almost 4g (cat. 374).

For the purpose of comparison, an average weight of Roman Republican *quadrantes* of the period broadly contemporary with the production of the Massalia and Ebusus coins is provided. Most of the AAPP *quadrantes* were struck in the period c206-144 BC, but there are two examples of *quadrantes* which were struck in the period c146-100 BC. By about this time 'the weight standard of the *as* was based on an *as* of less than an ounce', with most *asses* weighing in the region of 16g.[248] As there are only two coins in the AAPP assemblage, with a mean weight of 3.30g, 97 coins from the collections of the

---

[248] *RRC*, 596.

British Museum were assessed to provide a comparison. The BM examples range in weight from as low as 2.02g to 5.80g, and produce an average weight of 4.03g, which conforms neatly to the projected weight of a *quadrans* on the basis of the *as* of this period as described. As has been seen, neither the Massalia nor the Ebusus coins appear to be trying to conform to a standard as high as 4g, but at least for the Ebusus coins with an average weight hovering around 2g it would be tempting to argue that these were supposed to be half the weight of a contemporary Republican *quadrans*. On the other hand, a weight relationship with the Massalia coins, averaging about 1.5g, is not so obvious; and as there are only two such *quadrantes* in this assemblage – and the vast majority of Republican bronzes weigh a great deal more – to my mind it is hard to make a case for a relationship between the Roman Republican *quadrans* and the weight standard of the Campanian Ebusus coins.

2.3.5. Sizes of flan (Table 4)

The metrology implies some broad differences between the various sub-types of Massalia and Ebusus issues, but, because most of the material is very worn, ascertaining a weight standard is difficult. Another approach to the problem is diameter, since even if a coin is less than its minted weight as a result of circulation wear and burial degradation it is highly unlikely to have decreased in width. In this analysis no distinction was made between the different sub-types.

As Table 4 shows, the key difference is that around 80% of Ebusus coins (of all types) are between 13 and 16mm in diameter whilst around 95% of the Massalia coins are between 11 and 14mm in diameter. There are some outliers, notably a small proportion of Ebusus coins 17 to 18mm across; these are all likely to be imports. The same is likely for the small proportion of Massalia coins of 15 to 16mm in diameter, also likely to be imports. The number of anomalous local types is low, but most are around 14 to 16mm, which implies they have more in common with the Ebusus coins than Massalia, which was also the impression given by their weights and the fact that die-links can be found between the series.

Therefore even though the coins in the AAPP assemblage are in poor condition, it seems possible to discern some clear differences. Earlier Ebusus issues tend to be larger and heavier than later ones, and the Massalia coins are invariably lighter and smaller than the Ebusan types. But can this be taken further to suggest any denominational structure? One of the difficulties is that even those mints which set a denominational standard will not necessarily produce material of consistent size and weight. For example the undated Republican *asses* in the AAPP assemblage produced at Rome (cats 829-934, with Janus head obverse and ship prow reverse), fluctuate between 26 and 36mm in diameter and 13.81g to 39.05g in weight (although it may be the case that some of these are local imitations).[249] But these are all, nonetheless, *asses,* and were presumably valued as such in the denomination system, even if these fluctuations probably relate to number of episodes of striking.

---

[249] Crawford provides average weights for moneyer's bronze issues, but these can only be taken as a very rough guide: *RRC*, 51-55.

DIAMETER (mm)	Massalia	%	Anomalous	%	Ebusus	%
18+	0	0	0	0.0	0	0
18	0	0.0	0	0.0	9	2.3
17	0	0.0	1	6.7	17	4.4
16	2	0.7	3	20.0	43	11.2
15	5	1.7	4	26.7	110	28.6
14	43	14.5	3	20.0	105	27.3
13	77	26.0	2	13.3	58	15.1
12	111	37.5	2	13.3	31	8.1
11	53	17.9	0	0.0	11	2.9
10	5	1.7	0	0.0	1	0.3
Total	296		15		385	

Table 4. Diameters of Massalia, anomalous local types, and Ebusus, in the AAPP assemblage, irrespective of sub-types. The most commonly occurring diameters are indicated in solid outline.

Although the Ebusus 'symbol' types (Type 2) can vary in diameter between 10mm and 17mm, it is hard to make a convincing case for 'units' and 'half' units, particularly as the style of these pieces is so variable. In fact, if this type is divided into two groups, one of 14-17mm, and one of 10-13mm, then the weight range of the two types is not that dissimilar; the coins struck on the larger flan can range in weight between 1.29g and 4.03g, whilst the coins 10-13mm fluctuate between 0.98g and 3.17g. There seems to be no obvious way to ascertain if there was any attempt to create an Ebusus 'unit' and an Ebusus 'fractional' unit, unless one were to conduct a full and detailed die study, which would be extremely difficult given the generally poor state of preservation.

Despite these difficulties, there might be some sense in suggesting that the Massalia coins had a lower 'face value' than the Ebusus coins, as they are, on average, around a whole gram lighter in weight and invariably smaller in size. But what might such a relationship have been? They do not seem to have been intended as halves, thirds, or quarters of the Ebusus series, as their average weights show little obvious correlation. In fact, on average a Massalia coin equates to roughly two-thirds to three-quarters of an average Ebusus. Maybe at one point there *was* a relationship, but as production surged this became forgotten and ceased to have meaning. Which may imply that their 'face value' related more to their appearance than their size or weight, *i.e.* a coin with an image of Bes, however crude, had a different face value than a coin with a head on one side and a butting bull on the other.

2.4. The coinage of Rome

The locally produced coins provided most of the monetary stock at Pompeii in the late second to early first centuries BC (see 'Dating' discussion below, pp. 98-99). Like Massalia and Ebusus, Rome is also a special case as it forms a significant part of the assemblage, making up about 28% of the total (see Table 2). This is almost exactly the proportion noted by Vitale who calculated that 29% of pre-AD 79 coins originated in

Rome.[250] The presence of large numbers of Roman coins of both Republican and Imperial date might at first glance be related to what is, arguably, the single most influential event in the town's later history: after the defeat of the town at the hands of the Roman general Sulla in 89 BC the town had a Roman colony imposed on it as punishment. The main period of veteran settlement took place after *c.* 80 BC.[251] The impact of the imposition of at least two thousand veteran soldiers[252] and their families and dependants on the town's society and development must have been immense, and from the point of view of the coinage must have led to a major increase in the demand for 'small change'. But direct numismatic evidence for this historic event is by no means obvious, although it is not exactly clear what we might expect to see. As we have seen, the vast majority of Roman base metal coins in the assemblage can be dated to long before the colony was established, added to which the minting of bronze coins by Rome was sporadic after about the early first century BC and came to a halt altogether after the final bronze issues of Sulla in 82 BC.[253] The influx of veterans presumably increased the numbers of silver *denarii* in circulation, but because of their high intrinsic value, these coins rarely find their way into the pre-79 levels: the fleeing man at Oplontis is good evidence for the fact that silver coins were retained and kept separate from everyday 'small change' (discussed above, p. 6). In fact, the AAPP assemblage contains only 28 silver Republican coins (around 2% of the total), and over half (16) of these are silver-plated pieces anyway, designed, it is assumed, to deceive. The Roman bronze which made its way inside the town walls continued to circulate many decades after it was struck, given the fact that the *as* – the commonest type of Republican bronze denomination present in the assemblage – is more often than not extremely worn by the time it was lost or discarded. In addition, many of the Republican coins (and occasionally Imperial) were deliberately cut into halves, quarters, or possibly even smaller fractions, which can only have happened when the demand for 'small change' was intense: about 7% of the assemblage is made up of these deliberately cut pieces (cats 933-1040).[254] Contextual analysis suggests that these deliberately cut fractions were mainly circulating in the late first century BC and early first century AD (see p. 92). In any case, we know from the takings of the Bar of Lucius Vetudius Placidus on the via dell'Abbondanza that Republican coins circulated for a very long time after they were struck, right up to the time of the eruption (see p. 8 and Table 1). But the principal point is that the veterans did not visibly affect the characteristics of the 'local' coinage pool, and the copying of Roman prototypes, particularly the bridled horse's head types (see pp. 42 and 48) appears from the stratigraphic data to long pre-date the time of the colony.

[250] Vitale (2008), 30. Including illegible coins.

[251] Zanker (1998), 61ff.

[252] *Ibid.*, 62. Others suggest an even higher figure: 'The number of colonists is not known but it could have tallied with the size of a legion and been as high as 4,000-5,000': Descoeudres (2007), 16.

[253] *RRC*, 387, 596-97.

[254] There are no examples of cut fractions of either 'foreign' imports or local imitations.

2.4.1. Roman Republican coins in the AAPP assemblage

It is unfortunate that only 46 of the 161 Roman Republican coins (excluding cut halves and coins of Octavian) can be accurately dated; once again, heavy wear on the coins and corrosion means that in most cases it was not possible to discern enough details of inscriptions and other distinguishing motifs. Nevertheless some interesting patterns can be observed, if the number of coins is plotted by period of issue (Table 5 and Figure 8). A quarter of the dated coins come from the mid to late third century BC, including a few early *Dioscuri denarii* (cats 771-72) and issues thought to be Sicilian (cats 773-77). The next peak comes in the middle of the second century BC, with very few dated bronze coins earlier or later, although there may well be more in this group which are too worn to date. The highest peak per year are coins dated to 89-88 BC, the period of the Sullan attack, but as this is in reality only seven coins this cannot be taken to be statistically significant. Perhaps however what is of interest is the fact that the paucity of Roman Republican coins in the late second century to early first century BC seems to coincide with the period in which the major phase of imitation and local production of Ebusus and Massalia coins occurred (see below pp. 81-96).

As for denominations of Republican coins (excluding cut fractions – Table 6), *asses* make up just over half the total number, which is perhaps surprising given that these are physically the largest coins and therefore more easily spotted if accidentally dropped, so this must presumably be a reflection of the huge number of *asses* circulating in Pompeii and their popularity for commercial transactions.[255] It should also be reiterated that this is not a bias of recovery – smaller denominations tending to be missed by hand trowelling – because every context dug in the AAPP excavations was sieved through a fine mesh which led to a high proportion of smaller module coins being recovered. This contrasts with the Bathhouse hoard, in which of the 24 Republican coins only two are *asses*, although the hoard (probably a dropped purse) generally contains coins of low module so does not necessarily provide a good cross-section of the circulation pool at the time (see p. 66 and Appendix 2). The AAPP assemblage is more akin with the 'live' currency in the bar of L. Vetudius Placidus, where 14 of the 22 Republican bronze still circulating were *asses*.

The high volume of *asses* is also suggested by the popularity of these as halved coins, about 65% of all halves (see Table 7). There are very few *semisses* but a reasonable number of *trientes, quadrantes* and *sextantes* (Table 6). Of the silver coins of Republican date, of which there are 28, approximately 16 appear to be plated forgeries, although in some very corroded cases it is difficult to differentiate without metallurgical analysis what is plating and what is copper which has leached to the surface of a good quality silver coin.

---

[255] This corresponds well with research conducted by Vitale, who found that 60% of 211 Republican coins from published excavations were *asses*, the rest smaller denominations: Vitale (2008), 31.

DATED ROMAN REPUBLICAN		
	Total	by year
c. 241-200 BC	12	0.29
c. 199-180 BC	0	0.00
c. 179-70 BC	1	0.10
c. 169-158 BC	6	0.50
c. 157-146 BC	14	1.17
c. 145-122 BC	0	0.00
c. 121-90 BC	4	0.13
c. 89-88 BC	6	3.00
87-66 BC	1	0.04
Total	44	

Table 5. Dated Roman Republican coins in the AAPP assemblage.

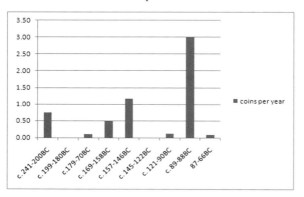

Figure 8. Dated Republican coins in the AAPP assemblage (coins per year.)

REPUBLICAN DENOMINATIONS		
	Total	%
Denarius (AR)*	20	12.4
Quinarius (AR)*	8	5.0
Litra (AE)	1	0.6
Uncia (AE)	6	3.7
As (AE)*	85	52.8
Semis (AE)	4	2.5
Triens (AE)	18	11.2
Quadrans (AE)	12	7.5
Sextans (AE)	6	3.7
Semuncia (AE)	1	0.6
Total	161	

*Denarii include 9 probable but very corroded and possibly plated pieces, and quinarii include 3 probable pieces; asses include one dated half (cat. 816)

Table 6. Republican denominations in the AAPP assemblage.

2.4.2. Deliberately cut coins

Although, as far as I am aware, there is no comprehensive survey as yet of deliberately halved and other fractioned bronze coins in the Roman Republican period, anecdotally the halving of coins appears to have been an extremely common practice when 'small change' was in short supply. 'Halved coins have been found in the nineteenth- and twentieth-century excavations by the hundreds'[256] and the AAPP assemblage is a continuation of that pattern, producing 108 examples, about 7% of the total (Table 7). Other Italian sites which have produced such fractions includes Cosa, Minturnae and Morgantina.[257] Halved coins appear to come from both urban and votive sites, an example of the latter being Bourbonne-les-Bains (Haute-Marne), dated to the time of Augustus, where around 94% of all the early Gaulish Roman provincial coins were halved.[258] Halved coins have also come from military sites, including Augst and Novaesium.[259] At Augst, 225 of the 283 Republican *asses* were halved and the assemblage also included other fractions, just as in this assemblage.[260] Py[261] states that Republican *asses* cut in halves, thirds and quarters are frequent in southern Gaul where they represent 18.3% of the known examples, proportions that are doubled on some sites, *e.g.* at Vieille-Toulouse; large numbers were also found at Narbonne.[262] This practice is not only confined to southern France because they have also been found at Ampurias.[263]

We know that halved coins were still in circulation at the time of the eruption, as evidenced by a halved *sestertius* found in the group of coins from the Bar of Asellina,[264]

	Total	%
Halved *asses*	71	66.4
Halved *semisses* and *trientes*	24	22.4
Cut quarters	11	10.3
Smaller fractions	1	0.9
Total	107	

Table 7. Deliberately cut Republican coins in the AAPP assemblage.

[256] Buttrey (1972), 31.

[257] Buttrey (1989).

[258] Sauer (1999), 155.

[259] Chantraine (1982); Peter (2001). I would like to thank Johan van Heesch for providing me with these references.

[260] Peter (2001), 41.

[261] Py (2006), 716; see also Feugere and Py (2011), 435.

[262] Amardel (1909).

[263] Ripoll *et al.* (1973-74).

[264] Taliercio Mensitieri (2005), 108-10; Stefani and Vitale (2005), 126, inv. Ill 8N.

but the vast majority of halves are of Republican date.[265] Buttrey's argument that the phenomenon can be dated to two phases, one in the penultimate decade of the first century BC and one in the 30s AD is to some extent contradicted by the evidence from the AAPP excavations (see 'Dating', p. 92), and has also been disputed by Sauer.[266]

Of the 108 deliberately cut coins in the AAPP assemblage, 70 are halved *asses*, 26 halved *semisses* or *trientes,* and there are also 11 quarters and one possible eighth (cat. 1039). The Janus head on the obverse of the Republican *as* provided a useful marker for forming two more or less equal halves, and it has been suggested that this was a way of creating supplementary *asses* during the Augustan period when official *asses* were in short supply.[267] But who created the halves is unclear, as is the issue of a weight standard. An examination of the weights represented in the AAPP assemblage demonstrates that the cut coins could fluctuate wildly, which is not surprising considering that the weight of full size *asses* are equally inconsistent (Figure 9). It is also unclear if the cutting was done inside the town walls, or if these cut halves were imports – maybe it was a combination of both. The fact that cut halves of Nemausus are extremely common in southern France might imply that these halves at least were imported from elsewhere (cats 1047-48: see below). Whatever the facts of the matter, it remains the case that cut Republican coins, and to a lesser extent early Imperial ones, were a common feature of the monetary pool of Pompeii and no doubt many urban centres across the Mediterranean. A further discussion of the significance of these fractioned coins, particularly with regard to their dating, is provided on p. 92.

2.4.3. Roman provincial coins of Imperial date

Uncertain mint, Italy (cats 1040-41)
Although some have argued for this being a Lyon issue, 'provenances support an Italian origin',[268] so these examples only add more weight to this argument. The issue has been dated to around 38 BC on the basis of stylistic parallels with issues of Agrippa.[269] Although often imitated, the AAPP examples appear from their weight and style to be official pieces.

---

[265] 'To my knowledge, no halved Augustan moneyers' or Tiberian *as* ... has ever been reported in Italy': Buttrey (1972), 39. In actuality there may be one in this assemblage, cat. 1056.

[266] Sauer (1999), 154-55.

[267] Buttrey (1972), 46: 'Halving was... the expedient by which *asses* were reinstated in the currency, the newly defined *dupondii* [*i.e.* Republican *asses*] being split to provide them'.

[268] *RPC* 1, 161.

[269] *Ibid.*

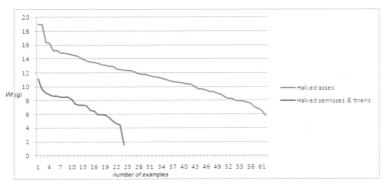

Figure 9. Weights of halved *asses* (in blue, 62 examples) and halved *semisses* and *trientes* (in red, 24 examples).

Nemausus (cats 1047-48)

These coins are almost certainly halves of Nemausus (modern Nîmes) with heads of Agrippa and Augustus, even if the legends cannot be read and the reverses are unclear (although it might be possible to make out part of the crocodile on cat. 1048). Deliberately halved Nemausus coins are extremely common finds in Gaul as are the full weight versions of what was clearly an immense issue.[270] Buttrey[271] highlights the earlier research of Morel-Fatio in the late nineteenth century who had seen 'over 1100 examples' in French Switzerland (although as Buttrey points out, it is unclear if these were all halves or a mixture of halves and full weight coins). Sauer's study of the 3,810 coins preserved in the museum at Bourbonne-les-Bains identified around 450 cut Nemausus.[272] As far as I am aware these are the only recorded examples of cut Nemausus halves from Pompeii and as I speculated above I wonder if they should be considered foreign imports. Four Nemausus coins have come from the River Liri at Minturnae, but it is not made clear in the report if these were full weight coins or halves.[273]

Alexandria (cats 1061-63)

It is unclear if these pieces are legitimate issues of Augustus or local copies as the legends are difficult to read and therefore might be garbled. The dating of the series, suggested to be the fourth of six, is problematic, as is the placing of the issue in the sequence.[274] Another turned up in the Casa di Amarantus excavations.[275] Fifteen further examples were found in the Liri.[276]

---

[270] *RPC* 1, 152-53; Giard (1971).

[271] Buttrey (1972), 32.

[272] Sauer (1999), 150.

[273] Stannard and Frey-Kupper (2008), 393, Table 8.

[274] *RPC* 1, 691-93.

[275] Stannard (unpublished), cat. 56.

[276] Stannard and Frey-Kupper (2008), 397, Table 8.

Patras (cat. 1185)

The single coin of Nero struck at the Aegean port of Patras, established as a Roman colony in 14 BC, is of a type thought likely to be linked with the emperors visit in AD 66-67 (celebrated by the 'ADVENTVS AVGVSTI' reverse). The weight of the AAPP example is remarkably close to the average weight of the coins of Patras of 8.97g.[277] I have not encountered any other examples at Pompeii, although two are known from the river Liri.[278]

2.4.4. Coins of Octavian to AD 79

Denominations

The three latest silver coins in the AAPP assemblage were struck in the early years of Octavian (32 to 21 BC; cats 1044-46). There are no silver coins of the Christian era. Notwithstanding the earlier silver pieces, which in any case are mostly plated (discussed above), this must reflect the clear split between 'ready cash', the bronze currency of everyday transactions, and the intrinsically valuable gold and silver coins retained as 'stores of wealth'. The 'till float' of L. Vetudius Placidus did not contain any silver coins either (Table 2 and Figure 10). Initially I was therefore puzzled by the fact that these three silver coins come from bars: the *denarius* (cat. 1044) from the Bar of Phoebus sited at the apex of the triangular insula and the two *quinarii* (cats 1045-46) from the Inn and Casa delle Vestali Bar respectively. But on closer inspection it transpires that the latter two coins were found in back rooms, not the bar counter areas directly on the street, where the most intensive coin loss is observed (see pp. 101-02 and Figure 19).

IMPERIAL DENOMINATIONS			Bar of L. Vetudius Placidus	
	Total	%		
Denarius (AR)	1	0.7	0	0.0
Quinarius (AR)	2	1.4	0	0.0
As	75	53.2	255	18.9
Dupondius	7	5.0	224	16.6
Sestertius	4	2.8	865	64.2
Quadrans	52	36.9	3	0.2
Total	141	100.0	1347	100.0

Table 8. Imperial denominations in the AAPP assemblage in comparison with the bar of L. Vetudius Placidus.

---

[277] *RPC* 1, 259.

[278] Stannard and Frey-Kupper (2008), 396, Table 8.

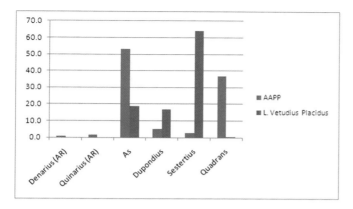

Figure 10. Imperial denominations in comparison with the bar of L. Vetudius Placidus.

As for the bronze coins of Octavian to Vespasian, in a similar manner to the Republican coin profile (see above), *asses* dominate, accounting for about half of all coins dating from Octavian to AD 79 (Table 8 and Figure 10). There are very few brass *dupondii* and *sestertii*, but a large number of Imperial *quadrantes*, particularly of Augustus and Claudius (although it should be pointed out that during Tiberius' long reign the denomination is represented by only a single type).[279] This denominational profile is in almost exact opposition to what is observed at the bar of L. Vetudius Placidus, where the vast majority of the coins were *sestertii* and most of the remainder *asses* and *dupondii*. In fact, there are only three *quadrantes* out of a total of 1,385 coins, which seems an extraordinarily low number. The only explanation might be that by AD 79, the *quadrans* had largely disappeared from circulation. Did the *quadrantes* of Octavian and his successors somehow fill a gap vacated by the loss of new issues of local imitations, perhaps the Campanian Ebusus coins? This is pure speculation. On average, the *quadrantes* are rather heavier and larger in diameter than the early Ebusus types and much heavier and larger than the latest ones, so a direct continuation is difficult to argue (as discussed above, pp. 51-54).

[279] *RIC* I, Tiberius, no. 32.

3 DATING THE PRE-79 COINS: MANUFACTURE AND USE

In the previous chapter, the range of coin types represented at Pompeii was discussed. At points some remarks were made on chronology, but in general terms the issue of dating was not addressed in any detail. Dating is the subject of this chapter.

The question of dating can be addressed through a number of different approaches:

- Comparison of the AAPP assemblage with other Pompeian assemblages – for example 'the Bathhouse hoard' (Appendix 2) and the coins from the bar of L. Vetudius Placidus.
- Assessing previous work on typology and other archaeological data sets; for example the work by Campo and Stannard on Ebusus[280] and Py and Frey-Kupper and Stannard on Massalia.[281]
- AAPP site phasing: as outlined above, some areas of the site have been phased making it possible to compare the numismatic and stratigraphic data (Appendix 1).
- AAPP contextual association: some contexts have well dated coins in association with the local issues, giving an insight into when the local coins were introduced into the circulation pool and how long they remained in circulation.

3.2. Comparing the AAPP assemblage with other Pompeian coin assemblages

Excavation of Regio VI, 1 established that the earliest evidence for human activity may date as early as the second half of the fourth century BC, as suggested by small amounts of pottery of this period.[282] There is no evidence that these early settlers were using coinage, but they probably *were* beginning to use coins by the time of the construction of the first substantial building located in the block, which lay beneath the Casa del Chirurgo.[283] In fact one of the earliest datable coins from the insula comes from Room 5 of the Casa del Chirurgo and dates to 214-212 BC (cat. 772). This coin is crucial to the dating of the house's foundation, as it provides a *terminus post quem* for its construction.

---

[280] For instance Campo (1976), Stannard (2005a).

[281] Py (2006); Frey-Kupper and Stannard (2010).

[282] Jones (2008), 141. Jones suggests that there is evidence of beaten earth floors dating to this period. Anderson (pers. comm.) suggests these may rather be layers of compressed ash from an earlier eruption; and that the pottery, reported in early excavation reports, is the only actual evidence for early occupation.

[283] *Ibid.*

Once the basic layout of the insula had been established and domestic and commercial activities were up and running, coinage began to form an increasingly important part of those activities. As has been shown, the numismatic evidence persuasively indicates that the population in the region used both imported coins from a number of locations around the Mediterranean, but also local (for sake of argument, 'Campanian') coins, copying prototypes mainly from Ebusus and Massalia. It is, however, very difficult to establish exactly when this copying process began, how long it went on, and how long these local issues were in use, and this is a matter not just pertinent to this insula block but to the town as a whole. As has already been discussed, the written sources are entirely silent on the subject (p. 15). It is not even clear which authority would have been responsible for coinage production, and there are no historical references to these local issues – we certainly have no idea what the Ebusus, Massalia and anomalous local denominations were termed by those who used them.[284] In addition, most numismatists have focussed their discussions of coin circulation in Pompeii on the time of the eruption,[285] with the exception of Stannard and Frey-Kupper,[286] which means that this topic has received less attention than it deserves.

But where does the AAPP assemblage fit in with other Pompeiian assemblages (Table 9)? It is not the earliest group: that is a hoard found in 1942 near the temple of Jupiter, which consisted of three silver and 134 bronze coins running down to c225 BC, most of which were Neapolis types.[287] This hoard must have been buried no later than the late third century BC. Crucially, it contained no Ebusus or Massalia coins, or indeed Roman Republican issues (although a number of coins could not be identified). This hoard probably, therefore, provides a *terminus post quem* for the production of local issues and the importation of Roman Republican coins.

Another important early assemblage – yet to be fully published – was excavated in 1984 at Gragnano, Castellamare di Stabia (better known as the Privati di Stabia deposit).[288] Over six hundred bronze coins were recovered, dating from the fourth until the end of the second century BC. Its earliest pieces are four fragments of *aes rude,* which – although they can be as early as the eighth century BC – are thought to be of fourth century date.[289] There are also early Roman *sextantes* on the libral standard, thus of the early to mid third century BC (*RRC* 18/3), and a coin of Paestum struck in 273 BC to commemorate the founding of the colony.

---

[284] In the catalogue they are referred to as 'AE unit'.

[285] For example Breglia (1950), Duncan-Jones (2003; 2007), Giove (2003).

[286] For example Stannard and Frey-Kupper (2008), Frey-Kupper and Stannard (2010).

[287] Duncan-Jones (2003), 162, n. 4; Maiuri (1942), 308. According to the latter publication the group contained a few Neapolis coins of the type with head of Apollo on the obverse and the foreparts of a bull on the reverse (*cf. HN* 568 or 574), not represented in this assemblage; most were obv. Apollo, rev. man-head bull being crowned by Victory reverse (*cf.* cats 1-6 this volume) and obv. head of Apollo, rev. tripod (*cf.* cats 7-8 this volume). Of the other mints recognised these included a coin of Cales (*cf. HN* 435). Apart from Maiuri's summary the coins have never been fully published.

[288] Miniero *et al.* (1997).

[289] Cantilena (1997).

Site/Location	Coin summary	Date range	References
Pompeii, Temple of Jupiter (VII, 8)	3 AR, 134 AE	down to c. 200 BC	Duncan-Jones (2003), 162; Maiuri (1942), 308*
Privati, Gragnano, Castellamare di Stabia	c. 600+ AE	4th c BC to c. 100 BC	Miniero et al. (1997)*
Pompeii, various locations	90 AE	late 4th c BC to c. AD 68	Ranucci (2008a), (2008b)
Pompeii, Republican baths ('Bathhouse hoard') (VIII, 5, 36)	90 AE	third century BC to c. 90 BC	Stannard (2005a), 122; Appendix 2 (this volume)
Pompeii, Casa di Amarantus (I, 9, 11-12)	12 AR, 171 AE	c. 3rd c BC to AD 79	Fulford and Wallace-Hadrill (1995-6); Stannard (2005a), 121*; Stannard (unpublished)
Pompeii, Forum excavations (VII, 8)	150 AE	Republic to AD 79	Arthur (1986); Stannard (2005a), 121-2*
Pompeii, Casa dei Postumii (VIII, 4, 4)	104 AE (?)	uncertain, includes Ebusus and Massalia	Stannard (2005a), 124*; Dickmann and Pirson (2005)
Pompeii, bar of Asellina (IX, 2, 11)	67, AR and AE	Republic to AD 79	Romagnoli and Vitale (2005)
Pompeii, bar of L. Vetudius Placidus (I, 1, 8)	1,285 AE	Republic to AD 79	Castiello and Oliviero (1997)

* summary lists or information only

Table 9. Comparable coin assemblages to the AAPP assemblage.

Coins of such early date are not present in the AAPP assemblage or indeed other well-excavated groups such as the Casa di Amarantus.[290] At the other end of the dating spectrum at Gragnano are Cyrenaican bronzes of the late second century BC and a Roman Republican *denarius* of 136 BC (*RRC* 237/1). These are the latest datable coins in the group and comparable examples are present in the AAPP assemblage. Both Ebusus and Massalia coins were also found at Gragnano, and, significantly, some of these are Campanian Ebusus type 3 (the 'rudimentary' type) which are the latest in the series. This implies that the local imitations of Ebusus and Massalia date from the late second century BC. The excavators believe that the votive deposit at Gragnano closes around 100 BC, and certainly prior to the Social War.[291]

Another important published set of coins excavated at Pompeii from below the AD 79 level were discovered during a series of excavations conducted by the Università degli Studi di Perugia between 2002 and 2007.[292] The excavations produced 144 coins in total, 130 of which were from excavated contexts, and 14 from surface collection (*i.e.* unstratified finds).

---

[290] Stannard (unpublished).

[291] Miniero *et al.* (1997), 17.

[292] Ranucci (2008a), (2008b). The project team conducted a number of small-scale excavations in different properties of the town in Regio VI 2, VI 5, VII 15, VIII 4 e VIII 6, and also investigated different aspects of the towns streets and plan at Regio VI 5-7 (Vicolo della Fullonica), VI 9-11 (Vicolo del Fauno), IX 7 (Vicolo di Tesmo) and IX 8 (Vicolo del Fauno ebbro): Ranucci (2008b), 151.

Although the bulk of the coins are of similar date range to the AAPP assemblage, there are a few earlier coins of the late fourth century BC: coins of Neapolis with the foreparts of a bull on the reverse (a type not present in the AAPP assemblage),[293] and of Siracusa (a different type to those in this assemblage).[294] Ebusus and Massalia imports and local coins make up about 40% of the whole assemblage, and include a single anomalous type with horse's head and horse reverse, a type not represented in the AAPP assemblage.[295] The excavations also produced Roman Republican and Imperial coins, coins of Cyrenaica, Panormus and a few non-Ebusan Spanish pieces (in a similar manner to the AAPP assemblage).

The next group of comparable coins is a hoard found in the sewers of a bathhouse at Regio VIII, 5, 36, referred to throughout this book as the Bathhouse hoard: a full list of the hoard is provided in Appendix 2.[296] Maiuri believed that the group was the contents of a purse, accidentally dropped by a bather and carried down to its resting place by the running waters. The hoard consists of 90 coins: 2 AE of Neapolis, 1 Sicilian AE, 15 Massalia or Campanian Massalia coins, 48 Ebusus and Campanian Ebusus coins, one Republican AR and 23 Republican AE. The Ebusan and Massalian coins, most of which are Campanian types (*i.e.* struck locally), make up exactly 70% of the assemblage. A few of the Roman Republican coins can be well dated: the earliest (Appendix 2, BH67) dates to *c.* 214-212 BC, and the latest are *semuncial* bronzes of around 91 BC,[297] with the very latest dated coin with left-facing prow (Appendix 2, BH80) struck in 86 BC. This coin provides a *terminus post quem* for the loss of the coins, which cannot have been deposited much after the late 80s BC.[298]

The Massalia coins in the Bathhouse hoard consist in the main of Campanian Massalia types with garbled legends (Type 2C, particularly 'ΑΜΟΣ'; see p. 39). All appear relatively fresh and not heavily circulated, suggesting production towards the end of the Republican coin sequence represented, perhaps late second century BC, to early first century BC. The Ebusus coins make up over half of the Bathhouse hoard and most are unworn, with the odd exception, *e.g.* BH66, Ebusus type 8B (see p. 49). The 'rudimentary' types dominate: 34 of the Ebusus coins are types 3A to C (with 3C by far the most common), and these appear to be the least circulated out of all the Ebusus types, which is logical given the fact that they are stylistically late in the sequence. So, like the Massalia coins, given the *terminus post quem* provided by the Republican coin dated to 86 BC, the implication is that the Ebusus coins were also struck not much before this date, around the time of the Sullan siege (see also pp. 86-92).

---

[293] See n. 100.

[294] Ranucci (2008b), Table 1, cat. 108.

[295] *Ibid.*, 250. I have also identified one of these coins in the assemblage of *c.* 70 coins found during excavations by the Via Consolare Project.

[296] Maiuri (1950). I would like to thank Dottssa Teresa Giove for allowing me to take impressions of the Bathhouse hoard in March 2009.

[297] Crawford states that 'the lower denominations are listed here without any very great conviction, since some may be. ... unofficial imitations': *RRC*, 340.

[298] A view shared by Stannard: Stannard (2005a), 122.

Other important groups of excavated coins from Pompeii (Casa di Amarantus, Forum excavations and the Casa dei Postumii) have been examined by Stannard in his 2005a paper, although a complete catalogue of the material in each assemblage is not provided.[299] Stannard has kindly provided me with his catalogue and study of the Casa di Amarantus assemblage, where he also provides details of other comparable assemblages.[300] Types relevant to this study have been discussed as appropriate (pp. 23-50).

Which brings us finally to two groups of 'live' coins from the bars of Lucius Vetudius Placidus and Asellina on the via dell'Abbondanza. These assemblages have already been discussed above (pp. 7-8 and Table 1), but it is worth reiterating that they are markedly different in character from the coin finds from the AAPP, the Casa di Amarantus and the Forum excavations. For example at the bar of Lucius Vetudius Placidus, coins of Vespasian, Domitian and Titus make up almost half the assemblage and most of the coins are Imperial *asses* (around 60%). A few Republican bronze coins, mostly *asses*, are also present, and also a few smaller denominations. These must have still been 'legal tender' at the time of the eruption when one might expect them to have long since fallen out of use, although the 'foreign' imports, a Ptolemaic coin from Cyrenaica of the early second century BC and a single Sicilian unit from Amestratus might rather be overlooked intruders. But one telling absence are the Campanian Ebusus and Campanian Massalia types. Despite being the principal types of coins for such a long period, they appear to have completely disappeared from circulation by AD 79.[301]

So what we can deduce from looking at assemblages comparable with the AAPP coins is that there is little evidence for large-scale coin use in Pompeii until the third century BC, and even the earlier groups of the late fourth century BC (for instance the assemblage from the Temple of Jupiter) come from quite specific contexts not able to be directly related to commercial exchange (notably the Privati di Stabia and Temple of Jupiter deposits). All the excavated Pompeii assemblages from non-religious contexts indicate that Roman Republican and imported Ebusus and Massalia coins appear in the second century BC, after which the latter two groups were copied locally. Most of these dropped out of use by the early decades of the first century AD when Roman Imperial coins began to appear in large numbers.

---

[299] Stannard (2005a).

[300] Stannard (unpublished).

[301] However it should be noted that two corroded Ebusus coins were found in a hoard of eruption date in 1984 discovered at Oplontis in Room 15 of the villa of Lucius Crassius Tertius: Castiglione Morelli (2000; the Ebusus coins are nos. 127 and 128). Unfortunately it is not clear from the report if these are Ebusus imports or Campanian copies, although as both are described as 'Bes? Bes?', suggesting that the figure is difficult to make out, this might imply the latter. The hoard totaled 409 coins, 2 gold, 189 silver and 218 bronze, with the earliest coin a *denarius* of Furius Purpurio (*RRC* 187 of 169-158 BC) and the latest 153 coins of Vespasian.

3.3. Dating the local coins on the basis of typology and archaeological data

So effectively the comparison with other assemblages shows that the AAPP assemblage is not one of the earliest known from Pompeii but can be dated to before and after the Sullan siege. But can we be more specific with regard to when these local coins arrived in Pompeii and when the main period of local production began? The discussion that follows addresses this question by examining how each local type relates to previous typological work, data derived from other archaeological strata and the stratigraphic data in the AAPP excavations.

The stratigraphic data from the AAPP excavations is set out in Appendix 1 (Tables 17-19). The data is derived from the three parts of the site that have been phased, the Inn, Inn Bar and Casa del Triclinio, the Casa del Chirurgo and the Shrine. In addition, pottery and lamp dates if available and the presence of cast or blown glass was also taken into account.

3.3.1. Dating evidence provided by the AAPP excavations

The most useful aspect of the data provided by this assemblage is the possibility of linking the coin evidence with the site stratigraphy and evidence provided by other categories of datable artefacts, particularly glass, certain classes of ceramics and archaeological evidence of the Sullan siege, for example lead slingshot. This work is not complete, but three parts of the block have been phased and some of the other non-numismatic material in them examined: the Inn and Casa del Triclinio to the north (plots 9 and 10), the Casa del Chirurgo (plots 5 and 6) and the Shrine (plot 4) (Figure 11). A summary of the archaeological data from these areas is provided here. These are not comprehensive accounts of the archaeology of these areas of the site, because this research is ongoing (and in any case, this volume is not the appropriate place to provide detailed information); instead the intention is to give a flavour of how these areas developed throughout their occupation and how the numismatic evidence ties in. The Shrine is discussed in a slightly different manner to the other two plots because it has been possible to conduct a more in-depth study of the numismatic material produced and what this can tell us about how the circulation pool changed over time. The specific data on the phasing, coins and other dated artefactual evidence is provided in Appendix 1 (Tables 17-19).

The Casa del Triclinio, the Inn and part of the Via Consolare (plots 9 and 10)

These two plots were the first properties encountered by those entering the town via the Porta Ercolano. The plot described as the Casa del Triclinio is a series of rooms at the extreme north-west of Regio VI, 1, the most recognisable feature of which is a *triclinium* bench situated in what was once an outside space, which gives its name to the 'house'. In its final form the adjacent Inn consisted of a series of rooms around a central courtyard, with the side facing the Via Consolare clearly commercial in character, particularly the bar counter in Room 1B (Figure 11). For most of the history of the insula these two plots were connected by a doorway (they were only separated during the post-Sullan rebuild, probably of the Augustan period)[302] so in many ways they ought to be viewed as one property. However as they were excavated as two separate plots they are discussed separately.

---

[302] Anderson (pers. comm.). Prior to this the Casa del Triclinio had been part of the Casa delle Vestali and accessed via a door in the western wall of the peristyle and a set of stairs: Robinson (pers. comm.).

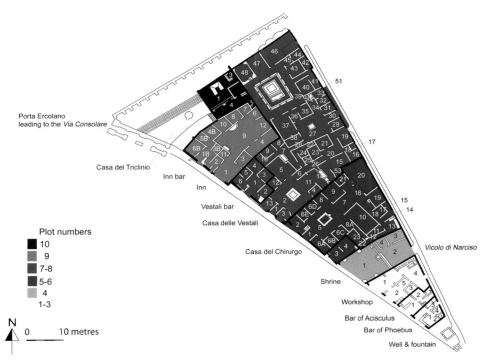

Figure 11. Plots and room numbers in Regio VI, 1.

The Inn: phasing and coins

The Inn (including the Inn Bar) produced 452 coins, accounting for almost 30% of the whole assemblage. The standing remains in this area of the insula can be dated back to the second century BC, a period during which 'the largely open landscape to the north and south [of the plot occupied by the Inn]... becomes filled with a range of small courtyard houses and commercial properties'.[303] Prior to this (phases 2 to 3 – late fourth to third centuries BC), the only evidence of activity in these plots comes in the form of a layer of grey-black sand (similar deposits of which are found beneath the tufa steps of the town's circuit wall) and a series of hard compacted earth layers. None of the contexts which can be dated to these phases produced any coins.

During phase 4, which can date no earlier than about 200 BC, and is more likely to date to the early second century BC, there is evidence that some structures, for instance an 'L' shaped wall, were built. These structures – their exact nature difficult to characterise as they are largely obliterated by later development – relate to the same general construction phase as the adjoining Casa delle Vestali to the south. Although only three deposits during this phase produced coins (Appendix 1, Table 17), these are of obvious importance because they are some of the earliest deposits in the insula block (although it should be noted that the most productive context in terms of coins (127.082) may date to phase 5).

---

[303] Jones and Robinson (2007), 393.

During the next phase (5), which is also pre-Sullan, there is evidence of expansion of these earlier structures so that the extent of the insula begins to encroach on the town's defensive ramparts. Two small industrial/commercial buildings were constructed by converting existing buildings between the Casa delle Vestali and the Porta Ercolano, and cutting into the ramparts for the first time.[304] A series of levelling fills were also laid down during this period (rooms 5B and 6B and rooms 1B and 3B – see Figure 11). One of the most distinctive features of this phase is a plaster-lined tank at the western end of room 1B. The layer of sediment found at the bottom of this tank contained many fish bones and scales, so it may have been used to produce salted fish or by-products such as *garum*.[305] The courtyard area in the centre of the plot was also apparently used to support the fish production activities. The number of coins that can be attributed to this phase rises dramatically to 87, spread across 17 or possibly 18 contexts (Appendix 1, Table 17). These contexts provide important evidence for the dating of locally produced coins (see pp. 81-89).

Phase 6 is post-Sullan and runs down to the mid/late first BC. The destruction caused by the Sullan siege, of which there is a great deal of evidence in the archaeological record in the form of different types of artillery – particularly lead slingshot, found in abundance in the central courtyard – appears to have led to the abandonment of industrial activities such as fish-processing, as the aforementioned tank was allowed to silt up before being filled with a dump of soil and rubble. It also necessitated the almost complete rebuilding of existing structures, with most of the walls in the plot being entirely new constructions. Another important new development occurred in the courtyard (Room 9), when aside from post-Sullan levelling, a ceramic vessel was set into the west of the room. Substantial quantities of charcoal and other evidence of heating suggest it was used for metalworking and it is entirely plausible that this may have supported a blacksmith's shop on the Via Consolare. Almost 40% (149 coins) of the total number of coins recovered from these plots can be dated to contexts in this phase. This may reflect a period of intensifying commercial activity, although as many of the contexts in the period can be characterised as post-Sullan destruction deposits, many of the coins may have been lost during earlier phases and dumped in this period during levelling activities.

In Phase 7, which dates to the late Augustan period at the earliest, and could even be as late as the mid first century AD, the Inn Bar was converted from a domestic space into a commercial property, almost certainly for the vending of hot food (a *thermopolium*); a bar counter was added in the mid first century AD.[306] Evidence for this change of use includes the construction of an oven in room 1B (Figure 11). This was part of a wider change in the use of the space from industrial activities, particularly metalworking (see above), to the creation of an Inn (*stabulum*). Like Phase 6 this phase also produces a large number of coins (102).

---

[304] Anderson (pers. comm.).

[305] For a discussion of the salting of fish at Pompeii see Ellis (2011b).

[306] Robinson (pers. comm.).

Phase 8 is likely to date to around the time of the earthquake of AD 62.[307] The main feature of this phase is the construction of upper storeys, which also occurs in other parts of the insula. In addition a bar counter was added in room 1B, an *opus signinum* floor was laid in rooms 1B and 6B, and both rooms were decorated with a white fresco with red stripes. Much of the building work had not been completed by the time of the eruption. The number of coins which can be attributed to this phase drops considerably to 23 (Appendix 1, Table 17).

Casa del Triclinio: phasing and coins
The Casa del Triclinio produced only 24 coins, barely 2% of the entire assemblage. The area was extensively damaged in the years following its discovery, particularly by an Allied bomb dropped on the insula in 1943, and its archaeology is also heavily disturbed because the whole plot was used as a spoil dump during Maiuri's investigations in about 1930.[308] Its name is also misleading, because there is no obvious living area and it is much more likely that it was a component of the adjacent Inn. The main features of the area, aside from the *triclinium*, include remains of brick pilasters indicative of a covered corridor, a series of small rooms including a Shrine with altar and niche to the east of the *triclinium* and an earth ramp connecting the *triclinium* with the Via Consolare. It is at present unclear to what extent this ramp relates to earlier excavations (*i.e.* much of it could be spoil), so the area is perhaps best characterised as a large open space on a gradient.

The same phasing scheme used for the Inn has been applied to the Casa del Triclinio. Although some features of Phase 2 have been identified, no deposits of phases 3 to 5 inclusive have been recovered, and therefore, not surprisingly, there are no coins that can be assigned to pre-Sullan phases. And even though all visible features therefore relate to post-Sullan expansion, there is very little which can be assigned to phase 6, apart from a curving wall of uncertain function and a large circular pit which may have functioned as a well or a cess-pit (or originally a well and later a cess-pit). Only one coin can be assigned to this phase (Appendix 1, Table 17). During Phase 7, the area was levelled with a series of dumps of domestic rubbish and building material which created a platform for the *triclinium*, also constructed during this phase (as were the Shrine and series of rooms to the east) and possibly an upper storey. A complicated system of water management was also instituted, most importantly for flushing toilets, which provides another strong indication that this area should be considered part of the Inn. Phase 7 produced three coins only (Appendix 1, Table 17).

During phase 8 further changes were made, probably predicated on the impact of the AD 62 earthquake. These include a simplification of the drainage system, perhaps to conserve water, and there is also evidence that new toilets were constructed and a new cess-pit dug. A new *cocciopesto* floor was also laid over some of the Casa del Triclinio, but this is extremely poorly preserved. The phase produced the highest number of coins, nine in total.

---

[307] It is difficult to be more precise; some features may pre-date, others post-date the earthquake; and it should also be borne in mind that there were probably a series of seismic events around this time: Anderson (pers. comm.).

[308] Maiuri (1930).

The phasing of the Inn and Casa del Triclinio can be summarised as follows:

1   Natural soil
2   fourth century to mid third century BC
3   mid third century BC
4   early second century BC
5   pre 89 BC
6   post 89 BC (mid to late first BC)
7   late Augustus to mid first AD
8   AD 62+
9   eruption and early modern
10   modern

The Casa del Chirurgo

The Casa del Chirurgo was named after a group of medical instruments found in the property on the 6th April 1771.[309] The house was excavated in its entirety over the course of the six AAPP excavation seasons in all areas where flooring was no longer intact, allowing a comprehensive picture of the development of the plot to be established.[310] The number of coins found in the Casa del Chirurgo is very low – only 58, or less than 4% of the assemblage – which probably reflects the fact that for most of the history of the house it was used as a domestic space with only two relatively small areas given over to commercial activities (see below).

Before the house was constructed there is evidence that the area was occupied in the late fourth century BC with the removal of over 1m in depth of the natural ground surface to create a terrace (Phase 2).[311] Very little remains of any subsequent early structures, with the only signs of occupation coming from the area that became room 23 (Figure 11). The next signs of development include the sinking of a number of pits into the beaten earth surface, including a large pit beneath room 10 in which was found twelve almost complete Greco-Italic amphorae and other debris; the amphorae allow for a dating of the fourth to second centuries BC. There are no coins that can be assigned to these early contexts.

The Casa del Chirurgo itself was not constructed until towards the end of the third century BC at the earliest (phase 3). It consisted of a nucleus of rooms looking towards the property's atrium, with several of the rooms (with the exception of the *tablinum*, room 7) also opening outwards onto a colonnade that surrounded the house on its southern and eastern sides. Dating to this construction phase was the provision of an *impluvium*, the main means by which rainwater could be collected, then fed into an underground cistern. Although only four coins can be dated to this phase (see Appendix 1, Table 18), one in particular (cat. 774) provides an important *terminus post quem* of 214-212 BC for the construction of the house, as it was discovered in a deposit which probably pre-dates the

---

[309] Bliquez (1994), 79-81.

[310] Anderson and Robinson (forthcoming).

[311] Although it should be made clear that the dating of Phase 2 is a matter of some conjecture: Anderson (pers. comm.).

The early levels produced high volumes of black-glossware, which help to date the phase to the late second to early first century BC.

Phase 4: although stratigraphically difficult to separate from phase 3, this phase represented a significant change in the use of the space. The industrial features of the previous phases (the tanks and cisterns) were put out of use and the area was further subdivided. One of the plaster-lined tanks (320.095) was decommissioned in the late first century BC on the evidence of red-slipware of Augustan date. A soakaway, constructed of two amphorae buried mouth to foot, seems to be associated with the phase. This phase is difficult to define exactly, but it is certainly after the Sullan siege of 89 BC.

Phase 5: It is arguable if this should be considered as a separate phase to Phase 4, as it is characterised by the laying of floors in the various rooms of the property and some degree of further subdividing the area. It seems that several soakaways in these smaller, now subdivided areas were part of the function of the space during this time. The phase has been dated to the late Republican period to the years of the early Empire.

Phase 6: This phase constitutes the penultimate configuration of the plot and represents a drastic change in its use. A wall (AAPP wall number 9) was built, dividing room 1 of this plot from room 2, and creating two larger spaces that spanned from the Via Consolare to the Vicolo di Narciso. Neat curb stones were added to the entrance on the via Consolare and a mortared stone underfloor laid for a white *cocciopesto* floor with black diamond decoration on the pavement and a white mosaic floor in the Shrine's main room. Four brick pillars on large masonry piers were built, probably to support a roof spanning the room; red plaster with a yellow band decorated the walls. The outside aspect was therefore of a broad frontage, which probably had a screen or gate for closing up at night. The Shrine was set back from the street making it visible only when standing directly in front of the building. The phase of re-modelling has been dated to the mid first century AD, and may post-date the earthquake of AD 62.

Phase 7: This phase includes a few changes to the initial layout of the Shrine. A plinth was constructed atop the mosaic floor, potentially for a statue or for further support of the roof – the exact purpose of the plinth is not clear. A large pit was cut into the centre of the plot with a sluice sloping away from it under the threshold stones: this was probably for some type of water feature. This phase is certainly post-earthquake of AD 62.

Phase 8: This phase encompasses modern activity, including the potential removal of the object resting in the cut of the pit in the centre of the room. However, this removal may have also have occurred in Phase 7. Other activities include the extensive reconstruction of the east and south walls, and consolidation of the wall plasters and remaining mosaic floor.

The phasing dates can be summarised as follows:

Phase 1	natural
Phase 2	mid to late second century BC
Phase 3	late second to early first BC
Phase 4	post Sulla
Phase 5	late Republic to early Imperial
Phase 6	mid first century AD to AD 62+
Phase 7	post AD 62
Phase 8	modern era

Coins from the Shrine

The Shrine[319] produced the second largest number of coins from any plot in the insula, 341 coins, about a quarter of the overall total (Table 10). Its coin density of 4.3 coins per m^2 is also one of the highest (Figure 19), and only surpassed by the Bar of Acisculus and the Inn Bar.

In terms of types represented, the coins from the Shrine are a little atypical (Table 19). The number of 'foreign' imports is rather lower than might be expected, but this is probably not statistically significant. The number of Ebusus coins is rather less than the norm, roughly 24% as opposed to 33%, if illegible coins are excluded. In contrast the number of Massalia coins is rather higher than average, roughly 39% as opposed to the normal c.24% across the insula (see also pp. 104-07). The figures for Rome are about average.

The phasing of the Shrine provides an opportunity to observe how the coin circulation pool changes during the development of the plot, which in turn may reflect that of the insula and wider Pompeii (Figure 12). A number of stratigraphic units (SUs) excavated within Room 1 of the Shrine[320] produced coins, and details of these are provided in Appendix 1, Table 19. Each SU has been phased on the basis of stratigraphic relationships and perceptions of how the plot developed, and not by using the numismatic evidence, although sometimes reference to pottery has been made. This means that the coins can be independently compared with the phasing data avoiding any circular arguments. The only disappointing aspect of this study is that the archaeological record for many of the stratigraphic units was often sketchy and these contexts can only be placed in 2 or sometimes 3 phases. Nevertheless it is still possible to gain a sense of how the circulation pool changed over time.

Phase 2, when the area was terraced, probably for an early building, produced no certain coins, and there is only one illegible coin from phases 2 to 3. Only two coins can be reliably dated to phase 3, both of which are unclassified Massalia coins, demonstrating that these were already circulating before 89 BC because the context from which they derive (310.088) is certainly pre-Sullan. A demonstration of the problems with the archaeology here is that two contexts which are perceived to be potentially as early as phase 3 in terms of the stratigraphy contain coins of Augustus and blown glass, so are almost certainly later even than phase 4. However, the 101 coins which can be reliably placed in phase 4 demonstrate the relative dominance of Massalia coins in the post-Sullan period, as they account for about half of the total, the next highest being 15 Ebusus (Figure 12). In Phase 5, which takes us into the early Imperial age, there are still relatively high numbers of Massalia coins, but when the contexts dated to phase 6 are factored in the number of Massalian coins falls; for instance only 14 of the 67 coins of phases 5 to 6 are Massalia/Campanian Massalia. Ebusus coins seem to stay in circulation rather longer, for instance of the 9 coins certainly from phase 6 there are no Massalia coins but two Campanian Ebusus. Not surprisingly, the later phases 5 to 6 are dominated by coins from Rome, both Republican and Imperial and also deliberately cut Republican coins.

[319] Only the coins from Room 1 of the Shrine (Figure 11) are included in this discussion.

[320] Although all 341 coins from the Shrine are represented in Table 10, stratigraphic data (Figure 12) was only available for the western half of the plot, collectively termed 'Room 1'.

| | Shrine Room 1 | | AAPP total | | |
	No.	%	No.	%	Excluding illeg.
'Foreign' imports	8	2.5	75	5.0	6.3
Massalia/Campanian Massalia	98	30.3	287	19.0	24.3
Anomalous local types	1	0.3	15	1.0	1.3
Ebusus and Campanian Ebusus	53	16.4	386	25.5	32.7
Roman Republican	28	8.7	162	10.7	13.7
Cut fractions	20	6.2	107	7.1	9.1
Octavian/Augustus to Claudius	32	9.9	142	9.4	12.0
Nero and later	0	0.0	7	0.5	0.6
Illegible/uncertain	83	25.7	331	21.9	
Total	323		1512		
Total (excl. illeg)			1181		

Table 10. The Shrine (Room 1) in comparison to the overall coin profile.

Industrial tanks

Four tanks were excavated in Room 1 of the Shrine and each produced a number of coins in their fills which were excavated in layers, or, when these were hard to distinguish, spits (Figure 13). Two of these tanks (310.202 and 320.095) provide 'closed' contexts, in which it may be possible to find further clues to the chronology of Pompeii's changing circulation pool.

A stone lime-slaking tank (310.202), excavated in 2003, produced 47 coins divided between five contextual levels. (As can be seen, the bottommost fill of the tank (310.089) produced no coins). The tank, which is believed to have been constructed in phase 3 and decommissioned in phase 4 after the Sullan siege, is dominated by Massalia/Campanian Massalia coins which account for just under 64%. The rest of the coins consist of a sprinkling of 'foreign' imports, Ebusus coins (1 or 2, 4B and 8B – although interestingly no 'rudimentary' type 3) and a small number of Republican bronzes including a cut quarter. There is no particular stratification discernible as such, with the earliest level with coins (310.090) producing roughly the same number of Massalia coins proportionately as the latest (310.220). Nevertheless the absence of any late Republican or Imperial coins allows us to suggest that the tank provides a useful snapshot of the coins in circulation in the late second to early first centuries BC, given that the tank was decommissioned after the siege of Sulla so we can expect the coins to span both the pre-Sullan and immediate post Sullan phase. In the tank are large numbers of coins of Massalia/Campanian Massalia or local copies, Ebusus coins of various types, both imported and locally copied, Republican AE and cut fractions and the odd 'foreign' import, in this case a coin from ?Vibo Valentia (cat. 24) and a coin of Cyrene (cat. 64).

The other tank (320.095), the fill of which was partially excavated in 2004 and completed in 2005, contained rather fewer coins (only 25), 40% of which are Massalia/Campanian Massalia. It too is believed to have been decommissioned after the Sullan siege. There appears to be more stratification in this tank than in the other tank (320.202) discussed above: the lowest stratigraphic level (320.088) contained *only* Massalia coins (of those coins which can be identified), whilst the latest fill has two Massalia coins,

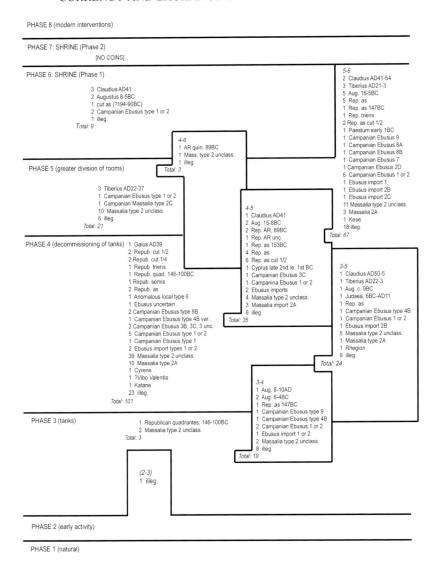

Figure 12. Coins in relation to the phasing of the Shrine.

three Ebusus, a Republican *as* struck in 147 BC and two early coins of Augustus from 10 to 8 BC, and the levels between either no coins, two Massalia and a single Ebusus. Once again this conforms quite neatly with the picture of coinage at the end of the first century BC and the beginning of the first century AD, when there were fewer Massalia coins in circulation but still Republican bronzes and Ebusus coins, and as is to be expected large numbers of Imperial issues.

Why these tanks produced these coins is unclear. Were they deliberately discarded, or dropped accidentally, and if so how? Or were the coins part of deposits taken from elsewhere used to infill the tanks when they became redundant? In the case of tank 320.202,

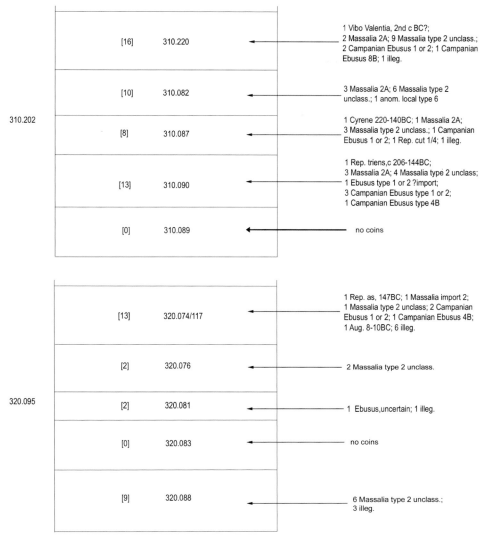

Figure 13. Two tanks in the Shrine and their coins. The total number of coins in each layer is given in square brackets.

the mixed nature of the coinage might imply that this happened as a single event, but the other tank (320.088) suggests a gradual infilling over a number of years.

The Shrine: summary
The Shrine is helpful for untangling the complexities of the pre-AD 79 'dead' coinage. Although there are some coins that appear highly residual – *e.g.* a Republican *as* of the mid second century BC turning up in Phase 5 – broadly speaking it is possible to use this evidence to suggest, in combination with other sets of data, a chronological sequence. Roman Republican coins were introduced into the town from the early second century BC, and continued to circulate in full and deliberately cut form right up to the time of the

eruption, as we know already from the 'live' assemblages recovered from the Bars of Asellina and L. Vetudius Placidus on the Via dell'Abbondanza (see p. 7). Massalia coins were also introduced around this time – probably in the mid to late second century BC – and rapidly copied. Although these coins were still circulating in the early decades of the Imperial period, all the evidence suggests that they had fallen out of use by the middle of the first century AD, as to a large extent had the Ebusus and Campanian Ebusus coins. Ebusus seems to have been introduced slightly later than Massalia, around the late second to early first century BC, and certainly before the Sullan siege of 89 BC. They too were rapidly copied. They continued to circulate into the early decades of the first century AD, but had certainly fallen out of use by the middle of the century.

The high volume of coinage from the Shrine in Regio VI, 1 must be testimony to the largely commercial activities taking place in the plot. Even if some of the coins found in the Shrine had been accidentally imported when floors were levelled for new buildings and activities, this surely cannot account for all of the coins found: the only way in which such a large number of coins could have been lost in the area is through close hand-to-hand exchange at high velocity, *i.e.* for the payment with 'small change' for vended goods. (Although we should be cautious as this level of loss needs to be kept in perspective: if the main period of occupation runs from *c.* 150 BC to AD 50 – phases 2 to 5 inclusive – this represents an average loss of fewer than two coins per year). There is no evidence to suggest that the area was ever used as a domestic property, and in any case the two known domestic properties did not produce large volumes of coin (see p. 101). So the Shrine, before it became such, was clearly an area where commercial activities were taking place. But in contrast to other areas of Regio VI, 1 that also produce high densities of coinage, there is no evidence for a bar counter, so a simple correlation between the purchase of food and drink and accidental coin loss cannot be made. So what was going on in the Shrine? Unfortunately the archaeological evidence is not conclusive. It is known that the space was subdivided in different ways for the creation of small rooms, none of which show any signs of being in any way grandiose, with two at the front onto Via Consolare possibly served by the series of rooms behind.[321] Within these rooms we know that there is evidence for both building, industrial and commercial activities: the lime-slaking tank provides evidence for the mortaring or plastering of walls, probably for industrial units within the plot itself, but maybe for the manufacture of plaster or mortar for other parts of the insula. The soakaway, perhaps a temporary latrine, provides very direct evidence for at least one episode of sustained building activity. Of course the evidence for building work cannot be associated directly with the use of 'small change', unless plaster and mortar is being sold physically, so other evidence for the creation of sustenance produce needs to be found. There are a few plaster-lined tanks, which were perhaps used to contain either water or *garum*, and would therefore hint at the vending of foodstuffs, but that unfortunately brings us back to the puzzling lack of a bar counter. But then maybe one was not needed; maybe these units were selling products direct to the customer.

[321] P. Daniel, 'AAPP 2203 AA 310 Excavation Report' (unpublished supervisor's report, 2003).

Other evidence for industrial activity includes metalworking debris pits, which were found to contain corroded iron objects, slag and hammerscale and in one instance hearth bottom slag. All this is indicative of smithing activity. The impression given of these activities to one excavator is that they were 'rather low tech, low scale and short-lived… [maybe even] a failed business'.[322] Yet they do at least show that metal products were being manufactured and therefore it is not a great leap of the imagination to suggest that they were being sold directly to the consumer.

3.3.2. Dating of specific types: Massalia, Anomalous local types and Ebusus

Having provided the background to the three areas of the insula which have been phased by the excavators, it is now possible to turn directly to a discussion of how this data provides indications of the dating of specific coin types. A summary of this information, in particular with regard to which types have been found in archaeological contexts which pre and post date the Sullan siege of 89 BC, is provided in Figure 14 (p. 85).

3.3.3. Massalia and Campanian Massalia

The dating evidence for the Massalia prototypes from which the Campanian Massalia types derive is discussed by Depeyrot.[323] Depeyrot's work was largely based on typological considerations: in more recent years, Depeyrot's classification has been reviewed in relation to the archaeological evidence from sites in southern France in a survey published by Michel Py and also Feugere and Py.[324]

Massalia Type 1 (Figure 6; Appendix 1, Tables 17-19)
In Py's survey of material from Lattes and related sites, the type has been dated to the first half of the second century BC, which conforms with the dating suggested by Depeyrot. Stratigraphic evidence includes a coin excavated at Nages (Depeyrot type 35-3) found in a layer attributed to the first quarter of the second century BC and another in the second quarter. Py concludes that the type was struck before 175 BC.[325]

Two coins of this type (cats 86 and 89) in this assemblage were found in a stratified context (127.091) in phase 4 of the Inn, early second century BC, as it included sherds of black-slip of the same date and an early lamp. These coins provide important evidence that coins from Massalia were being imported into Pompeii as early as the early to mid second century BC, and Type 1 (with Apollo bust left) would appear to pre-date types 2 onwards (with Apollo bust right) of which examples are far more numerous. Another coin (cat. 85) was found in a context dated to phase 5 of the Inn Bar (pre 89 BC; 127.078).

---

[322] *Ibid.*

[323] Depeyrot (1999).

[324] Py (2006); Feugere and Py (2011).

[325] Py (2006), 193-94.

Massalia type 2A (Figure 6; Appendix 1, Tables 17-19)
The prototype was dated by Depeyrot to around 150 to 130 BC,[326] and supplementary data from excavations suggests that the type was in use before 125 BC (evidence from Le Baou-Roux) and the last three quarters or the second half of the second century BC (Nages) and other sites. Lattes produced numerous examples in archaeological contexts of the late second century BC.[327]

From the Inn/Triclinium area of the insula there are 12 coins of type 2A which are evenly spread between contexts dating from phase 4 (early second century BC) to phase 7 (late Aug./mid first century AD). Two coins (cats 116 and 123) come from a context in the Inn Bar (127.082) believed to be one of the earliest in this area of the site – in fact, the excavators originally placed the context in Phase 2, fourth to mid third century BC, but the coins suggest that this was too early in the phasing sequence so the context has been re-assigned to phase 4. Another coin (cat. 114) comes from one (612.027) of only four contexts in the Casa del Chirurgo assigned to phase 3 (*c.* 200 BC to 150 BC). This evidence therefore broadly correlates with the data collated by Py,[328] although, perhaps surprisingly, there is a suggestion at Pompeii that these Massalia coins were in circulation somewhat earlier than 150 BC, perhaps even the early part of the second century BC.

There are a number of coins of this type from the Shrine which date to phase 4 (post Sulla), *e.g.* contexts 310.220, 310.090. Another type 2A coin comes from a context (510.047/510.051) poorly dated to phases 3-5, but thought to be more likely phase 3 which would be pre-Sulla if correct (Appendix 1, Table 19).

Massalia Type 2B (Figure 6; Appendix 1, Tables 17-19)
Examples of the prototype found in southern France in archaeological contexts suggest that the type was struck before 125 BC, with many examples from contexts dated generally before 100 BC.[329] In the AAPP assemblage there is one worn and doubtful coin (cat. 147) from a context (123.054) in the Inn dated to phase 6, *i.e.* post 89 BC. A coin (cat. 149 – probably of this type) comes from a context in the Shrine (510.015/510.043) which despite producing a high volume of black-glossware, suggestive of an early date, is considered unstratified.

Massalia type 2C (Figure 6; Appendix 1, Tables 17-19)
Py dates the prototypes (PBM 45-8) to the last quarter of the second century BC, with some before 125 BC.[330] Of note is the fact that all the Campanian Massalia coins in the

---

[326] Depeyrot (1999), 64.

[327] Py (2006), 215.

[328] *Ibid.*

[329] Py (2006), 234.

[330] Py (2006), 234: Py refers to many examples found at Le Baou-Roux which can be dated to before 125 BC, and says that stratigraphically many examples have been found in contexts of the last quarter of the second century BC. See also Stannard (forthcoming).

Bathhouse hoard (Appendix 2) are of this type; this confirms that the type was in circulation in the first quarter of the first century BC.[331]

In this assemblage there is one coin (cat. 159) of Type 2C (this example probably with legend 'ΑΟΣΣ', although the coin is very worn) from a phased context (271.235) in the Inn, a deposit placed in phase 6 (post 89 BC) a post-Sullan destruction deposit given that it contained seventeen slingshot. An important piece of dating evidence is a single Republican silver *quinarius* in the same archaeological layer which was struck in 89 BC. The implication is that this particular coin of Campanian Massalia Type 2C was already in circulation by the time of the Sullan siege. The only other example of a phased coin (cat. 153) comes from the Shrine (510.022) where it has been placed in Phase 5, again post 89 BC (possibly as late as early Imperial; of interest is the fact that all sixteen coins in the deposit were Massalia types). Although having only two coins from phased contexts is hardly conclusive, taken in combination with the evidence from the Bathhouse hoard and the likely date for striking the prototypes, dating Massalia Type 2C – which, as has been seen, were locally struck – to the late second to early first century BC, certainly before the Sullan siege, would seem reasonable on current evidence.

Massalia Type 2C variant (Figure 6; Appendix 1, Tables 17-19)
Two coins of this sub-type come from phased contexts: cat. 164 from the Inn (182.011), the only coin from the context that has been placed in Phase 6 (post-89 BC). The other comes from another Inn deposit (271.234) that produced a large number of coins (29) mostly Campanian Ebusus, but also evidence of the Sullan siege, for instance slingshot and stone balls. This small amount of dating evidence does not contradict the dating of the main Type 2C group, to which this variant is likely to belong, *i.e.* it too was probably struck in the late second to early first century BC.

Massalia Type 3 (Figure 6; Appendix 1, Tables 17-19)
Only one (cat. 369) of the two coins of this type comes from a phased deposit in the Inn (120.018) which has been assigned to phase 7 (late Augustus to mid first century AD), although originally the excavators placed it in phase 6 (post 89 BC).[332] Associated finds in the deposit, such as Italian *sigillata* and blown glass, suggest the deposit is late, so little helpful evidence is provided for when this type was struck. Stylistic considerations would suggest the late second century to early first century BC.

3.3.4. Anomalous local types

Some of the prototypes on which these types were likely to have been based provide a *terminus post quem* for their production. As discussed above (see p. 41), the prototype for the bridled horse's head appears to be a Roman Republican type (*RRC* 25) dated to 241-235 BC. Another Roman type (*RRC* 44/2) has been suggested as the model for type 5 and is dated to the late third century BC onwards. Less easy to ascertain are the possible prototypes

---

[331] See p. 66 and Stannard (forthcoming).

[332] Phase 6 may however be late first BC: Anderson (pers. comm.).

of the toad types; Stannard has suggested Luceria and Venusia, both struck in 211-200 BC.[333] The die-links with the Ebusus series provide further dating evidence.

Types 1A and 1B (Figure 6; Appendix 1, Tables 17-19)
The single example of a Type 1A coin comes from a context (617.097) which is yet to be phased, although contextual association (see pp. 89-92) suggests a strong likelihood of a pre-Sullan date, possibly even mid second century BC, as all the other coins in the context are likely to be either Massalia or Ebusus imports. One of the Type 1B coins (cat. 372) comes from a context (271.259) which is probably pre-Sullan, Inn/Triclinium Phase 5; although this was originally placed in phase 6 (post 89 BC) by the excavators, who point out that this particular context and others in the area are difficult to interpret, so there is some uncertainty over the context's date; however the other five coins in the same context are a Cyrene, *c.* 250-120 BC, two Massalia coins and a Campanian Ebusus (and one illegible), none of which were definitely struck post-Sulla. The other type 1B coin (cat. 371) is from a context where it is the only coin (140.155). This is sufficient evidence, when taken in conjunction with the die-links with the Campanian Ebusus series, to suggest that these two types were struck in the mid second to early first century BC. Further discoveries may refine the dating.

Anomalous local Type 2 (Figure 6; Appendix 1, Tables 17-19)
This particular example comes from a context that is yet to be phased (140.147), as with the die-linked Campanian Ebusus type 6 coin (cat. 745). Nevertheless the context from which it derives ought to provide some clues as to the date of this issue, as it was one of the most coin rich contexts in the excavations, producing a total of 33 coins. Although the overwhelming majority of these coins are most likely to be of pre-Sullan date (for example imports from Paestum, Sicyon, Samos and Cyrene, and a number of imports and Campanian Massalia and Ebusus types and a Republican as dated to 169-158 BC) the context contained three coins of Octavian of 10-5 BC and 7 BC. So the only means of dating the issue is the die sharing of the horse's head, suggesting that this is also a late second century to early first century BC type.

Anomalous local types 3A and 3B (Figure 6; Appendix 1, Tables 17-19)
There is one example of a Type 3A coin (cat. 374) in a phased context from the Inn (271.250). The context has been placed in phase 5, which is pre-Sulla. Both type 3B coins (cats 378-79) come from phased contexts in the Inn: one from a context placed in pre-Sullan phase 5 (271.243), one of 26 coins in the same context, all of which are types which were likely struck pre-Sulla, being a mixture of Massalia and Ebusus coins and Republican bronzes. The other coin comes from a layer (271.234) that is certainly post-Sulla because of the presence of both slingshot and stone balls. Both types can therefore safely be dated to the late second to early first century BC, possibly earlier; they were certainly in circulation by the time of the Sullan siege.

---

[333] *HN* Italy, nos. 682 and 725; Stannard (forthcoming).

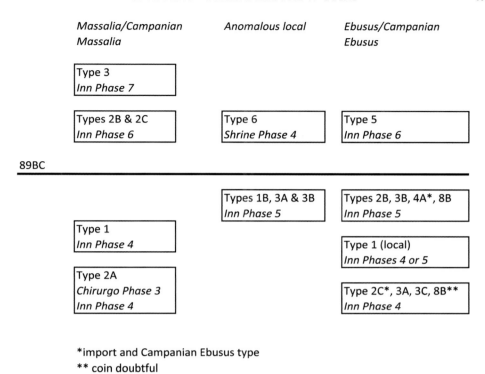

*import and Campanian Ebusus type
** coin doubtful

Figure 14. Massalia/Campanian Massalia, anomalous local and Ebusus/Campanian Ebusus types which have been found in contexts which pre and post date the Sullan horizon.

Anomalous local types 4-6 (Figure 6; Appendix 1, Tables 17-19)
The context (032.007) from which the single example of type 4 derives has not been phased, but does include another reasonably well-dated coin, a bronze of Neapolis (cat. 8) that is dated to the early third century BC. This does not tell us when the type was struck but does at least imply that the type was early, so a second century BC date is suggested. Note also the possibility that the toad is modelled on coins of the late third century BC (see p. 43).

Type 5 is the only coin in its context (502.029) and as the context has not been phased there is no useful dating evidence for when it was struck. Stylistic considerations therefore are the only means of determining the date, and at present a second to early first century BC date is therefore suggested until more examples come to light. There is a good case for the prototype being a Roman coin of the late third century BC (see p. 43).

Type 6, of which there is only one example (cat. 384), comes from a stratified context (310.082) in the Shrine, one of five fills of a lime-slaking tank (310.202). Nine other coins were found in the same context, all of which were imported Massalia or Campanian Massalia coins. The tank is thought to have been constructed in phase 3, which is late second to early first century BC; the fills are later (phase 4), and although none of the coins can certainly be dated to after the Sullan attack the fills are likely to be post-Sullan, and although this does not exclude the possibility that this coin was struck before 89 BC, perhaps mid second to early first century BC is the best assessment of the date of production until more examples come to light.

3.3.5. Ebusus and Campanian Ebusus

The seminal work on the Ebusus series has been conducted by Campo.[334] Principally using style and metrology as a guide, Campo divided the series into a number of typological phases. All the Ebusus coins found in the AAPP excavations and indeed in other parts of Pompeii come from Campo's period II, which she dates from the Second Punic War to the middle of the second century BC, *i.e. c.* 214-150 BC. It should be noted that no examples of Campo Phases III (*c.* 125-75 BC) or IV (*c.* AD 14 to 54) coins have been found at Pompeii, *i.e.* the types with Punic inscriptions on the reverse (Campo XIX) or the Imperial issues struck between the reigns of Tiberius to Claudius (Campo XX to XXIII). As has already been discussed, the principal work on the classification of the Campanian Ebusus types has been conducted by Stannard (see p. 45).

Dating evidence for Ebusus Type 1 (Figure 6; Appendix 1, Tables 17-19)
Four Ebusus imports of type 1 have been discovered in dated contexts. Three can be assigned to phase 6 of the Inn/Triclinium, *i.e.* post 89 BC; for instance there is one example (cat. 391) in a context (180.001) which also included evidence of the Sullan attack in the form of destruction debris. This demonstrates that the imports must have arrived in Pompeii prior to 89 BC, which entirely accords with previous perceptions of when the type first appeared in southern Italy.[335]

Of interest is a Type 1 coin which stylistically is almost certainly a local imitation (cat. 410), given the way in which the figure has been rendered and the small module size of 11mm. This comes from a context (127.082) considered by the excavators to date to one of the earliest phases of development in the Inn Bar. Originally the context was assigned to Phase 2 (fourth to mid third century BC), but the coinage demonstrates that it cannot be quite this early, so the suggestion, that it is reassigned to phase 4, early second century BC, or even phase 5, pre 89 BC, has been accepted.[336] This is another indication that the imitation of imported Ebusus coins was already under way by the time of the Sullan siege, and may have been in progress since perhaps the middle of the second century BC.

Ebusus Types 2A-D (Figure 6; Appendix 1, Tables 17-19)
There are two Type 2B (cornucopia) Ebusus imports in dated contexts (cats 416 (180.015) and 419 (120.051)), both assigned to phase 5, thus pre 89 BC; this again confirms that the Ebusus imports were arriving at Pompeii before the Sullan attack. There is one example of the imported caduceus type 2C in a pre Sullan context in the Inn, Phase 4 (cats 427), as well as one example of a local imitation (cat. 431), which, in a similar manner to Type 1 coins shows that the type was being imitated pre-Sulla (see above).

---

[334] Campo (1976; 1993; 1994).

[335] For example Stannard (2005a).

[336] Anderson (pers. comm.).

Only one example of the entirely local type 2D with caduceus and dolphin has been found in a phased context: cat. 436, from Room 1 of the Shrine. The context in which this coin was discovered (320.061) produced a large number of coins (65 in total) ranging in date from Republican *asses*, including one dated to 147 BC (cat. 800) through to Claudius (AD 50-54) and has been assigned on stratigraphic grounds to phases 5-6 (potentially as early as the late Republican period or as late as the earthquake of AD 62). This provides insufficient evidence for when the coin was struck, as it seems likely be highly residual. Stylistically it appears that it may have been struck before the Sullan siege.

Ebusus Type 3A-C (Figure 6; Appendix 1, Tables 17-19)
Type 3 coins are the most distinctive local Ebusus products and are relatively easily recognised. None can be dated to phases 2 to 4 in the Inn/Triclinium or to phases 2 to 3 in the Casa del Chirugo. There are a small number of Type 3 coins in Phase 5 Inn/Triclinium, thus prior to the Sullan attack. This includes one Type 3 unclassified coin (cat. 721), one of a group of 26 coins none of which can be definitely dated after Sulla. The context also included a small quantity of cast glass, which does not contradict a pre-Sullan date, as cast glass had a long antiquity. There is an isolated type 3B coin in the Inn Bar (cat. 631) in a context which the excavators believed was pre-Sullan (166.063).

Perhaps the best stratigraphic evidence for Type 3 comes from a context (120.039) in room 4 of the Inn (Figure 11). This context contained only two coins, one Type 3A (cat. 614) and one Type 3C (cat. 637). Importantly, the context is stratigraphically earlier in the sequence than contexts which contained clear evidence for the Sullan attack in the form of ballista bolts and other destruction debris. Thus we can be confident that some, if not all, of the 'rudimentary' Type 3 Campanian Ebusus coins were struck before 89 BC. This concurs with evidence from the Privati deposit (see p. 64) and also the Bathhouse hoard (see p. 66 and Appendix 2). However as most of the Type 3 coins come from later Phases (6 to 8), with the majority clustering in phases 6 and 7 (Inn/Triclinium) and 5 and 6 (Chirugo), it is possible that they continued to be struck after the Sullan attack.

Ebusus Type 4A-B (Figure 6; Appendix 1, Tables 17-19)
There are two examples of probable imports of type 4A (cats 730 and 731) both of which were found in contexts in the Inn believed to be pre-Sullan (271.243 and 271.250). One context (271.243) produced 26 coins, all of which can reasonably be dated to before the Sullan attack; the same can be said of the seven coins from the other (271.250). There is also a single example (cat. 734) of a Type 4A coin believed to be a local imitation which was found in a context in the Inn placed in Phase 5, which is a pre 89 BC phase (180.015). This context produced 13 coins, all of which can be safely ascribed to a pre-Sullan phase (including one probable Canusium coin dated to 250-225 BC (cat. 10)).

Six out of the seven coins of type 4B (cats 736-42) come from room 1 of the Shrine, which is notable but not easily explained. One coin (cat. 737) was found in a context in the Shrine (510.015) that produced 12 coins all of which can be safely ascribed to a pre-Sullan era, including one Republican coin dated to 153 BC (cat. 790, although the coin is very worn, so the attribution is doubtful). The layer also included a high volume of black-slip ware, again suggesting a second century BC date, but the layer is now considered by the excavators to be unreliable.[337]

The variant of type 4B with illegible legend (cat. 742) also comes from the Shrine, in this instance a lime-slaking tank. The context in question (310.090) produced 12 coins, all of which could have been struck before the Sullan siege and stratigraphically the fill of the tank has been placed in phase 4, which as discussed above (p. 77) is believed to be post-Sullan when the tanks were decommissioned. It would seem likely that all the coins are residual but the stratigraphic evidence cannot prove that this type is 'pre-Sullan' (see p. 79 and Figure 13).

Ebusus Type 5 (Figure 6; Appendix 1, Tables 17-19)
One example (cat. 744) has been placed in Phase 6 of the Inn; *i.e.* mid to late first century BC; a small quantity of blown glass in the same context (164.014) implies at least an Augustan date. The other example (cat. 743) comes from the same unstratified context (510.015) as the example of type 4B discussed above. Therefore at present, it can only be dated stylistically by comparison with the other horse's head types which most likely pre-date the Sullan siege.

Ebusus Type 6 (Figure 6; Appendix 1, Tables 17-19)
Unfortunately this coin (cat. 745) comes from an area of the site (the Workshop) that has not yet been phased (interestingly, this also produced the die-linked coin cat. 373; in fact, they were both found in the same context, 140.147. This has parallels with the apparent cluster of Type 4B coins in the Shrine). However given the die-links with the types with bridled horse's head, it would appear that this coin most likely dates to the late second century BC.

Ebusus Type 7 (Figure 6; Appendix 1, Tables 16-18)
The single example in this assemblage (cat. 746) comes from phases 5-6 of the Shrine and was found in one of the most productive contexts in the whole assemblage, producing a total of 65 coins (320.061). This is a thick deposit of compacted levelling layers and because of the presence of Imperial coins, including one of Claudius of AD 50-54, it is clearly late and does not help date the production of this type. The presence of a broadly comparable coin in the Bathhouse hoard (see p 66 and Appendix 2, cat. BH65) therefore is the only useful indicator of date, probably at best early first century BC. Further examples might be able to indicate if the type was struck before or after the Sullan siege.

Ebusus Type 8A-B (Figure 6; Appendix 1, Tables 17-19)
Only one coin of type 8A (with bust left) (cat. 748) comes from a phased context, in room 1 of the Shrine (320.061) which has been placed in phases 5-6 (late Republic to mid first century AD) and is the same context which produced a single coin of type 7 (see above) so offers no useful dating evidence, apart from the likelihood that this coin is residual. So only stylistic considerations can be used to assess the date, and on this basis, given the full rather than 'rudimentary' figure of Bes, it can be suggested that the type dates to the late second to early first centuries BC.

---

[337] Weiss (pers. comm.).

There is better evidence for the dating of Type 8B. Cat. 754 comes from one of the earliest contexts in the Inn Bar (127.082) and was originally phased by the excavators to phase 2 (fourth century BC to mid third century BC), but has been moved to Phase 4 (early second century BC) largely on the basis of the coins which include Massalia imports (see above). The only problem however is that this particular coin is extremely worn so is not certainly of this type. Another coin (cat. 759, with unusual type of bust) comes from what is believed to be a Phase 5 context in the Inn (pre 89 BC; 271.243), although originally the excavators placed it in phase 6; it has now been accepted as likely to be a pre-Sullan deposit, particularly as none of the 26 coins in the context are firmly post Sullan and there is no other material evidence in the layer to suggest that it is a post Sullan layer (for example ballista bolts or post-destruction debris). Two are from either late or unstratified contexts (320.061, cat. 761; 510.020, cat. 757) but the others (cats 756 and 758) are from tank fills of phase 4, therefore post-Sulla, but potentially residual as it is believed that the tanks were constructed before the Sullan siege and infilled after; so the coins may have been struck before the Social War if these layers represent re-deposition (see pp. 77-79). It should also be noted that the single example of this type in the Bathhouse hoard (Appendix 2, cat. BH66) is worn in comparison to the other Ebusus types in the group, which might also imply a date earlier in the striking sequence. Taken as a whole the evidence would suggest that the type had almost certainly been struck before the Sullan siege, probably mid to late second century BC.

Dating evidence for Ebusus Type 9 (Figure 6; Appendix 1, Tables 17-19)
Both coins of this type come from the Shrine (cats 762-63). One is from a very productive context (320.061) discussed above, assigned to phases 5-6 which may be as late as the mid first century AD; this coin is therefore highly likely to be residual. The other comes from a context (510.016) that has not been phased because it is contaminated backfill. Therefore only stylistic observations can be made; the presence for example of the anomalous local type with Mars head and toad[338] in the Bathhouse hoard (see Appendix 2, BH18) would suggest that this type can probably be dated to the late second to early first century BC for the time being, until better stratigraphic evidence can be found (and it is hoped more examples of the type).

3.4. Contextual association

Another approach to the issue of dating of local types (in particular Ebusus and Massalia) is to examine the presence of well-dated coins in the same archaeological contexts as local imitative types. Well-dated coins usually mean Roman Republican and Roman Imperial coins, although on occasion other 'foreign' imports are sufficiently well-dated to be of some use. The dated coins may not be the latest coins in a particular context, as local imitations may have been struck later, but to give an idea on when the material was struck and particularly when these were being used this approach is instructive.

---

[338] Stannard (2005a), Group V, 1.

	Massalia Type 2		Anom. local (Types 1-3)		Ebusus Type 1 & 2		Ebusus Type 3		Ebusus Type 4		Ebusus Type 8		Repub. cut fractions	
Date range	no.	%	no.	%	No.	%	no.	%	no.	%	no.	%	no.	%
pre-200 BC	4	3.7	0	0.0	4	3.9	1	2.3	0	0.0	0	0.0	3	5.9
200 BC – 151 BC	7	6.4	0	0.0	3	2.9	1	2.3	1	14.3	0	0.0	0	0.0
150 BC – 101 BC	54	49.5	6	100.0	53	52.0	25	56.8	5	71.4	3	42.9	9	17.6
100 BC – 51 BC	6	5.5	0	0.0	5	4.9	3	6.8	0	0.0	0	0.0	6	11.8
50 BC – 1 BC	11	10.1	0	0.0	8	7.8	5	11.4	1	14.3	0	0.0	15	29.4
AD 1 – AD 50	12	11.0	0	0.0	19	18.6	6	13.6	0	0.0	3	42.9	15	29.4
AD 51 – AD 79	15	13.8	0	0.0	10	9.8	3	6.8	0	0.0	1	14.3	3	5.9
Total	109	100.0	6	100.0	102	100.0	44	100.0	7	100.0	7	100.0	51	100.0

Table 11. Contextual association.

To create Table 11, the chronology was divided into broad 50-year phases and each instance of an association between undated locally struck coins and dated coins counted. As an example, AA165, SU 12 (165.012) from the Inn Bar rm. 1B&3b (See 'Concordance') contained 11 coins: a coin of Rhegium which can be dated to the third century BC, two Ebusus types 1 or 2, both probably imports, a number of illegible coins and one coin of Tiberius dating to AD 35-37. This means that the two Ebusus coins are placed in the 'AD 1-50' dating bracket, as the Tiberius coin is the latest dateable coin in the context. Less accurate, in terms of date, are the Roman Republican bronzes, as most of these are too worn to be dated any more closely than *c*. 206-144 BC. When the local issues are found in association with these they are counted in the 150-101 BC bracket, as this is the latest possible date (even if statistically most of these will probably be one dating bracket earlier). Deliberately halved and further fractioned Republican coins were not considered to provide reliable dates, as it is not known when the fractioning was enacted (see pp. 57-58). The other point to note is that no distinction was made between imports and Campanian issues as this was simply too complicated to factor in to the calculations; but note that this only effects Massalia 2, Ebusus 1 and 2 and Ebusus 4 as the other categories are purely local types.

As can be seen in Table 11, almost exactly half of the dated Massalia coins are in contexts which fall into the 150-101 BC dating bracket, which implies that this is the principal period during which these coins were circulating. There are a few in earlier contexts, but this is probably because the dated coins in those contexts were lost many decades after they were struck, so it should *not* be taken to indicate that Massalia coins were in circulation in the late third century BC or the first half of the second century BC. The rest of the Massalia coins are relatively evenly spread over the final four dating brackets, continuing to be found in association with coins as late as the post-AD 50 period. However, the presence of Massalia coins in the most recent dating bracket is slightly misleading, as all

15 coins come from a single context (320.061), which had only a single coin of Claudius as its latest datable coin. Therefore in reality, the evidence for Massalia coins still circulating in the mid first century AD is poor; most had dropped out of use by this point, and it would not be unreasonable to suggest that they did not circulate much beyond the Augustan period.

There are really too few anomalous local types to provide much useful contextual dating evidence, so only the types with bridled horse's head were counted (Types 1-3). However all six of these were found in association with coins in the 150-101 BC dating bracket, entirely in keeping with the other dating evidence for these types which is persuasively pre-Sullan (see p. 84). Although the sample is too small to make any sweeping statements, it would not be unreasonable to suggest that what seem to be relatively small issues were mid to late second century types which quickly fell out of use and did not survive much beyond the early decades of the first century BC, if even into the post-Sullan period.

As for Ebusus, these are broadly similar in the way they behave to the Massalia coins, but with some subtle differences. Ebusus types 1 or 2 are almost identical in behaviour to the Massalia Type 2 coins, *i.e.* around half fall into the 150-101 BC bracket, a handful in association with earlier coins and a few more of the late first century BC running up to the middle of the first AD. However just like Massalia (see above), it is a single context (320.061) from the Shrine which accounts for all 10 of the Ebusus 1 or 2 types in the post-AD 51 period, so it is likely that most had dropped out of use some time before this date, although it will be noted that there are marginally more of this type in the period AD 1-50 than of Massalia (18.6% to 11% respectively). Ebusus 3, a purely local type with the distinctive 'rudimentary' style more or less mirrors Ebusus 1 and 2, despite being, on typological grounds, later in terms of production. Again this does not contradict the dating evidence from the phasing, as it seems highly likely that these coins were already in circulation in the late second to early first century BC. Ebusus type 3 also peter out in the early part of the first century AD.

Perhaps most of interest are Ebusus types 4 and 8. Type 4 has a butting bull reverse, and although the number of these found in association with dated coins is very low – only seven in total – it is perhaps significant that five of these come from the second half of the second century BC, and only one is found in a later context. Again this would appear to work well with the stratigraphic data that suggests a pre-Sullan date for their manufacture and use (see pp. 87-88). Ebusus Type 8 on the other hand, with an identically low number of examples to Ebusus Type 4, appears to hang around for longer, with 4 of the 7 coins coming from 'AD' contexts. This perhaps reflects the fact that these are purely local issues, *i.e.* they are not based on an imported Ebusus prototype, which may suggest a slightly later production and circulation pattern – but the numbers are too low to really be sure. Future discoveries may help refine their dating.

It will be noticed that in Table 11, only a relatively small proportion of the total number of Ebusus and Massalia coins have been included (only 269 coins out of a total of 673). This is because there are a number of contexts in the AAPP excavations which *only* contain Ebusus, Massalia and sometimes anomalous local coins, either as one type or a mixture of both or all three (sometimes the context also includes a number of illegible coins and a single undated Roman Republican coin). These contexts are listed in Table 12. Clearly these contexts could not be counted in the creation of Table 11 because they are not associated with any well-dated coins. These contexts are very important as they show that for a number of periods during Pompeii's Oscan phase, Massalia/Campanian Massalia, Ebusus/Campanian Ebusus and the anomalous local types were the principal currency in use: an examination of the coins from the Shrine also supports this view (see pp. 76-81). All the evidence suggests that this phase in the town's life corresponded with the last decades of the second century BC and the first decades of the first century BC.

The final two columns of Table 11 list Republican cut fractions. The underlying reasons for the creation of halves and further fractions is not particularly well understood (see p. 57), but counting examples found in association with well dated coins produces some interesting results as to their main period of use. It is apparent that the cut fractions tend to come from later contexts than the Massalia, Ebusus and anomalous local types. Almost 60% of the cut coins come from the period 50 BC to AD 50, with far fewer in earlier contexts and only a small number post AD 50. We can only speculate on why this is the case, but it is tempting to suggest that this was the period in which the Ebusus and Massalia coins were dropping out of use and Republican bronze coins and cut fractions were becoming more commonly used. Furthermore it might be tempting to associate this with the imposition of the colony on Pompeii after 80 BC. It was not until many decades later that bronze coins began to be struck again at Rome in volume, with *asses* and *quadrantes* from Augustus and his successors gradually making up the bulk of Pompeiian 'small change' in the early decades of the first century AD.

It is also possible to review Buttrey's research in the light of this new dating evidence.[339] In his paper, he argues that there were two phases of halving, one in the late first century BC (probably from the 20s BC) and one in the 30s of the first century AD.[340] In doing so, Buttrey rejects an earlier suggestion by Cesano[341] that halving in Italy began before 42 BC, a conclusion she reached largely on the basis of an examination of the coin hoard from Terni.[342] Buttrey argues that during the Augustan period, the earlier Janus headed Republican *asses* were 'redefined' as *dupondii*: 'possibly before the reformed coins [*i.e.* the Augustan bronze series] appeared'.[343] He therefore suggests that the old Republican bronzes, which by this stage were very worn, often to the extent that the Janus head was no longer visible, were deliberately halved to form *asses*: 'the newly defined dupondii being split into two to provide them'.[344] These '*asses*' then circulated alongside the newly introduced bronze.

---

[339] Buttrey (1972).

[340] As stated previously (p. 58), this has been disputed by Sauer, whose examination of the coins from Bourbonne-les-Bains suggests that it is not possible to isolate two distinct phases of halving but 'a continuous process' from the late first century BC into the early first century AD: Sauer (1999), 155.

[341] Cesano (1915).

[342] Buttrey (1972), 38.

[343] *Ibid.*, 46.

[344] *Ibid.*

Context	Massalia & Campanian Massalia	Anomalous local	Ebusus & Campanian Ebusus	Other/illeg.	Total
018.014	2	0	0	0	2
025.002	2	0	1	0	3
049.064	0	0	2	0	2
065.038	0	0	2	1	3
088.019	0	0	2	0	2
088.024	0	0	2	0	2
088.028	0	0	2	0	2
120.018	2	0	1	2	5
120.039	0	0	2	0	2
120.066	1	0	1	1	3
123.056	2	0	0	1	3
123.061	1	0	1	0	2
123.091	2	0	0	0	2
127.076	0	0	2	0	2
127.082	7	0	4	2	13
127.091	4	0	0	0	4
140.086	1	0	1	0	2
140.174	2	0	1	0	3
142.014	0	0	2	0	2
180.008	1	0	2	1	4
182.016	1	0	2	0	3
182.030	0	0	7	3	10
184.009	1	0	1	0	2
271.263	1	0	1	0	2
310.082	10	0	0	0	10
310.088	2	0	0	0	2
310.090	7	0	3	1	11
310.220	10	0	3	2	15
311.234	0	0	2	0	2
320.076	2	0	0	0	2
320.088	6	0	0	3	9
321.033	4	0	1	4	9
323.002	3	0	3	3	9
500.018	1	0	2	0	3
500.049	2	0	0	0	2
502.036	1	0	4	4	9
502.048	5	0	3	0	8
503.064	0	0	2	0	2
510.014	2	0	1	1	4
510.022	12	0	0	4	16
510.023	2	0	0	0	2
600.002	0	0	2	0	2
612.023	1	0	2	0	3
617.097	3	1	1	1	6
Total	*103*	*1*	*68*	*34*	*206*

Table 12. Contexts that contain exclusively, or mainly, Massalia, anomalous local, or Ebusus coins.

The dating evidence from the AAPP excavations does not entirely contradict Buttrey's thesis but does lend support to Cesano's suggestion that, at least in Italy, halving was occurring in the early to mid first century BC. The evidence for this is twofold. Firstly, as shown in Table 11, 18 out of 51 fractional coins are found in association with dated coins between pre 200 BC and 51 BC. None of these examples can be pushed as late as the Augustan era for when they were lost, because in all the contexts from which they derive the lack of later coins would have to be accounted for. However it will be noted that the bulk of the fractioned coins (around 60%) are found in contextual association with coins of the second half of the first century BC to the first half of the first century AD, which broadly does lend support to Buttrey's thesis, although it is of course impossible to know if *all* these coins had been fractioned in one episode and all in the 20s BC.[345]

Secondly, a number of fractioned coins come from contexts which have been dated on stratigraphic grounds long before the Augustan period, although there is a curiosity: the handful of the very earliest examples all are cut quarters. There are two cut quarters from the Inn and the Inn Bar (cats 1033 and 1038) placed in phase 5, a pre-Sullan context, another in a context (161.016) with evidence of the Sullan attack (a lead slingshot) and another from phase 4 of the Shrine (cat. 1037, the period after the Sullan siege). All the rest of the fractions where there is available dating evidence come from post-Sullan contexts. Two further contexts suggest the presence of halved coins in the decades following the Sullan siege: four deliberately halved and one possible one-eighth appear in a context (161.014) with twelve other coins all of which are either full size Republican *asses* or 'foreign' imports (Megara, Volcae Arecomici) and only one an Augustan coin struck in 15 BC; and another relatively coin-rich context (271.235, with 13 coins in total) which had two cut halves in association with mostly Massalia, Ebusus and two uncut Republican coins including a *quinarius* struck in 89 BC, but perhaps more tellingly two early lamps and 17 lead slingshot. If this context is a post-Sullan destruction deposit, it is highly likely that the material contained within it had been circulating for some time, before the Sullan siege in the case of the lamps and the Ebusus and Massalia coins; and highly unlikely therefore that the deposit can be pushed into the late first century BC to coincide with Buttrey's theoretical first phase of halving.

So it would therefore appear plausible that some halved Republican *asses* and other fractions were in circulation from before the Sullan siege (maybe not in large numbers, but they were around), but indeed became more common later as Buttrey suggests, from let us say the mid first century BC onwards, and conceivably to coincide with Buttrey's theoretical first halving phase. They stayed in circulation up until the middle of the first century AD – the AAPP stratigraphic data provides evidence for this, *e.g.* a number of halved coins in phase 7 of the Inn (*e.g.* contexts 123.024, 222.012; see Table 17 for further examples); and as has been seen, they are also found in 'live' assemblages (see p. 8).

---

[345] Although it should be noted that Buttrey himself concedes: 'One cannot prove that halving did not occur earlier [*i.e.* before the 20s BC]': Buttrey (1972), 43.

Massalia & Campanian Massalia	External dating evidence	AAPP production evidence	AAPP circulation evidence
Type 1	200-175 BC	early 2nd c BC	150-100 BC (most); fallen out of use by 1st decades of 1st c AD.
Type 2A	c170 BC to 100 BC	early 2nd c BC	
Type 2B	before 125 BC to 100 BC	pre-Sulla?	
Type 2C	125-100 BC (prototypes)	c. 125 BC – 90 BC	
Type 3	n/a	no stratigraphic evidence	
Anomalous local types			
Type 1A	*tpq* 241-235 BC? *RRC* 25	mid 2nd c BC? Contextual association only	
Type 1B	*tpq* 241-235 BC? *RRC* 25	pre 89 BC	
Type 2	*tpq* 241-235 BC? *RRC* 25	pre 89 BC (contextual association only)	
Type 3A	*tpq* 241-235 BC? *RRC* 25	pre 89 BC	
Type 3B	*tpq* 241-235 BC? *RRC* 25	pre 89 BC	
Type 4	*tpq* 211-200 BC? (Luceria/Venusium)	no stratigraphic evidence; found with Neapolis so 2nd c BC?	
Type 5	*tpq* late 3rd c BC? *RRC* 44/2	no stratigraphic or contextual evidence	
Type 6	n/a	mid 2nd to early 1st century BC	
Ebusus & Campanian Ebusus			
Type 1	c214-150 BC (Campo Phase II)	mid 2nd c BC to early 1st c BC?	150-100 BC (most); fallen out of use by 1st decades of 1st c AD.
Type 2A	c214-150 BC (Campo Phase II)	no dating evidence	
Type 2B	c214-150 BC (Campo Phase II)	pre 89 BC	
Type 2C	c214-150 BC (Campo Phase II)	pre 89 BC (imports and imitations)	
Type 2D	n/a	pre-89 BC? Stylistic evidence only	
Type 3 (A to C)	n/a	pre 89 BC	
Type 4A	c214-150 BC (Campo Phase II)	pre 89 BC	200 BC to 100 BC?
Type 4B	n/a	mid 2nd c BC to 89 BC?	200 BC to 100 BC?
Type 5	n/a	pre 89 BC	
Type 6	n/a	no direct dating evidence, but prob. late 2nd c BC	
Type 7	n/a	no direct dating evidence, but association with Bathhouse hoard suggests late 2nd - early 1st c BC	
Type 8A	n/a	no dating evidence	150 BC to AD 50?
Type 8B	n/a	mid to late 2nd c BC	150 BC to AD 50?
Type 9	n/a	no direct dating evidence, but by association with Bathhouse hoard late 2nd - early 1st c BC	

Table 13. Summary of dating evidence for Massalia, Ebusus and local anomalous types.

3.5. Massalia, Ebusus and anomalous local types: conclusions

Having examined the stratigraphic data, contextual information, previous work on typology and comparable assemblages, it is possible to provide the following commentary on the main types circulating in Pompeii in the pre-Imperial period (Table 13).

Firstly, Massalia. The work of Depeyrot and Py on the French data[346] indicates that the prototypes for the Campanian Massalia coins were struck in the early part of the second century BC (Types 1 and 2A) and possibly into the late second century BC (Types 2B and 2C). Stratigraphic evidence from the AAPP excavations indicates that the imports of these prototypes also dates to the early to mid second century BC and the imitation of these coins began very soon after. There is unfortunately too little stratigraphic data for types 2C and type 3, both local products, but the little data that is available indicates production in the late second century BC, almost certainly before the Sullan siege. Contextual association and stratigraphic evidence shows that the main period of circulation was probably 150 to 100 BC, although Massalia coins were still circulating after the Sullan siege, but not much beyond the last decades of the first century BC. Most had certainly dropped out of circulation by the middle of the first AD, and would appear to be entirely absent from abandoned assemblages of AD 79, *i.e.* the final year of the town's life.

As for the anomalous local types, the only convincing prototype is Rome, the bridled horse seen on *RRC* 25, which is of the late third century BC, pointing towards a *terminus post quem* for the production of the local types. As we have seen, there is also important evidence from die-links with some of the Ebusan types. In addition most of these anomalous types appear from contextual association and some limited stratigraphic evidence to be pre-Sullan. We might therefore perhaps see all these coins as second century types; the contextual association suggests circulation in the second half of the second century BC, with no evidence that they circulated after the Sullan attack. Further discoveries of these coins will improve our understanding of them; it would also be instructive to establish if any have been found outside the town walls of Pompeii, as it appears that all discoveries so far have come from within.

As for Ebusus, we know from the work of Campo that the prototypes (and therefore some of the imports) date to the late third to the mid second century BC. In terms of production, most Ebusus coins, including the Campanian Ebusus 'rudimentary' types (Type 3), can safely be dated to the pre-Sullan period, although more refined dates are difficult to find; but late second century BC seems reasonable. Two local types, 4B and 8B, could however be of earlier date, *i.e.* early to mid second century BC. In terms of circulation, much like the Massalia coins the main period of use seems to be 150-100 BC, with circulation of the Ebusus coins continuing after the Sullan siege but only a few Ebusus coins surviving into the Christian era. Two Ebusus types might be different, type 4 could be earlier, 8 possibly late; but the numbers are too low to be certain of this.

---

[346] Depeyrot (1999); Py (2006).

3.6. Date profile of the Imperial period coins (Table 14, Figure 14)

ROMAN IMPERIAL COINS	AAPP			L. Vetudius Placidus		
	Total	by year	%	Total	by year	%
Octavian/Augustus (27 BC-AD 14)	68	1.6	45.3	23	0.5	1.7
Tiberius (AD 14-37)	33	1.4	22.0	188	7.8	14.0
Gaius (AD 37-41)*	13	2.6	8.7	79	15.8	5.9
Claudius (AD 41-54)	29	2.1	19.3	231	16.5	17.2
Nero (AD 54-68)**	4	0.3	2.7	166	11.1	12.4
Vespasian (AD 69-79)***	3	0.3	2.0	653	59.4	48.7
Total	150			1340		

*for L. Vetudius Placidus includes Agrippa.
** for L. Vetudius Placidus includes 51 Julio-Claudan uncertain and Galba
*** for L. Vetudius Placidus includes Titus and Domitian

Table 14. 'Dead' Imperial coins from the AAPP assemblage in comparison with 'live' Imperial coins from the bar of L. Vetudius Placidus.

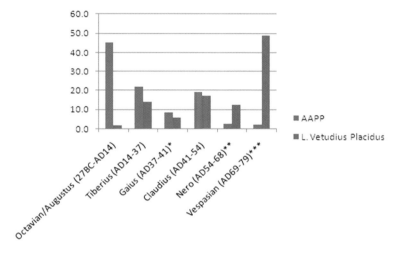

Figure 15. Date profile of the Imperial coins in the AAPP assemblage in comparison with the coins from the bar of L. Vetudius Placidus.

Having established that the local coins had largely fallen out of use by the late first century BC, we can now conclude our examination of the coinage pool by looking at the dating of the Imperial material.

Just less than half of the Imperial AAPP coins date to Octavian/Augustus, after which there is a gradual decline in numbers to Claudius (about one-fifth) and then a steep drop from the reigns of Nero and Vespasian and no coins at all of Titus. This is to be expected, given the fact that the AAPP project excavated below the AD 79 level; during the early days of excavation when the properties were cleared, we can expect that large numbers of 'live' coins would have been found which had been abandoned *in situ*, especially in the areas of the street-side bars and commercial units; what is known of the coins found during previous campaigns of clearance and excavation is summarised on pp. 21. This is why the date profile of the bar of L. Vetudius Placidus is almost exactly opposite that of the AAPP, with just less than half the coins dating to the last decade of the town's life, roughly the same proportion of coins dating to Claudius and far fewer coins of Gaius or earlier (Figure 15). The picture of coin loss and withdrawal from circulation which comes from comparing these assemblages could hardly be more clear.

3.7. Overall date profile

Date bracket	Total	%
pre 200 BC	32	2.8
200 BC – 151 BC	226	19.8
150 BC – 101 BC	594	52.0
100 BC – 51 BC	131	11.5
50 BC – 28 BC	10	0.9
Octavian/Augustus (27 BC-AD 14)	68	5.9
Tiberius (AD 14-37)	33	2.9
Gaius (AD 37-41)	13	1.1
Claudius (AD 41-54)	29	2.5
Nero (AD 54-68)	4	0.3
Vespasian (AD 69-79)	3	0.3
Total	1143	

Table 15. Date range of the coins in the AAPP assemblage (excluding illegible and undated coins).

As we can be reasonably confident that most of the local Pompeii coins were struck in the late second to early first century BC, it is possible to gain a crude impression of the overall date profile of the material in the APPP assemblage (Table 15 and Figure 16). The clear picture which emerges is that most coins found in the excavations date to between about 200 BC and 50 BC, with a small number of earlier coins (all 'foreign' imports) and far fewer coins of later date (second half of the first century BC onwards), with the exception of coins of Augustus which feature quite prominently. It should be stressed that this is a crude calculation by virtue of the fact that we have no clear sense of when the local imitations were *no longer* manufactured, although there is very little evidence for production much beyond about 80 BC. It must also be remembered that this analysis does not tell us very much about the date of coin use, for it is clear from the heavily worn state of the vast majority of coins in the assemblage that they could circulate for many decades after they were struck, which would again mean that for those periods where it seems the number of coins is very low this may be a false impression.

Nevertheless, it is fair to say that there seems to have been a period of quite intensive coin activity during the second to early first century BC. During this period, a large number of Roman Republican coins were imported into the town, as well as issues from

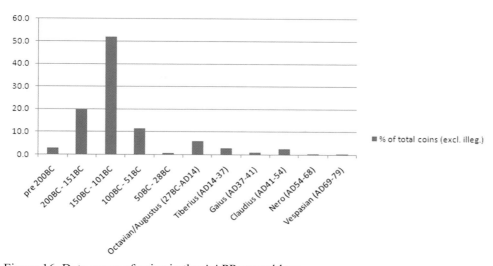

Figure 16. Date range of coins in the AAPP assemblage.

other 'foreign' mints, particularly Ebusus and Massalia. The latter types, as we have seen, were then copied in very large numbers. These three groups as well as a few other 'foreign' imports made up the monetary stock of the town during this period and perhaps beyond, although as we have seen there is little evidence that Ebusus and Massalia coins were still being used much beyond the reign of Augustus. After Augustus' reign it seems that the Roman Republican coins continued to circulate but the vast majority of the Ebusus, Massalia and other local imitations dropped out of circulation. Whether this was a deliberate rejection of these local imitations in favour of newly imported coins from Rome, perhaps related to the imposition of the *colonia*, is unclear.

4 COIN DISTRIBUTION ACROSS REGIO VI, 1

4.1.1. Overall coin distribution and density

The excavation of the entirety of Regio VI, insula 1 from 1994 to 2006 (for further information, see p. 2) provides an opportunity to examine how coins were distributed across the insula and how this relates to the functions of different parts of the block. Although coins were recovered from all properties within the insula, the distribution of coins recovered is not evenly spread. Figure 17 shows at a very basic level which rooms in each property produced coins, excluding the areas shown in red which were not dug because of intact floors. It is immediately clear that the sterile areas for coins are almost exclusively in the domestic properties (Casa delle Vestali and Casa del Chirurgo), and these blank areas also tend to be on the quieter Vicolo di Narciso eastern side. Figure 18 takes this analysis one step further by adding the number of coins found in different parts of the insula. Strong differences are again apparent between the domestic and commercial spaces. Only a tiny proportion of the rooms in the Casa delle Vestali and Casa del Chirurgo produced more than ten coins, and no areas produced more than fifty, with the vast number of excavated areas producing less than ten. In contrast the commercial areas, bars and workshops hardly ever include areas with less than ten coins and some have rooms that produced 200+ or even 300+ coins, as is the case with the Shrine (see pp. 74-81).

The analysis can be taken a step further still to factor in the room areas excavated to produce coin density (Figure 19).[347] This brings out the differences between the commercial areas, bars and domestic spaces even more acutely. It is obvious that the highest level of coin loss is in the southern part of the block (the so-called 'commercial triangle'), particularly the Shrine and the Workshop, and to the north in commercial premises situated near the Porta Ercolano (the Inn, Inn Bar and Casa delle Vestali bar), and that the domestic spaces (Casa delle Vestali, Casa del Chirurgo and the Casa del Triclinio) are almost devoid of coin, with usually only 0.1 to 0.4 coins per metre^2.

By putting all the data together in tabular form the point is further reinforced (Table 16). This shows that over 80% of coins from the insula come from the most northerly and most southerly parts, *i.e.* the Inn and its related areas and the 'commercial triangle' to the south from the Shrine to the public well and fountain. Recasting this in terms of function, it is clear that almost half the coins come from bars and hostelry type facilities. The Shrine and Workshop account for most of the rest, and these areas were also commercial in character,

---

[347] Ideally the calculation would have been made using the volume of soil extracted from each stratigraphic unit. Although there is information on the number of buckets of soil which some of these units produced, the information was too inconsistent to be of practical use.

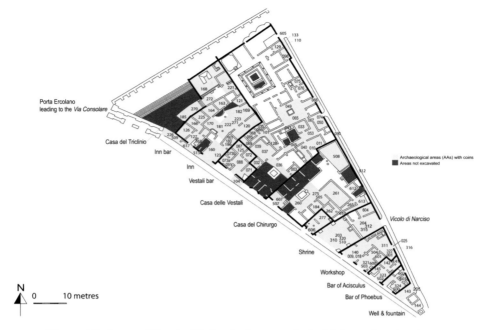

Figure 17. Areas of Regio VI, insula 1, excavated which produced coins.

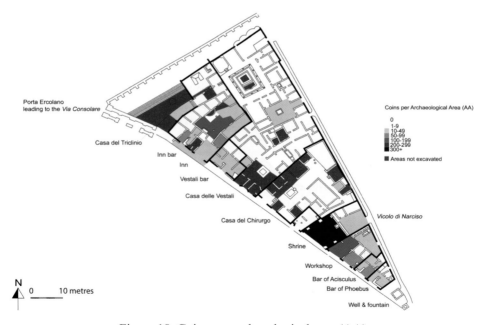

Figure 18. Coins per archaeological area (AA).

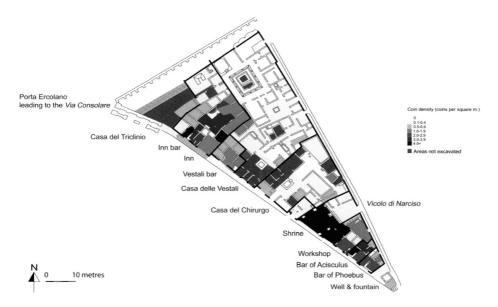

Figure 19. Coins per square meter per archaeological area (AA).

the Shrine itself an area of commercial units for most of its history, only becoming a Shrine in the last few years of Pompeii's existence (see p. 74). The domestic spaces produce little more than a tenth of the whole assemblage.

Such a pattern of coin loss must relate to the fact that the commercial areas, be they bars or workshops, were the areas where the most daily transactions were taking place so were the most likely areas for 'small change' to be accidentally dropped and trodden into the ground which eventually formed the archaeological record.

4.1.2. Coin distribution by type

The distribution of coins by broad type has also been examined.

Distribution of 'foreign' coins (Figure 20)

There is no particular pattern to the distribution of 'foreign' imports, with coins found in both northern and southern parts of the insula in equal numbers (37 in the south, *i.e.* the Casa del Chirurgo and properties to the south, 37 to the north of and including the Casa delle Vestali). Neither are there any particular discernible patterns by type, *i.e.* coins from all over the Mediterranean are found on all parts of the insula. The only unusual aspect of these coins is that a relatively high proportion of coins – 11 of a total of 74, or about 15% – come from rooms in the Casa del Chirurgo and the Casa delle Vestali not considered as commercial premises.

Plot name/no.			Plot	Totals	%	Function	Totals	%
Inn [9]	355	23.5	'Commercial triangle' [1-3]	773	51.1	Bars, Inn, taberna	709	46.9
Shrine [4]	340	22.5	Casa del Triclinio and Inn [9]	477	31.5	'The Shrine'	340	22.5
Workshop [1-3]	249	16.5	Casa delle Vestali [7-8]	171	11.3	Workshop	249	16.5
Bar of Acisculus [1-3]	126	8.3	Casa del Chirurgo [5-6]	59	3.9	Houses	171	11.3
Inn Bar [9]	98	6.5	Streets	28	1.9	Streets	28	1.8
Casa delle Vestali [7-8]	98	6.5	Unstratified	4	0.3	Well and fountain	11	0.7
Vestali Bar [7-8]	73	4.8				Unstratified	4	0.3
Casa del Chirurgo [5-6]	49	3.2						
Bar of Phoebus [1-3]	47	3.1						
Casa del Triclinio [10]	24	1.6						
Via Consolare	15	1.0						
Vicolo di Narciso	13	0.9						
Well & fountain	11	0.7						
Chirurgo shop [5-6]	10	0.7						
Unstratified	4	0.3						
Total	1512		Total	1512		Total	1512	

Table 16. Location of coins in the AAPP assemblage in descending order of quantities by property, plots and function.

Distribution of Massalia and Campanian Massalia (Figure 21)

All three Massalia types are found in all areas of the insula which produce coins; the rarer Type 1 (Apollo head left) only turn up in 'commercial' areas, but the numbers are too low for this to be of any significance. Looking at the Massalia coins as a collective group, the vast majority are found in the commercial areas, with a very low number of coins (only 13, or 4.5%) coming from domestic spaces, which is much less than that seen for 'foreign' coins (see above) or Roman coins (see below). There is also a bias towards the south of the insula block: 197 coins, or approx. 69%, come from the southern 'commercial triangle' and the Casa del Chirurgo. Why there should be this southern bias is not clear. The Massalia coins were the smallest denomination in use during the late second to first centuries BC, and being therefore the very definition of 'small change' it is not surprising that they were lost in relatively large numbers. But why more appear to have been lost (and therefore supposedly used) in the south of the insula than the north is not easily explained. Perhaps it reflects

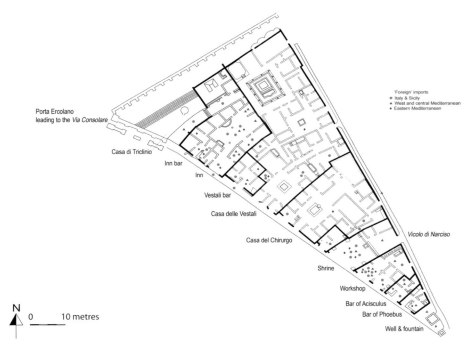

Figure 20. Distribution of 'foreign' coins in Regio VI, 1.

Figure 21. Distribution of Massalia, Campanian Massalia and anomalous local coins in Regio VI, 1.

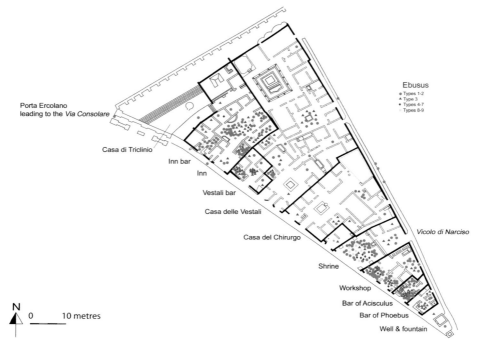

Figure 22. Distribution of Ebusus and Campanian Ebusus coins in Regio VI, 1.

Figure 23. Distribution of Roman coins in Regio VI, 1.

a chronological period during which the southern plots were more in use as commercial premises than in the north; or, or and additionally, perhaps there was a phase when Massalia coins were more common that the Ebusus coins, so were lost in greater numbers. However the dating is not refined enough for either the chronology of the insula or of the coinage to make such a distinction.

The anomalous local types appear in both northern and southern parts of the insula, with marginally more in the north than the south.

Distribution of Ebusus and Campanian Ebusus (Figure 22)
The distribution pattern of Ebusus coins is broadly similar to the Massalia coins, with a predictably heavy concentration in the commercial areas. The north/south balance however is much more even than the Massalia distribution, which as has been seen favours the southern properties: 189 Ebusus coins from the north, 195 from the south. Given that Massalia and Ebusus coins appear to have circulated more or less in tandem there is no obvious explanation for this, unless there is a subtlety to the chronology which also applies to the use of space in the insula.

The number of coins from the domestic spaces is 37, just under 10%, double that of the Massalia types but about the same as Roman (see below). Curiously, room 27 of the Casa delle Vestali, the atrium which leads into the back suite of rooms, produced 11 of these 'domestic' Ebusus coins: only 12 identifiable coins were excavated in this room (the other is Roman) but why they were found here is a puzzle.

Distribution of Roman coins (Figure 23)
Roman coins of the Republican and Imperial periods, including cut fractions, are evenly distributed amongst the areas where they have been unearthed. The overall distribution pattern is broadly similar to the other groups but with some subtle differences. Around 10% (43 coins) come from the domestic spaces, so about the same as Ebusus but rather more than Massalia and less than other 'foreign' imports. The north/south ratio is also about equal, with marginally more Roman coins coming from the southern plots (213 coins) than the northern (200).

When the distribution of the Roman coins is examined more closely and compared with the Massalia and Ebusus types some interesting patterns emerge. For instance, behind the Bar counter of Acisculus, 14 Roman coins were found, most of which were late in date, in comparison with only four Massalia; it is tempting to speculate that the Bar was in more heavy use during the later decades than earlier. And yet it is the other way around with the area to the south of the bar counter (Bar of Acisculus – Room 1), which produced only 5 Roman coins but 19 Massalia. Room 6 of the Inn, which numismatically is one of the most productive rooms in the whole insula block (Figure 19) produced relatively small numbers of Massalia coins (6 only) but large numbers of Roman and Ebusus. At the present time it is not clear why this is the case – further work on the archaeology of this particular room may shed some light.

5 CONCLUSIONS AND FURTHER RESEARCH

The primary purpose of this book is to provide a catalogue of the 1,512 coins recovered from the excavations conducted by the Anglo-American Project in Pompeii, in order that one of the largest excavated assemblages of coins from Pompeii is available to others.[348] In the preceding pages I have tried to set this material in context, drawing on evidence from both written and archaeological sources, for the use of coinage in Pompeii up until the time of the eruption of Vesuvius. As we have seen, coins did not appear in the town much before the third century BC, and did not enter common usage until the next century. By the time of the Social War, it appears that substantial numbers of imported bronze coins were in use in Pompeii, principally from three places of origin: Massalia, Ebusus and to a lesser extent Rome. In addition there were a handful of coins in circulation originating from other mints in modern Italy and towns dotted around both the western and eastern Mediterranean (see p. 23). At some point in the late second century BC, and certainly before the siege of Sulla in 89 BC, local copies of coins of Ebusus and Massalia, and a smaller number of 'anomalous local' types, began to circulate. The quality of these coins was highly variable, with the early Massalia and Ebusus types closely modelled on imported prototypes and of 'good' quality, the latest types (Campanian Ebusus in particular) bearing only a passing resemblance to the imports on which they were based, often made of poor fabrics and of fluctuating size and weight.

Debate continues as to where these local coins were manufactured. Stannard and Frey-Kupper, in their thoughtful study of coins from Paestum/Panormus and Ebusus/Massalia,[349] argue that these coins were struck 'with near certainty [at] Pompeii in the early first century BC'.[350] They base their argument on two principal aspects of these coins: the large numbers found at Pompeii, in comparison to other sites in central Italy (for example Minturnae, where Paestum/Panormus coins are more prevalent) and a number of die-links between the Campanian Ebusus coins and the 'anomalous local' types, many of which are unique to this assemblage.[351] Although these arguments are persuasive, we still have to be cautious, which is why I have termed these coins 'Campanian' types throughout this publication. A key research question yet to be answered is how widely these local types spread – again as Stannard and Frey-Kupper point out: 'The relative number of canonical [*i.e.* coins originating in Ebusus and Massalia] to imitation coins [*i.e.* coins struck locally] is difficult to

---

[348] The importance of the assemblage, coming as it does from below the AD 79 destruction level, is amplified by the fact that only an estimated '2% of the town has been investigated stratigraphically below the level of AD79': Coarelli and Pesardo (2011), 37.

[349] Stannard and Frey-Kupper (2008).

[350] *Ibid.*, 354.

[351] *Ibid.*, 360.

establish because of small samples and because very few specimens have been illustrated in publications.'[352] Clearly more museum collections and discoveries from archaeological excavation need to be made available for study, with images a necessity, in order that these local types can be distinguished from imports. What, for example, has been found at nearby Herculaneum, probably the second most scrutinised victim of the events of AD 79?[353] If Ebusus and Massalia coins have been discovered there, how many are imports and how many are local copies? Anecdotally, I get the impression that many disagree that Pompeii is the primary focus of these coins,[354] or at least there are other sites which have also produced these coins in number; but until the evidence is presented, this is going to remain a question to which we do not have a definite answer. In addition, if it transpires that the local Campanian types are present in a number of different places, what does this tell us about who was responsible for their manufacture? Was it a single town authority who 'supplied' a number of different urban centres, either directly or because coins used in one town gradually trickled down to others? Or were these coins struck as the result of some kind of collective regional response to the need for 'small change'? The latter seems highly unlikely, given that, as Michael Crawford reminds us (my italics): 'It is perhaps worth repeating that coinage is struck at Rome, *as in other ancient states*, to serve the needs of the state, not to supply the consumer.'[355]

Another key question concerning these local coins is why imitate Massalia and Ebusus? Clearly more needs to be done to understand commercial links between Massalia, Ebusus and the Bay of Naples in the late Republican period. The exchange of commodities was clearly taking place, and we know something of the products involved (for example, Campanian black-slip wares: see p. 35) – but the scale, diversity and chronological span of the trade is yet to be properly characterised.[356] If it transpires that large volumes of goods were moving between these places, this may account for the disproportionately large number of Ebusus and Massalia coins arriving in Pompeii in comparison to other towns with which Pompeii traded; assuming that the argument forwarded by Stannard and Frey-Kupper that the coins themselves were a commodity and arrived as a block is rejected (see p. 34).

Beyond the scale of the importation of these coins, however they arrived, are there additional reasons why the distinctive iconography was chosen to be copied? Might it be that Bes' association with wine and merrymaking (see p. 44) seemed an appropriate motif for a coin which – as we have seen from the coinage distribution (p. 107) – was heavily

---

[352] *Ibid.*, 370.

[353] I have not come across any studies of coins found below the AD 79 destruction levels at Herculaneum: I would welcome suggestions on where this information might be available, if it exists.

[354] Much discussion on this topic ensued after I presented a paper at the first Workshop Internazionale di Numismatica (Rome, 28-30 September 2011).

[355] *RRC*, xiii.

[356] A point alluded to by Stannard and Frey-Kupper (2008), 374: 'there is... as yet no systematic database of provenanced finds of amphorae and ceramics from the late Republican period in Italy and Sicily'.

used in local bars? Intriguingly, paintings of both Bes *and* a bull (admittedly standing, but nevertheless the same beast) have been found in the *sacrarium* of the temple of Isis, uncannily similar to the two main motifs on the local coins.[357] Although these paintings are later in date, does this suggest some connection with the cult of Isis and the production of these Ebusus and Massalia types? I have also pointed out elsewhere[358] that the turtle and toad, which appear on anomalous local types unique to Pompeii (see p. 43), are symbols found in association with another imported cult, that of the Phrygian deity Sabazius. Evidence for the worship of Sabazius at Pompeii is relatively easy to find, and includes in particular a number of bronze hands, thought to have been fixed to wooden staffs, and also two jars found near an altar in the garden of house II.i.12, probably craters for the communal sharing of ritual alcohol.[359] These cult objects sport a number of different symbols, including depictions of toads and turtles. Sabazius was originally associated with agriculture and fertility, and later with rebirth and immortality; and rituals concerned with Sabazius, in a similar manner to Bes, included music, dancing, and the consumption of wine.[360] Intriguingly, also like Bes, Sabazius through the use of toad symbolism was associated with the protection of women in childbirth – although what this might have to do with coinage is difficult to fathom.[361] Of course, it is unlikely that a connection between the iconography of these particular coins and Egyptian and Phrygian cults will ever be proved, but at the very least it is worth noting, and reminds us that iconography is chosen for a reason by those responsible for coinage production. Again this is an area which would benefit from further research.

This study of the coins from the AAPP excavations has at least been able to refine our understanding of when these locally struck types were circulating and how the circulation pool changed over time; it has also provided crucial stratigraphic evidence, largely lacking in previous research.[362] By comparing the coins with the contextual data, it has been shown that both imported Ebusus and Massalia coins and the locally struck types that copied them circulated both sides of the Social War, but probably not much beyond the middle of the first century BC. Of great importance to the dating is the location of the insula block, serendipitously positioned in an area of the town which bore the brunt of the siege by Sulla in 89 BC, thus allowing the observation in the archaeology of an invaluable and distinctive destruction horizon. By the later decades of the first century BC, as has

---

[357] d'Alessio (2009), 71 figs. 87 & 88.

[358] Hobbs (forthcoming).

[359] Vermaseren (1985), 10.

[360] This also provides a connection with Dionysus. In relation to the vessels and others like them from Pompeii, Allen (1989, 31) states: 'Not only do these vessels remind one of the Dionysiac connection claimed for Sabazius, but their real importance is that they point to communal wine-drinking by Sabazius-worshippers'.

[361] Allen (1989), 24: '... frogs were associated well into Roman times with birth ... together with representations of Bes [frogs] seem to have been used to dispel evil spirits on the occasion of childbirth'.

[362] In this respect this research is able to complement research done by others, particularly Stannard and Frey-Kupper (*e.g.* Stannard 2005a, Stannard and Frey-Kupper 2008).

been seen, for example, from contextual association (p. 89) it appears that these local coins, the production of which had long since ceased, had largely fallen out of use. The period from about the mid first century BC until coins of Octavian and his successors began to appear in number seems to have been somewhat of a vacuum in terms of supply; it is not entirely clear what coins were in use during these few decades, with the evidence presented here suggesting that Pompeii relied largely on Roman Republican coins, by now heavily worn and often fractioned (see p. 57). After this bronze coinage produced in Rome appear to have flooded in, such that by the time of the eruption Roman coins dominated; this allows a bridge to be built with those 'live' coinage assemblages abandoned *in situ*, which show that the circulation pool at the time of the eruption was very different from the earliest periods (see p. 61).

What effect the settlement of Roman veterans from about the 80s BC had on the circulation pool in Pompeii is also unclear. Were the local coins, the iconography of which had little to do with Rome, and the metrology of which does not appear to relate to the Roman system (see p. 52) deliberately withdrawn? Or was it simply that, given they do not appear to have been struck much after the early first century BC, they gradually dropped out of circulation? Interestingly, Pompeii's use of imitative coins did not cease with the use of the local Campanian types: in this assemblage, it will be seen that there are a number of *quadrantes* that too seem likely to be imitative.[363] Were these too struck locally, or imported from elsewhere? This is another area that would benefit from more research, particularly as to the frequency of these imitative Roman coins in Pompeii and other places in the region.[364] In combination with a study of the Campanian local types as discussed, this would lead to a much clearer picture of the circulation of bronze coins in central Italy in the second century BC into the early decades of Empire.

We can at least be confident that there is nothing particularly special about this assemblage, *i.e.* it certainly provides a representative sample of the circulation pool of Pompeii in the last three centuries of the town's existence. In the summer of 2010 I examined coins excavated by the Via Consolare Project[365] from a small trench in Regio VII near to the modern café. Although to date only a small number of coins have emerged (about 70 in total), the assemblage is dominated by Ebusus and Massalia imports and copies, a few local anomalous types, coins from Rome, and a small number of imported Greek coins – entirely as I expected to see. In addition I advised a Spanish team excavating at the Casa di Arianna (Regio VII, 4, 31-51)[366] under the direction of Albert Ribera (Servicio de Investigación Arqueológica Municipal de Valencia): again the assemblage is very similar. And Giacomo Pardini (University of Salerno) is currently studying a set of about 991 coins from excavations conducted by the Pompeii Archaeological Research Project: Porta

---

[363] For instance, possible imitative units and *quadrantes* of Octavian (cats 1040, 1043, 1064, 1077-78, 1085, 1088, 1091, 1097-99, 1100, 1103) and Claudius (cats. 1172, 1179-80).

[364] This has also been noted by Stannard and Frey Kupper: 'Many imitations of Roman *quadrantes* – of varying degrees of verisimilitude – also circulated widely in central Italy' (2008, 378).

[365] http://www.sfsu.edu/~pompeii/.

[366] http://www.fastionline.org/micro_view.php?fst_cd=AIAC_338&curcol=sea_cd-AIAC_909.

Stabia[367] – and once again has similar proportions of the different groups to those documented in this volume. When these assemblages are also published, the number of coins documented from below the AD 79 level will provide a substantial database for future generations of researchers.

These further discoveries also provide support to the notion that the number of coins in circulation during the late second century BC to early first century AD was indisputably very substantial. Earlier I suggested that the ubiquity of coins in Pompeii at the time of the eruption was clear from even the 33,000 or so coins recorded (p. 8). A rough calculation for the preceding centuries can be made on the basis of the coins examined in this book. Given that the AAPP excavations produced around 1,500 coins from an excavated area of approximately 1,270 square metres, it can be projected that if the whole of Pompeii were to be excavated down to the natural ground surface, its surface area of 66 hectares or 660,000 square metres might produce something in excess of 775,000 (mostly bronze) coins.[368] Of course this is a rather crude calculation, for there were many areas of the town where fewer coins are likely to have been lost, but it does give some idea of the vast number of coins which must have been in circulation during the last two centuries or so of the town's life; and this is irrespective of the fact that we are only talking here about coins *lost*, *i.e.* those which found their way into the archaeological record. The number of coins actually in circulation in the second century BC to the first century AD must surely have run into the millions. It is interesting to reflect on this, given that coinage in the modern developed world is increasingly playing second fiddle to cashless transactions using debit and credit cards and virtual money in the form of electronic transfers, such that a time can be envisaged when coinage will no longer be used at all. In this imagined scenario, understanding the origins and use of coinage within nascent economies such as that of Pompeii will become more important than ever.

---

[367] http://classics.uc.edu/pompeii/ – at the time of writing, these include 520 coins from Regio VIII, 7 and 440 coins from Regio I, 1.

[368] Stannard and Frey-Kupper (2008) arrived at a similar figure for the number of the commonest 'rudimentary' Bes type in circulation: '... we can hypothesis the issue as 70 pairs of dies [the number of die varieties Stannard counted] multiplied by 10,000 coins a pair, or 700,000 coins.'

BIBLIOGRAPHY

Abbreviations[1]

BMC Greek	*The British Museum Catalogue of Greek Coins* (London 1873-1929)
CIL	*Corpus Inscriptionum Latinarum*, Berlin
HN	N. K. Rutter, (ed.). *Historia Numorum. Italy* (London 2001)
RIC	C. H. V. Sutherland, *The Roman Imperial Coinage, Vol. 1 from 31 BC to AD 69* (London 1984).
RPC	A. Burnett, M. Amandry, P. Pau Ripollès, *Roman Provincial Coinage, Vol. 1* (London, Paris 1992).
RRC	M. H. Crawford, *Roman Republican Coinage* (Cambridge 1974).
RSP	Rivista di Studi Pompeiani
SNG ANS	*Sylloge Nummorum Graecorum: the Collection of the American Numismatic Society* (New York 1961-)
SNG	Copenhagen *Sylloge Nummorum Graecorum: The Royal Collection of Coins and Medals Danish National Museum* (43 volumes, Copenhagen 1942-)
SNG Morcom	*Sylloge Numorum Graecorum, vol. 10. The John Morcom Collection of Western Greek Bronze Coins* (1995)

d'Alessio 2009: M. T. d'Alessio, *I culti a Pompei. Divinità, luoghi e frequentatori (VI secolo a.C.–79 d.C.)* (Rome 2009).

Allen 1995: D. F. Allen (M. Mays ed.) *Catalogue of Celtic coins in the British Museum. Vol. III. Bronze coins of Gaul* (London 1995).

Amardel 1909: G. Amardel, 'Note sur quelques monnaies recueillies aux environs de Narbonne', *Bulletin de la Commission Archéologique di Narbonne* 10 (1909), 587-92.

D'Ambrosio and de Caro 1983: A. D'Ambrosio and S. de Caro, *Un impegno per Pompei: Fotopiano e documentazione della Necropoli di Porta Nocera* (Milan 1983).

Anderson, Jones, and Robinson forthcoming: M. Anderson, R. Jones, and D. Robinson, forthcoming. *The Casa del Chirurgo (VI.i.9-10.23)*. AAPP Final Reports Volume 1 (Oxford forthcoming).

Andreau 1974: J. Andreau, *Les Affaires de Monsieur Jucundus*. Collection de l'École Française de Rome 19 (Rome 1974).

Andreau 1999: J. Andreau, *Banking and business in the Roman World* (Cambridge 1999).

Andreau 2008: J. Andreau, 'The Use and Survival of Coins and of Gold and Silver in the Vesuvian Cities', in Harris (2008), 208-25.

---

[1] Used in Chapters 1-5 and the Catalogue.

de Angelis 2011: F. de Angelis, 'Playful Workers. The Cupid Frieze in the Casa dei Vettii', in E. Poehler, M. Flohr and K. Cole (eds), *Pompeii. Art, industry and infrastructure* (Oxford and Oakville 2011), 62-73.

Anniboletti 2005: L. Anniboletti, 'Progetto Regio VI. Sacello del Vicolo di Narciso (VI 2, 16-21)', in Guzzo and Guidobaldi (2005), 381-82.

Arthur 1986: P. Arthur, 'Problems of the Urbanization of Pompeii: excavations 1980-81', *The Antiquaries Journal* 66 (1986), 29-44.

Baxter and Cool 2008: M. J. Baxter and H. E. M. Cool, 'Notes on the statistical analysis of some loom-weights from Pompeii', *Archeologia e Calcolatori* 19 (2008), 239-56.

Beard 2008: M. Beard, *Pompeii. The life of a Roman town* (London 2008).

Bliquez 1994: L. J. Bliquez, *Roman Surgical Instruments and Other Minor Objects in the National Archaeological Museum of Naples* (Mainz 1994).

Borgongino and Stefani 2001-02: M. Borgongino and G. Stefani, 'Intorno all data dell'eruzione del 79 d. C.', *RSP* (2001-02), 177-215.

Breglia 1950: L. Breglia, 'Circolazione monetale ed aspetti di vita economica a Pompei', in G. Macchiavoli (ed.), *Pompeiana. Racolta di Studi per il second centenaio degli scavi di Pompei* (Naples 1950).

Brizio 1892: E. Brizio, 'Nocera Umbra – resti di un antico santuario riconosciuti in contrada 'Campo la Piana', *Notizie degli Scavi di antichità* (1892), 308-13.

Burnett 1998: A. Burnett, 'Roman coins from India and Sri Lanka', in O. Bopearachchi and D. P. M. Weerakkody, *Origin, Evolution and Circulation of Foreign Coins in the Indian Ocean* (New Dehli 1998), 179-90.

Burns forthcoming: M. Burns, 'Pompeii under siege: a missile assemblage from the Social War', *Journal of Roman Military Equipment Studies*, forthcoming.

Buttrey 1972: T. V. Buttrey, 'Halved coins, the Augustan reform and Horace, Odes 1.3', *American Journal of Archaeology* 76 (1972), 31-48.

Buttrey 1989: T. V. Buttrey, *Morgantina Studies: Vol. 2, the coins* (Princeton 1989).

Camodeca 1992: G. Camodeca, *L'archivio puteolano dei Sulpicii*, Publicazioni del Dipart-imento di Diritto Romano e Storia della Scienza Romanistica dell'Universita' degli Studi di Napoli Federico II, IV (Naples 1992).

Campo 1976: M. Campo, *Las monedas de Ebusus* (Barcelona 1976).

Campo 1993: M. Campo, 'Las monedas de Ebusus', in VII Jornadas de arqueologia fenico-púnica, *Trabajos del Museo Archeológico de Ibiza* 31 (1993), 147-71.

Campo 1994: M. Campo, 'Les Monedes de l'Eivissa Púnica', in *La moneda a l'Eivissa Púnica* Palma (1994), 39-98.

Cantilena 1997: R. Cantilena, 'Le monete', in Miniero *et al.* (1997), 39-49.

Cantilena 2008: R. Cantilena, *Pompei. Rinvenimenti monetali nella Regio VI*, Istituto Italiano di Numismatica, Studi e Materiali 14 (Rome 2008).

Cantilena and Giove 2001: R. Cantilena and T. Giove (eds), *La collezione numismatica. Per una storia monetaria del mezzogiorno* (Naples 2001).

Castiello and Oliviero 1997: D. Castiello and S. Oliviero, 'Il ripostiglio del termopolio I.8.8 di Pompeii', *Annali Istituto Italiano di Numismatica* 44 (1997), 93-205.

Castiglione Morelli 2000: V. Castiglione Morelli, 'Un gruzzolo dalla stanza degli 'Ori di Oplontis', *RSP* 11 (2000), 187-234.

Castiglione Morelli 2003: V. Castiglione Morelli, 'Lo scheletro n.27 e il suo "tesoro" monetale', in A. d'Ambrosio, P. G. Guzzo and M. Mastroroberto (eds), *Storie dal un'eruzione. Pompeii Ercolano Oplontis* (Milano 2003), 174-97.

Cerchiai *et al.* 2001: L. Cerchiai, L. Jannelli and F. Longo, *Citta greche dell Magna Grecia e della Sicilia* (Verona 2001).

Cesano 1915: L. Cesano, 'Contributo allo studio delle monete antiche dimezzate', *Rivista Italiana di Numismatica* 28 (1915), 11-38.

Chantraine 1982: H. Chantraine, *Die Antiken Fündmünzen von Neuss Gesamtkatalog der Ausgragungen 1955-1978*, Novaesium VIII (Berlin 1982).

Ciampoltrini 1998: G. Ciampoltrini, 'L'insediamento Etrusco nelle valle del Serchio fra IV e III secolo a.c.', *Studi Etruschi* 52 (1998), 173-210.

Coarelli and Pesando 2011: F. Coarelli and F. Pesando, 'The urban development of NW Pompeii: the Archaic period the 3rd c. B.C.', in S. J. R. Ellis (ed.), *The making of Pompeii. Studies in the history and urban development of an ancient town* (JRA Supplement 85, Portsmouth, Rhode Island 2011), 37-58.

Cool forthcoming: H. E. M. Cool, *The small finds and vessel glass from Insula VI, 1, Pompeii* (forthcoming).

Cooley 2009: M. Cooley, 'When did Vesuvius erupt?', *Omnibus* 57 (January 2009), 13-14.

Cooley and Cooley 2004: A. E. Cooley and M. G. L. Cooley, *Pompeii. A sourcebook* (Abingdon 2004).

Crawford 1973: M. H. Crawford, 'Paestum and Rome. The Form and function of a subsidiary coinage', in Centro internazionale di studi numismatici (ed.), *La monetazione di bronzo di Poseidonia-Paestum, Atti del III Convegno del Centro internazionale di studi numismatici*, Annali Instituto Italiano di Numismatica Supplemento 18-19 (1973), 47-109.

Crawford 1982: M. H. Crawford, 'Unofficial imitations and small change under the Roman Republic', *Annali Istituto Italiano di Numismatica* 29 (1982), 139-64.

Crawford 1985: M. H. Crawford, *Coinage and money under the Roman Republic: Italy and the Mediterranean economy* (London 1985).

Crawford 1987: M. H. Crawford, 'Sicily', in A. M. Burnett and M. H. Crawford (eds), *The coinage of the Roman world in the late Republic: proceedings of a colloquium held at the British Museum in 1985*. BAR International Series 326 (Oxford 1987).

Crawford 2011: M. H. Crawford, *Imagines Italicae* (London 2011).

Dasen 1993: V. Dasen, *Dwarfs in ancient Egypt and Greece* (Oxford 1993).

Depeyrot 1999: G. Depeyrot, *Les monnaies Hellénistiques de Marseille*, Collection Moneta 16 (Wetteren 1999).

Descoeudres 2007: J-P. Descoeudres, 'History and historical sources', in J. J. Dobbins and P. W. Foss (eds). 2007, 9-27.

Dickmann and Pirson 2005: J. A. Dickmann and F. Pirson, 'Il progetto 'Casa dei Postumii': un complesso architettonico a Pompei come esemplificazione della storia dell'insediamento, del suo sviluppo e delle sue concezioni urbanistiche', in P. G. Guzzo and M. P. Guidobaldi (eds) (2005), 156-69.

Dobbins and Foss 2007: J. J. Dobbins and P. W. Foss (eds), *The World of Pompeii* (London and New York 2007).

Duncan-Jones 2003: R. Duncan-Jones, 'Roman coin circulation in the cities of Vesuvius', in E. Lo Cascio (ed.), *Credito e moneta nel mondo Romano. Atti degli Incontri capresi di storia dell'economica antica (Capri 12-14 Ottobre 2000)*, (Bari 2003), 161-80.

Duncan-Jones 2007: R. Duncan-Jones, 'Coin evidence from Pompeii and the Vesuvian cities', in Centro Internazionale di Studi Numismatici Napoli (ed.), *Presenza e circolazione della monete in area Vesuviana. Atti del XIII convegno organizzato dal centro internazionale di studi numismatici dall'università di Napoli 'Federico II'. Napoli 30 Maggio-1 Giugnio 2003* (Napoli 2007), 11-26.

Eschebach 1993: L. Eschebach, *Gebäudeverzeichnis und Stadtplan der antiken Stadt Pompeji* (Köln 1993).

Ellis 2011a: S. J. R. Ellis (ed.), *The making of Pompeii. Studies in the history and urban development of an ancient town*, JRA Supplment 85 (Portsmouth, Rhode Island 2011).

Ellis 2011b: S. J. R. Ellis, 'The rise and re-organization of the Pompeian salted fish industry', in S. J. R. Ellis (ed.), 2011, 59-88.

Esposito 2003: R. Esposito, 'Lo scavo nell'insula VI, 9', *RSP* 14 (2003), 299-304.

Feugère and Py 2011: M. Feugère and M. Py, *Dictionnaire des monnaies découvertes en Gaule méditerranéenne (530-27 avant notre ère)* (Paris 2011).

Frey-Kupper and Stannard 2010: S. Frey-Kupper and C. Stannard, 'Les imitations pseudo-Ebusus/Massalia en Italie central. Typologie et structure, presence dans les collections et dans les trouvailles de France', *Revue Numismatique* 166 (2010), 109-47.

Garnsey *et al.* 1983: P. Garnsey, K. Hopkins and C. R. Whittaker (eds), *Trade in the Ancient Economy*, (Berkley and Los Angeles 1983).

Geertman 2007: H. Geertman, 'The urban development of the pre-Roman city', in J. J. Dobbins and P.W. Foss (eds) (2007), 82-97.

Giard 1971: J. B. Giard, 'Nimes sous Auguste', *Schweizer Münzblätter* (1971), 68-73.

Giove 2003: T. Giove, 'La circolazione monetale a Pompei', in A. d'Ambrosio, P. G. Guzzo and M. Mastroroberto (eds), *Storie dal un'eruzione. Pompeii Ercolano Oplontis* (Milano 2003), 26-33.

Giove forthcoming: T. Giove, *Pompei. Rinvenimenti Monetali nella Regio I* (Rome forthcoming).

Goudineau 1983: C. Goudineau, 'Marseilles, Rome and Gaul from the third to first century BC', in P. Garnsey *et al.* (1983), 76-86.

Guzzo 2011: P. G. Guzzo, 'The orgins and development of Pompeii: the state of our understanding and some working hypotheses', in S. J. R. Ellis (ed.), *The making of Pompeii. Studies in the history and urban development of an ancient town* (JRA Supplement 85, Portsmouth, Rhode Island 2011), 11-18.

Guzzo and Guidobaldi 2005: P. G. Guzzo and M. P. Guidobaldi (eds), *Nuove ricerche a Pompei e Ercolano, Atti del Convegno Internazionale, Roma 28-30 Novembre 2002*, Studi della Soprintendenza Archeologica di Pompei 10 (Naples 2005).

Harris 2008a: W. V. Harris (ed.), *The monetary systems of the Greeks and Romans* (Oxford 2008).

Harris 2008b: W. V. Harris, 'The Nature of Roman Money', in Harris (2008a), 174-207.

Hobbs 1996: R. Hobbs, *British Iron Age coins in the British Museum* (London 1996).

Hobbs 2003: R. Hobbs, 'Coins from the AAPP excavations, Pompeii', *Numismatic Chronicle* 163 (2003), 377-79.

Hobbs 2005: R. Hobbs, 'Coins from the AAPP excavations, Pompeii: update 1', *Numismatic Chronicle* 165 (2005), 377-81.

Hobbs 2011: R. Hobbs, 'Coinage and currency in ancient Pompeii', in N. Holmes (ed.), *Proceedings of the XIVth International Numismatic Congress Glasgow 2009* (Glasgow 2011), 732-41.

Hobbs forthcoming: R. Hobbs, 'The commercial life of insula VI, 1: the coins from the excavations of the Anglo-American Project in Pompeii', in A. Aréval, D. Bernal and D. Cottica (eds), *Acts of the scientific meeting, Ebusus y Pompeya. Testimonios Monetales di una relación, 12-13 November 2010, Escuela Española de Historia y Arquologia en Roma* (forthcoming).

Hollander 2008: D. B. Hollander, 'The Demand for Money in the Late Roman Republic', in W. V. Harris (ed.) (Oxford 2008), 112-36.

Johnson 1984: S. E. Johnson, 'The present state of Sabazius research', *Aufstieg und Niedergang der römischen Welt* II, 17.3 (1984), 1583-1613.

Jones 2006: D. Jones, *The bankers of Puteoli: Finance, Trade and Industry in the Roman World* (Stroud 2006).

Jones 2008: R. F. Jones, 'The urbanisation of Insula VI 1 at Pompeii', in P. G. Guzzo and M. P. Guidobaldi (eds), *Nuove ricerche archeologiche nell'area Vesuviana (scavi 2003-2006). Atti del convegno internazionale, Roma, 1-3 febbraio 2007* (Rome 2008), 139-46.

Jones and Robinson 2004: R. F. Jones and D. Robinson, 'The making of an elite house: the House of the Vestals at Pompeii', *Journal of Roman Archaeology* 108 (2004), 107-30.

Jones and Robinson 2005: R. Jones and D. Robinson, 'Water, wealth and social status at Pompeii. The House of the Vestals in the first century', *American Journal of Archaeology* 109 (2005), 695-710.

Jones and Robinson 2007: R. F. Jones, and D. Robinson, 'Intensification, heterogeneity and power in the development of Insula (VI.1)', in J. J. Dobbins and P. Foss (eds), (2007), 389-406.

Lane 1989 : E. N. Lane, *Corpus Cultus Iovis Sabazii (CCIS) v. III. Conclusions* (Leiden 1989)

La Tour 1892 : H. de La Tour, *Atlas des monnaies gauloises* (Paris 1892).

Lindgren 1989: H. C. Lindgren, *Ancient Greek bronze coins: European mints from the Lindgren collection* (California 1989).

Maiuri 1930: A. Maiuri, 'Saggi nella 'Casa del Chirurgo' (Regio VI, Ins. 1, n.10)', *Notizie degli Scavi di antichità* (1930), 381-95.

Maiuri 1942: A. Maiuri, 'Ara dinanzi al Tempio di Giove', *Notizie degli Scavi di antichità* (1942), 304-08.

Maiuri 1950: A. Maiuri, 'Pompei – Scoperta di un edificio termale nella Regio VIII, Insula 5, nr. 36', *Notizie degli Scavi di antichità* (1950), 116-36.

McKenzie-Clark forthcoming: J. McKenzie-Clark, *The Vesuvian red-slip ware from Regio VI, 1* (forthcoming)

Miniero et al. 1997: P. Miniero, A. d'Ambrosio, A. Sodo, G. Bonifacio, G. V.di Giovanni, G. Gasperetti and R. Cantilena, 'Il santuario campano in località Privati presso Castellamare di Stabia. Osservazioni preliminari', *RSP* 8 (1997), 11-56.

Painter 2001: K. S. Painter, *The insula of the Menander at Pompeii. Volume IV: The silver treasure* (Oxford 2001).

Parker 1992: A. J. Parker, *Ancient Shipwrecks in the Mediterranean and Roman Provinces*, BAR Int. Series 580 (Oxford 1992).

Peter 2001: M. Peter, *Untersuchungen zu den Fundmünzen aus Augst und Kaiseraugst*, Studien zu Fundmünzen der Antike 17 (Berlin 2001).

Py 2006 : M. Py, *Les monnaies préaugustéenne de Lattes et la circulation monétaire proto-historique en Gaule méridionale* (Lattes 2006).

Ranucci 2008a: S. Ranucci, 'Moneta straniera a Pompei in età Repubblicana: nuove acquisizioni', in J. Uroz, J. M. Noguera and F. Coarelli, (eds), *Iberia e Italia. Modelos Romanos de Integración territorial*, Actas de IV Congreso Hispano-Italiano Histórico-Arqueológico (Murcia 2008), 249-58.

Ranucci 2008b: S. Ranucci, 'Circolazione monetaria a Pompei. La documentazione numismatica dagli scavi dell'università di Perugia', *Annali dell'Istituto Italiano di Numismatico* 54 (2008), 151-74.

Reece 2002: R. Reece, *Coinage in Roman Britain* (Stroud 2002).

Ripoll *et al.* 1973-74: E. Ripoll, J. M. Nuix and L. Villaronga, 1973-4. 'Las monedas partidas procedentes de las excavaciones de Emporion', *Numisma* 23-4 (1973-74), 75-90.

Ripollès *et al.* 2009: P. P. Ripollès, E. Collado, C. Delegido, and D. Durá, 'La moneda en el area rural de Ebusus (Siglos IV-1 a.C.)', *Ús i circulació de la moneda a la Hispània Citerior. XIII Curs d'Història Monetària d'Hispània* (Barcelona 2009), 105-35.

Robinson 2005: D. Robinson, 'Re-thinking the social organisation of trade and industry in first century AD Pompeii' in A. MacMahon and J. Price (eds) *Roman working lives and urban living* (Oxford, 2005) 88-107.

Rostowzew 1903: M. Rostowzew, *Tesserarum Urbis Romae et Suburbi Plumbearum Sylloge*. (St. Petersburg, 1903).

Sauer 1999: E. Sauer, 'The Augustan coins from Bourbonne-les-Bains (Haute Marne). A mathematical approach to dating a coin assemblage', *Revue Numismatique* 6 (154) (1999), 145-82.

De Sena and Ikaheimo 2003: E. C. De Sena and J. P. Ikaheimo, 'The supply of amphora-borne commodities and domestic pottery in Pompeii 150BC-AD79: preliminary evidence from the House of the Vestals', *European Journal of Archaeology* 6(3) (2003), 301-21.

Stannard 1998: C. Stannard, 'Overstrikes and imitative coinages in central Italy in the late Republic', in A. Burnett, A. U. Wartenberg and R. B. Witschonke (eds), *Coins of Macedonia and Rome. Essays in honour of Charles Hersch* (London 1998), 209-29.

Stannard 2005a: C. Stannard, 'The monetary stock at Pompeii at the turn of the second and first centuries BC: pseudo-Ebusus and pseudo-Massalia', in P. G. Guzzo and M. P. Guidobaldi (eds), 2005, 120-43.

Stannard 2005b: C. Stannard, 'Numismatic evidence for relations between Spain and central Italy at the turn of the second and first centuries BC', *Schweizerische Numismatische Rundschau* 84 (2005), 47-79.

Stannard forthcoming: C. Stannard, 'Are Ebusus and Pseudo-Ebusus/Massalia at Pompeii a sign of intensive contacts with the island of Ebusus?', in A. Aréval, D. Bernal and D. Cottica (eds), *Acts of the scientific meeting, Ebusus y Pompeya. Testimonios Monetales di una relación, 12-13 November 2010, Escuela Española de Historia y Arquologia en Roma* (forthcoming).

Stannard unpublished: C. Stannard, 'Ebusus and Pseudo-Ebusus under Pompeii' (unpublished publication of the coins from the excavations of the Casa di Amarantus).

Stannard and Frey-Kupper 2008: C. Stannard and S. Frey-Kupper, ''Pseudo-mints' and small change in Italy and Sicily in the late Republic', *American Numismatic Review* (Second Series), 20, (2008), 351-404.

Stazio 1955: A. Stazio, 'Rapporti tra Pompei ed Ebusus nelle Baleari alla luce dei rinvenimenti monetali', *Annali dell'Istituto Italiano di Numismatico* 2 (1955), 33-57.

Stefani and Vitale 2005: G. Stefani and R. Vitale, 'Il termopoli di Asellina', in G. Stefani (ed.) *Cibi e sapori a Pompei e dintorni. Antiquarium di Boscoreale 3 Febbraio – 26 Giugno 2005* (Castellamare di Stabia 2005), 115-28.

Taliercio Mensitieri 1986: M. Taliercio Mensitieri, 'Il bronzo di Neapolis', in *La monetazione di Neapolis nella Campania antica, Atti del VII Convegno del Centro Inter-nazionale di Studi Numismatici, Napoli, 20-24 Aprile 1980* (Naples 1986), 219-73.

Taliercio Mensitieri 2005: M. Taliercio Mensitieri (ed.), *Pompei. Rinvenimenti monetali nella Regio IX* (Rome 2005).

Tchernia 1978: A. Tchernia, *L'Épave romaine de la Madrague de Giens (Var), Campagnes 1972-1975: fouilles de l'Institut d'archéologie méditerranéeanne* (Gallia Supplement 34, Paris 1978).

Tchernia 1983: A. Tchernia, 'Italian wine in Gaul at the end of the Republic', in P. Garnsey *et al.* (eds) 1983, 87-104.

Tchernia 2009: A. Tchernia, 'L'exportation du vin: interpretations actuelles de l'exception gauloise', in J. Carlsen and E. Lo Cascio (eds), *Agricoltura e scambi nell'Italia tardo-Repubblicana* (Bari 2009), 91-113.

Vermaseren 1985: M. J. Vermaseren, *Corpus Cultus Iovis Sabazii (CCIS), v. I. The hands* (Leiden 1985).

Villaronga 1994: L. Villaronga, *Corpus nummum Hispaniae ante Augusti Aetatem* (Madrid 1994).

Vitale 2008: R. Vitale, 'Il numerario di piccolo taglio dai rinvenimenti monetali di Pompei', in H. Asolati e G. Gorini (eds) *I ritrovamenti monetali e i processi inflativi nel mondo antico e medievale: Atti del IV congresso internazionale di numismatica e di storia monetaria, Padova, 12-13 ottobre 2007* (2008), 29-51.

Warren 1984: J. A. Warren, 'The autonomous bronze coinage of Sicyon (Part 2)', *Numismatic Chronicle* 144 (1984), 1-24.

Weber 1922-29: L. Forrer, *The Weber Collection. Descriptive catalogue of the collection of Greek coins formed by Sir Hermann Weber (1922-29)* (London 1922-29).

Zanker 1998: P. Zanker, *Pompeii. Public and private life* (Cambridge Massachusetts 1998).

CATALOGUE

CATALOGUE

REGIONAL IMPORTS (from Italy, excluding Rome) (1-36)

Neapolis (Campania) (1-8)
Arpi (Apulia) (9)
Canusium (Apulia) (10)
Paestum (Lucania) (11-20)
Thurii (Lucania) (21-23)
Vibo Valentia? (Bruttium) (24)
Rhegion (Bruttium) (25-31)
Katane (Sicilia) (32-33)
Leontinoi (Sicilia) (34)
Siracusa (Sicilia) (35)
Motya, Sicilia? Croton, Bruttium? (36)

'FOREIGN' IMPORTS (from outside Italy) (37-82)

Epidamnos-Dyrrachium (Illyria) (37-38)
Megara (Attica) (39)
Sicyon (Corinthia) (40-44)
Boeotia (uncertain mint) (45-46)
Samos (Ionia) (47-48)
Volcae Arecomici (southern Gaul) (49)
Carmo, Sevilla (Hispania) (50)
Kese (Tarraco) (Hispania) (51)
Also Kese? Other Spanish? (52-53)
Hispano-Carthaginian (54)
Cyrene (Cyrenaica) (56-67)
Uncertain mint (Cyprus) (68-72)
Jerusalem/Judaea (Palestine) (73-75)
Uncertain probable foreign imports (76-82)

MASSALIA & EBUSUS IMPORTS AND CAMPANIAN TYPES (83-770)

Massalia imports and Campanian Massalia (83-369)
Anomolous local types (370-384)
Ebusus imports and Campanian Ebusus (385-770)

ROME

Roman Republican (771-932)
Deliberately cut fractions (933-1039)
Octavian/Augustus (27 BC - AD 14) (1040-1110)
Tiberius (AD 14–37) (1111-1139)
Gaius (AD 37-41) (1140-1152)
Claudius (AD 41-54) (1153-1181)
Nero (AD 54-68) (1182-1185)
Vespasian (AD 69-79) (1186-1188)

ILLEGIBLE (1189-1512)

Notes

Catalogue numbers run sequentially from 1 to 1512. With the exception of illegible coins (cats. 1189-1512), none of which are illustrated in the plates, coins **not** illustrated are indicated with an asterisk beside the cat. no., *e.g.* '57*.'

NR – specifies not recorded (*i.e.* weight or diameter).

A note on weights: most are given to two decimal places; those to only one decimal place are due to a lack of a more accurate set of scales being available on site at the time the coin in question was weighed. Therefore if a weight is given as, for example, 1.3g, this should not be read as '1.30g'. Superscript is used to indicate effects on weight, *i.e.* 'b' for broken, 'f' for fragment. 'h' – halved, 'q' quartered.

References to coin catalogues, sylloges etc. normally give the cat. nos. (*e.g.* HN 577); if page numbers are relevant instead these are specified.

The properties which make up Regio VI, 1, are given in the form used throughout the text (*e.g.* 'Casa del Chirurgo'). Room numbers are provided in Figure 11 p. 69. Excavation codes are in the format AA (Archaeological Area) then context: *e.g.* 142.045, is AA 142, context 45. This is followed by the small find number (*e.g.* '180'). A concordance between the excavation codes and the catalogue numbers is provided at the end of the book.

REGIONAL IMPORTS (from Italy, excluding Rome)

Neapolis (Campania)

AE unit. *obv.* head of Apollo, laureate, r.; *rev.* man-headed bull stg. r., above trident. c. 300 BC? cf *HN* 577

1. 21mm 7.52g	142.045, 180 Bar of Acisculus - rm. 2	very worn but probably this type; Cales also possible (*HN* 436)

AE unit. *obv.* head of Apollo, laureate, l.; *rev.* man headed bull stg. r., Victory flying above crowning head, in exergue 'IΣ'. c. 275-250 BC? *SNG* Copenhagen (1-3: Italy) 504-27; *HN* 589

2. 19mm 4.14g	270.036, 354 Casa del Triclinio – ramp	inscription illeg.
3. 18mm 4.78g	271.234, 97 Inn - rm. 9	inscription illeg.

AE unit. *obv.* head of Apollo r.; *rev.* man-faced bull stg. r., Victory flying above, 'ΝΕΟΠΟΛΙΤΩΝ'. c. 250-225 BC? *SNG* Copenhagen (1-3: Italy) 486-503; Taliercio Mensitieri (1986), Group IV D; *HN* 595

4. 14mm 4.06g	140.143, 275 Workshop - rm. 1	rev. illeg.
5. 13mm 2.43g	277.036, 137 Casa del Chirurgo - rms. 3&4	inscription illeg.
6. 12mm 1.76g	003.090, 1318 Casa delle Vestali - rm. 11/4	inscription illeg.

AE unit. *obv.* male head l.; *rev.* tripod, 'ΝΕΟΠΟΛΙΤΩΝ'. c. 300-275 BC. *SNG* ANS 165-66; *HN* 583

7. 14mm 2.0g	003.022, 1750 Casa delle Vestali - rm. 11/4	
8. 13mm 1.59g	032.007, 211 Casa delle Vestali - rm. 12	uncertain; symbols in field

Arpi (Apulia)

AE unit. *obv.* head of Athena r., with Corinthian helmet; *rev.* bunch of grapes, inscription. c. 215-212 BC. *SNG* Copenhagen (1-3: Italy) 612-13; *HN* 650

9. 15mm 3.64g	088.049, 331 Casa delle Vestali Bar - rm. 1	probably this type, but very worn; inscription illeg.

Canusium (Apulia)

AE triens. *obv.* head of Herakles r.; *rev.* club, on either side 'KA NY', four pellets. c. 250-225 BC. *HN* 661

10. 14mm 3.21g	180.015, 68 Inn - rm. 3	possibly this type, but very worn; inscription illeg.

Paestum (Lucania)

AE triens (?). *obv.* heads of Dioscuri r.; *rev.* swan r., above 'M.SAI C.HEL'. Late second to early first c. BC? Crawford (1973) 23/2a; *HN* 1235

11. 16mm 3.53g	222.002, 71 Inn - rm. 9	obv. and rev. inscription illeg.
12. 15mm 1.36g	140.147, 222 Workshop - rm. 1	possibly this type

AE semis. *obv.* helmeted head of Athena r.; *rev.* clasped hands, above 'L.FAD', below 'L.SAT'. Probably late first c. BC[1]. Crawford (1973) 32; *HN* 1250

13. 15mm 3.12g	507.028, 19 Casa del Chirurgo shop - rm. 2	obverse and reverse die-linked with Stannard and Frey-Kupper (2008) 14
14. 14mm 3.69g	168.004, 2 Casa del Triclinio – clean	very worn; garbled legend. For reverse *cf.* Stannard and Frey-Kupper (2008) 16

AE semis. *obv.* female head r., to l. 'MINEIA M F'; *rev.* two storey building, on either side of upper floor 'P S', lower floor 'S C'. Early first c. BC. Crawford (1973) 38a-c; *HN* 1258

15. 15mm 3.21g	069.018, 30 Casa delle Vestali - rm. 10	inscriptions illeg.
16. 13mm 3.29g	310.043, 145 Shrine - rm. 1	inscriptions illeg.

AE unit. *obv.* bust r., before lituus, 'C LOLLI M DOI II VIR'; *rev.* female fig. std. r. AD 14-37 (Tiberius). *RPC* 1, 604

17. 19mm 4.8g	610.026, 208 Casa del Chirurgo - rm. 12	inscription illeg.
18. 16mm 6.1g	032.005, 2 Casa delle Vestali - rm. 12	inscription illeg.

AE unit. *obv.* laureate head r., 'L LICINIVS IIVIR'; *rev.* Victory walking r., with palm branch and wreath. AD 14-37 (Tiberius). *RPC* 1, 613

19. 15mm 2.9g	513.029, 523 via Consolare – Inn area	inscription illeg.

AE unit. *obv.* laureate head r., 'A VERGILIVS OPT IIVIR'; *rev.* Mars stg. l., on pedestal, holding standard and sword. AD 14-37 (Tiberius). *RPC* 1, 617

20. 15mm 3.72g[b]	140.027, 55 Workshop - rm. 1

Thurii (Lucania)

AE unit. *obv.* head of ?Demeter l., behind 'ΘΟΥΡΙΑ'; *rev.* bull butting l. After 300 BC. *SNG* Copenhagen (1-3: Italy) 1513-14; *HN* 1932

21. 16mm 4.1g	011.020, 913 Casa delle Vestali - rm. 153	probably this type
22. 15mm 2.86g	323.070, 156 Bar of Acisculus - rm. 1	uncertain – very corroded
23. 15mm 2.16g	140.166, 344 Workshop - rm. 1	extremely corroded

Vibo Valentia (Bruttium)

AE sextans. *obv.* laureate head of Apollo r.; *rev.* lyre, 'VALENTIA'. c. second c. BC? *SNG* ANS 494-96; *HN* 2266

24. 12mm 1.3g	310.220, 411 Shrine - rm. 1	possibly this type but inscription difficult to read

---

[1] Stannard and Frey-Kuper (2008), after Crawford (1973), date this to the 40's BC.

Rhegion (Bruttium)

AE triantes. *obv.* jugate bearded busts of Asclepius and Hygeia r.; *rev.* Artemis stg. facing, with dog and 'IIII'. c. 215-150 BC? *SNG* Copenhagen (1-3: Italy) 1979; *SNG* ANS 761-62; *HN* 2555

25. 18mm 3.28g	120.037, 415 Inn - rm. 4	
26. 16mm 2.87g	221.001, 1 Casa del Triclinio - rm. 4	
27. 15mm 3.61g	322.050, 233 Workshop - rm. 4	obv. illeg.; rev. v. faint traces of stg. figure
28. 15mm 2.86g	085.017, 277 Casa delle Vestali - rm. 9	
29. 15mm 2.45g	165.012, 52 Inn Bar - rm. 1b and 3b	probably this type but extremely worn

AE triantes. *obv.* jugate busts r.; *rev.* figure stg. l., holding branch, bird and sceptre. c. 215-150 BC? *SNG* ANS 776-85; *HN* 2559

30. 15mm 3.99g	226.013, 21 Via Consolare – Porta Ercolano
31. 15mm 2.6g	510.024, 71 Shrine - rm. 1

Katane (Sicilia)

AE unit. *obv.* jugate heads of Serapis and Isis r.; *rev.* two corn ears, around 'καταναιωχ'. Third to second c. BC. *SNG* Copenhagen (4-5: Sicily) 188

32. 13mm 1.76g	510.004, 26 Shrine - rm. 1	reverse illeg.
33. 12mm 1.6g	503.070, 153 Workshop - rm. 2	

Leontinoi (Sicilia)

AE unit. *obv.* bust of Demeter l., illeg.; *rev.* corn ear tied together, 'to left 'ΤΙΝΩΝ'. Late third c. BC? *SNG* Copenhagen (4-5: Sicily) 366; *SNG* Morcom 609

34. 16mm 3.62g	222.001, 2 Inn - rm. 9

Siracusa (Sicilia)

AE unit. *obv.* head of Poseidon l., illeg.; *rev.* ornamental trident flanked by dolphins. Hieron II, c. 275-215 BC. *BMC* Greek 2, 603; *SNG* Copenhagen (4-5: Sicily) 844-56; *SNG* Morcom 827-30

35. 19mm 6.3g	123.024, 115 Inn - rm. 1

Motya, Sicily? Or Croton, Bruttium?

AE unit. *obv.* bust r.; *rev.* crab, otherwise illeg. Third to second c. BC? *cf. SNG* Copenhagen (1-3: Italy) 1823 and *HN* 2226 (Croton); *SNG* Morcom 645 (Motya)

36. 10mm 1.19g	265.085, 88 Casa del Chirurgo - rm. 11

'FOREIGN' IMPORTS (from outside Italy)

Epidamnos/Dyrrachium (Illyria)

AR drachm. *obv.* cow standing r., looking back at suckling calf; *rev.* square containing double stellate pattern 'T' in field. Third to second c. BC. *cf. BMC* Greek 6, no. 31

37. 16mm 2.63g   500.005, 97 Bar of Phoebus - rm. 1   pierced

AE unit. *obv.* laureate head of Apollo r.; *rev.* serpents intertwined around a staff. Third to first c. BC? Lindgren (1989), II 1425

38. 15mm 3.24g   121.028, 175 Inn - rm. 6   another example in the British
                                                               Museum, C&M 1922,0317.70
                                                               (unpublished)

Megara (Attica)

AE unit. *obv.* laureate head of Apollo r.; *rev.* tripod, 'ΜΕΓΑ'. c. second c. BC. *BMC* Greek 11, 16-18; *SNG* Copenhagen (13-14: Aetolia-Euboea) 471

39. 14mm 4.3g   161.014, 64 Inn - rm. 3

Sicyon (Corinthia)

AE unit. *obv.* dove flying l.; *rev.* 'ΣΙ' inside wreath. c. 196-150 BC. Warren (1984), groups 8 or 10

40. 15mm 1.62g   204.109, 174 Shrine - rm. 2
41. 13mm 1.97g   140.073, 156 Workshop - rm. 1
42. 13mm 1.78g   316.006, 8 Vicolo di Narciso
43. 13mm 1.7g   311.010, 54 Workshop - rm. 4

AE unit. *obv.* dove flying l.; *rev.* bust of Apollo r. Early first c. BC? Warren (1984), group 12

44. 14mm 1.81g   140.147, 220 Workshop - rm. 1   light for type?

Boeotia (uncertain mint)

AE unit. *obv.* head of Demeter, facing; *rev.* Poseidon stg. l., resting foot on rock and leaning on trident. c. second c. BC? *BMC* Greek 8, p. 41 cats. 81-89

45. 18mm 2.22g   182.013, 31 Inn - rm. 12
46. 16mm 4.22g   270.006, 178 Casa del Triclinio - ramp

Samos (Ionia)

AE unit. *obv.* head of Hera, r., pellet border; *rev.* peacock stg. on caduceus, r., 'ΣΑΜΙΩΝ'. Late second to first c. BC? *BMC* Greek 16, Ionia 201; *SNG* Copenhagen (22-24: Ionia) 1722

47. 19mm 6.78g   073.039, 43 Casa delle Vestali Bar - rm. 1   probably this type
48. 17mm 6.07g   140.147, 337 Workshop - rm. 1

Volcae Arecomici (southern Gaul)

AE unit. *obv.* female bust r., to l. VOLCAE'; *rev.* togate fig. stg. l., before palm tree, behind 'AREC'. c. 70-30 BC, or 60-40 BC (Py (2006), 481). Allen (1995) 215-30; Feugère and Py (2011) VLC-2677

49. 13mm 1.57g   161.014, 72 Inn - rm. 3   distinctive casting sprue

Carmo, Sevilla (Hispania)

AE unit. *obv.* head of ?Hercules r.; *rev.* two ears of corn, between 'CARMO'. Second to first c. BC. *SNG* Copenhagen (43: Spain-Gaul) 141-42; Villaronga (1994), pp. 384-85

50. 22mm 14.58g   142.002, 305 Bar of Acisculus - rm. 2

Kese (Tarraco) (Hispania)

AE unit. *obv.* head of Mercury r., behind caduceus; *rev.* horse galloping r. Second c. BC. Villaronga (1994), p. 162, no. 28

51. 12mm 1.48g   144.071, 131 Well and fountain - n. of Well

Also Kese? Or other Spanish?

AE unit. *obv.* bust r.; *rev.* horse stg. r.; - otherwise illegible

52. 14mm 3.06g   223.108, 171 Inn - rm. 9
53. 15mm 1.91g[b]   320.061, 337 Shrine - rm. 1

Hispano-Carthaginian

AE unit. *obv.* head of Tanit l.; *rev.* horse r., above star. Second c. BC? Villaronga (1994), p. 67, no. 28; Ranucci (2008b), cat. 99

54. 14mm 3.51g   121.028, 177 Inn - rm. 6

Cyrene (Cyrenaica)

AE unit. *obv.* diademed head of Ptolemy I, r.; *rev.* head of Libya r., legend before 'ΠΤΟΛΕΜΑΙΟΥ', behind 'ΒΑΣΙΛΣΩΣ'. Circular lathe-marks on each side. c. 250-120 BC. *BMC* Greek 29, 42 ff.; *SNG* Copenhagen (40: Egypt: the Ptolemies) 437-53

55. 20mm 3.4g	160.042, 42 Inn - rm. 1	most similar to *SNG* Copenhagen 451
56. 17mm 3.33g	127.032, 114 Inn Bar - rm. 1b	*cf.* SNG Copenhagen 446
57*. 17mm 1.85g	140.147, 206 Workshop - rm. 1	*cf.* SNG Copenhagen 446
58. 16mm 3.93g	140.172, 395 Workshop - rm. 1	*cf.* SNG Copenhagen 446
59. 15mm 1.78g	145.005, 22 Bar of Acisculus - behind counter	
60. 15mm 2.70g	072.006, 134 Casa delle Vestali Bar - rm. 3	
61. 14mm 3.05g	505.008, 100 Casa del Chirurgo - rm. 5&8a	
62. 14mm 2.23g	271.259, 359 Inn - rm. 9	
63. 13mm 2.52g	143.058, 68 Well and fountain. - s. of Well	*cf.* SNG Copenhagen 439 and 445
64. 13mm 1.38g	310.087, 627 Shrine - rm. 1	*cf.* SNG Copenhagen 439 and 445

65. 13mm 1.20g[b]	032.005, 217 Casa delle Vestali - rm. 12	cf. SNG Copenhagen 439 and 445
66. 12mm 2.3g	049.081, 181 Casa delle Vestali - rm. 27	cf. SNG Copenhagen 439 and 445
67. 12mm 1.6g	127.050, 168 Inn Bar - rm. 1b	cf. SNG Copenhagen 439 and 445

Uncertain mint (Cyprus)

AE unit. *obv.* bust r.; *rev.* head-dress of Isis, 'ΠΤΟΛΕΜΒΑΣΙΛ'. Late second to early first c. BC. *SNG* Copenhagen (40: Egypt: the Ptolemies) 685-90; Weber (1922-29), 8295

68*. 14mm 2.64g	324.023, 111 Bar of Phoebus - rm. 1	
69. 13mm 2.6g	120.016, 178 Inn - rm. 4	probably this type, but very unclear
70. 12mm 2.31g	503.020, 13 Workshop - rm. 2	
71. 12mm 1.74g	166.028, 56 Inn Bar - rm. 5B	
72. 11mm 1.5g	310.200, 416 Shrine - rm. 1	

Jerusalem/Judaea (Palestine)

AE unit. *obv.* ear of corn, 'KAICAPOC'; *rev.* palm tree, pellets. 6 BC to AD 11 (Augustus). *RPC* I, 4954-57

73. 16mm 1.97g	140.027, 54 Workshop - rm. 1
74. 14mm 2.09g	310.117, 284 Shrine - rm. 1

AE unit. *obv.* bunch of grapes with vine leaf on stem, 'HPWΔHC'; *rev.* crested helmet, to l. caduceus, 'EΘNAPXN'. 4 BC to AD 6 (Herod Archelaus). *RPC* 1, 4917

75. 15mm 2.08g	073.001, 3 Casa delle Vestali Bar - rm. 1

UNCERTAIN COINS WITH LEGENDS OR ICONOGRAPHY – PROBABLY 'FOREIGN' IMPORTS

AE unit. *obv.* Janus head; *rev.* standing figure? inscription which includes 'AICA' (?), or possibly 'AIST'.

76. 17mm 1.74g	140.147, 216 Workshop - rm. 1

AE unit. *obv.* bust r., illeg; *rev.* tripod, to one side 'ANOΣ' (?).

77. 19mm 5.7g	500.030, 171 Bar of Phoebus - rm. 1

AE unit. *obv.* bust r.; *rev.* sphinx (or griffin?) std. l., otherwise illeg.

78. 19mm 4.71g	145.005, 20 Bar of Acisculus - behind counter	very worn

AE unit. *obv.* bare headed bust r.; *rev.* prow r.?, before three pellets, above illegible inscription

79. 20mm 3.9g	610.021, 72 Casa del Chirurgo - rm. 12

AE unit. *obv.* laureate bust r.; *rev.* bust with triangular shaped beard, before uncertain inscription, possibly including 'Λ Λ'. Sabratha? North Africa. Early first c. AD?

| 80. 16mm 2.34g | 275.004, 34 Casa del Chirurgo - rm. 5 | *cf. RPC* 817 (this is the closest parallel, but is a larger module coin) |

AE unit. *obv.* bust r., pellet border; *rev.* fig. std. l., pellet border

| 81. 14mm 1.81g | 320.061, 336 Shrine - rm. 1 | obv. has parallels with *RRC* 343, but this is a copper coin |

AE/Pb? unit. *obv.* bust r., below 'C.DOMIT' inside tablet; *rev.* illeg. inscription

| 82. 15mm 2.86g | 181.139, 77 Inn - rm. 9 | context dated to phase 7 (late Augustus to mid 1st c. AD); the only broadly similar parallel is Rostowzew (1903), no. 1202 |

MASSALIA IMPORTS AND CAMPANIAN MASSALIA

Massalia imports

TYPE 1

AE unit. *obv.* head of Apollo l.; *rev.* bull butting r., above ΜΑΣΣΑ', below exergual line 'ΛΙΗΤΩΝ'. c. 200-175 BC. Depeyrot (1999) 34-35; Py (2006) 390-404. Diameter: 12-14 mm. Wt. range: 1.26-1.67g Average wt.: 1.40g [5 examples]

83. 14mm 2.5g	503.018, 178 Workshop - rm. 2	traces of inscription below exergual line
84. 14mm 1.67g	025.002, 11 Workshop - back entrance to rm. 4	above ']ΣΣΑ'
85. 14mm c1g	127.078, 405a Inn Bar - rm. 1b	above bull 'ΜΑΣ[ΣΑ]', below exergual line 'ΛΙΗ['
86. 13mm 1.69g[b]	127.091, 395 Inn Bar - rm. 1b	above bull 'ΜΑΣΣΑ'
87. 13mm 1.26g	140.174, 388 Workshop - rm. 1	above bull 'ΜΑΣΣΑ'
88. 12mm 1.44g	088.053, 335 Casa delle Vestali Bar - rm. 1	illeg. inscription above and below bull
89. 12mm 1.32g	127.091, 574 Inn Bar - rm. 1b	above bull 'Μ]ΑΣΣ[Α'
90. 12mm 1.29g	140.192, 464 Workshop - rm. 1	inscription illegible

variant

| 91. 12mm 1.3g | 503.086, 167 Workshop - rm. 2 | below exergual line 'ΔΙΑ' (?) |

Massalia imports/Campanian Massalia

TYPE 2A

AE unit. *obv.* head of Apollo r.; *rev.* bull butting r., above 'ΜΑΣΣΑ', below exergual line 'ΛΙΗΤΩΝ'. c 170-100 BC. Depeyrot (1999) 39-40; Stannard (2005a), Figure 11, no. 85; Py (2006) 405-92. Diameter: 11-16 mm. Wt. range: 1.00-2.7g Average wt.: 1.41g [42 examples]

92. 16mm 2.21g[b]	140.000, 76 Workshop - rm. 1	No visible legend
93. 16mm 1.88g	140.027, 79 Workshop - rm. 1	'ΜΑΣΣΑ'
94. 15mm 2.5g	500.018, 187 Bar of Phoebus - rm. 1	'ΜΑΣ]Σ[Α'

95. 15mm 1.97g	140.046, 72	Workshop - rm. 1	'[ΜΑΣΣ]Α'
96. 15mm 1.85g	320.061, 306	Shrine - rm. 1	']ΣΣΑ'
97. 15mm 1.26g	310.220, 410	Shrine - rm. 1	irregular shaped flan; 'ΜΑΣΣΑ'
98. 14mm 2.7g	617.097, 2	Via Consolare - outside Inn	'Μ]ΑΣΣ[Α'; behind Apollo head traces of letter
99. 14mm 1.80g	085.008, 150	Casa delle Vestali - rm. 9	'ΜΑΣ[ΣΑ]'
100. 14mm 1.68g	310.090, 632	Shrine - rm. 1	'ΜΑΣΣΑ'; behind Apollo head traces of letter or symbol
101. 14mm 1.54g[b]	320.073, 441	Shrine - rm. 1	'ΜΑΣΣΑ'
102. 14mm 1.38g	502.039, 105	Bar of Acisculus - rm. 1	'[ΜΑ]ΣΣΑ'; behind Apollo head traces of letter or symbol
103. 14mm 1.36g	310.090, 637	Shrine - rm. 1	'[Μ]ΑΣΣΑ'
104. 14mm 1.23g	324.014, 72	Bar of Phoebus - rm. 1	'ΜΑΣ]ΣΑ'; 'Λ]ΙΗΤ[ΩΝ'
105. 14mm 1.17g	320.062, 13	Shrine - rm. 1	'ΜΑ]ΣΣΑ'
106. 13mm 2.13g	310.220, 403	Shrine - rm. 1	'[Μ]ΑΣΣΑ'
107. 13mm 1.98g	120.066, 525	Inn - rm. 4	'[ΜΑ]ΣΣ[Α]'
108. 13mm 1.86g	127.089, 403	Inn Bar - rm. 1b	'Μ]ΑΣΣ[Α'
109. 13mm 1.85g	320.067, 631	Shrine - rm. 1	'ΛΙΗ[ΤΩΝ]'
110. 13mm 1.67g	320.074, 390	Shrine - rm. 1	'ΜΑ]ΣΣ[Α]'
111. 13mm 1.62g[b]	140.027, 86	Workshop - rm. 1	'ΜΑΣΣΑ' (very faint)
112. 13mm 1.6g	513.041, 132	Via Consolare - Inn area	'Λ]ΙΗΤΩΝ'
113. 13mm 1.51g	140.000, 469	Workshop - rm. 1	'Μ[ΑΣΣΑ]'; 'ΛΙΗ[ΤΩΝ]'
114. 13mm 1.4g	612.027, 232	Casa del Chirurgo - rms. 17-18	['Μ]ΑΣΣΑ'; 'Λ]ΙΗΤ[ΩΝ'
115. 13mm 1.42g	140.027, 123	Workshop - rm. 1	'ΜΑ]ΣΣΑ'
116. 13mm 1.33g	127.082, 389	Inn Bar - rm. 1b	'[Μ]ΑΣΣΑ'
117. 13mm 1.26g[b]	310.087, 623	Shrine - rm. 1	'ΜΑΣ]ΣΑ'; below exergue illegible inscription
118. 13mm 1.21g	272.017, 118	Casa del Triclinio - rm. 4	'ΜΑΣ]ΣΑ'; behind Apollo head possible letter
119. 13mm 1.15g	223.029, 141	Inn - rm. 9	'Μ]ΑΣΣΑ'
120. 13mm c. 1g	223.007, 0d	Inn - rm. 9	probably 'ΜΑΣΣΑ'
121. 12mm 1.8g	018.014, 350	Workshop - rm. 1	'ΜΑ[ΣΣΑ]'
122. 12mm 1.76g	502.048, 84	Bar of Acisculus - rm. 1	'Λ]ΙΗΤ[ΩΝ]'
123. 12mm 1.62g	127.082, 388	Inn Bar - rm. 1b	'ΜΑΣΣ[Α'
124. 12mm 1.56g	310.082, 622	Shrine - rm. 1	'ΜΑ]ΣΣΑ'
125. 12mm 1.26g	320.061, 317	Shrine - rm. 1	'ΜΑΣΣΑ'
126. 12mm 1.26g	310.082, 610	Shrine - rm. 1	'ΜΑ]ΣΣ[Α'
127. 12mm 1.22g	142.043, 131	Bar of Acisculus - rm. 2	'ΜΑ]ΣΣΑ'
128. 12mm 1.21g	271.250, 257	Inn - rm. 9	'Μ]ΑΣΣ[Α'
129. 12mm 1.21g	310.090, 621	Shrine - rm. 1	'ΜΑΣ]ΣΑ'
130. 12mm 1.18g	140.147, 214	Workshop - rm. 1	'ΜΑΣ]ΣΑ'
131. 12mm 1.16g	140.073, 157	Workshop - rm. 1	'ΜΑΣ]ΣΑ' just about visible
132. 12mm NR	271.235, 257	Inn - rm. 9	'ΜΑΣΣΑ'
133. 11mm 1.72g	025.002, 8	Workshop - back entrance to rm. 4	'ΜΑ]ΣΣΑ'
134. 11mm 1.31g	161.042, 104	Inn - rm. 3	'ΜΑ]ΣΣ[Α'
135. 11mm 1.31g	145.013, 111	Bar of Acisculus - behind counter	'ΜΑ]ΣΣ[Α'
136. 11mm 1.24g	320.061, 359	Shrine - rm. 1	'ΜΑΣ]Σ[Α'
137. 11mm 1.20g	180.008, 82	Inn - rm. 3	'ΜΑ]ΣΣΑ'
138. 11mm 1.12g	222.061, 395	Inn - rm. 9	'Μ]ΑΣΣ[Α'

139. 11mm 1.11g[b] 320.061, 617 Shrine - rm. 1   'M]ΑΣΣΑ'

140*. 11mm 1.08g 310.082, 612 Shrine - rm. 1   'M]ΑΣΣ['

141. 11mm 1.06g 502.048, 89 Bar of Acisculus - rm. 1   '[M]ΑΣΣΑ'

142. 11mm 1.06g 123.091, 570 Inn - rm. 1   'ΜΑ]ΣΣΑ'

143. 11mm 1.06g 271.235, 262 Inn - rm. 9   'ΜΑ]ΣΣΑ'

144. 11mm 1.03g 510.047, 94 Shrine - rm. 1   below exergual line faint
traces of inscription

145. 11mm 1.00g 321.033, 117 Workshop - rm. 2   'ΜΑ]ΣΣΑ'

Imitation? no exergual line

146. 12mm 1.44g 127.082, 397 Inn Bar - rm. 1b   below bull 'IΛTI' (?)

Massalia imports/Campanian Massalia

TYPE 2B

AE unit. *obv.* Head of Apollo r.; *rev.* bull butting r., above 'ΜΑΣΣΑ', below exergual line 'ΔΑ'. c 125-100 BC. Depeyrot (1999), type 47/9; Py (2006), 518-29. Diameter: 12-13mm Wt. range: 1.2-1.71g Average wt.: 1.60g [2 examples]

147. 13mm 1.7g[b] 123.054, 451 Inn - rm. 1   'ΔΑ'? Extremely worn

148. 13mm 1.4g 500.049, 151 Bar of Phoebus - rm. 1   probably 'ΔΑ'

149. 13mm 1.2g 510.015, 128 Shrine - rm. 1   probably this type

150. 12mm 1.71g 502.018, 95 Bar of Acisculus - rm. 1

151. 12mm 1.52g 142.045, 174 Bar of Acisculus - rm. 2   possibly 'ΔΑ'. Reverse die-linked to Stannard 4.195 (unpublished)

Campanian Massalia (local imitations)

TYPE 2C

AE unit. *obv.* Head of Apollo r.; *rev.* bull bullting r., various garbled inscriptions, above and below bull. c. 125-90 BC. Stannard (2005a) Figure 12, nos. 103-07. Wt. range: 1.2-1.66g Average wt.: 1.49g [6 examples]

ΑΜΣΣ (Stannard (2005a) Figure 11, no. 91, from the Bathhouse hoard, Appendix 2 BH7)

152. 12mm 1.0g[b] 009.000, 19 Workshop - rm. 1   unstratified

153. 12mm 1.3g 510.022, 58 Shrine - rm. 1

ΑΜ[O]Σ

154. 12mm 1.54g 184.009, 22 Casa del Chirurgo - rm. 6c   reverse die-linked to a coin in the Bathhouse hoard (Appendix 2 BH8)

ΑΟΜΣ (la Tour (1892), 2227 and 2242; Stannard (2005a) Figure 11, nos. 92-96)

155. 13mm 1.38g 221.010, 21 Casa del Triclinio - rm. 4

156. 12mm 1.2g 050.071, 172 Casa delle Vestali - rm. 19

ΑΟΣΣ (la Tour (1892), 2228; Bathhouse hoard, Appendix 2 BH14, reverse only)

157. 12mm 1.30g   140.154, 174 Workshop - rm. 1
158. 12mm 1.3g   140.147, 215 Workshop - rm. 1
159. 12mm 1.66g   271.235, 256 Inn - rm. 9   very worn, but probably this
                                                            type

0ΑΣΣ

160. 12mm 1.64g   502.037, 9 Bar of Acisculus - rm. 1   above bull '0ΑΣΣ [ ]' sigmas
                                                            retrograde

ΜΑΑ? (Stannard (2005a), Figure 11, nos. 98-99)

161. 13mm 1.47g   123.091, 579 Inn - rm. 1
162. 12mm 1.47g^b 321.033, 113 Workshop - rm. 2   obv. and rev. die-linked to a
                                                            coin in the Bathhouse hoard
                                                            (Appendix 2 BH13)

Variant

AE unit. *obv.* head of Apollo r.; *rev.* bull butting r., below no exergual line, small ?animal (calf?). Late second to early first c. BC? Wt. range 1.34-1.75g. Av. wt.: 1.55g [3 examples]

163. 13mm 1.75g   088.006, 23   Casa delle Vestali Bar - rm. 1
164. 13mm 1.56g   182.011, 48   Inn - rm. 12
165. 13mm 1.34g   271.234, 101 Inn - rm. 9

TYPE 2 (unclassifiable) – Massalia imports and Campanian Massalia

AE unit. *obv.* head of Apollo r.; *rev.* bull butting r. Sometimes traces of inscriptions above or below bull, but too worn or corroded to classify. Mid. second c. BC to early first c. BC? Diam. 10-15mm

[15mm]
166. 15mm c. 1g   270.018, 108 Casa del Triclinio – ramp

[14mm] Av. wt.: 1.71g [25 examples]
167*. 14mm 2.79g   271.243, 197 Inn - rm. 9
168.* 14mm 2.36g   180.015, 48   Inn - rm. 3
169.* 14mm 2.19g   140.046, 85   Workshop - rm. 1
170. 14mm 2.06g   140.027, 58   Workshop - rm. 1
171. 14mm 2.04g   204.109, 199 Shrine - rm. 2
172. 14mm 1.99g   310.082, 630 Shrine - rm. 1
173.* 14mm 1.85g   310.090, 674 Shrine - rm. 1
174.* 14mm 1.84g   140.038, 128 Workshop - rm. 1
175.* 14mm 1.81g   085.020, 151 Casa delle Vestali - rm. 9
176.* 14mm 1.8g   612.023, 311 Casa del Chirurgo - rms. 17-18
177. 14mm 1.8g   617.097, 85   Via Consolare - outside Inn
178. 14mm 1.78g   323.047, 109 Bar of Acisculus - rm. 1
179.* 14mm 1.76g   140.147, 200 Workshop - rm. 1
180. 14mm 1.7g   617.097, 3   Via Consolare - outside Inn
181.* 14mm 1.69g   127.091, 381 Inn Bar - rm. 1b

182.* 14mm 1.67g 127.082, 399 Inn Bar - rm. 1b
183.* 14mm 1.62g 145.013, 88 Bar of Acisculus - behind counter
184.* 14mm 1.62g 310.092, 197 Shrine - rm. 1
185.* 14mm 1.56g 320.061, 314 Shrine - rm. 1
186.* 14mm 1.51g 321.033, 119 Workshop - rm. 2
187.* 14mm 1.51g 145.013, 105 Bar of Acisculus - behind counter
188.* 14mm 1.50g 088.021, 106 Casa delle Vestali Bar - rm. 1
189.* 14mm 1.43g 073.034, 52 Casa delle Vestali Bar - rm. 1
190.* 14mm 1.41g 310.220, 408 Shrine - rm. 1
191.* 14mm 1.37g 310.087, 638 Shrine - rm. 1
192. 14mm 1.33g 310.087, 672 Shrine - rm. 1
193.* 14mm 1.3g^b 500.049, 152 Bar of Phoebus - rm. 1
194.* 14mm 1.22g 310.220, 398 Shrine - rm. 1
195. 14mm 0.94g^b 180.116, 100 Inn - rm. 3
196.* 14mm 0.87g^b 310.087, 673 Shrine - rm. 1
197. 14mm 0.73g 091.025, 76 Casa delle Vestali Bar - rm. 5/6

[13mm] Average wt.: 1.55g [28 examples]
198.* 13mm 2.88g 123.019, 62 Inn - rm. 1
199. 13mm 2.12g 271.235, 266 Inn - rm. 9
200. 13mm 1.93g 310.220, 413 Shrine - rm. 1   behind Apollo head traces of monogram?

201.* 13mm 1.9g 600.035, 250 Workshop - rm. 2
202.* 13mm 1.85g 126.028, 259 Inn Bar - rm. 6b
203. 13mm 1.85g 310.106, 251 Shrine - rm. 1   above bull illegible inscription
204. 13mm 1.82g 510.014, 40 Shrine - rm. 1
205.* 13mm 1.70g 140.086, 145 Workshop - rm. 1
206.* 13mm 1.7g^b 510.015, 125 Shrine - rm. 1
207.* 13mm 1.67g 310.220, 401 Shrine - rm. 1
208. 13mm 1.63g 310.197, 683 Shrine - rm. 1
209.* 13mm 1.61g^b 323.007, 16 Bar of Acisculus - rm. 1
210.* 13mm 1.60g 088.006, 22 Casa delle Vestali Bar - rm. 1
211. 13mm 1.58g 140.069, 81 Workshop - rm. 1   possible last 'A' visible above bull

212. 13mm 1.57g 140.027, 82 Workshop - rm. 1
213.* 13mm 1.56g^b 310.220, 402 Shrine - rm. 1
214.* 13mm 1.52g 180.001, 1 Inn - rm. 3
215.* 13mm 1.47g 510.020, 44 Shrine - rm. 1
216.* 13mm 1.47g^b 140.027, 83 Workshop - rm. 1
217.* 13mm 1.46g 321.033, 121 Workshop - rm. 2
218.* 13mm 1.45g 310.082, 620 Shrine - rm. 1
219.* 13mm 1.45g 140.027, 124 Workshop - rm. 1
220. 13mm 1.44g 323.002, 80 Bar of Acisculus - rm. 1
221.* 13mm 1.43g 310.220, 655 Shrine - rm. 1
222.* 13mm 1.4g 140.073, 326 Workshop - rm. 1
223.* 13mm 1.38g 310.082, 613 Shrine - rm. 1
224.* 13mm 1.36g 180.001, 2 Inn - rm. 3
225.* 13mm 1.34g^b 127.082, 392 Inn Bar - rm. 1b
226.* 13mm 1.31g 310.197, 356 Shrine - rm. 1
227.* 13mm 1.27g^b 126.052, 142 Inn Bar - rm. 6b

228.* 13mm 1.26g 140.166, 325 Workshop - rm. 1
229.* 13mm 1.26g 142.048, 177 Bar of Acisculus - rm. 2
230.* 13mm 1.25g 271.234, 71 Inn - rm. 9
231. 13mm 1.22g   141.019, 21 Bar of Acisculus - rm. 3
232. 13mm 1.2g   510.015, 121 Shrine - rm. 1
233.* 13mm 1.19g^b 310.082, 640 Shrine - rm. 1
234.* 13mm 1.11g^b 310.304, 602 Shrine - rm. 1
235.* 13mm 1.08g 182.114, 253 Inn - rm. 12
236.* 13mm c1g   127.078, 405d Inn Bar - rm. 1b
237.* 13mm 0.94g 310.223, 406 Shrine - rm. 1
238.* 13mm c. 0.5g 222.002, 475 Inn - rm. 9
239. 13mm NR   320.107, 1002 Shrine - rm. 1   exergual line, but no
                                                          inscription visible below

[12mm] Average wt.: 1.31g [64 examples]
240.* 12mm 1.91g 510.020, 46 Shrine - rm. 1
241.* 12mm 1.86g 265.085, 87 Casa del Chirurgo - rm. 11
242. 12mm 1.83g   140.162, 528 Workshop - rm. 1
243.* 12mm 1.79g^b 510.022, 61 Shrine - rm. 1
244.* 12mm 1.73g 140.073, 158 Workshop - rm. 1.
245. 12mm 1.71g   310.220, 614 Shrine - rm. 1   traces of illegible inscription
                                                          above bull

246.* 12mm 1.70g 310.082, 605 Shrine - rm. 1
247.* 12mm 1.70g 271.263, 1001 Inn - rm. 9
248. 12mm 1.69g   140.147, 209 Workshop - rm. 1
249.* 12mm 1.67g^b 320.073, 442 Shrine - rm. 1
250.* 12mm 1.66g^b 271.259, 351 Inn - rm. 9
251.* 12mm 1.61g 322.063, 1004 Workshop - rm. 4
252.* 12mm 1.61g 271.259, 357 Inn - rm. 9
253.* 12mm 1.61g 502.048, 108 Bar of Acisculus - rm. 1
254.* 12mm 1.61g 320.061, 301 Shrine - rm. 1
255.* 12mm 1.57g 088.015, 69 Casa delle Vestali Bar - rm. 1
256.* 12mm 1.56g 321.033, 120 Workshop - rm. 2
257.* 12mm 1.56g 320.061, 350 Shrine - rm. 1
258. 12mm 1.55g   121.033, 179 Inn - rm. 6   possible 'N' below exergual
                                                          line

259.* 12mm 1.52g 510.022, 51 Shrine - rm. 1
260.* 12mm 1.52g 310.135, 250 Shrine - rm. 1
261. 12mm 1.49g   127.082, 382 Inn Bar - rm. 1b
262. 12mm 1.49g   050.068, 361 Casa delle Vestali - rm. 19
263.* 12mm 1.48g 320.088, 512 Shrine - rm. 1
264.* 12mm 1.47g 310.220, 412 Shrine - rm. 1
265.* 12mm 1.47g^b 169.003, 57 Inn - rm. 12
266. 12mm 1.46g   142.037, 104 Bar of Acisculus - rm. 2
267.* 12mm 1.46g 510.042, 109 Shrine - rm. 1
268.* 12mm 1.42g 127.057, 224 Inn Bar - rm. 1b
269.* 12mm 1.42g^b 510.034, 70 Shrine - rm. 1
270.* 12mm 1.4g   510.022, 53 Shrine - rm. 1
271. 12mm 1.39g   310.088, 598 Shrine - rm. 1
272.* 12mm 1.38g 320.061, 322 Shrine - rm. 1

273.* 12mm 1.37g 140.147, 336 Workshop - rm. 1
274.* 12mm 1.36g 142.035, 100 Bar of Acisculus - rm. 2
275. 12mm 1.33g 310.082, 616 Shrine - rm. 1
276. 12mm 1.33g 123.056, 577 Inn - rm. 1
277.* 12mm 1.33g 324.025, 124 Bar of Phoebus - rm. 1
278.* 12mm 1.33g 320.061, 309 Shrine - rm. 1
279.* 12mm 1.32g 320.061, 356 Shrine - rm. 1
280.* 12mm 1.3g 120.044, 532 Inn - rm. 4
281. 12mm 1.28g 123.061, 441 Inn - rm. 1
282.* 12mm 1.28g 510.014, 14 Shrine - rm. 1
283.* 12mm 1.28g 320.061, 622 Shrine - rm. 1
284. 12mm 1.23g 502.048, 88 Bar of Acisculus - rm. 1
285.* 12mm 1.22g 323.002, 75 Bar of Acisculus - rm. 1
286.* 12mm 1.22g^b 120.018, 181 Inn - rm. 4
287.* 12mm 1.22g^b 142.037, 102 Bar of Acisculus - rm. 2

288. 12mm 1.20g 145.013, 87 Bar of Acisculus - behind counter   unusual style of bust – not Apollo?

289. 12mm 1.2g 009.002, 18 Workshop - rm. 1
290.* 12mm 1.2g 510.023, 63 Shrine - rm. 1
291. 12mm 1.2g 127.091, 401 Inn Bar - rm. 1b
292. 12mm 1.19g 088.013, 66 Casa delle Vestali Bar - rm. 1
293.* 12mm 1.16g 140.174, 398 Workshop - rm. 1
294. 12mm 1.15g 140.166, 348 Workshop - rm. 1
295. 12mm 1.13g^b 614.029, 38 Casa del Chirurgo - rm. 11
296.* 12mm 1.12g 310.090, 625 Shrine - rm. 1
297.* 12mm 1.10g 140.177, 465 Workshop - rm. 1
298.* 12mm 1.08g 510.004, 34 Shrine - rm. 1
299.* 12mm 1.07g 310.090, 634 Shrine - rm. 1
300. 12mm 1.05g 072.026, 101 Casa delle Vestali Bar - rm. 3
301. 12mm 1.05g^b 310.220, 407 Shrine - rm. 1
302.* 12mm 1.02g 510.022, 55 Shrine - rm. 1
303.* 12mm 1.02g 320.068, 240 Shrine - rm. 1
304.* 12mm c1g 140.027, 161 Workshop - rm. 1
305.* 12mm c1g 127.078, 405b Inn Bar - Rm 1b
306. 12mm c1g 311.229, 315 Workshop - rm. 4
307.* 12mm c1g 223.007, 0b Inn rm. 9
308.* 12mm 0.99g 142.038, 107 Bar of Acisculus - rm. 2
309.* 12mm 0.99g 127.082, 396 Inn Bar - rm. 1b
310.* 12mm 0.98g 271.234, 87 Inn - rm. 9
311.* 12mm 0.98g 323.017, 176 Bar of Acisculus - rm. 1
312. 12mm 0.97g 182.016, 69 Inn - rm. 12
313.* 12mm 0.96g 140.147, 211 Workshop - rm. 1
314.* 12mm 0.95g 073.010, 4 Casa delle Vestali Bar - rm. 1
315.* 12mm 0.95g 510.022, 57 Shrine - rm. 1
316.* 12mm 0.95g 510.022, 49 Shrine - rm. 1
317.* 12mm 0.92g 510.043, 135 Shrine - rm. 1
318. 12mm 0.88g 141.034, 22 Bar of Acisculus - rm. 3
319.* 12mm 0.86g 018.013, 287 Workshop - rm. 1
320.* 12mm 0.86g 271.234, 75 Inn - rm. 9
321.* 12mm 0.75g 310.090, 636 Shrine - rm. 1   very thin flan

[11mm] Average wt.: 1.25g [29 examples]

322.* 11mm 1.79g 320.074, 397 Shrine - rm. 1
323.* 11mm 1.65g 320.076, 389 Shrine - rm. 1
324.* 11mm 1.64g 271.243, 196 Inn - rm. 9
325.* 11mm 1.6g   503.054, 156 Workshop - rm. 2
326. 11mm 1.48g   310.169, 604 Shrine - rm. 1
327.* 11mm 1.47g^b 221.259, 352 Casa del Triclinio - rm. 4
328. 11mm 1.44g   510.022, 62 Shrine - rm. 1
329.* 11mm 1.43g 320.061, 355 Shrine - rm. 1
330.* 11mm 1.42g 320.061, 333 Shrine - rm. 1
331.* 11mm 1.42g^b 320.088, 511 Shrine - rm. 1
332.* 11mm 1.39g 018.014, 298 Workshop - rm. 1
333. 11mm 1.39g   127.078, 289 Inn Bar - rm. 1b
334.* 11mm 1.34g 502.048, 85 Bar of Acisculus - rm. 1
335.* 11mm 1.30g^b 123.056, 578 Inn - rm. 1
336.* 11mm 1.3g   310.088, 600 Shrine - rm. 1
337.* 11mm 1.3g   607.261, 170 Casa del Chirurgo - rm. 2
338.* 11mm 1.28g 323.047, 108 Bar of Acisculus - rm. 1
339.* 11mm 1.27g 271.235, 261 Inn - rm. 9
340.* 11mm 1.26g 320.061, 615 Shrine - rm. 1
341. 11mm 1.24g   502.048, 86 Bar of Acisculus - rm. 1
342. 11mm 1.23g   323.002, 78 Bar of Acisculus - rm. 1
343.* 11mm 1.21g 140.166, 1001 Workshop - rm. 1
344.* 11mm 1.20g 320.088, 507 Shrine - rm. 1
345. 11mm 1.16g   323.030, 133 Bar of Acisculus - rm. 1
346.* 11mm 1.14g 510.022, 54 Shrine - rm. 1
347. 11mm 1.14g   271.234, 106 Inn - rm. 9
348. 11mm 1.1g   009.002, 328 Workshop - rm. 1
349.* 11mm 1.1g   510.024, 72 Shrine - rm. 1
350.* 11mm 1.06g 182.109, 268 Inn - rm. 12
351.* 11mm 1.02g 320.088, 506 Shrine - rm. 1
352.* 11mm 0.98g^f 510.004, 25 Shrine - rm. 1
353. 11mm 0.97g   502.036, 5 Bar of Acisculus - rm. 1
354. 11mm 0.97g   101.018, 113 Casa delle Vestali - rm. 7
355.* 11mm 0.96g 510.022, 50 Shrine - rm. 1
356.* 11mm 0.95g 320.088, 513 Shrine - rm. 1
357.* 11mm 0.90g^b 323.047, 107 Bar of Acisculus - rm. 1   almost a third of the coin is missing

358.* 11mm 0.83g 510.022, 56 Shrine - rm. 1
359.* 11mm 0.74g 090.016, 102 Vicolo di Narciso – back of Chirurgo
360.* 11mm 0.72g^f 140.163, 328 Workshop - rm. 1
361.* 11mm NR   222.003, 0d Inn - rm. 9

[10mm] Average wt.: 1.01g [3 examples]

362.* 10mm 1.25g^b 127.057, 218 Inn Bar - rm. 1b
363.* 10mm 1.09g 320.076, 388 Shrine - rm. 1
364.* 10mm 1.06g 000.000, 0 unstratified
365. 10mm 0.89g   320.061, 323 Shrine - rm. 1
366.* 10mm 1.3g^f 032.006, 213 Casa delle Vestali - rm. 12
367.* – mm 0.60g^f 320.088, 510 Shrine - rm. 1

Campanian Massalia

TYPE 3

AE unit. *obv.* helmeted bust of Mars r.; *rev.* bull butting r. late second c. BC to early first c. BC?
Stannard and Frey-Kupper (2008) 33, 34, 36. Wt. range: 1.2-1.48g

368. 13mm 1.2g   600.026, 199   Workshop - rm. 2   below exergual line 'ΔA'
369. 12mm 1.48g   120.018, 173   Inn - rm. 4   Mars is bearded; above bull
                                                           'MA' (?)

ANOMOLOUS LOCAL TYPES

HORSE'S HEAD

TYPE 1A

AE unit. *obv.* bull butting l.; *rev.* horse head with bridle, r. Mid second c. BC? Frey-Kupper and
Stannard (2010) Figure 1, 14

370. 14mm 2.0g   617.097, 83   Via Consolare - outside Inn   Pellet below bull ?and
                                                            exergual line; obverse die
                                                            linked to cat. 732

TYPE 1B

AE unit. *obv.* bull butting r.; *rev.* horse head with bridle, r. c. 150-89 BC. Frey-Kupper and Stannard
(2010) 6. Av. wt.: 1.54g [2 examples]

371. 13mm 1.70g   140.155, 330   Workshop - rm. 1   reverse die-linked to cat. 744
372. 13mm 1.38g   271.259, 356   Inn - rm. 9

TYPE 2

AE unit. *obv.* ?bull leaping r., below serpent; *rev.* horse head with bridle, r. c. 150-89 BC. Stannard and
Frey-Kupper (2008) 40; Frey-Kupper and Stannard (2010) Figure 1, 7

373. 15mm 1.44g   140.147, 219   Workshop - rm. 1   obverse die-linked to Stannard
                                                             (2005a), Group I, 2 and cat.
                                                             745; reverse die-linked to cats.
                                                             377 & 743. Die break on obverse

TYPE 3A

AE unit. *obv.* bust of Apollo, l.; *rev.* horse head with bridle, r. c. 150-89 BC. Frey-Kupper and Stannard
(2010) Figure 1, 10. 14-17mm Av. wt.: 2.80g [2 examples]

374. 17mm 3.74g   271.250, 402   Inn - rm. 9   probably this type. Pellet
                                                             below horse head
375. 15mm 2.8g   037.007, 57   Casa delle Vestali - rm. 5   pellet below horse head
376. 15mm 1.86g   140.073, 175   Workshop - rm. 1   pellet below horse's head?
377. 14mm 1.6g   600.036, 282   Workshop - rm. 2   no pellet; reverse die-linked to
                                                                cats. 373 and 743

TYPE 3B

AE unit. *obv.* bust of Apollo, r.; *rev.* horse head with bridle, r. c. 150-89 BC. Stannard (2005a), Group II, 2; Stannard (2005b) Group III, 2; Stannard and Frey-Kupper (2008) 39; Frey-Kupper and Stannard (2010) Figure 1, 4. 15-16mm

378. 16mm 2.04g[b]   271.234, 88 Inn - rm. 9   probably this type
379. 15mm 3.21g   271.243, 182 Inn - rm. 9   probably this type

Uncertain sub-types with horse head reverse but illegible obverse

380. 16mm 2.8g   037.050, 201 Casa delle Vestali - rm. 5
381. 16mm 2.16g[b]   271.234, 95 Inn - rm. 9

TOA/D/TURTLE/EAGLE

TYPE 4

AE unit. *obv.* toad; *rev.* bull butting r. Second c. BC? Stannard and Frey-Kuper (2008) 35; Frey-Kupper and Stannard (2010) Figure 1, 24

382. 14mm 1.4g   032.007, 212 Casa delle Vestali - rm. 12   traces of inscription above
                                                                    bull including 'A'

TYPE 5

AE unit. *obv.* bearded head of Mars r., behind anchor, below 'X'. *rev.* turtle. Second to early first c. BC? Frey-Kupper and Stannard (2010) Figure 1, 22

383. 12mm 1.9g   502.029, 3 Bar of Acisculus - rm. 1

TYPE 6

AE unit. *obv.* bust of ?Minerva r.; *rev.* eagle stg. facing. Mid. second to early first c. BC? Stannard (forthcoming) 39

384. 12mm 1.40g   310.082, 608 Shrine - rm. 1

EBUSUS AND CAMPANIAN EBUSUS

BES ON BOTH OBVERSE AND REVERSE

TYPE 1 (without symbols)

AE unit. *obv.* and *rev.* full figure of Bes facing, feet together, right arm raised holding hammer, a serpent in his left, no symbol visible in field. c. Mid 2nd to early 1st c. BC. Campo (1976) Group XVIII, 50; Campo (1994) 127-28; *cf.* Stannard (2005a) Figure 4, no. 4. Diameter: 14–18 mm. Weight range: 1.46-3.75g. Average wt.: 2.67g [15 examples]

Ebusus imports (probable)

385. 18mm 2.56g   502.042, 83 Bar of Acisculus - rm. 1
386.* 18mm 2.46g   271.263, 000 Inn - rm. 9
387. 18mm 2.37g   271.235, 254 Inn - rm. 9
388. 17mm 3.39g   145.008, 30 Bar of Acisculus - behind counter
389. 17mm 2.58g   032.017, 164 Casa delle Vestali - rm. 12
390. 17mm 2.0g   503.073, 141 Workshop - rm. 2
391. 16mm 2.88g   180.001, 5 Inn - rm. 3

392. 16mm 2.60g   165.012, 49 Inn Bar - rms. 1b&3b
393. 16mm 2.47g   032.005, 214 Casa delle Vestali - rm. 12
394. 16mm 2.17g   140.147, 221 Workshop - rm. 1
395. 16mm 2.1g   205.011, 22 Vicolo di Narciso – nr. well and fountain
396. 15mm 3.75g   320.061, 349 Shrine - rm. 1
397. 15mm 3.10g   065.038, 90 Casa delle Vestali - rm. 27
398. 15mm 3.01g   321.034, 128 Workshop - rm. 2
399. 15mm 2.52g   312.082, 368 Shrine - rm. 2
400. 15mm 1.46g   502.006, 2 Bar of Acisculus - rm. 1
401. 14mm 2.79g   142.014, 20 Bar of Acisculus - rm. 2

Campanian Ebusus (probable local imitations)

AE unit. As above (no visible symbol in field), but imitative style (*e.g.* head poorly rendered, body full but 'loose' style; also normally smaller and lighter in weight). Late second to early first c. BC? Stannard (2005a) Group V. 11-16mm Wt. range: 1.33-3.19g Average wt.: 2.14g [6 examples]

402. 16mm 2.62g   140.147, 212 Workshop - rm. 1
403. 15mm 3.19g   510.014, 15 Shrine - rm. 1
404. 14mm 2.23g   067.034, 91 Casa delle Vestali - rm. 20
405. 14mm 1.53g   025.002, 9 Workshop - back entrance to rm. 4
406. 14mm 1.33g   140.069, 138 Workshop - rm. 1
407. 13mm 1.7g   503.064, 169 Workshop - rm. 2
408. 13mm 1.60g[b] 088.024, 328 Casa delle Vestali Bar - rm. 1
409. 13mm c1g   311.234, 349a Workshop - rm. 4
410. 11mm 1.92g   127.082, 390 Inn Bar - rm. 1b   very worn

TYPE 2 (with symbols)

TYPE 2A [flower]

AE unit. *obv.* and *rev.* full figure of Bes facing, feet together, right arm raised holding hammer, a serpent in his left. On one or both sides four-petalled flower to right of figure in field. c. 214-150 BC. Campo (1976) Group XVIII, 53; Campo (1994) 130-34; Stannard (2005a) Figure 4, no. 8. 15-16mm. 1.9-2.3g

Ebusus imports

411. 16mm 2.3g   617.097, 1 Via Consolare - outside Inn   symbol on both obv. and rev.
412. 15mm 1.9g   600.002, 56 Workshop - rm. 2   possibly this type but very
                                                                 worn

TYPE 2B [cornucopia]

AE unit. *obv.* and *rev.* full figure of Bes facing, feet together, right arm raised holding hammer, a serpent in his left. On one or both sides cornucopia to right of figure in field. c. 214-150 BC. Campo (1976) Group XVIII, 62; Campo (1994) 147-49. 15-17mm. Average wt.: 2.83g [7 examples]

Ebusus imports (probable)

413. 17mm 3.39g	140.069, 80 Workshop - rm. 1	cornocupia not well defined
414. 16mm 3.04g	120.068, 533 Inn - rm. 4	symbol one side only
415. 16mm 2.9g	510.024, 73 Shrine - rm. 1	symbol one side only
416. 16mm 2.61g	180.015, 47 Inn - rm. 3	symbol one side only
417. 15mm 2.94g	320.061, 360 Shrine - rm. 1	symbol on obverse and reverse
418. 15mm 2.86g	145.017, 107 Bar of Acisculus - behind counter	symbol on obverse and reverse
419. 15mm 2.8g	120.051, 420 Inn - rm. 4	symbol on obverse and reverse
420. 15mm 2.68g	143.035, 67 Well & Fountain - s. of Well	symbol on obverse and reverse
421. 15mm 2.32g	072.021, 132 Casa delle Vestali Bar - rm. 3	symbol on obverse and reverse
422. 14mm 2.3g	140.069, 137 Workshop - rm. 1	one side too corroded

Campanian Ebusus (probable local imitations)

AE unit. *obv.* and *rev.* as above, but imitative style, smaller flan. Stannard (2005a) Group V, 6

423. 12mm 2.2g	612.023, 304 Casa del Chirurgo - rms. 17-18	one side very corroded

TYPE 2C [caduceus]

Ebusus imports (probable)

AE unit. *obv.* and *rev.* full figure of Bes facing, feet together, right arm raised holding hammer, a serpent in his left. On one or both sides caduceus in field. c. 214-150 BC. Campo (1976) Group XVIII, 58-60[2]; Campo (1994) 139-46. Stannard (2005a) Figure 4, no. 7. 15-16mm. Av. wt.: 2.43g [5 examples]

424. 16mm 2.70g	165.082, 132 Inn Bar - rm. 1b&3b	?symbol ?both sides
425. 16mm 1.87g	225.035, 66 Inn Bar - rm. 4b	?symbol ?both sides
426. 16mm 1.7g	612.022, 212 Casa del Chirurgo - rms. 17-18	?caduceus. Very worn
427. 15mm 2.64g	271.243, 184 Inn - rm. 9	symbol on obverse and reverse
428. 15mm 2.50g	320.061, 340 Shrine - rm. 1	symbol on one side only
429. 15mm 2.5g	037.007, 1 Casa delle Vestali - rm. 5	symbol on one side only
430. 15mm 2.43g	088.019, 323 Casa delle Vestali Bar - rm. 1	symbol on one side only

---

[2] But note that 59-60 have punic letter shin to right in field. It is not possible to say if any of the coins here have this because they are too worn.

Campanian Ebusus (probable local imitations)

AE unit. *obv.* and *rev.* as above, but imitative style, smaller flan. c. 125-89 BC? Stannard (2005a) Group V, 5. 12-14mm. Av. wt.: 2.05g [4 examples]

431. 14mm 2.63g	180.015, 58	Inn - rm. 3	odd fabric - lead?
432. 14mm 2.58g	125.075, 211	Casa delle Vestali Bar - rm. 4	symbol on obverse and reverse
433. 14mm 1.7g	602.012, 70	Bar of Phoebus - rm. 3	?caduceus ?both sides
434. 13mm 1.81g	127.082, 576	Inn Bar - rm. 1b	symbol on obverse and reverse
435. 12mm 1.18g	032.008, 136	Casa delle Vestali - rm. 12	symbol one side only (but other might be off flan)

Campanian Ebusus (local imitations)

TYPE 2D [caduceus and dolphin]

AE unit. *obv.* and *rev.* as above, but imitative style, smaller flan; on one side caduceus, on other dolphin. Pre-89 BC? Frey-Kupper and Stannard (2010) 27.1. 12-13mm. 1.45-1.63g Average wt.: 1.50g [3 examples]

436. 13mm 1.45g	320.061, 329	Shrine - rm. 1
437. 12mm 1.63g	140.147, 218	Workshop - rm. 1
438. 12mm 1.41g	110.020, 111	Vicolo di Narciso - back of Chirurgo probably this type

Campanian Ebusus (probable local imitations)

Cornucopia or caduceus?

AE unit. *obv.* and *rev.* full figure of Bes facing, feet together, right arm raised. On one or both sides cornucopia or caduceus in field, but ill defined. 12-13mm

439. 13mm 2.35g	180.015, 44	Inn - rm. 3
440. 13mm 1.81g	180.135, 110	Inn - rm. 3
441. 12mm 1.51g	204.072, 150	Shrine - rm. 2
442. 12mm 1.28g	140.147, 228	Workshop - rm. 1
443. 12mm 1.22g	032.005, 216	Casa delle Vestali - rm. 12

Ebusus imports/ local imitations

Types with Punic symbols and letters

AE unit. *obv.* and *rev.* full figure of Bes facing, feet together, right arm raised. In field symbol of goddess Tanit. Mid to late second c. BC. Campo (1976) Group XVIII 64; Campo (1994) 150-51

444. 14mm 1.6g	602.012, 90	Bar of Phoebus - rm. 3 probably an imitation

AE unit. *obv.* and *rev.* full figure of Bes facing, feet together, right arm raised. In field Punic letter 'mem' to left of Bes on one side. Mid to late second c. BC. Campo (1976) Group XVIII 57; Campo (1994) 138

445. 17mm 2.91g	142.048, 175	Bar of Acisculus - rm. 2 probably an import

TYPE 1 OR 2

Ebusus imports or probable Campanian Ebusus (local imitations); arranged by diameter.

AE unit. *obv.* and *rev.* full figure of Bes facing, feet together, right arm raised holding hammer, a serpent in his left. On one or both sides symbol in field or no symbol, but too worn or corroded to identify. Second to early first c. BC? Campo (1976), various. Stannard (2005a), Group V, various. 13-17mm

[18mm; Wt. range 2.5-2.56g]
446.* 18mm 2.56g 142.043, 133 Bar of Acisculus - rm. 2   Ebusus import
447.* 18mm 2.50g[b] 101.016, 115 Casa delle Vestali - rm. 7   Ebusus import

[17mm; Wt. range 2.08-3.51g; Average wt.: 3.05g; 7 examples]
448.* 17mm 3.51g 320.092, 152 Shrine - rm. 1   Ebusus import
449.* 17mm 3.42g 142.037, 103 Bar of Acisculus - rm. 2   Ebusus import
450.* 17mm 3.39g 502.048, 103 Bar of Acisculus - rm. 1   Ebusus import
451.* 17mm 3.28g 271.235, 264 Inn - rm. 9   Ebusus import
452. 17mm 2.84g   503.037, 82 Workshop - rm. 2   Ebusus import; illegible
                                                          symbol in field
453.* 17mm 2.83g 180.146, 148 Inn - rm. 3   Ebusus import
454.* 17mm 2.34g[b] 182.030, 181 Inn - rm. 12   Ebusus import
455. 17mm 2.08g   502.036, 6 Bar of Acisculus - rm. 1   Ebusus import; possible
                                                          symbol but illegible

[16mm; Wt. range 1.96-2.99g; Average wt.: 2.45g; 12 examples]
456.* 16mm 2.99g 142.010, 19 Bar of Acisculus - rm. 2   Campanian Ebusus?
457. 16mm 2.8g   510.015, 120 Shrine - rm. 1   Campanian Ebusus (head in
                                                          outline)
458.* 16mm 2.77g 182.030, 180 Inn - rm. 12   Ebusus import?
459.* 16mm 2.73g 203.165, 188 Shrine - rm. 1   probable Ebusus import
460.* 16mm 2.62g 270.032, 369 Casa del Triclinio - ramp too worn to judge
461.* 16mm 2.58g 182.109, 236 Inn - rm. 12   probably Campanian Ebusus,
                                                          very worn
462.* 16mm 2.47g[b] 182.016, 67 Inn - rm. 12   Ebusus import
463. 16mm 2.43g   503.035, 92 Workshop - rm. 2   Ebusus import
464.* 16mm 2.41g[b] 271.250, 401 Inn - rm. 9   probable Ebusus import
465.* 16mm 2.40g 310.090, 626 Shrine - rm. 1   Ebusus import?
466.* 16mm 2.35g 271.243, 183 Inn - rm. 9   Ebusus import
467.* 16mm 2.32g 310.169, 599 Shrine - rm. 1   probable Ebusus import but
                                                          very worn
468.* 16mm 2.31g[b] 145.013, 110 Bar of Acisculus - behind counter probable Ebusus import but
                                                          very worn
469.* 16mm 2.23g 165.005, 40 Inn Bar - rm. 1b&3b   probable Ebusus import but
                                                          very worn
470.* 16mm 2.05g 271.234, 103 Inn - rm. 9   too corroded to judge
471.* 16mm 2.05g[b] 140.069, 244 Workshop - rm. 1   too corroded to judge
472.* 16mm 1.96g 184.003, 25 Casa del Chirurgo - rm. 6c too corroded to judge

[15mm. Weight range: 1.2-4.03g; Average wt.: 2.58g; 39 examples]
473.* 15mm 4.03g 142.011, 36 Bar of Acisculus - rm. 2   probable Ebusus import but
                                                          very corroded

474.* 15mm 3.42g 145.013, 68 Bar of Acisculus - behind counter   Ebusus import

475.* 15mm 3.32g 311.050, 293 Workshop - rm. 4   very worn and corroded but probably Ebusus import

476.* 15mm 3.32g 311.050, 293a Workshop - rm. 4   Campanian Ebusus? Very worn

477. 15mm 3.31g 129.015, 159 Casa delle Vestali - rm. 44   Campanian Ebusus?

478.* 15mm 3.17g 320.020, 62 Shrine - rm. 1   probably Campanian Ebusus

479.* 15mm 3.13g 160.015, 49 Inn - rm. 1   Campanian Ebusus?

480. 15mm 3.1g 120.063, 617 Inn - rm. 4   Campanian Ebusus

481.* 15mm 3.05g 127.076, 286 Inn Bar - rm. 1b   probably Campanian Ebusus

482. 15mm 3.03g 127.020, 59 Inn Bar - rm. 1b   Ebusus import?

483.* 15mm 2.98g 120.066, 530 Inn - rm. 4   Pompeii Campanian. Fabric contains lead?

484.* 15mm 2.96g 271.243, 178 Inn - rm. 9   too corroded to judge

485.* 15mm 2.94g 127.057, 217 Inn Bar - rm. 1b   too corroded to judge

486.* 15mm 2.89g 181.179, no. no. Inn - rm. 9   too corroded to judge

487.* 15mm 2.86g 120.067, 527 Inn - rm. 4   Ebusus import? Very corroded

488.* 15mm 2.83g 271.243, 186 Inn - rm. 9   Ebusus import? Very worn

489. 15mm 2.82g 165.012, 75 Inn Bar - rm. 1b&3b   Ebusus import?

490.* 15mm 2.76g 127.057, 220 Inn Bar - rm. 1b   Ebusus import

491.* 15mm 2.74g 088.076, 318 Casa delle Vestali Bar - rm. 1   too corroded to judge

492.* 15mm 2.73g 311.097, 242 Workshop - rm. 4

493.* 15mm 2.70g 271.243, 193 Inn - rm. 9   probably Ebusus import

494. 15mm 2.6g 500.018, 185 Bar of Phoebus - rm. 1   Ebusus import?

495.* 15mm 2.54g 120.037, 418 Inn - rm. 4   Ebusus import; symbols in field too worn to identify

496.* 15mm 2.52g 312.051, 193 Shrine - rm. 2   Campanian Ebusus

497.* 15mm 2.47g 180.008, 81 Inn - rm. 3   probably Ebusus import but very worn

498.* 15mm 2.42g 065.017, 15 Casa delle Vestali - rm. 27   probably Ebusus import but very worn

499.* 15mm 2.3g 311.031, 366 Workshop - rm. 4   too corroded to judge

500.* 15mm 2.24g 271.242, 146 Inn - rm. 9   Campanian Ebusus

501.* 15mm 2.22g 203.006, 66 Shrine - rm. 1   Campanian Ebusus, odd brown fabric, cracked

502.* 15mm 2.2g 600.052, 377 Workshop - rm. 2   too corroded to judge

503.* 15mm 2.19g^b 320.061, 620 Shrine - rm. 1   Campanian Ebusus

504.* 15mm 2.15g^b 180.020, 43 Inn - rm. 3   probably Campanian Ebusus

505.* 15mm 2.14g 140.083, 142 Workshop - rm. 1   probably Campanian Ebusus

506.* 15mm 2.13g 271.243, 194 Inn - rm. 9   Ebusus import?

507.* 15mm 2.10g 271.243, 18 Inn - rm. 9   Campanian Ebusus?

508.* 15mm 2.08g 222.012, 310 Inn - rm. 9   probably Campanian Ebusus but very worn and corroded

509.* 15mm 2.05g 142.014, 24 Bar of Acisculus - rm. 2   probably Campanian Ebusus

510.* 15mm 2.03g 182.016, 43 Inn - rm. 12   probably Campanian Ebusus but very worn

511.* 15mm 1.97g 310.239, 603 Shrine - rm. 1   probably Campanian Ebusus but extremely worn

512.* 15mm 1.96g 320.025, 123 Shrine - rm. 1   Ebusus import?

513.* 15mm 1.95g 180.131, 108 Inn - rm. 3   Campanian Ebusus

514.	15mm 1.9g	503.009, 168	Workshop - rm. 2	Ebusus import
515.	15mm 1.9g	512.051, 118	Vicolo di Narciso - back of Casa del Chirurgo	Ebusus import
516.	15mm 1.9g	503.054, 157	Workshop - rm. 2	Campanian Ebusus
517.	15mm 1.87g	127.076, 287	Inn Bar - rm. 1b	Campanian Ebusus, unidentifiable symbol in field
518.*	15mm 1.76g	180.015, 4	Inn - rm. 3	Campanian Ebusus
519.	15mm 1.71g[b]	045.045, 113	Casa delle Vestali - rm. 26	Campanian Ebusus, unidentifiable symbol in field
520.*	15mm 1.68g	311.069, 124	Workshop - rm. 4	probably Campanian Ebusus but very worn and corroded
521.*	15mm 1.68g	204.109, 200	Shrine - rm. 2	probably Campanian Ebusus but extremely worn
522.*	15mm 1.6g	018.017, 166	Workshop - rm. 1	Campanian Ebusus
523.*	15mm 1.2g	180.001, 4	Inn - rm. 3	probably Campanian Ebusus but very corroded

[14mm. Wt. range: 1.2-2.93g; Average wt.: 2.13g; 31 examples]

524.*	14mm 2.93g	271.250, 403	Inn - rm. 9	Campanian Ebusus
525.*	14mm 2.81g	142.020, 23	Bar of Acisculus - rm. 2	Ebusus import?
526.*	14mm 2.78g	271.250, 410	Inn - rm. 9	Ebusus import? very worn
527.*	14mm 2.77g	140.103, 171	Workshop - rm. 1	Campanian Ebusus, unidentifable symbol in field
528.*	14mm 2.76g	180.008, 84	Inn - rm. 3	Campanian Ebusus
529.*	14mm 2.68g	180.120, 103	Inn - rm. 3	Campanian Ebusus
530.*	14mm 2.5g	612.053, 376	Casa del Chirurgo - rms. 17-18	Campanian Ebusus, extremely worn
531.*	14mm 2.5g	613.024, 88	Casa del Chirurgo - rm. 13	Campanian Ebusus
532.	14mm 2.41g	142.011, 98	Bar of Acisculus - rm. 2	Campanian Ebusus? but good style
533.*	14mm 2.38g	088.019, 326	Casa delle Vestali Bar - rm. 1	Campanian Ebusus
534.*	14mm 2.33g	165.082, 133	Inn Bar - rm. 1b&3b	Ebusus import? But small flan size
535.*	14mm 2.31g	509.012, 18	Via Consolare – Porta Ercolano	probably Campanian Ebusus
536.*	14mm 2.29g	140.086, 144	Workshop - rm. 1	Campanian Ebusus?
537.*	14mm 2.26g	320.117, 608	Shrine - rm. 1	Campanian Ebusus
538.	14mm 2.23g	323.055, 197	Bar of Acisculus - rm. 1	Ebusus import despite size?
539.*	14mm 2.22g	271.000, 420	Inn - rm. 9	Campanian Ebusus
540.*	14mm 2.21g	203.165, 142a	Shrine - rm. 1	Campanian Ebusus
541.*	14mm 2.2g	037.031, 347	Casa delle Vestali - rm. 5	probably Campanian Ebusus
542.*	14mm 2.14g	065.017, 93	Casa delle Vestali - rm. 27	Campanian Ebusus?
543.*	14mm 2.05g	163.024, 49	Inn - rm. 8	Campanian Ebusus?
544.*	14mm 2.03g	140.069, 139	Workshop - rm. 1	Campanian Ebusus?
545.*	14mm 2.02g	271.243, 191	Inn - rm. 9	
546.*	14mm 2.00g	165.082, 135	Inn Bar - rm. 1b&3b	Campanian Ebusus? very worn
547.*	14mm 2.0g	164.014, 35	Inn - rm. 10	probably Campanian Ebusus but very corroded
548.*	14mm 1.96g	310.220, 611	Shrine - rm. 1	probably Campanian Ebusus but very corroded

549.* 14mm 1.93g 271.243, 188 Inn - rm. 9
550. 14mm 1.88g 140.162, 333 Workshop - rm. 1   Campanian Ebusus
551.* 14mm 1.88g 320.061, 319 Shrine - rm. 1   Campanian Ebusus
552.* 14mm 1.83g 140.069, 133 Workshop - rm. 1   Campanian Ebusus
553.* 14mm 1.68g 182.030, 189 Inn - rm. 12   Campanian Ebusus
554.* 14mm 1.64g 500.005, 93 Bar of Phoebus - rm. 1   Campanian Ebusus
555.* 14mm 1.61g 140.073, 174 or 274 Workshop - rm. 1 Campanian Ebusus
556.* 14mm 1.6g 510.015, 124 Shrine - rm.1   Campanian Ebusus
557.* 14mm 1.44g 180.116, 111 Inn - rm. 3   Campanian Ebusus; very thin
                                                         flan

558. 14mm 1.35g 065.041, 85 Casa delle Vestali - rm. 27   Campanian Ebusus
559. 14mm 1.29g 140.069, 136 Workshop - rm. 1   Campanian Ebusus
560.* 14mm 1.2g 612.019, 125 Casa del Chirurgo - rms. 17-18   Campanian Ebusus

NOTE: all the remaining Type 1 or 2 coins are considered to be Campanian Ebusus, local imitations

[13mm. Wt. range: 1.2-2.57g; Average wt.: 1.84g, 26 examples]
561.* 13mm 2.57g 182.117, 242 Inn - rm. 12   very worn grey fabric with
                                                        visible brown core

562.* 13mm 2.52g 065.058, 157 Casa delle Vestali - rm. 27
563.* 13mm 2.46g^b 320.061, 318 Shrine - rm. 1
564.* 13mm 2.45g 320.061, 344 Shrine - rm. 1
565.* 13mm 2.36g 120.018, 218 Inn - rm. 4   lead?
566.* 13mm 2.21g 271.234, 91 Inn - rm. 9
567.* 13mm 2.20g 275.038, 78 Casa del Chirurgo - rm. 5
568.* 13mm 2.18g 160.042, 67 Inn - rm. 1
569.* 13mm 2.17g 145.004, 62 Bar of Acisculus - behind counter
570.* 13mm 2.03g 166.003, 33 Inn Bar - rm. 5b
571.* 13mm 2.00g 271.243, 195 Inn - rm. 9
572.* 13mm c 2.0g 223.007, 0a Inn - rm. 9   uncertain symbol in field
573.* 13mm 1.93g 271.242, 145 Inn - rm. 9
574.* 13mm 1.93g 222.011, 405 Inn - rm. 9   double struck?
575.* 13mm 1.85g 320.061, 313 Shrine - rm. 1
576.* 13mm 1.83g 222.011, 351 Inn - rm. 9
577.* 13mm 1.8g^b 003.090, 1317 Casa delle Vestali - rm. 11/4
578.* 13mm 1.65g 271.234, 104 Inn - rm. 9
579.* 13mm 1.64g 310.087, 624 Shrine - rm. 1
580.* 13mm 1.6g 510.020, 42 Shrine - rm. 1
581.* 13mm 1.59g 321.052, 155 Workshop - rm. 2
582.* 13mm 1.57g 140.027, 56 Workshop - rm. 1
583.* 13mm 1.55g 323.002, 79 Bar of Acisculus - rm. 1
584.* 13mm 1.51g 503.014, 102 Workshop - rm. 2
585.* 13mm 1.48g 088.028, 337 Casa delle Vestali Bar - rm. 1
586.* 13mm 1.46g 088.024, 67 Casa delle Vestali Bar - rm. 1
587.* 13mm 1.43g 140.069, 135 Workshop - rm. 1
588.* 13mm 1.34g 320.048, 182 Shrine - rm. 1
589.* 13mm 1.24g 271.243, 176 Inn - rm. 9
590.* 13mm 1.21g 320.061, 305 Shrine - rm. 1
591.* 13mm 1.2g 001.003, 320 Workshop - rm. 4
592.* 13mm 1.09g^b 271.259, 358 Inn - rm. 9

[12mm. Wt. range: 0.94-1.72g. Average wt.: 1.39g; 11 examples]
593.* 12mm c 2g   311.234, 349 Workshop - rm. 4
594.* 12mm 1.72g 271.235, 260 Inn - rm. 9
595.* 12mm 1.64g 120.050, 417 Inn - rm. 4
596.* 12mm 1.62g 320.117, 606 Shrine - rm. 1
597.* 12mm 1.50g 271.254, 361 Inn - rm. 9
598.* 12mm 1.44g 311.009, 86 Workshop - rm. 4
599.* 12mm 1.42g[b] 271.234, 108 Inn - rm. 9
600.* 12mm 1.33g 140.166, 346 Workshop - rm. 1
601.* 12mm 1.31g 180.015, 67 Inn - rm. 3
602.* 12mm 1.25g 071.037, 237 Casa delle Vestali Bar - rm. 2
603.* 12mm 1.14g 310.090, 615 Shrine - rm. 1
604. 12mm c1g   205.011, 35 Vicolo di Narciso – nr. well and fountain
605.* 12mm 0.94g 510.047, 114 Shrine - rm. 1

[11mm. Wt. range: 0.98-1.95g. Average wt.: 1.41g; 6 examples]
606.* 11mm 1.95g 310.220, 409 Shrine - rm. 1
607.* 11mm 1.78g 127.032, 115 Inn Bar - rm. 1b
608.* 11mm 1.42g 310.090, 633 Shrine - rm. 1
609. 11mm 1.21g   085.013, 152 Casa delle Vestali - rm. 9   illegible symbol in field
610.* 11mm 1.09g 502.036, 4 Bar of Acisculus - rm. 1   very worn
611.* 11mm 0.98g 065.038, 91 Casa delle Vestali - rm. 27

[10mm]
612.* 10mm 1.49g 271.234, 10 Inn - rm. 9   odd brown fabric

[no diameter]
613.* - mm 2.18g[f] 166.003, 32 Inn Bar - rm. 5b   fragments only

Campanian Ebusus (all Type 3 are local imitations)

TYPE 3A

AE unit. *obv.* and *rev.* rudimentary figure of Bes, right arm raised on **both** obverse and reverse
sometimes holding staff behind head; left hand by side, sometimes with serpent. c. 125-89 BC?
Stannard (2005a) Group VI (*e.g.* 47-51). Diameter: 13-15mm Weight range: 1.25-2.90g. Average wt.:
1.94g [10 examples]

614.* 15mm 2.90g 120.039, 424a Inn - rm. 4
615. 15mm 2.19g   065.017, 96 Casa delle Vestali - rm. 27
616. 15mm 1.66g   140.166, 1002 Workshop - rm. 1   die-linked to cat. 617
617. 15mm 1.25g   123.019, 56 Inn - rm. 1   die-linked to cat. 616
618. 15mm c1g   222.003, 0a Inn - rm. 9
619. 14mm 2.27g   088.006, 24 Casa delle Vestali Bar - rm. 1
620. 14mm 2.12g   140.147, 201 Workshop - rm. 1   very corroded
621.* 14mm 1.83g 323.002, 69 Bar of Acisculus - rm. 1   very worn and corroded
622. 14mm 1.71g   123.005, 32 Inn - rm. 1   ring in left field
623. 14mm 1.61g   271.234, 94 Inn - rm. 9
624. 13mm 1.85g   225.022, 94 Inn Bar - rm. 4b   one side appears even more
                                                                garbled than normal

TYPE 3B

AE unit. *obv.* and *rev.* rudimentary figure of Bes, right arm raised on 'obverse', left arm on 'reverse'. c. 125-89 BC? Stannard (2005a) Group VI (*e.g.* 52). Diameter: 14-18mm Weight range: 1.18-2.33g. Average wt.: 1.82g [9 examples]

625. 18mm 2.33g   140.147, 226 Workshop - rm. 1   clear casting sprues
626.* 16mm 1.3g   603.000, NN Bar of Phoebus - rm. 4
627.* 16mm 1.23g   146.166, 100 Well/ Fntn. - north of Well   extremely worn
628.* 15mm 2.26g   140.174, 399 Workshop - rm. 1
629. 15mm 2.14g   145.004, 53 Bar of Acisculus - behind counter
630. 15mm 2.1g   182.030, 179 Inn - rm. 12
631. 15mm 2.01g   166.063, 74 Inn Bar - rm. 5b   very worn
632. 15mm 1.93g   510.004, 28 Shrine - rm. 1
633. 15mm 1.71g   184.006, 16 Casa del Chirurgo - rm. 6c
634. 15mm 1.18g   032.005, 4 Casa delle Vestali - rm. 12
635. 14mm 1.61g   262.008, 59 Casa del Chirurgo - rm. 23
636. 14mm 1.2g[b] 503.045, 145 Workshop - rm. 2

TYPE 3C

AE unit. *obv.* and *rev.* rudimentary figure of Bes, left arm raised on **both** obverse and reverse: slanted 'T' symbol usually visible on both obverse and reverse to left of figure in field. c. 125-89 BC? Campo (1976) 71; Stannard (2005a) group VI, 7 (*e.g.* 57). Diameter: 13-18mm Weight range: 1.18-2.84g. Average weight: 1.96g [49 examples]

637. 18mm 2.84g   120.039, 424 Inn - rm. 4
638. 18mm 2.72g   503.064, 147 Workshop - rm. 2
639. 18mm 1.56g   142.047, 179 Bar of Acisculus - rm. 2   very worn and corroded
640. 17mm 2.17g   204.034, 85 Shrine - rm. 2
641. 17mm 2.0g   049.064, 122 Casa delle Vestali - rm. 27
642.* 16mm 2.57g   123.017, 55 Inn - rm. 1   casting sprue
643. 16mm 2.37g   324.059, 181 Bar of Phoebus - rm. 1
644. 16mm 2.0g   600.002, 90 Workshop - rm. 2
645. 16mm 1.98g   184.008, 15 Casa del Chirurgo - rm. 6c
646.* 16mm 1.95g   123.038, 449 Inn - rm. 1
647. 16mm 1.87g   184.009, 21 Casa del Chirurgo - rm. 6c
648. 16mm 1.6g   500.013, 161 Bar of Phoebus - rm. 1
649. 16mm 1.47g   145.004, 33 Bar of Acisculus - behind counter
650. 15mm 2.69g   310.268, 524 Shrine - rm. 1   very worn and corroded, but
                                                                     probably this type
651. 15mm 2.42g   510.004, 29 Shrine - rm. 1
652.* 15mm 2.4g   500.018, 186 Bar of Phoebus - rm. 1   very worn and corroded
653.* 15mm 2.23g   088.009, 336 Casa delle Vestali Bar - rm. 1
654.* 15mm 2.20g   088.009, 109 Casa delle Vestali Bar - rm. 1   very worn and corroded
655. 15mm 2.2g   604.021, 190 Shrine - rm. 3
656. 15mm 2.16g   182.030, 178 Inn - rm. 12
657. 15mm 2.10g   181.132, 96 Inn - rm. 9
658.* 15mm 2.07g   073.014, 25 Casa delle Vestali Bar - rm. 1
659. 15mm 1.98g   140.073, 169 Workshop - rm. 1
660. 15mm 1.96g   123.024, 116 Inn - rm. 1

661.* 15mm 1.89g   145.004, 65 Bar of Acisculus - behind counter
662. 15mm 1.8g   600.021, 161 Workshop - rm. 2
663. 15mm 1.73g^b   502.048, 87 Bar of Acisculus - rm. 1
664. 15mm 1.72g   181 or 182, unknown Inn - rm. 9
665. 15mm 1.63g   222.012, 241 Inn - rm. 9
666.* 15mm 1.58g^b 142.011, 97 Bar of Acisculus - rm. 2   very worn and corroded, but
                                                                  probably this type
667. 15mm 1.55g   182.030,102 Inn - rm. 12
668.* 15mm 1.48g   088.028, 334 Casa delle Vestali Bar - rm. 1
669. 14mm 2.39g   123.061, 447 Inn - rm. 1
670.* 14mm 2.28g   272.010, 61 Casa del Triclinio - rm. 4   very worn
671. 14mm 2.27g   036.003, 108 Casa delle Vestali - rm. 2
672. 14mm 2.2g   502.050, 158 Bar of Acisculus - rm. 1
673. 14mm 2.2g^b   502.070, 140 Bar of Acisculus - rm. 1
674.* 14mm 2.14g   222.014, 403 Inn - rm. 9
675. 14mm 2.03g   145.013, 106 Bar of Acisculus - behind counter
676.* 14mm 2.0g   502.070, 170 Bar of Acisculus - rm. 1
677. 14mm 1.99g   271.234, 86 Inn - rm. 9
678. 14mm 1.98g   065.017, 27 Casa delle Vestali - rm. 27
679. 14mm 1.95g   088.009, 329 Casa delle Vestali Bar - rm. 1
680. 14mm 1.95g   125.009, 3 Casa delle Vestali Bar - rm. 4
681. 14mm 1.92g   086.006, 85 Casa delle Vestali - rm. 8
682. 14mm 1.91g   088.021, 68 Casa delle Vestali Bar - rm. 1
683. 14mm 1.83g   032.011, 171 Casa delle Vestali - rm. 12
684.* 14mm 1.82g   123.019, 52 Inn - rm. 1
685.* 14mm 1.80g   065.017, 95 Casa delle Vestali - rm. 27   probably this type
686.* 14mm 1.8g   507.080, 138 Casa del Chirurgo shop - rm. 2
687.* 14mm 1.77g   140.099, 159 Workshop - rm. 1
688.* 14mm 1.71g   123.038, 220 Inn - rm. 1
689. 14mm 1.7g   123.017, 53 Inn - rm. 1
690.* 14mm 1.67g   323.055, 198 Bar of Acisculus - rm. 1
691.* 14mm 1.65g   140.147, 339 Workshop - rm. 1   very corroded
692.* 14mm 1.55g   502.036, 8 Bar of Acisculus - rm. 1
693.* 14mm 1.53g   121.091, 432 Inn - rm. 6   very worn
694. 14mm 1.41g   312.030, 132 Shrine - rm. 2
695. 14mm 1.28g   127.020, 58 Inn Bar - rm. 1b
696. 13mm 2.38g   271.234, 93 Inn - rm. 9
697. 13mm 1.9g   502.058, 160 Bar of Acisculus - rm. 1
698. 13mm 1.81g   324.019, 86 Bar of Phoebus - rm. 1
699.* 13mm 1.60g   323.002, 76 Bar of Acisculus - rm. 1

TYPE 3, ANOMOLOUS

AE unit. *obv.* and *rev.* rudimentary figure of Bes, arms raised on **both** obverse and reverse? c. 125-89 BC?

700. 15mm 2.31g^b   204.036, 98 Shrine - rm. 2

TYPE 3

AE unit. *obv.* and *rev.* rudimentary figure of Bes, too worn or corroded to categorise further

701.* 17mm 2.3g	500.013, 163 Bar of Phoebus - rm. 1	very worn and corroded
702.* 16mm 2.16g	145.013, 109 Bar of Acisculus - behind counter	very corroded
703.* 15mm 3.52g	140.162, 517 Workshop - rm. 1	
704.* 15mm 1.81g	180.021, 54 Inn - rm. 3	
705.* 15mm 1.27g	180.003, 20 Inn - rm. 3	very corroded and poor condition
706.* 15mm 1.1g^b	500.013, 162 Bar of Phoebus - rm. 1	
707.* 15mm c1g	277.065, 244 Casa del Chirurgo - rms. 3&4	
708.* 14mm 2.34g	502.036, 7 Bar of Acisculus - rm. 1	
709.* 14mm 2.31g	123.024, 114 Inn - rm. 1	very worn, but probably this type
710.* 14mm 2.2g	120.016, 425 Inn - rm. 4	
711.* 14mm 1.83g	510.004, 22 Shrine - rm. 1	
712.* 14mm 1.82g	088.007, 26 Casa delle Vestali Bar - rm. 1	
713.* 14mm 1.80g	323.055, 196 Bar of Acisculus - rm. 1	very worn and corroded
714.* 14mm 1.76g	324.047, 253 Bar of Phoebus - rm. 1	very corroded, but probably this type
715.* 14mm 1.66g	311.077, 125 Workshop - rm. 4	very badly corroded
716.* 14mm 1.63g	065.038, 97 Casa delle Vestali - rm. 27	
717.* 14mm 1.57g	120.016, 175 Inn - rm. 4	
718.* 14mm 1.52g	222.001, 6 Inn - rm. 9	
719.* 14mm 1.4g	502.011, 146 Bar of Acisculus - rm. 1	very corroded
720.* 13mm 1.94g^b	311.076, 160 Workshop - rm. 4	badly cracked and disintegrating; unusual fabric
721.* 13mm 1.86g	271.243, 177 Inn - rm. 9	very worn
722.* 13mm 1.40g^b	222.012, 151 Inn - rm. 9	
723.* 13mm 1.33g	088.006, 25 Casa delle Vestali Bar - rm. 1	very worn and corroded
724.* 13mm 1.3g	612.023, 291 Casa del Chirurgo rms 17-18	very worn and corroded
725.* 13mm 1.29g	271.234, 98 Inn - rm. 9	
726. 13mm 1.19g	123.042, 177 Inn - rm. 1	
727.* 12mm 2.52g	321.042, 151 Workshop - rm. 2	very worn and corroded
728.* NR NR	037.007, 2 Casa delle Vestali - rm. 5	fragments only

BES COMBINED WITH AN ANIMAL

TYPE 4A

Ebusus imports (probable)

AE unit. *obv.* full figure of Bes facing, right arm raised holding hammer, serpent in l.; *rev.* bull butting l. c. 214-150 BC Campo (1976) Group XII 14-17; Stannard (2005a), fig. 4, no. 6. Diameter: 14-15mm Weight range: 2.58-3.0g

729. 15mm 3.0g	000.000, no no. unstratified	
730. 15mm 2.58g	271.243, 187 Inn - rm. 9	
731. 14mm 1.71g^b	271.250, 399 Inn - rm. 9	

Campanian Ebusus (probable local imitations)

AE unit. *obv.* full figure of Bes facing, right arm raised holding hammer, serpent in l.; *rev.* bull butting l. pre 89 BC? Campo (1976) group XIII, 18; Stannard (2005a) Group I, 5; Frey-Kupper and Stannard (2010) Figure 1, 16. Diameter: 14-15mm Weight range: 1.75-2.28g. Average weight: 1.95g [3 examples]

732. 15mm 2.28g   140.147, 224 Workshop - rm. 1   pellet below bull ?and exergual line. Reverse die-linked to cat. 370

733.* 14mm 1.82g 271.234, 85 Inn - rm. 9   reverse almost illegible; doubtful

734. 14mm 1.75g   180.015, 62 Inn - rm. 4

Variant

735. 14mm 1.9g   603.024, 68 Bar of Phoebus - rm. 4   ?dolphin in field to right of figure? Obverse v. similar to type 2D

TYPE 4B

Campanian Ebusus (probable local imitations)

AE unit. *obv.* full figure of Bes facing, right arm raised holding hammer, serpent in l.; *rev.* bull butting r. mid 2nd c. BC – 89 BC? Campo (1976) Group XIV; Stannard (2005a) Group I, 1. Diameter: 12-14mm Weight range: 1.23-2.28g. Average weight: 1.58g [5 examples]

736.* 14mm 1.30g 321.033, 136 Workshop - rm. 2
737. 13mm 2.1g   510.015, 129 Shrine - rm. 1   appears to be obv. and rev. die-linked with Stannard (2005a) Figure 5, no. 15 (Pompeii old excavations P14184)

738. 12mm 2.28g 510.020, 43 Shrine - rm. 1
739. 12mm 1.69g 510.001, 21 Shrine - rm. 1
740. 12mm 1.23g 510.023, 64 Shrine - rm. 1
741. 12mm 1.41g 320.117, 607 Shrine - rm. 1

variant

AE unit. *obv.* full figure of Bes facing, right arm raised holding hammer, serpent in l.; *rev.* bull butting r., indistinct legend above - a variation of 'ΜΑΣΣΑ'?. Second to early first c. BC? Stannard (2005a) Group I, 4; Frey-Kupper and Stannard (2010) Figure 1, 18

742. 12mm 1.41g 310.090, 675 Shrine - rm. 1   letter 'A' possible, rest of legend illegible. Obverse and reverse die-linked to Stannard (2005a) 22 (Pompeii forum excavations, Arthur (1986))

TYPE 5

Campanian Ebusus

AE unit. *obv.* full figure of Bes, right arm raised holding hammer, serpent in l.; *rev.* bridled horse head, r. c. 150-89 BC. Campo (1976) Group XVI, 22; Stannard (2005a) Group II, 1. Diameter: 13-14mm Weight range: 1.4-1.63g

743.	14mm 1.4g	510.015, 130 Shrine - rm. 1	symbol (flower?) in field on reverse. Reverse die-linked to Stannard (2005a) 28
744.	13mm 1.63g	164.014, 36 Inn - rm. 10	die-linked to cats. 371 and 482

TYPE 6

Campanian Ebusus

AE unit. *obv.* full figure of Bes, right arm raised holding hammer, serpent in l.; *rev.* ?bull leaping r., serpent below. Late second c. BC? Stannard (2005a) Group I, 2; Stannard and Frey-Kupper (2008) 38; Frey-Kupper and Stannard (2010) Figure 1, 8

745.	14mm 1.68g	140.147, 213 Workshop - rm. 1	very worn. Die-linked to cat. 373

TYPE 7

Campanian Ebusus

AE unit. *obv.* figure of Bes facing, right arm raised holding hammer, serpent in l.; *rev.* toad. Late 2nd to early first c. BC? Stannard (2005a) Group IV, 2; Frey-Kupper and Stannard (2010) Figure 2, 25

746. 13mm 1.55g   320.061, 335 Shrine - rm. 1

BES COMBINED WITH A BUST

Campanian Ebusus (local imitations)

TYPE 8A

AE unit. *obv.* full figure of Bes stg., right arm raised holding hammer, serpent in l.; *rev.* bust of Apollo l. Late second to early first c. BC? Campo (1976) group XVI, 21; Stannard (2005a) Group II, 5. Diameter: 12-14mm Weight range: 1.32-1.38g

747. 14mm 1.66[b]g   140.046, 61 Workshop - rm. 1
748.* 12mm 1.38g 320.061, 302 Shrine - rm. 1
749. 12mm 1.32g   032.005, 215 Casa delle Vestali - rm. 12

Campanian Ebusus

TYPE 8B

AE unit. *obv.* full figure of Bes stg., right arm raised holding hammer, serpent in l.; *rev.* bust of Apollo r. Mid to late second c. BC? Stannard (2005a) Group II, 3-4. Diameter: 11-16mm Weight range: 0.91-2.73g. Average weight: 1.80g [7 examples]

750.*	16mm 2.19g	311.048, 84	Workshop - rm. 4		extremely worn, reverse doubtful
751.	15mm 2.1g	600.036, 285	Workshop - rm. 2		
752.*	15mm 2.17g	161.016, 102	Inn - rm. 3		extremely worn, doubtful
753.	14mm 2.73g	120.010, 120	Inn - rm. 4		
754.*	14mm 1.14g^b	127.082, 398	Inn Bar - rm. 1b		reverse doubtful
755.	13mm 1.3g^b	503.072, 143	Workshop - rm. 2		
756.	13mm 1.73g	310.220, 400	Shrine - rm. 1		
757.*	12mm 1.49g^b	510.020, 45	Shrine - rm. 1		extremely worn, doubtful
758.	12mm 1.70g	320.009, 93	Shrine - rm. 1		
759.	11mm 1.59^{b}g	271.243, 192	Inn - rm. 9		distinctive style of bust on reverse
760.*	11mm 1.17g	271.234, 92	Inn - rm. 9		
761.*	11mm 0.91g	320.061, 331	Shrine - rm. 1		

Campanian Ebusus

TYPE 9

AE unit. *obv.* full fig. of Bes, right arm raised holding hammer, serpent in l.; *rev.* bust of Mars r. Late second to early first c. BC? Frey-Kupper and Stannard (2010) Figure 1, 21

762. 14mm 2.28g   510.016, 41 Shrine - rm. 1
763. 14mm 1.63g   320.061, 320 Shrine - rm. 1

UNCERTAIN BES COINS, IMPOSSIBLE TO CATEGORISE

AE unit. obv. & rev. figure of Bes, otherwise illeg.

764.*	17mm 3.14g	071.037, 239	Casa delle Vestali Bar - rm. 2		flat one one side, plano-convex on other, casting sprue
765.*	16mm 2.62g	127.057, 216	Inn Bar - rm. 1b		'bun' shaped flan, casting sprue
766.*	15mm 3.25g	032.020, 160	Casa delle Vestali - rm. 12		dumpy flan, red and green oxides
767.*	14mm NR	222.003, 0b	Inn - rm. 9		
768.*	13mm 2.23g	120.051, 421	Inn - rm. 4		shape of flan and fabric suggests Ebusus
769.*	13mm 1.98g	125.009, 45	Casa delle Vestali Bar - rm. 4		doubtful, could be Massalia
770.*	12mm 1.89g^b	320.081, no no.	Shrine - rm. 1		extremely corroded

ROMAN REPUBLICAN

DATED COINS (AR and AE)

AE litra. *obv.* helmeted head of Mars r.; *rev.* horse head r., below 'ROMA'. Rome, 241-235 BC. *RRC* 25/3

771. 16mm c 2g   604.042, 430 Shrine - rm. 3   poorly preserved. Inscription illeg.

AE uncia. *obv.* helmeted head of Roma, r.; *rev.* ship prow, above 'ROMA'. Rome, 215-212 BC. *RRC* 41/10

772. 18mm 5.09g   260.014, 78 Casa del Chirurgo - rm. 5

AE uncia. *obv.* helmeted head of Roma r.; *rev.* ship prow, above 'ROMA' and corn ear. Sicily, c. 214-212 BC. *RRC* 42/4

773.* 21mm 6.99g 324.024, 94 Bar of Phoebus - rm. 1   possibly this type, but very corroded

774. 20mm 6.77g   277.156, 1003 Casa del Chirurgo - Rms. 3&4
775. 20mm 6.45g   142.051, 216 Bar of Acisculus - rm. 2
776. 20mm 5.93g   142.011, 95 Bar of Acisculus - rm. 2
777. 20mm 5.47g   120.044, 713 Inn - rm. 4

AE sextans. *obv.* head of Mercury r.; *rev.* ship prow, above 'ROMA', below 2 dots, before 'C'. Sardinia, 211 BC. *RRC* 63/6

778. 18mm 3.87g   323.047, 110 Bar of Acisculus - rm. 1

AR denarius. *obv.* head of Roma r., behind 'X'; *rev.* Dioscuri riding horses, below 'ROMA'. Rome, late third c. BC. *RRC* 50ff.

779. 20mm 4.65g   127.039, 165 Inn Bar - rm. 1b   extremely corroded
780.* 20mm 4.26g 223.007, 66 Inn - rm. 9   probably this type, but very worn

781.* 20mm 4.20g 144.006, 204 Well/ Fntn. - n. of Well   probably this type, but very worn

782. 19mm 4.14g   121.028, 176 Inn - rm. 6   probably this type, but very worn

AE as. *obv.* Janus head; *rev.* ship prow, above 'MAT' (monogram). Rome, 179-170 BC. *RRC* 162/3

783. 27mm 19.80g 323.048, 206 Bar of Acisculus - rm. 1   possibly this type, but very worn

AE as. *obv.* Janus head; *rev.* ship prow, above 'A.CAE'. Rome, 169-158 BC. *RRC* 174/1

784. 33mm 25.56g 140.147, 205 Workshop - rm. 1

AE as. *obv.* Janus head; *rev.* ship prow, above butterfly on vine branch, below 'ROMA'. Rome 169-158 BC. *RRC* 184/1

785. 35mm 33.58g 160.015, 48 Inn - rm. 1   possibly this type, but very worn

786. 32mm 34.18g 165.082, 130 Inn Bar - rm. 1b&3b
787. 31mm 21.56g 140.002, 3 Workshop - rm. 1   probably this type, but very
                                                                  worn

AE as. *obv.* Janus head; *rev.* ship prow, above 'P.BLAS'. Rome, 169-158 BC. *RRC* 189/1

788. 30mm 24.79g 073.026, 57 Casa delle Vestali Bar - rm. 1

AE as. *obv.* Janus head; *rev.* ship prow, above 'AT' monogram. Rome, 169-158 BC. *RRC* 192/1

789. 32mm 28.6g   120.044, 535 Inn - rm. 4   possibly this type, but
                                                                  extremely worn

AE as. *obv.* Janus head; *rev.* ship prow, above 'C.MAIANI'. Rome, 153 BC. *RRC* 203/2

790. 33mm 27.4g   510.015, 119 Shrine - rm. 1   probably this type, but
                                                                  extremely worn
791. 31mm 25.42g 310.243, 607 Shrine - rm. 1
792. 30mm 32.10g 086.014, 149 Casa delle Vestali - rm. 8
793. 29mm 24.37g 222.011, 354 Inn - rm. 9   very worn

AE as. *obv.* Janus head; *rev.* ship prow, above 'L.SAVF'. Rome, 152 BC. *RRC* 204/2

794. 29mm 20.71g 222.003, 278 Inn - rm. 9

AE as. *obv.* Janus head; *rev.* ship prow, above 'P.SVLA'. Rome, 151 BC. *RRC* 205/2

795. 30mm 28.6g   503.054, 154 Workshop - rm. 2   probably this type, but
                                                                  extremely worn

AE as. *obv.* Janus head; *rev.* ship prow, above 'SAFRA', before dolphin. Rome, 150 BC. *RRC* 206/2

796. 32mm 26.01g 320.005, 232 Shrine - rm. 1

AE as. *obv.* Janus head; *rev.* ship prow, above 'Q.MARC', before 'LIBO'. Rome, 148 BC. *RRC* 215/2

797. 29mm 18.93g 088.006, 65 Casa delle Vestali Bar - rm. 1   very worn

AE quadrans. *obv.* Head of Hercules r., 3 dots behind; *rev.* ship prow, below 'ROMA', above 'Q.MARC', before 'LIBO'. Rome, 148 BC. *RRC* 215/5

798. 21mm 6.05g   160.049, 68 Inn - rm. 1
799.* 20mm 5.8g^b 600.027, 210 Workshop - rm. 2   very worn, but probably this
                                                                  type

AE as. *obv.* Janus head; *rev.* ship prow, above 'C TER. LVC', below 'ROMA'. Rome. 147 BC. *RRC* 217/2

800. 31mm 27.18g 320.061, 347 Shrine - rm. 1   probably this type, but very
                                                                  worn

801. 30mm 25. 24g 310.062, 710 Shrine - rm. 1
802. 30mm 21.30g 320.074, 632 Shrine - rm. 1

AE as. *obv.* Janus head; *rev.* ship prow, above 'CAESTI' and puppy, below 'ROMA'. Rome, 146 BC. *RRC* 219/2

803. 30mm 29.8g   011.024, 186 Casa delle Vestali - rm. 15/53

AR denarius. *obv.* helmeted head of Roma, r.; *rev.* quadriga, below 'CARB', ROMA'. Rome, 121 BC. *RRC* 279/1

804. 22mm 3.96g   123.019, 54 Inn - rm. 1   probably this type, but very
                                                                          worn

AR denarius. *obv.* head of Roma, behind 'X', legend before 'M. CIPI. M.F', behind 'X'; *rev.* biga with rider and palm, below rudder and 'ROMA'. Rome, c. 115-114 BC. *RRC* 289/1

805. 18mm 3.51g   180.010, 40 Inn - rm. 3

AR denarius. *obv.* helmeted head of Roma r.; *rev.* Victory in triga r. with head of last horse turned back. Rome, 111 or 110 BC. *RRC* 299/1a or b

806. 18mm 3.45g   085.017, 278 Casa delle Vestali - rm. 9   legend below triga illegible

AR quinarius. *obv.* bust of Victory r.; *rev.* Pegasus, below 'Q.TITI'. Rome, 90 BC. *RRC* 341/3

807. 12mm 1.96g   163.024, 50 Inn - rm. 8

AR denarius. *obv.* female bust r. with hair tied in band; *rev.* Victory std. r., in exergue 'VICTRIX'. Rome, 89 BC. *RRC* 343/1

808. 18mm 4.32g   088.009, 324 Casa delle Vestali Bar - rm. 1   gummy deposit on surface.
                                                                          Legends on obv. and rev.
                                                                          illleg.

AR quinarius. *obv.* head of Liber r., behind 'M.CATO'; *rev.* Victory std. r., in exergue 'VICTRIX'. Rome, 89 BC. *RRC* 343/2a or 2b

809. 14mm 2.00g   271.235, 259 Inn - rm. 9
810. 13mm 2.02g   310.169, 618 Shrine - rm. 1   plated, or base silver?
811. 13mm 1.89g   203.080, 86 Shrine - rm. 1
812. 12mm 1.87g   018.011, 26 Workshop - rm. 1

AR denarius. *obv.* bearded head of King Tatius r.; *rev.* killing of Tarpeia, 'L.TITVRI'. Rome, 89 BC. *RRC* 344/2

813. 17mm 3.75g   310.263, 628 Shrine - rm. 1

AR denarius. *obv.* bust r., illeg.; *rev.* Victory in biga r.: below 'CN LENTVL'. Rome, 88 BC. *RRC* 345/1

814. 18mm 4.2g   500.014, 184 Bar of Phoebus - rm. 1   possibly this type, but very
                                                                          worn

AR denarius. *obv.* head of Apollo r., with hair tied in band, 'Q.POMPONI' 'MVSA'; *rev.* Hercules playing lyre r. Rome, 66 BC. RRC 410/1

815. 17mm 2.83g[p]   040.036, 369 Casa delle Vestali - rm. 14   plated coin with clear copper core, loop for suspension. Reverse almost illegible

AE as (halved). *obv.* Janus head; *rev.* prow. Spain and Sicily, 45 BC onwards. RRC 479 (Pompeiis Magnus)

816. 29mm 11.6g[h]   018.011, 25 Workshop - rm. 1

UNDATED ROMAN REPUBLICAN

SILVER AND SILVER PLATED

817. 19mm 4.11g   133.008, 84 Vicolo di Narciso - n. end   obv. helmeted bust r.?
818. 18mm 3.66g   065.017, 94 Casa delle Vestali - rm. 27   obv. bearded laureate bust r., illeg. AR or core of AR

819.* 18mm 3.26g   069.001, 2 Casa delle Vestali - rm. 10
820.* 18mm 1.79g   033.005, 160 Casa delle Vestali - rm. 21   obv. helmeted bust r., illeg. Probably core of a denarius

821.* 17mm 3.58g   185.013, 49 Casa del Triclinio - ramp
822. 16mm 3.37g   310.092, 180 Shrine - rm. 1   obv. and rev. uncertain objects in field; very worn. AR plated

823.* 16mm 3.07g   223.007, 64 Inn - rm. 9   AR plated. Obv. bust r., rev. fig. stg. l.?

824.* 16mm 1.94g   120.010, 121 Inn - rm. 4   obv. faint traces of bust r.?.; rev. illeg., apart from winged fig. to r. off flan?

825.* 15mm 2.49g   140.172, 396 Workshop - rm. 1   obv. bust r.? rev. figure std. r.? AR plated

826.* 13mm 1.94g   225.041, 74 Inn Bar - rm. 4b   rev. slight traces of design and pellet border

827.* 12mm 0.99g   204.026, 133 Shrine - rm. 2   deep purple corrosion
828.* 11mm 1.3g   037.007, 56 Casa delle Vestali - rm. 5   obv. bust r.?

AE as. *obv.* Janus head; *rev.* ship prow, sometimes with additional details, for example inscriptions or symbols. Mostly mint of Rome. c. 206-144 BC

829.* 36mm 34.18g 320.067, 472 Shrine - rm. 1   very worn
830.* 36mm 33.56g 145.011, no no. Bar of Acisculus - behind counter very worn
831.* 36mm 23g   185.008, 97 Casa del Triclinio - ramp
832.* 34mm 31.32g 271.243, 185 Inn - rm. 9   extremely worn
833.* 34mm 29.43g 500.005, 117 Bar of Phoebus - rm. 1   extremely worn
834. 34mm 29.35g 039.013, 261 Casa delle Vestali - rm. 5
835.* 33mm 39.3g 261.043, 13 Casa del Chirurgo - rm. 10   very heavy
836.* 33mm 39.05g 181.017, 1 Inn - rm. 9   very worn
837.* 33mm c38g   322.055, 252 Workshop - rm. 4
838.* 33mm 28.28g 088.007, 21 Casa delle Vestali Bar - rm. 1   extremely worn
839. 33mm 26.50g 140.175, 400 Workshop - rm. 1   above prow ']MA' (bar of A slanted)
840.* 33mm 25.21g 186.003, 25 Inn - rm. 3   extremely worn

841. 33mm 23.29g 140.069, 74 Workshop - rm. 1   extremely worn
842. 33mm 21.91g 161.014, 61 Inn - rm. 3   below prow 'ROMA'; worn
843.* 33mm 20.67g[b] 180.015, 45 Inn - rm. 3
844.* 33mm NR   120.016, 427 Inn - rm. 4   very worn
845.* 32mm 28.89g 125.023, 63 Casa delle Vestali Bar - rm. 4
846.* 32mm 28.79g 161.014, 62 Inn - rm. 3
847.* 32mm 27.82g 120.016, 426 Inn - rm. 4   below prow 'ROM[A]'
848. 32mm 27.2g 123.005, 31 Inn - rm. 1   extremely worn
849. 32mm 27.14g 271.243, 190 Inn - rm. 9   'bow' in field on obverse;
    below prow 'ROM[A]'

850.* 32mm 22.24g 510.004, 90 Shrine - rm. 1
851.* 32mm 20.03g 123.038, 221 Inn - rm. 1
852.* 31mm 34.36g 222.011, 394 Inn - rm. 9   extremely worn
853.* 31mm 31.45g 225.041, 105 Inn Bar - rm. 4b   very worn
854.* 31mm 30.92g 508.026, 107 Casa del Chirurgo - rms. 16&20   extremely worn
855.* 31mm 29.05g 161.014, 63 Inn - rm. 3   extremely worn
856.* 31mm 28.54g 510.047, 101 Shrine - rm. 1   very worn
857. 31mm 25.39g 142.037, 106 Bar of Acisculus - rm. 2   above prow illegible
    inscription

858.* 31mm 25.0g 186.003, 34 Inn - rm. 3
859.* 31mm 24.87g 600.005, 98 Workshop - rm. 2   very worn
860.* 31mm 24.01g 186.146, 153 Inn - rm. 3   very worn
861.* 31mm 22.43g[b] 510.002, 1 Shrine - rm. 1
862.* 30mm 34.36g 320.061, 346 Shrine - rm. 1   very corroded
863. 30mm 28.52g 320.061, 304 Shrine - rm. 1   very worn
864.* 30mm 28.5g 120.010, 124 Inn - rm. 4
865.* 30mm 28.0g 600.033, 226 Workshop - rm. 2   extremely worn
866.* 30mm 27.86g 088.026, 104 Casa delle Vestali Bar - rm. 1   extremely worn
867.* 30mm 27.9g 120.010, 179 Inn - rm. 4   obv. illeg., rev. ship prow
868.* 30mm 26.57g 320.061, 338 Shrine - rm. 1   very worn
869.* 30mm 25.75g 161.014, 65 Inn - rm. 3   very worn
870.* 30mm 24.61g 320.073, 439 Shrine - rm. 1   extremely worn, but faint
    traces of Janus head

871. 30mm 24.54g 182.028, 73 Inn - rm. 12
872.* 30mm 23.96g 140.166, 353 Workshop - rm. 1   very worn, powdery corrosion
873.* 30mm 23.93g 161.016, 86 Inn - rm. 3   very worn
874. 30mm 23.73g 142.037, 101 Bar of Acisculus - rm. 2   very worn
875. 30mm 23.23g 275.016, 50 Casa del Chirurgo - rm. 5   below prow 'ROM[A]
876. 30mm 22.99g 222.011, 396 Inn - rm. 9
877. 30mm 22.75g 320.073, 321 Shrine - rm. 1
878.* 30mm 22.16g 088.007, 64 Casa delle Vestali Bar - rm. 1   before prow 'I', illeg
879. 30mm 21.74g 086.010, 172 Casa delle Vestali - rm. 8   below prow 'ROMA'
880.* 30mm 21.28g 320.061, 324 Shrine - rm. 1   extremely worn
881.* 30mm 20.98g 140.166, 347 Workshop - rm. 1
882.* 30mm 20.00g 607.314, 300 Casa del Chirurgo rm. 2   worn
883.* 30mm 19.61g 181.114, 147 Inn - rm. 9   extremely worn
884.* 30mm 19.03g 222.001, 8 Inn - rm. 9   extremely worn
885.* 30mm 18.02g 142.043, 132 Bar of Acisculus - rm. 2
886.* 30mm 13.81g 011.007, 834 Casa delle Vestali - rm. 15/53   Punched hole in centre
887.* 29mm 23.34g 203.165, 142 Shrine - rm. 1   extremely worn

888. 29mm 21.94g 510.004, 27 Shrine - rm. 1   below prow 'RO]MA'
889. 29mm 21.69g 088.052, 327 Casa delle Vestali Bar - rm. 1   traces of illegible inscription
                                                                       above prow
890.* 29mm 19.19g 320.061, 341 Shrine - rm. 1   extremely worn
891.* 28mm 20.12g 086.008, 173 Casa delle Vestali - rm. 8   very worn
892.* 28mm 19.16g 145.004, 32 Bar of Acisculus - behind counter   very corroded
893.* 26mm 9.3g 500.013, 164 Bar of Phoebus - rm. 1   extremely worn and corroded

AE semis. *obv.* head of Saturn r., behind 'S'; *rev.* ship prow, before 'S', below prow 'ROMA'. Mostly
Rome, c. 206-144 BC

894. 27mm 18.28g 088.021, 322 Casa delle Vestali Bar - rm. 1
895. 25mm 9.84g   168.100, 139 Casa del Triclinio - clean
896.* 24mm 8.24g 121.033, 178 Inn - rm. 6
897.* 22mm 6.93g 510.004, 32 Shrine - rm. 1   probably this denomination
                                                                       but very worn

AE triens. *obv.* head of Minerva r., above 4 dots; *rev.* ship prow, below 4 dots. Rome, c. 206-144 BC

898. 26mm 13.0g 503.067, 174 Workshop - rm. 2
899. 25mm 12.21g 127.077, 378 Inn Bar - rm. 1b
900. 25mm 11.68g 262.009, 43 Casa del Chirurgo - rm. 23   above prow 'ROMA'
901.* 25mm 10.46g 261.043, 29 Casa del Chirurgo - rm. 10
902. 25mm 10.08g 271.250, 400 Inn - rm. 9
903.* 25mm 9.16g 142.048, 178 Bar of Acisculus - rm. 2   extremely worn
904.* 24mm 11.52g 271.243, 204 Inn - rm. 9
905.* 24mm 10.9g 502.050, 155 Bar of Acisculus - rm. 1
906.* 24mm 7.6g   510.015, 131 Shrine - rm. 1   probably this denomination
907.* 23mm 14.61g 181.179, 126 Inn - rm. 9   very worn
908. 23mm 11.96g 180.015, 63 Inn - rm. 3
909. 23mm 10.9g   123.059, 440 Inn - rm. 1   illeg. inscription above
910. 23mm 10.42g 123.054, 444 Inn - rm. 1   very clear 'ROMA' above
                                                                       prow
911. 23mm 9.18g   120.044, 719 Inn - rm. 4   above prow 'ROMA'
912.* 21mm 9.76g 320.061, 326 Shrine - rm. 1   extremely worn and corroded
                                                                       but probably this
                                                                       denomination
913.* 21mm 7.94g 271.234, 96 Inn - rm. 9   above 'MA[?'
914.* 20mm NR   221.111, 126 Casa del Triclinio - rm. 4   probably this type, but very
                                                                       corroded
915.* 18mm 6.73g 310.090, 635 Shrine - rm. 1

AE quadrans. *obv.* head of Hercules r., above or behind 3 dots; *rev.* ship prow r., above 'ROMA',
below 3 dots. Rome, mostly 206-144 BC

916.* 28mm 8.52g 143.115, 104 Well/ Fntn. - s. of Well
917.* 27mm 14.71g 165.094, 222 Inn Bar - rm. 1b&3b
918.* 25mm 8.5g   260.012, 4 Casa del Chirurgo - rm. 5   below prow 3 pellets, traces of
                                                                       legend above
919.* 22mm 9.16g 101.015/017, 114 Casa delle Vestali - rm. 7   extremely worn -
                                                                       denomination doubtful
920. 22mm 6.24g   160.042, 66 Inn - rm. 1   above 'R]OMA'
921. 20mm 6.64g   071.020, 188 Casa delle Vestali Bar - rm. 2   above 'R.MA'

922.* 19mm 3.04g 145.013, 112 Bar of Acisculus - behind counter
923.* 18mm 6.76g 271.235, 268 Inn - rm. 9

AE sextans. *obv.* head of Mercury, r.; *rev.* ship prow, above 'ROMA', below 2 dots. Rome, probably 206-144 BC

924.* 21mm 8.66g 180.015, 66 Inn - rm. 3
925. 18mm 2.3g   037.008, 58 Casa delle Vestali - rm. 5   above prow ']MA'
926. 17mm 4.55g   165.082, 137 Inn Bar - rm. 1b&3b
927. 16mm 1.58g   096.017, 27 Casa delle Vestali - rm. 42   above prow 'R.MA'
928. 14mm 1.48g   127.079, 292 Inn Bar - rm. 1b

AE quadrans. *obv.* head of Hercules r., above or behind 3 dots; *rev.* ship prow r., above 'ROMA', below 3 dots. Rome, c. 146 - c.100 BC

929. 17mm 3.32g   165.012, 34 Inn Bar - rm. 1b&3b   three dots above prow
930. 16mm 3.28g   310.215, 404 Shrine - rm. 1

AE semuncia. *obv.* head of Mercury r.; *rev.* ship prow, wreath as border. First c. BC? Crawford (1982) 46

931. 11mm 0.62g   222.011, 277 Inn - rm. 9

Republican fraction?

AE unit. *obv.* bust r., illeg.; *rev.* illeg.

932. 14mm 1.89g   087.010, 20 Casa delle Vestali Bar - rm. 4   local type?

DELIBERATELY CUT FRACTIONS

Cut *asses*. Janus head, ship prow types. Rome, mostly c. 206-144 BC

933.* 33mm 18.91g^h 128.035, 410 Casa delle Vestali - rm. 7
934. 33mm 14.58g^h 223.031, 182 Inn - rm. 9
935. 32mm 19.04g^h 271.235, 265 Inn - rm. 9
936.* 32mm 14.81g^h 161.014, 71 Inn - rm. 3
937.* 32mm 13.14g^h 140.147, 202 Workshop - rm. 1
938.* 32mm 12.9g^h 120.016, 215 Inn - rm. 4
939.* 31mm 16.38g^h 073.030, 56 Casa delle Vestali Bar - rm. 1
940.* 31mm 15.16g^h 322.037, 144 Workshop - rm. 4
941. 31mm 14.76g^h 032.005, 5 Casa delle Vestali - rm. 12
942.* 31mm 14.48g^h 222.116, 352 Inn - rm. 9
943. 31mm 13.47g^h 145.013, 69 Bar of Acisculus - behind counter
944.* 31mm 13.37g^h 140.162, 334 Workshop - rm. 1
945.* 31mm 12.0g^h 513.041, 133 Via Consolare - Inn area   below prow 'ROM['
946.* 31mm 11.46g^h 310.197, 415 Shrine - rm. 1   very encrusted with corrosion
947.* 31mm 11.04g^h 040.036, 129 Casa delle Vestali - rm. 14
948. 31mm 10.63g^h 120.037, 413 Inn - rm. 4   below prow 'ROM[A]'
949.* 31mm 10.34g^h 145.005, 18 Bar of Acisculus - behind counter
950.* 31mm 9.66g^h 310.039, 193 Shrine - rm. 1
951.* 30mm 15.16g^h 140.046, 75 Workshop - rm. 1
952.* 30mm 14.27g^h 072.006, 133 Casa delle Vestali Bar - rm. 3
953.* 30mm 13.92g^h 161.014, 66 Inn - rm. 3

954.* 30mm 13.60g^h 140.066, 78 Workshop - rm. 1
955. 30mm 13.08g^h 320.071, 408 Shrine - rm. 1
956.* 30mm 12.4g^h 500.041, 182 Bar of Phoebus - rm. 1
957.* 30mm 12.45g^h 222.012, 150 Inn - rm. 9
958. 30mm 12.35g^h 073.027, 76 Casa delle Vestali Bar - rm. 1
959.* 30mm 12.33g^h 500.005, 113 Bar of Phoebus - rm. 1
960. 30mm 11.80g^h 076.006, 47 Casa delle Vestali - rm. 32   below prow 'ROMA'
961.* 30mm 11.50g^h 140.151, 327 Workshop - rm. 1
962.* 30mm 11.40g^h 035.009, 131 Casa delle Vestali - rm. 8
963.* 30mm 10.37g^h 271.235, 258 Inn - rm. 9
964. 30mm 10.00g^h 140.072, 168 Workshop - rm. 1
965.* 30mm 10.00g^h 161.006, 34 Inn - rm. 3
966.* 30mm 9.65g^h 165.012, 54 Inn Bar - rm. 1b&3b
967.* 30mm 9.31g^h 311.031, 1 Workshop - rm. 4
968.* 30mm 9.05g^h 161.014, 69 Inn - rm. 3
969.* 30mm 7.98g^h 123.017, 35 Inn - rm. 1
970.* 30mm 7.90g^h 223.031, 185 Inn - rm. 9
971.* 30mm 7.72g^h 140.147, 204 Workshop - rm. 1
972. 30mm 6.5g^h 605.004, 87 Vicolo di Narciso - by city wall
973.* 30mm NR   222.042, 128 Inn - rm. 9
974.* 29mm 13.68g^h 320.062, 287 Shrine - rm. 1
975. 29mm 12.93g^h 320.021, 165 Shrine - rm. 1   monogram about prow.
                                                          Possibly LPLH, RRC 134/2
                                                          (Rome, 194-190 BC)

976.* 29mm 12.56g^h 123.024, 63 Inn - rm. 1
977.* 29mm 12.10g^h 127.057, 294 Inn Bar - rm. 1b
978.* 29mm 11.24g^h 503.003, 10 Workshop - rm. 2
979. 29mm 10.95g^h 320.073, 443 Shrine - rm. 1
980.* 29mm 10.69g^h 161.014, 67 Inn - rm. 3
981.* 29mm 10.01g^h 225.035, 67 Inn Bar - rm. 4b
982.* 29mm 9.49g^h 140.172, 394 Workshop - rm. 1
983. 29mm 8.86g^h 161.013, 60 Inn - rm. 3
984.* 29mm 8.3g^h 500.030, 175 Bar of Phoebus - rm. 1
985.* 29mm c. 8g^h 310.044, 132 Shrine - rm. 1
986.* 29mm 7.97g^h 323.055, 199 Bar of Acisculus - rm. 1
987.* 29mm 6.78g^h 009.013, 8 Workshop - rm. 1
988.* 29mm 6.0g^h 205.011, 11 Vicolo di Narciso - nr. well and fountain
989.* 28mm 16.25g^h 223.007, 65 Inn - rm. 9
990.* 28mm 14.92g^h 320.061, 311 Shrine - rm. 1
991.* 28mm 11.84g^h 320.061, 312 Shrine - rm. 1
992. 28mm 11.80g^h 180.001, 3 Inn - rm. 3   below prow 'ROMA'
993.* 28mm 10.56g^h 320.073, 440 Shrine - rm. 1
994.* 28mm 9.29g^h 182.013, 32 Inn - rm. 12
995.* 28mm 8.52g^h 310.197, 399 Shrine - rm. 1
996. 28mm 8.47g^h 222.012, 148 Inn - rm. 9
997.* 28mm 8.25g^h 320.011, 400 Shrine - rm. 1
998.* 28mm c. 8g^h 165.008, 62 Inn Bar - rm. 1b&3b
999.* 28mm 7.56g^h 073.001, 2 Casa delle Vestali Bar - rm. 1
1000.* 28mm 7.02g^h 120.016, 172 Inn - rm. 4
1001.* 28mm 5.79g^f 165.012, 74 Inn Bar - rm. 1b&3b

1002.* 28mm 1.56g^h 323.002, 77 Bar of Acisculus - rm. 1
1003. 27mm 10.75g^h 161.006, 35 Inn - rm. 3

AE lesser fractions (probably, as opposed to *asses*), deliberately halved. Rome, mostly c. 206-144 BC

1004.* 27mm 9.68g^h 320.061, 354 Shrine - rm. 1
1005. 27mm 9.11g^h 508.015, 75 Casa del Chirurgo - Rms. 16&20
1006. 27mm 8.86g^h 140.177, 401 Workshop - rm. 1
1007. 27mm 8.66g^h 018.011, 24 Workshop - rm. 1
1008. 27mm 8.5g^h 503.054, 181 Workshop - rm. 2
1009.* 27mm 7.32g^h 324.004, 48 Bar of Phoebus - rm. 1
1010.* 27mm 5.89g^h 322.067, 306 Workshop - rm. 4
1011.* 27mm 5.02g^h 140.172, 397 Workshop - rm. 1
1012.* 26mm 11.12g^h 320.061, 351 Shrine - rm. 1
1013.* 26mm 8.65g^h 222.004, 404 Inn - rm. 9
1014.* 26mm 8.47g^h 310.169, 617 Shrine - rm. 1   very corroded
1015.* 26mm 7.46g^h 310.092, 199 Shrine - rm. 1
1016.* 26mm 7.22g^h 018.011, 178 Workshop - rm. 1
1017.* 26mm 6.53g^h 140.147, 217 Workshop - rm. 1
1018.* 25mm 8.08g^h 324.006, 31 Bar of Phoebus - rm. 1
1019.* 25mm 7.36g^h 310.128, 286 Shrine - rm. 1   bust right?; illegible
1020.* 25mm 6.47g^h 320.061, 345 Shrine - rm. 1
1021.* 25mm 4.64g^h 140.027, 59 Workshop - rm. 1
1022.* 25mm 4.45g^h 182.109, 238 Inn - rm. 12
1023.* 24mm 5.54g^h 140.162, 529 Workshop - rm. 1   very worn
1024.* 23mm 5.91g^h 182.032, 317 Inn - rm. 12
1025.* 20mm 1.57g^h 067.019, 53 Casa delle Vestali - rm. 20
1026.* NR 5.94g^h 000.000, no. no. unstratified
1027.* NR NR   121.084, 344 Inn - rm. 6   very fragile

Cut quarters: usually of Janus head, ship prow types. Second to first c. BC?

1028.* 26mm 8.7g^q 050.030, 110 Casa delle Vestali - rm. 19
1029. 22mm 7.04g^q 161.016, 105 Inn - rm. 3
1030. 25mm 5.7g^q 503.018, 179 Workshop - rm. 2   traces of ship prow
1031. 22mm 5.23g^q 035.006, 130 Casa delle Vestali - rm. 8
1032.* 22mm 4.5g^q 503.018, 180 Workshop - rm. 2
1033. 15mm c 2g   127.078, 405e Inn Bar - Rm 1b
1034. 14mm 3.75g^f 067.019, 52 Casa delle Vestali - rm. 20
1035.* NR 4.53g^f 120.016, 479 Inn - rm. 4
1036.* –mm 3.40g^q 320.039, 106 Shrine - rm. 1
1037.* –mm 2.04g^f 310.087, 631 Shrine - rm. 1
1038.* –mm 1.94g^f 120.051, 419 Inn - rm. 4

Cut eighth? Second to first c. BC?

1039. –mm 1.02g^f 161.014, 75 Inn - rm. 3

OCTAVIAN/ AUGUSTUS (27 BC – AD 14)

AE unit. *obv.* bare headed bust r., 'CAESAR DIVI F'; *rev.* laureate head of Caesar, r., 'DIVOS IVLIVS'. Uncertain (Italy), c. 38 BC. *RRC* 535/1; *RPC* I 620

1040. 29mm c13g 127.006, 38 Inn Bar - rm. 1b	extremely worn and underweight. Imitation?
1041. 28mm 10.30g 144.139, 136 Well/ Fntn. - n. of Well	extremely corroded, only ']ESA[' visible

AE unit. *obv.* bare headed bust r., behind 'DIVI F', before star; *rev.* laurel wreath, 'DIVOS IVLIVS'. Uncertain (Italy), c. 38 BC. *RRC* 535/2; *RPC* I 621

1042. 31mm 21.61g 140.072, 170 Workshop - rm. 1	
1043. 30mm 11.58g 222.012, 50 Inn - rm. 9	very worn and light weight; imitation?

AR denarius. *obv.* Victory on prow, r.; *rev.* Octavian in quadriga r., in exergue 'CAESAR DIVI F'. Uncertain mint (Italy), c. 32-29 BC. *RIC* I Aug. 263

1044. 16mm 3.06g 324.004, 54 Bar of Phoebus - rm. 1	'possibly struck at Brindisium' (*RIC* I, 30)

AR quinarius. *obv.* bare headed bust r., 'CAESAR IMP VII'; *rev.* Victory stg. l. on 'cista mistica', serpents to l. and r., 'ASIA RECEPTA'. Rome, 29-27 BC. *RIC* I Aug. 276

1045. 15mm 1.61g 170.001, 1 Inn - rm. 9

AR quinarius. *obv.* bare headed bust r., 'AVGVSTVS'; *rev.* Victory stg. l. on prow. ?North Peloponnese mint, c. 21 BC. *RIC* I Aug. 474

1046. 15mm 2.85g 072.029, 89 Casa delle Vestali Bar - rm. 3	AE core or AR plated?

AE as (halved). *obv.* heads of Agrippa (to l.) and Augustus to r., below 'DIVI F'; *rev.* palm-shoot and chained crocodile. Nemausus, c. 27 BC-c. AD 14. *RPC* I 522-25; *RIC* I Aug. 155-61

1047. 25mm 5.68g^h 270.001, 21 Casa del Triclinio – ramp	probably this type but rev. illeg.
1048. 25mm 4.88g^h 270.017, 135 Casa del Triclinio – ramp	probably this type, but rev. illeg.

AE as. *obv.* bare headed bust r., 'CAESAR AVGVSTVS TRIBVNIC POTEST'; *rev.* 'C ASINIVS GALLVS IIIVIR AAAFF', 'S C'. Rome, after 16 BC. *cf. RIC* I Aug. 373

1049. 27mm 10.14g 140.027, 57 Workshop - rm. 1

AE as. *obv.* bare headed bust r., 'CAESAR AVGVSTVS TRIBVNIC POTEST'; *rev.* 'C CASSIVS CELER III VIR AAA FF', 'S C'. Rome, 16 BC. *RIC* I Aug. 376

1050. 28mm 10.81g 142.002, 18 Bar of Acisculus - rm. 2

AE as. *obv.* bust r., 'CAESAR AVGVSTVS TRIBVNIC POTEST'; *rev.* 'C GALLIVS LVPERCVS IIIVIR AAA FF', 'SC'. Rome, c. 16 BC. *RIC* I Aug. 379

1051. 27mm 12.31g 144.026, 24 Well/ Fntn. - n. of Well	probably this type, but much of legend obscured by corrosion

AE as. *obv.* bare headed bust r.; *rev.* 'S C', legend obscured. c. 16 BC. *RIC* I Aug. p. 69-71

1052. 25mm 5.09g^h 320.061, 353 Shrine - rm. 1   deliberately halved. Moneyer
                                                                                                                       uncertain

AE as. *obv.* bare headed bust r., 'CAESAR AVGVSTVS TRIBVNIC POTEST'; *rev.* 'CN PISO CN F
IIIVIR AAAFF', 'SC'. Rome, 15 BC. *RIC* I Aug. 382

1053. 28mm 11.35g 120.015, 177 Inn - rm. 4
1054. 26mm 11.43g 000.000, NR unstratified
1055. 25mm 10.72g 161.013, 59 Inn - rm. 3
1056. 27mm 6.12g^h 270.017, 136 Casa del Triclinio – ramp   countermarked 'AVG' (?)
                                                                                                                       Garbled inscription? Possibly
                                                                                                                       this type

AE dup. *obv.* laurel wreath, 'AVGVSTVS TRIBVNIC POTEST'; *rev.* 'L SVRDINVS III VIR AAA
F', 'S C'; Rome, 15 BC. *cf. RIC* I Aug. 384

1057. 29mm 11.40g 073.027, 75 Casa delle Vestali Bar - rm. 1   countermarked 'SEVE' (?)
                                                                                                                       (reversed 'S')

AE as. *obv.* bare headed bust r., 'CAESAR AVGVSTVS TRIBVNIC POTEST'; *rev.* 'L SVRDINVS
IIIVIR AAAFF', 'SC'. Rome, 15 BC. *RIC* I Aug. 386

1058. 30mm 11.34g 161.014, 68 Inn - rm. 3   probably this type
1059. 25mm 9.52g 310.243, 523 Shrine - rm. 1

AE as. *obv.* bare headed bust r., 'CAESAR AVGVSTVS TRIBVNIC POTEST'; *rev.* 'C PLOTIVS
RVFVS IIIVIR AAAFF', 'SC'. Rome, 15 BC *RIC* I Aug. 389

1060. 25mm 10.15g 503.042, 111 Workshop - rm. 2

AE unit. *obv.* Head of Augustus r., 'ΚΑΙ – ΣΑΡ'; *rev.* crescent, above star, below crescent
'ΣΕΒΑΣΤΟΣ'. Alexandria, c. 10-5 BC? *RPC* I 5021

1061. 15mm 1.8g 040.002, 38 Casa delle Vestali - rm. 14
1062. 14mm 2.81g 277.038, 168 Casa del Chirurgo - rms. 3-4
1063. 14mm 2.1g 140.147, 208 Workshop - rm. 1

AE quad. *obv.* clasped hands and caduceus, 'LAMIA SILIVS AMMIVS'; *rev.* 'III VIR AAAFF' 'S
C'. Rome, c. 9 BC. *RIC* I Aug. 420

1064. 16mm 2.95g 310.000, 191 Shrine - rm. 1   imitation?
1065. 16mm 2.98g 120.021, 125 Inn - rm. 4
1066. 16mm 2.92g 612.017, 164 Casa del Chirurgo - rms. 17-18
1067. 15mm 3.15g 145.005, 23 Bar of Acisculus - behind counter

AE quad. *obv.* simpulum and lituus, 'LAMIA SILIVS ANNIVS'; *rev.* 'III VIR AAA FF' 'S C'. Rome,
9 BC. *RIC* I Aug 421

1068. 19mm 3.18g 310.032, 64 Shrine - rm. 1
1069. 17mm 3.1g 612.017, 165 Casa del Chirurgo - rms. 17-18
1070. 16mm 3.2g   127.020, 60 Inn Bar - rm. 1b
1071. 16mm 3.10g 071.037, 236 Casa delle Vestali Bar - rm. 2

AE quad. *obv.* 'S C', cornucopia, 'LAMIA SILVIVS ANNIVS'; *rev.* 'III VIR AAA FF', bowl. Rome, c. 9 BC. *RIC* I Aug. 422

1072.	18mm 3.23g	310.106, 206	Shrine - rm. 1	extremely corroded
1073.	18mm 2.82g	320.000, 219	Shrine - rm. 1	obv. illegible
1074.	17mm 3.31g	507.032, 20	Casa del Chirurgo shop - rm. 2	
1075.	17mm 3.06g	071.018, 97	Casa delle Vestali Bar - rm. 4/2	
1076.	15mm 3.1g	204.109, 198	Shrine - rm. 2	
1077.	14mm 2.8g	043.004, 743	Casa delle Vestali - rm. 22	imitation?

AE quadrans, uncertain type, Rome, c. 9-8 BC. *RIC* I Aug. 420 to 423

1078. 16mm 3.04g 186.003, 9 Inn - rm. 3   imitation?

AE quad. *obv.* clasped hands holding caduceus, 'PVLCHER TAVRVS REGVLVS'; *rev.* 'IIIVIRAAAFF' 'SC'. Rome, 8 BC. *RIC* I Aug. 423

1079. 17mm 3.25g 127.059, 237 Inn Bar - rm. 1b

AE quad. *obv.* 'PVLCHER TAVRVS REGVLVS' 'SC', cornucopia; *rev.* 'III VIR AAA FF III', altar. Rome, 8 BC. *RIC* I Aug. 425

1080. 16mm 2.64g 169.005, 13 Inn - rm. 12

AE as. *obv.* bare headed bust r., 'CAESAR AVGVST PONT MAX TRIBVNIC POT'; *rev.* '?] AAA FF' 'S C'. Rome, 7 BC. *RIC* I Aug 427, 431 or 435

1081. 27mm 11.2g 504.004, 91 Workshop - Rms. 5&3

AE as. *obv.* bust l., 'CAESAR AVGVST PONT MAX TRIBVNIC POT'; *rev.* 'P LVRIVS AGRIPPA IIIVIR AAA FF' 'SC'. Rome, 7 BC. *RIC* I Aug. 428

1082.	27mm 11.72g	320.061, 334	Shrine - rm. 1	
1083.	26mm 9.87g	265.004, 36	Casa del Chirurgo - rm. 11	
1084.	24mm 8.98g	320.061, 343	Shrine - rm. 1	
1085.	25mm 6.89g	140.147, 207	Workshop - rm. 1	probably an imitation

AE as. *obv.* bare headed bust r., 'CAESAR AVGVST PONT MAX TRIBVNIC POT'; *rev.* 'M MAECILIVS TVLLVS III VIR AAA FF' 'SC'. Rome, 7 BC. *RIC* I Aug. 435

1086. 27mm 10.71g 145.004, 64 Bar of Acisculus - behind counter
1087. 25mm 11.32g 140.147, 229 Workshop - rm. 1   probably this type, but reverse
                                              difficult to read
1088. 25mm 10.50g 322.002, 61 Workshop - rm. 4   appears imitative

AE as. *obv.* bare headed bust l., 'CAESAR AVGVST PONT MAX TRIBVNIC POT'; *rev.* 'M MAECILIVS TVLLVS III VIR AAA FF' 'SC'. Rome, 7 BC. *RIC* I Aug. 436

1089. 27mm 9.73g 142.001, 21 Bar of Acisculus - rm. 2

AE as. *obv.* bare headed bust r., 'CAESAR AVGVST PONT MAX TRIBVNIC POT'; *rev.* 'VOLVSVS VALER MESSAL IIVIR AAA FF', 'S C'. Rome, 6 BC. *RIC* I Aug. 441

1090. 25mm 10.75g 203.055, 80 Shrine - rm. 1

AE quad. *obv.* 'APRONIVS MESSALLA AAAFF' 'SC'; *rev.* 'GALVS SISENNA III VIR', altar. Rome, c. 6-5 BC. *RIC* I Aug. 443 var.

1091. 18mm 3.06g 320.025, 124 Shrine - rm. 1   acc. to fn. 447 in RIC, this is an imitation

AE quad. *obv.* 'GALVS APRONIVS AAA FF' 'SC'; *rev.* 'MESSALLA SISENNA III VIR', altar. Rome, 5 BC. *RIC* I Aug. 447 var.

1092. 17mm 3.90g 145.004, 34 Bar of Acisculus - behind counter

AE quad. *obv.* 'GALVS MESSALLA AAAFF' 'SC'; *rev.* 'SISENNA APRONIVS III VIR', altar. Rome, 5 BC. *RIC* I Aug. 450 var.

1093. 20mm 2.57g 071.020, 113 Casa delle Vestali Bar - rm. 2
1094. 16mm 3.1g 601.017, 112 Workshop - Rms. 5&3

AE quad. *obv.* 'MESSALLA APRONIVS AAA FF' 'S C'; *rev.* 'GALLVS SISENNA III VIR', altar. Rome, 5 BC. *RIC* I Aug. 453 var.

1095. 17mm 3.03g 203.002, 9 Shrine - rm. 1

AE quad. *obv.* 'MESALLA SISENNA AAAFFII' 'SC'; *rev.* 'GALVS APRONIVS III VIR', altar. Rome, 5 BC. *RIC* I Aug. 458 var. (*cf.* p. 77, fn. 447)

1096. 18mm 2.96g 140.038, 127 Workshop - rm. 1

AE quad. *obv.* 'P BETILIENVS BASSVS' 'S C'; *rev.* 'III VIR AAA FF', altar. Rome, 4 BC. *RIC* I Aug. 465

1097. 16mm 2.61g 073.001, 1 Casa delle Vestali Bar - rm. 1   imitation?
1098. 16mm 1.86g 320.025, 74 Shrine - rm. 1   obv. garbled 'BETILIENVS BASSVS' 'SC', imitation; style poor and low weight
1099. 14mm 2.57g 142.025, 99 Bar of Acisculus - rm. 2   imitation? Rather light

AE quad. *obv.* 'L VALERIUS CATALLVS' 'SC'; *rev.* 'IIIVIRAAAFF', garlanded altar. Rome, 4 BC. *RIC* I Aug. 468

1100. 16mm 2.72g 009.002, 327 Workshop - rm. 1   imitation?
1101. 15mm 4.23g 320.061, 308 Shrine - rm. 1

uncertain *quadrantes*, Rome, c. 15-8 BC

1102. 19mm 4.23g 310.040, 66 Shrine - rm. 1   obv. illeg.; rev. ']APRONIVS[(RIC I Aug. 449ff.]

1103. 18mm 2.69g 310.092, 198 Shrine - rm. 1   probably an imitation
1104. 18mm NR 320.011, 28 Shrine - rm. 1   obv. and rev. inscriptions illegible; large chunk of corrosion attached to surface

1105. 17mm 2.04g 071.013, 90 Casa delle Vestali Bar - rm. 2   obv. altar with bowl shaped top, illeg.; rev. ']NO[' (?), around 'S C', illeg.

1106. 16mm 3.3g 603.005, 63 Bar of Phoebus - rm. 4   'S C' and altar, legend unclear

Tiberius under Augustus

AE as. *obv.* bare headed bust r., 'TI CAESAR AVGVST F IMPERAT V'; *rev.* 'PONTIFEX TRIBVN POTESTATE XII', 'SC'. Rome, AD 8-10. *RIC* I Aug. 469

1107. 30mm 10.78g 121.051, 303 Inn - rm. 6
1108. 27mm 11.20g 320.074, 398 Shrine - rm. 1
1109. 27mm 9.5g   500.031, 176 Bar of Phoebus - rm. 1
1110. 27mm NR   607.299, 255 Casa del Chirurgo - rm. 2   reverse almost illeg., but
                                                                   probably this type

TIBERIUS (AD 14-37)

AE as. *obv.* bare headed bust. l., 'TI CAESAR DIVI AVG F AVGVST IMP VII'; *rev.* female std. r., 'PONTIF MAXIM TRIBVN POTEST XVII'. Rome, AD 15-16. *RIC* I Tib. 34

1111. 27mm 10.87g 140.162, 332 Workshop - rm. 1

AE as. *obv.* radiate Aug. l., above star, before thunderbolt, 'DIVVS AVGV-STVS PATER'; *rev.* female std. r., feet on stool, 'S C'. Rome, c. AD 15-16. *RIC* I Tib. 72

1112. 28mm 10.99g 145.004, 63 Bar of Acisculus - behind counter

AE as. *obv.* bust l., 'TI CAESAR DIVI AVG F AVGVST IMP VIII'; *rev.* 'PONTIF MAXIM TRIBVN POTEST XXIII' 'S C'. Rome, AD 21-22. *RIC* I Tib. 44

1113. 28mm 10.84g 310.032, 68 Shrine - rm. 1
1114. 28mm 10.79g 145.002, 21 Bar of Acisculus - behind counter
1115. 27mm 10.46g 165.012, 35 Inn Bar - rm. 1b&3b   probably this type

AE as. *obv.* bare headed bust l., 'DRVSVS CAESAR TI AVGF DIVI AVG N'; *rev.* 'PONTIF TRIBVN POTEST ITER S C'. Rome, AD 21-22. *RIC* I Tib. 45

1116. 30mm 9.71g 165.009, 42   Inn Bar - rm. 1b&3b
1117. 29mm 11.01g 320.061, 348 Shrine - rm. 1
1118. 29mm c10g   322.025, 105 Workshop - rm. 4
1119. 27mm 11.25g 169.005, 14   Inn - rm. 12
1120. 25mm 10.79g 166.003, 41   Inn Bar - rm. 5b

AE as. *obv.* radiate bust l., 'DIVVS AVGVSTVS PATER'; *rev.* altar, 'PROVIDENT' 'SC'. Rome, AD 22/3-?30. *RIC* I Tib. 81

1121. 30mm 11.08g 165.008, 56   Inn Bar - rm. 1b&3b   very corroded
1122. 29mm 10.88g 186.003, 10   Inn - rm. 3
1123. 29mm 9.2g   120.016, 14   Inn - rm. 4   very worn
1124. 28mm 11.38g 223.004, 39   Inn - rm. 9
1125. 28mm 11.34g 320.064, 418 Shrine - rm. 1
1126. 28mm 10.98g 166.003, 11   Inn Bar - rm. 5b
1127. 28mm 10.97g 320.064, 424 Shrine - rm. 1   obverse die-linked to cat.
                                                               1129
1128. 28mm 10.91g 310.116, 609 Shrine - rm. 1
1129. 28mm 10.60g 320.061, 315 Shrine - rm. 1   obverse die-linked to cat.
                                                               1127

1130. 28mm 9.92g 315.012, 21 Shrine - rm. 2
1131. 27mm 10.52g 165.017, 76 Inn Bar - rm. 1b&3b
1132. 25mm 10.16g 277.085, 272 Casa del Chirurgo - rms. 3&4
1133. 25mm 11.00g 145.004, 66 Bar of Acisculus - behind counter

AE as. *obv.* laureate bust l., 'TI CAESAR DIVI AVG F AVGVST IMP VIII'; *rev.* 'PONTIF MAX TR POT XXVII', rudder, globe. Rome, AD 35-36. *RIC* I Tib. 58

1134. 29mm 12.0g 140.027, 60 Workshop - rm. 1

AE as. *obv.* laureate bust l., 'TI CAESAR DIVI AVG F AVGVST IMP VIII'; *rev.* 'PONTIF MAX TR POT XXXIIX', rudder, globe. Rome, AD 36-37. *RIC* I Tib. 64

1135. 27mm 13.07g 320.064, 417 Shrine - rm. 1

AE as. *obv.* bust l., 'DIVVS AVGVSTVS PATER'; *rev.* eagle stg. on globe, 'S C'. Rome, c. AD 34-37. *RIC* I Tib. 82

1136. 27mm 10.47g 145.009, 61 Bar of Acisculus - behind counter

AE as. *obv.* bust radiate l., 'DIVVS AVGVSTVS PATER'; *rev.* winged thunderbolt, 'S C'. Rome, AD 34-37. *RIC* I Tib. 83

1137. 30mm 10.39g 068.001, 18 Casa delle Vestali - rm. 9
1138. 29mm 9.87g 323.062, 242 Bar of Acisculus - rm. 1
1139. 28mm 11.15g 127.055, 167 Inn Bar - rm. 1b

GAIUS (AD 37-41)

AE as. *obv.* bust l., 'GERMANICVS CAESAR TI AVGVST F DIVI AVG N'; *rev.* 'CAESAR AVG GERMANICVS PON M TR POT' 'S C'. Rome, AD 37-38. *RIC* I Gaius 35

1140. 27mm 10.18g 068.007, 69 Casa delle Vestali - rm. 9

AE as. *obv.* bare headed bust l., 'M AGRIPPA L F COS III'; *rev.* Neptune stg. facing, 'S C'. Rome, AD 37-41 (undated). *RIC* I Gaius 58

1141. 30mm 10.59g 311.027, 32 Workshop - rm. 4
1142. 29mm 11.18g 322.002, 62 Workshop - rm. 4
1143. 28mm 10.51g 127.020, 51 Inn Bar - rm. 1b
1144. 27mm 10.8g 500.039, 183 Bar of Phoebus - rm. 1
1145. 24mm 7.4g   604.044, 535 Shrine - rm. 3   possibly this type, but
                                                              extremely worn and
                                                              underweight. Imitation?

AE as. *obv.* bust l., 'C CAESAR AVG GERMANICVS PON M TR POT'; *rev.* Vesta on throne, 'VESTA' 'S C'. Rome, AD 37-38. *RIC* I Gaius 38

1146. 30mm 10.0g 053.011, 2 Casa delle Vestali - rm. 20
1147. 27mm 11.06g 165.008, 66 Inn Bar - rm. 1b&3b   coin bent
1148. 27mm 10.84g 145.004, 67 Bar of Acisculus - behind counter

AE quad. *obv.* 'C CAESAR DIVI AVG PRON AVG', 'S C', pileus; *rev.* 'PON M TRP III PP COS DES III' 'RCC'. Rome, AD 39. *RIC* I Gaius 39

1149. 17mm 2.90g 186.003, 22 Inn - rm. 3   very worn
1150. 15mm 3.33g 320.026, 51 Shrine - rm. 1

AE as. *obv.* bare headed bust l., 'GERMANICVS CAESAR TI AVG F DIVI AVG N'; *rev.* 'C CAESAR DIVI AVG PRON AVG PM TRP IIII PP', 'SC'. Rome, AD 40-41. *RIC* I Gaius 50

1151. 29mm 11.16g 140.069, 132 Workshop - rm. 1

AE quad. *obv.* 'C CAESAR DIVI AVG P RON AVG', 'SC'; *rev.* 'PON M TRP III PP COS TERT' 'RCC'. Rome, AD 40-41. *RIC* I Gaius 52

1152. 17mm 3.3g   612.009, 47 Casa del Chirurgo - rms. 17-18

CLAUDIUS (AD 41-54)

AE quad. *obv.* 'TI CLAVDIVS CAESAR AVG', 3 legged modius; *rev.* 'PON M TR P IMP COS DES IT', 'SC'. Rome, AD 41. *RIC* I Claud. 84

1153. 19mm 3.52g 310.040, 69   Shrine - rm. 1
1154. 19mm 3.19g 310.033, 108 Shrine - rm. 1
1155. 18mm 3.11g 145.005, 19   Bar of Acisculus - behind counter
1156. 17mm 2.87g 311.038, 47   Workshop - rm. 4
1157. 17mm 2.76g 320.020, 63   Shrine - rm. 1
1158. 17mm 2.25g 310.037, 109 Shrine - rm. 1
1159. 15mm 3.42g 310.092, 287 Shrine - rm. 1

AE quad. *obv.* 'TI CLAVDIVS CAESAR AVG' around hand and scales, 'PNR'; *rev.* 'PON M TR P IMP COS DES IT SC'. Rome, AD 41. *RIC* I Claud. 85

1160. 19mm 2.5g   164.024, 56 Inn - rm. 10

AE quad. *obv.* 'TI CLAVDIVS CAESAR AVG', 3 legged modius; *rev.* 'PON M TR P IMP COS II' 'SC'. Rome, AD 42. *RIC* I Claud. 88

1161. 18mm 3.30g 186.002, 6   Inn - rm. 3
1162. 18mm 3.3g   606.013, 87   Casa del Chirurgo - rm. 3 entrance
1163. 18mm 2.81g 071.020, 187 Casa delle Vestali Bar - rm. 2
1164. 17mm 2.61g 068.001, 1   Casa delle Vestali - rm. 9
1165. 17mm 1.97g 186.002, 7   Inn - rm. 3

AE quad. *obv.* 'TI CLAVDIVS CAESAR AVG', hand and scales, 'PNR'; *rev.* 'POM M TRP IMP COS II' 'SC'. Rome, AD 42. *RIC* I Claud. 89

1166. 16mm 2.61g 277.085, 271 Casa del Chirurgo - rms. 3&4

AE quad. *obv.* 'TI CLAVDIVS CAESAR AVG' around 3 legged modius; *rev.* 'PON M TRP IMP PP COS II', 'S C'. Rome, AD 42. *RIC* I Claud. 90

1167. 19mm 2.68g 265.001, 1   Casa del Chirurgo - rm. 11
1168. 18mm 3.8g   507.078, 139 Casa del Chirurgo shop - rm. 2

AE dup. *obv.* female bust r. 'ANTONIA AVGVSTA'; *rev.* Claudius stg. l., 'TI CLAVDIVS CAESAR AVG P M TR P IMP', 'S C'. Rome, c. AD 41-50. *RIC* I Claud. 92

1169. 28mm 14.8g 507.072, 81 Casa del Chirurgo shop - rm. 2

AE sest. *obv.* bust l., 'NERO CLAVDIVS DRVSVS GERMANICVS IMP'; *rev.* Claudius std. l., 'TI CLAVDIVS CAESAR AVG PM TRP IMP', 'S C'. Rome, c. AD 41-50. *RIC* I Claud. 93

1170. 35mm 26.77g 032.003, 3 Casa delle Vestali - rm. 12

AE as. *obv.* bare headed bust l., 'TI CLAVDIVS CAESAR AVG PM T R T IMP'; *rev.* Constantia I stg. facing, 'CONSTANTIAE AVGVSTI', 'S C'. Rome, c. AD 41-50. *RIC* I Claud. 95

1171. 27mm 9.80g 165.009, 41 Inn Bar - rms. 1b&3b
1172. 25mm 7.82g 121.059, 304 Inn - rm. 6   probably this type. Imitation?

AE sest. *obv.* laureate bust r., 'TI CLAVDIVS CAESAR AVG PM T R T IMP'; *rev.* Spes, draped adv. l., 'SPES AVGVSTA', 'SC'. Rome, c. AD 41-50. *RIC* I Claud. 99

1173. 33mm 19.7g 601.033, 209 Workshop - Rms. 5&3
1174. 32mm 17.83g 126.022, 84 Inn Bar - rm. 6b

AE as. *obv.* Germanicus r., 'GERMANICVS CAESAR TI AVG F DIVI AVG N'; *rev.* 'TI CLAVDIVS CAESAR AVG GERM P M TR P IMP P P', 'S C'. Rome, c. AD 50-54. *RIC* I Claud. 106

1175. 29mm 7.79g 120.010, 123 Inn - rm. 4   very worn, probably this type

AE as. *obv.* bare headed bust l., 'TI CLAVDIVS CAESAR AVG PM TR P IMP P P'; *rev.* Libertas stg. r., 'LIBERTAS AVGVSTA' 'SC'. Rome, AD 50-54. *RIC* I Claud. 113

1176.* 30mm 11.36g 165.009, 136 Inn Bar - rm. 1b&3b
1177. 29mm 10.27g 071.018, 92 Casa delle Vestali Bar - rm. 2
1178. 28mm 12.38g 310.116, 405 Shrine - rm. 1
1179. 26mm 8.57g 120.016, 31 Inn - rm. 4   imitation?
1180. 24mm 6.75g 223.004, 38 Inn - rm. 9   imitation?

AE as. *obv.* bare headed bust l., 'TI CLAVDIVS CAESAR AVG PM TR P IMP P P'; *rev.* Minerva with shield and javelin adv. r., 'S C'. Rome, c. AD 50-54. *RIC* I Claud. 116

1181. 29mm 11.18g 320.061, 310 Shrine - rm. 1

NERO (AD 54-68)

AE dup. *obv.* rad. bust r., 'NERO CLAVD CAESAR AVG GER PM TR P IMP P P'; *rev.* Roma std. l. 'ROMA' 'SC'. Rome, c. AD 65. *RIC* I Nero 295

1182. 27mm 13.42g 164.002, 1 Inn - rm. 10

AE dup. *obv.* laureate bust r., 'IMP NERO CAESAR AVG GERM'; *rev.* Victory with shield l., 'S C'. Rome, c. AD 66. *RIC* I Nero 351

1183. 30mm 12.64g 076.001, 1 Casa delle Vestali - rm. 32
1184. 30mm 10.97g 071.013, 91 Casa delle Vestali Bar - rm. 2   probably this type, but very
                                                                                 corroded

AE unit. *obv.* radiate bust l., 'NERO CAESAR AVG GERM'; *rev.* trireme, 'ADVENTVS AVGVSTI' 'C P'. Patras, Achaea, c. AD 66-67. *RPC* I 1273

1185. 22mm 8.98g 166.006, 36 Inn Bar - rm. 5b

VESPASIAN (AD 69-79)

AE sest. *obv.* bust r., 'IMP CAES VESPASIAN AVG PM TR P P P COS III'; *rev.* Mars adv. r. with spear and trophy, 'S C'. Rome, AD 71. *RIC* II Vesp. 203

1186. 35mm 27.78g 075.011, 75 Casa delle Vestali - rm. 33

AE dup. *obv.* radiate bust r., 'IMP CAES VESPASIAN AVG COS IIII'; *rev.* Roma std. l., 'ROMA VICTRIX', 'S C' in exergue. Rome, AD 72-73. *RIC* II Vesp. 297

1187. 25mm 13.85g 222.001, 1 Inn - rm. 9

Titus under Vespasian

AE dup. *obv.* radiate bust r., 'T CAES IMP PON TRP COS II CENS'; *rev.* Felicitas stg. l., 'FELICITAS PVBLICA' 'S C'. Rome, AD 73. *RIC* II Vesp. 614

1188. 28mm 13.23g 165.006, 55 Inn Bar - rm. 1b&3b   the context no. may be incorrect, as it is a threshold stone; more likely 165.009 (Anderson pers. comm.)

ILLEGIBLE

All AE unless indicated otherwise

1189. 40mm 33.41g 185.008, 17 Casa del Triclinio - ramp
1190. 37mm 31.61g 185.013, 51 Casa del Triclinio - ramp
1191. 37mm 29.99g 185.013, 50 Casa del Triclinio - ramp
1192. 35mm 22.76g 324.024, 95 Bar of Phoebus - rm. 1
1193. 32mm 23.8g 502.050, 165 Bar of Acisculus - rm. 1
1194. 32mm 16.7g 045.034B, 173 Casa delle Vestali - rm. 26   obv. bust r., illeg. Early imperial?
1195. 32mm 9.47g 160.002, 25 Inn - rm. 1   very thin flan - not a coin? Illegible inscription
1196. 30mm 22.92g 072.025, 102 Casa delle Vestali Bar - rm. 3   Rome?, early 1st AD?
1197. 30mm 21.95g 324.059, 178 Bar of Phoebus - rm. 1
1198. 30mm 13.76g 120.010, 122 Inn - rm. 4
1199. 29mm 18.45g 320.026, 85 Shrine - rm. 1
1200. 29mm 10.39g 185.008, 18 Casa del Triclinio - ramp   early imperial?
1201. 28mm 18.65g 120.044, 529 Inn - rm. 4
1202. 28mm 11.00g 140.073, 176 Workshop - rm. 1
1203. 27mm 12.17g 071.018, 98 Casa delle Vestali Bar - rm. 2
1204. 26mm 15.26g 271.234, 100 Inn - rm. 9
1205. 26mm 11.33g 310.116, 639 Shrine - rm. 1   shape of flan suggests Republican
1206. 26mm 10.24g 120.018, 216 Inn - rm. 4   probably an imperial as, but very corroded

1207. 25mm 9.15g 127.039, 169 Inn Bar - rm. 1b   obv. faint traces of bust l.?.; rev. illeg.

1208. 25mm 7.58g 140.147, 203 Workshop - rm. 1
1209. 24mm 13.58g 271.243, 198 Inn - rm. 9
1210. 24mm 11.32g 320.061, 330 Shrine - rm. 1   looks likely to be early imperial

1211. 24mm 7.77g 510.004, 24 Shrine - rm. 1
1212. 23mm 3.39g^f 165.082, 138 Inn Bar - rm. 1b&3b   not deliberately cut
1213. 22mm 6.93g 271.234, 105 Inn - rm. 9
1214. 22mm 5.72g 018.011, 27 Workshop - rm. 1   very corroded piece of metal, too thick to be a single coin; either two coins fused together or not a coin

1215. 22mm 4.59g 504.007, 17 Workshop - Rms. 5&3
1216. 21mm 9.55g 182.110, 235 Inn - rm. 12
1217. 21mm 8.07g 181.067, 40 Inn - rm. 9   two odd protrusions from edge of flan

1218. 21mm 8.06g 182.030, 191 Inn - rm. 12
1219. 21mm 5.2g   600.002, 91 Workshop - rm. 2
1220. 21mm 4.89g 185.013, 61 Casa del Triclinio - Ramp
1221. 21mm 4.55g^b 510.004, 36 Shrine - rm. 1   probably a Republican AE
1222. 21mm 3.68g 142.011, 93 Bar of Acisculus - rm. 2
1223. 20mm 6.81g 074.001, 113 Casa delle Vestali - rm. 19
1224. 20mm 6.50g 168.078, 104 Casa del Triclinio - clean
1225. 20mm 6.39g 182.030, 192 Inn - rm. 12   may be two coins fused together

1226. 20mm 6.15g 073.042, 73 Casa delle Vestali Bar - rm. 1   obv. bust? illeg.
1227. 20mm 6.0g   018.012, 342 Workshop - rm. 1
1228. 20mm 5.62g 320.067, 630 Shrine - rm. 1
1229. 20mm 5.3g   262.006, 21 Casa del Chirurgo - rm. 23
1230. 20mm 3.63g 105.000, no no. Casa delle Vestali - rm. 46
1231. 20mm 4.16g 320.061, 328 Shrine - rm. 1   early imperial?
1232. 20mm 3.55g 145.004, 36 Bar of Acisculus - behind counter
1233. 20mm 3.4g   502.038, 177 Bar of Acisculus - rm. 1   possibly bust r.?
1234. 20mm 2.84g 320.046, 267 Shrine - rm. 1   unusual grey fabric – lead? Not a coin?

1235. 19mm 5.35g 121.063, 305 Inn - rm. 6
1236. 19mm 5.32g 123.054, 445 Inn - rm. 1
1237. 19mm 4.78g 271.234, 109 Inn - rm. 9
1238. 19mm 4.32g 065.017, 13 Casa delle Vestali - rm. 27
1239. 19mm 4.11g 500.005, 112 Bar of Phoebus - rm. 1
1240. 19mm 4.1g   127.050, 166 Inn Bar - rm. 1b
1241. 19mm 3.85g 182.028, 72 Inn - rm. 12
1242. 19mm 3.8g   612m 613, 614, no no. Surgeon rm. 11 or 13, 17&18
1243. 19mm 3.38g 320.074, 391 Shrine - rm. 1
1244. 19mm 3.31g 123.056, 581 Inn - rm. 1
1245. 19mm 2.5g   123.054, 448 Inn - rm. 1
1246. 18mm 7.33g 140.166, 349 Workshop - rm. 1
1247. 18mm 5.02g 125.030, 124 Casa delle Vestali Bar - rm. 4
1248. 18mm 4.82g 123.054, 443 Inn - rm. 1

1249. 18mm 4.82g 140.105, 225 Workshop - rm. 1
1250. 18mm 4.74g 310.032, 67 Shrine - rm. 1   early imperial?
1251. 18mm 4.23g 180.003, 25 Inn - rm. 3
1252. 18mm 3.72g 165.012, 57 Inn Bar - rm. 1b&3b
1253. 18mm 4.4g   140.172, 618 Workshop - rm. 1
1254. 18mm 3.80g 182.160, 237 Inn - rm. 12
1255. 18mm 3.6g   510.043, 136 Shrine - rm. 1
1256. 18mm 3.5g   602.078, 174 Bar of Phoebus - rm. 3
1257. 18mm 3.39g 140.097, 329 Workshop - rm. 1
1258. 18mm 3.2g   600.044, 338 Workshop - rm. 2
1259. 18mm 2.95g 128.002, 83 Casa delle Vestali - rm. 7
1260. 18mm 1.24g 143.004, 21 Well/ Fntn. - s. of Well   obv. faint traces of bust r.? rev.
                                                                illeg.

1261. 18mm 1.11g^f 145.013, 165 Bar of Acisculus - behind counter
1262. 17mm 6.50g 271.243, 199 Inn - rm. 9
1263. 17mm 5.93g 169.003, 11 Inn - rm. 12
1264. 17mm 4.74g 140.038, 125 Workshop - rm. 1
1265. 17mm 4.4g   606.043, 183 Casa del Chirurgo - rm. 3 entrance
1266. 17mm 4.37g 203.134, 131 Shrine - rm. 1
1267. 17mm 4.24g 320.061, 316 Shrine - rm. 1   obv. bust r.?; rev. 2 figures ?
1268. 17mm 4.16g 275.093, 113 Casa del Chirurgo - rm. 5
1269. 17mm 3.61g 145.005, 29 Bar of Acisculus - behind counter
1270. 17mm 3.39g 260.120, 140 Casa del Chirurgo - rm. 5   not a coin?
1271. 17mm 3.38g 322.043, 160 Workshop - rm. 4
1272. 17mm 2.98g 142.011, 37 Bar of Acisculus - rm. 2
1273. 17mm 2.9g   123.019, 113 Inn - rm. 1
1274. 17mm 2.5g   603.005, 21 Bar of Phoebus - rm. 4
1275. 17mm 2.37g 144.071, 75 Well/ Fntn. - n. of Well   obv. bust r., rev. illeg.
1276. 17mm 2.36g 164.002, 2 Inn - rm. 10
1277. 17mm 1.97g 142.048, 176 Bar of Acisculus - rm. 2
1278. 17mm 1.91g 009.002, 329 Workshop - rm. 1   casting sprue, one side flat,
                                                                other side plano-convex

1279. 17mm 1.86g 166.064, 85 Inn Bar - rm. 5b
1280. 17mm NR   226.005, 11 Via Consolare - Porta Ercolano
1281. 17mm NR   127.078, 405c Inn Bar - rm. 1b
1282. 17mm 1.71g 145.004, 31 Bar of Acisculus - behind counter
1283. 16mm 5.20g 320.000, 370 Shrine - rm. 1
1284. 16mm 4.72g 310.092, 179 Shrine - rm. 1
1285. 16mm 3.89g 322.050, 232 Workshop - rm. 4
1286. 16mm 3.61g 165.012, 50 Inn Bar - rm. 1b&3b
1287. 16mm 3.59g 140.162, 335 Workshop - rm. 1
1288. 16mm 3.59g 140.162, 530 Workshop - rm. 1
1289. 16mm 3.56g 073.023, 48 Casa delle Vestali Bar - rm. 1   AR?
1290. 16mm 3.29g 120.016, 176 Inn - rm. 4
1291. 16mm 3.05g 320.081, 570 Shrine - rm. 1
1292. 16mm 2.98g 127.057, 221 Inn Bar - rm. 1b
1293. 16mm 2.8g   617.099, 51 Via Consolare - outside Inn
1294. 16mm 2.65g 140.175, 505 Workshop - rm. 1
1295. 16mm 2.5g   009.002, 326 Workshop - rm. 1
1296. 16mm 2.5g   123.042, 178 Inn - rm. 1

1297. 16mm 2.4g   222.002, 69 Inn - rm. 9
1298. 16mm 2.33g 110.017, 110 Vicolo di Narciso – back of Chirurgo
1299. 16mm 2.31g 088.049, 332 Casa delle Vestali Bar - rm. 1
1300. 16mm 2.3g   600.039, 301 Workshop - rm. 2
1301. 16mm 2.29g^b 222.012, 149 Inn - rm. 9
1302. 16mm 1.7g   127.082, 393 Inn Bar - rm. 1b
1303. 16mm 1.70g 142.011, 96 Bar of Acisculus - rm. 2
1304. 16mm 1.45g 142.008, 130 Bar of Acisculus - rm. 2
1305. 15mm 4.66g 503.004, 11 Workshop - rm. 2
1306. 15mm 4.22g 322.050, 230 Workshop - rm. 4
1307. 15mm 3.9g   120.051, 416 Inn - rm. 4   obv. fig.?; rev. animal?
1308. 15mm 3.79g 035.005, 1 Casa delle Vestali - rm. 8
1309. 15mm 3.45g 310.155, 285 Shrine - rm. 1
1310. 15mm 3.20g 066.003, 16 Vicolo di Narciso - outside door 25
1311. 15mm 3.13g 071.037, 240 Casa delle Vestali Bar - rm. 2
1312. 15mm 2.95g 087.025, 40 Casa delle Vestali Bar - rm. 4   faint traces of design
1313. 15mm 2.8g   600.036, 281 Workshop - rm. 2   obv. bust r.; rev. illeg.
1314. 15mm 2.7g   508.053, 137 Casa del Chirurgo - Rms. 16&20 obv. bust l.; rev. illeg.
1315. 15mm 2.69g 180.008, 83 Inn - rm. 3
1316. 15mm 2.59g 271.243, 205 Inn - rm. 9
1317. 15mm 2.56g 312.082, 369 Shrine - rm. 2
1318. 15mm 2.53g 320.061, 300 Shrine - rm. 1
1319. 15mm 2.53g 271.243, 181 Inn - rm. 9
1320. 15mm 2.48g 127.059, 288 Inn Bar - rm. 1b
1321. 15mm 2.39g 310.087, 629 Shrine - rm. 1
1322. 15mm 2.37g^b 510.014, 39 Shrine - rm. 1
1323. 15mm 2.35g 120.066, 526 Inn - rm. 4   AR?
1324. 15mm 2.3g   617.097, 84 Via Consolare - outside Inn
1325. 15mm 2.29g 510.047, 116 Shrine - rm. 1   obv. bust r.?; rev. illeg.
1326. 15mm 2.16g 271.234, 107 Inn - rm. 9
1327. 15mm 2.14g 320.117, 604 Shrine - rm. 1
1328. 15mm 2.10g^b 321.033, 116 Workshop - rm. 2
1329. 15mm 2.07g 320.050, 198 Shrine - rm. 1
1330. 15mm 2.04g 126.017, 32 Inn Bar - rm. 6b
1331. 15mm 1.96g 185.002, 16 Casa del Triclinio - Ramp
1332. 15mm 1.95g^b 142.007, 236 Bar of Acisculus - rm. 2
1333. 15mm 1.94g^b 180.015, 109 Inn - rm. 3
1334. 15mm 1.92g 271.234, 99 Inn - rm. 9
1335. 15mm 1.9g   049.064, 121 Casa delle Vestali - rm. 27
1336. 15mm 1.8g   182.030, 188 Inn - rm. 12
1337. 15mm 1.75g 140.162, 331 Workshop - rm. 1
1338. 15mm 1.72g 140.175, 484 Workshop - rm. 1
1339. 15mm 1.70g 223.005, 184 Inn - rm. 9
1340. 15mm 1.70g 223.028, 143 Inn - rm. 9   obv. bust r.; rev. illeg.
1341. 15mm 1.66g 320.088, 505 Shrine - rm. 1
1342. 15mm 1.65g 145.013, 108 Bar of Acisculus - behind counter
1343. 15mm 1.63g^b 500.005, 99 Bar of Phoebus - rm. 1
1344. 15mm 1.52g 180.080, 60 Inn - rm. 3   obv. bust r.; rev. illeg.
1345. 15mm 1.52g^b 140.147, 223 Workshop - rm. 1   probably AR
1346. 15mm 1.46g 222.001, 6A Inn - rm. 9

1347. 15mm 1.46g^b 142.011, 94 Bar of Acisculus - rm. 2
1348. 15mm 1.45g 165.096, 221 Inn Bar - rm. 1b&3b
1349. 15mm 1.42g 163.024, 48 Inn - rm. 8
1350. 15mm 1.41g 164.026, 9 Inn - rm. 10
1351. 15mm 1.4g   037.037, 348 Casa delle Vestali - rm. 5
1352. 15mm 1.23g 180.020, 101 Inn - rm. 3
1353. 15mm NR   323.002, 74 Bar of Acisculus - rm. 1
1354. 14mm 3.73g 271.234, 180 Inn - rm. 9
1355. 14mm 3.52g 320.048, 188 Shrine - rm. 1
1356. 14mm 2.75g 088.026, 107 Casa delle Vestali Bar - rm. 1   obv. bust r.?; rev. illeg.
1357. 14mm 2.72g 096.020, 74 Casa delle Vestali - rm. 42
1358. 14mm 2.59g 140.038, 126 Workshop - rm. 1
1359. 14mm 2.53g 311.009, 85 Workshop - rm. 4
1360. 14mm 2.34g 120.050, 423 Inn - rm. 4
1361. 14mm 2.3g   607.233, 6 Casa del Chirurgo - rm. 2
1362. 14mm 2.14g 165.012, 51 Inn Bar - rm. 1b&3b
1363. 14mm 2.07g 127.082, 379 Inn Bar - rm. 1b
1364. 14mm 2.07g^b 165.012, 53 Inn Bar - rm. 1b&3b
1365. 14mm 2.03g 120.067, 534 Inn - rm. 4
1366. 14mm 1.9g   310.087, 671 Shrine - rm. 1
1367. 14mm 1.87g 510.004, 35 Shrine - rm. 1
1368. 14mm 1.82g 127.078, 291 Inn Bar - rm. 1b
1369. 14mm 1.76g 271.000, 20 Inn - rm. 9
1370. 14mm 1.67g 180.014, 26 Inn - rm. 3   obv. ?bust r.; rev. illeg.
1371. 14mm 1.67g 320.049, 223 Shrine - rm. 1
1372. 14mm 1.6g   140.069, 131 Workshop - rm. 1
1373. 14mm 1.56g 165.083, 129 Inn Bar - rm. 1b&3b
1374. 14mm 1.50g 320.117, 60 Shrine - rm. 1
1375. 14mm 1.4g   140.147, 338 Workshop - rm. 1
1376. 14mm 1.36g 127.082, 402 Inn Bar - rm. 1b
1377. 14mm 1.24g^b 320.061, 327 Shrine - rm. 1
1378. 14mm 1.23g 011.011, 706 Casa delle Vestali - rm. 15/53
1379. 14mm 1.17g^b 180.009, 55 Inn - rm. 3
1380. 14mm 1.16g 140.043, 130 Workshop - rm. 1
1381. 14mm 1.12g^b 180.015, 57 Inn - rm. 3   obv. bust r.?; rev. illeg.
1382. 14mm 0.86g^f 140.144, 463 Workshop - rm. 1
1383. 14mm 0.85g^f 104.007, 60 Via Consolare - Casa delle Vestali front
1384. 14mm 1.43g 140.069, 141 Workshop - rm. 1   obv. helmeted bust r.?; rev. illeg.
1385. 14-18mm 3.36g^f 065.072, 186 Casa delle Vestali - rm. 27
1386. 13mm 3.34g 088.021, 105 Casa delle Vestali Bar - rm. 1
1387. 13mm 3.07g 510.004, 16 Shrine - rm. 1
1388. 13mm 2.73g 271.234, 70 Inn - rm. 9   obv. bust r.?; rev. illeg.
1389. 13mm 2.59g 203.091, 110 Shrine - rm. 1
1390. 13mm 2.37g 271.243, 179 Inn - rm. 9
1391. 13mm 2.3g   510.028, 65 Shrine - rm. 1
1392. 13mm 2.21g 067.019, 50 Casa delle Vestali - rm. 20
1393. 12mm 2.83g 503.020, 12 Workshop - rm. 2
1394. 12mm 2.18g 181.179, 125 Inn - rm. 9
1395. 13mm 2.08g^b 067.019, 51 Casa delle Vestali - rm. 20

1396. 13mm c2g   223.007, 0c Inn - rm. 9
1397. 13mm 1.97g   312.030, 432 Shrine - rm. 2
1398. 13mm 1.94g   088.021, 110 Casa delle Vestali Bar - rm. 1
1399. 13mm 1.84g[b] 182.030, 195 Inn - rm. 12
1400. 13mm 1.8g   603.017, 60 Bar of Phoebus - rm. 4
1401. 13mm 1.78g   186.003, 23 Inn - rm. 3
1402. 13mm 1.76g   321.033, 115 Workshop - rm. 2
1403. 13mm 1.72g   510.004, 37 Shrine - rm. 1
1404. 13mm 1.64g   320.074, 393 Shrine - rm. 1
1405. 13mm 1.61g   510.051, 115 Shrine - rm. 1
1406. 13mm 1.60g   320.061, 339 Shrine - rm. 1
1407. 13mm 1.6g   500.017, 144 Bar of Phoebus - rm. 1
1408. 13mm 1.58g   140.038, 129 Workshop - rm. 1
1409. 13mm 1.58g   144.009, 25 Well/ Fntn. - n. of Well
1410. 13mm 1.55g   320.061, 342 Shrine - rm. 1
1411. 13mm 1.48g   320.061, 332 Shrine - rm. 1
1412. 13mm 1.48g   140.056, no no. Workshop - rm. 1
1413. 13mm 1.43g[b] 510.047, 110 Shrine - rm. 1
1414. 13mm 1.18g   120.018, 428 Inn - rm. 4
1415. 13mm 1.16g   140.164, 324 Workshop - rm. 1
1416. 13mm 1.16g   271.234, 90 Inn - rm. 9
1417. 13mm 1.1g[f] 600.002, 93 Workshop - rm. 2
1418. 13mm 1.07g[b] 140.166, 345 Workshop - rm. 1
1419. 13mm 0.8g   607.236, 39 Casa del Chirurgo - rm. 2
1420. 12mm 2.03g   322.058, 274 Workshop - rm. 4
1421. 12mm 2.01g   182.049, 293 Inn - rm. 12   obv. faint traces of bust r.; rev.
                                                                 illeg.

1422. 12mm 2.00g   073.023, 47 Casa delle Vestali Bar - rm. 1
1423. 12mm 1.89g   223.024, 140 Inn - rm. 9
1424. 12mm 1.83g   161.005, 23 Inn - rm. 3
1425. 12mm 1.78g[b] 140.147, 210 Workshop - rm. 1
1426. 12mm 1.73g   510.024, 78 Shrine - rm. 1
1427. 12mm 1.71g   320.061, 358 Shrine - rm. 1
1428. 12mm 1.69g   009.002, 330 Workshop - rm. 1
1429. 12mm 1.67g   310.106, 252 Shrine - rm. 1
1430. 12mm 1.52g   271.234, 89 Inn - rm. 9
1431. 12mm 1.51g[b] 510.004, 31 Shrine - rm. 1
1432. 12mm 1.50g   323.047, 111 Bar of Acisculus - rm. 1
1433. 12mm 1.48g   320.061, 616 Shrine - rm. 1
1434. 12mm 1.43g   088.021, 325 Casa delle Vestali Bar - rm. 1 obv. illeg.; rev. standing
                                                                 figure?

1435. 12mm 1.37g   140.084, 143 Workshop - rm. 1
1436. 12mm 1.35g   320.074, 392 Shrine - rm. 1
1437. 12mm 1.33g[b] 166.064, 101 Inn Bar - rm. 5b
1438. 12mm 1.28g   140.027, 53 Workshop - rm. 1
1439. 12mm 1.28g   510.047, 106 Shrine - rm. 1
1440. 12mm 1.26g   510.024, 74 Shrine - rm. 1
1441. 12mm 1.23g   140.069, 140 Workshop - rm. 1   obv. ?bust r.; rev. illeg.
1442. 12mm 1.20g   065.038, 30 Casa delle Vestali - rm. 27
1443. 12mm 1.20g[b] 320.040, 140 Shrine - rm. 1

1444. 12mm 1.15g 180.020, 85 Inn - rm. 3
1445. 12mm 1.14g 261.043, 30 Casa del Chirurgo - rm. 10
1446. 12mm 1.1g   510.015, 126 Shrine - rm. 1
1447. 12mm 1.06g 140.027, 84 Workshop - rm. 1
1448. 12mm 1.06g 310.268, 525 Shrine - rm. 1
1449. 12mm 1.03g 320.061, 307 Shrine - rm. 1
1450. 12mm 0.94g^b 510.004, 23 Shrine - rm. 1
1451. 12mm 0.9g   503.086, 166 Workshop - rm. 2
1452. 12mm 0.87g 161.014, 70 Inn - rm. 3
1453. 12mm 0.62g^b 142.037, 105 Bar of Acisculus - rm. 2
1454. 12mm c. 0.5g 222.003, 0c Inn - rm. 9
1455. 12mm 0.37g^b 320.061, 303 Shrine - rm. 1
1456. 11mm 1.91g 310.164, 289 Shrine - rm. 1   obv. bust l.; rev. illeg.
1457. 11mm 1.72g 320.061, 357 Shrine - rm. 1
1458. 11mm 1.68g 127.057, 222 Inn Bar - rm. 1b
1459. 11mm 1.5g   510.050, 104 Shrine - rm. 1
1460. 11mm 1.48g 181.132, 71 Inn - rm. 9
1461. 11mm 1.43g 510.022, 52 Shrine - rm. 1
1462. 11mm 1.39g 311.050, 55 Workshop - rm. 4
1463. 11mm 1.29g^b 510.022, 47 Shrine - rm. 1
1464. 11mm 1.28g 120.037, 414 Inn - rm. 4   not a coin?
1465. 11mm 1.06g^b 510.024, 76 Shrine - rm. 1
1466. 11mm 1.04g 510.024, 77 Shrine - rm. 1
1467. 11mm 1.02g 320.061, 352 Shrine - rm. 1
1468. 11mm 0.95g 310.220, 658 Shrine - rm. 1
1469. 11mm 0.86g 140.147, 227 Workshop - rm. 1
1470. 11mm 0.47g 133.008, 85 Vicolo di Narciso - n. end   AR? obv. bust r.?; rev. illeg.
1471. 11mm -NR   205.000, 58 Vicolo di Narciso - nr. well & fountain
1472. 10mm 1.24g^f 320.074, 396 Shrine - rm. 1
1473. 10mm 0.99g 320.061, 621 Shrine - rm. 1
1474. 10mm 0.89g^b 323.002, 73 Bar of Acisculus - rm. 1
1475. 10mm 0.86g 510.022, 48 Shrine - rm. 1
1476. 10mm 0.75g 310.079, 192 Shrine - rm. 1
1477. 10mm 0.59g^f 510.004, 33 Shrine - rm. 1
1478. 10mm 0.21g 010.004, 75 Casa delle Vestali - rm. 15/53
1479. 9mm 0.99g   271.235, 263 Inn - rm. 9
1480. 9mm 0.39g   513.018, 80 Via Consolare - Inn area
1481. 10mm NR   601.036, 215 Workshop - rms. 5&3
1482. NR 24.15g   510.050, 79 Shrine - rm. 1
1483. NR 10.11g   033.004, 159 Casa delle Vestali - rm. 21
1484. NR 3.3g   600.033, 222 Workshop - rm. 2
1485. NR 3.27g^f 324.004, 52 Bar of Phoebus - rm. 1
1486. NR 2.69g   018.007, 343 Workshop - rm. 1
1487. NR 2.02g^f 510.028, 67 Shrine - rm. 1
1488. NR 2.10g^f 271.243, 230 Inn - rm. 9
1489. NR 1.77g^f 510.028, 69 Shrine - rm. 1
1490. NR 1.76g^f 510.034, 68 Shrine - rm. 1
1491. NR 1.67g^b 321.033, 118 Workshop - rm. 2
1492. NR 1.6g^f 510.015, 127 Shrine - rm. 1
1493. NR 1.46g^f 271.259, 360 Inn - rm. 9

1494. NR 1.40g^f 510.004, 30 Shrine - rm. 1
1495. NR 1.15g^f 510.028, 66 Shrine - rm. 1
1496. NR 1.14g^f 510.022, 59 Shrine - rm. 1
1497. NR c1g^f 311.229, 316 Workshop - rm. 4
1498. NR 0.83gf   510.022, 60 Shrine - rm. 1
1499. NR 0.7g^f 510.015, 122 Shrine - rm. 1
1500. NR 0.5g^f 502.054, 159 Bar of Acisculus - rm. 1
1501. NR 0.5g^f 510.043, 134 Shrine - rm. 1
1502. NR 0.54g^f 320.073, 557 Shrine - rm. 1
1503. NR 0.54g^f 320.088, 508 Shrine - rm. 1
1504. NR 0.53gf   320.088, 509 Shrine - rm. 1
1505. NR 0.2g^f 500.038, 148 Bar of Phoebus - rm. 1
1506. NR 0.2g^f 500.038, 149 Bar of Phoebus - rm. 1
1507. NR 0.2g^f 510.043, 123 Shrine - rm. 1
1508. NR 0.1g^f 500.030, 142 Bar of Phoebus - rm. 1
1509. NR 0.05g^f 500.038, 150 Bar of Phoebus - rm. 1
1510. NR NR   050.041, 200 Casa delle Vestali - rm. 19   powder only
1511. NR NR   123.042, 179 Inn - rm. 1
1512. NR NR   163.063, 75 Inn - rm. 8

APPENDIX 1

Table 17. Inn, Casa del Triclinio, Via Consolare (plots 9 & 10)

Description	Context	Phase	Date	Coins [cat. nos.] [Totals]	Other dating evidence	Comments
Phase 4 – early 2nd century BC						
Inn - rm. 12	182.117	4	early 2nd c BC	1 Ebusus TYPE 1 or 2 [561] [Total: 1]	no other dated material	
Inn Bar - Rm. 1b	127.082	4	early 2nd c BC	2 Massalia imports TYPE 2A [116, 123] & 1 possible imitation [146], 4 Mass. unclass. [182, 225, 261, 309], 1 Campanian Ebusus TYPE 1 [410], 1 Campanian Ebusus TYPE 2C [434], 1 Campanian Ebusus TYPE 8B [754], 3 illeg. [1302, 1363, 1376] [Total: 13]	no other dated material	possibly phase 4/5
Inn Bar - Rm. 1b	127.091	4	early 2nd c BC	2 Massalia import TYPE 1 [86, 89], 2 Massalia unclass. [181, 29] [Total: 4]	black-gloss ware (1st half 2nd c BC, lamp (4th – 3rd c BC)	
Phase 5 – pre 89 BC						
Inn - rm. 3	180.120	5	pre 89 BC	1 Ebusus TYPE 1 OR 2, an import [529] [Total: 1]	no other dated material	
Inn - rm. 3	180.015	5	pre 89 BC	1 Canusium, 250-225 BC (probably) [10], 1 Massalia TYPE 2 unclass. [168 – but as it's 14mm probably an import], 1 Ebusus import TYPE 2B [416], 1 Campanian Ebusus TYPE 2C [431], 1 Campanian Ebusus TYPE 2 unclass. [439], 1 Ebusus TYPE 1 OR 2 probable import [518], 1 Campanian Ebusus TYPE 1 OR 2 [601], 1 Campanian Ebusus TYPE 4A [734], 1 Repub. *as* [843] + 1 *triens* [908]+ 1 *sextans* [924]. c. 206-144 BC, 2 illeg. [1333, 1381] [Total: 13]	no other dated material	
Inn - rm. 3	180.116	5	pre 89 BC	1 Massalia TYPE 2 unclass. [195], 1 Campanian Ebusus TYPE 1 OR 2 [557] [Total: 2]	no other dated material	lowest fill of pit (180.017)
Inn - rm. 3	180.146	5	pre 89 BC	1 Ebusus import TYPE 1 OR 2 [453] [Total: 1]	no other dated material	
Inn - rm. 4	120.039	5	pre 89 BC	2 Campanian Ebusus, 1 3A [614] & 1 3C [637] [Total: 2]	no other dated material	

Description	Context	Phase	Date	Coins [cat. nos. / Totals]	Other dating evidence	Comments
Inn - rm. 4	120.051	5	pre 89 BC	1 Ebusus import TYPE 2B [419], 1 Ebusus unclass. [768], 1 cut Rep. quarter [1038], 1 illeg. [1307] [Total: 4]	no other dated material	
Inn - rm. 4	120.063	5	pre 89 BC	1 Campanian Ebusus TYPE 1 OR 2 [480] [Total: 1]	red-slip ware (prior AD 1-40; prior 10-1 BC)	
Inn - rm. 4	120.066	5	pre 89 BC	1 Massalia import TYPE 2A [107], 1 Campanian Ebusus TYPE 1 OR 2 [483], 1 AR illeg. [1323] [Total: 3]	red-slip ware, 3rd c. BC	
Inn - rm. 4	120.067	5	pre 89 BC	1 probable Ebusan import TYPE 1 OR 2 [487], 1 illegible [1365] [Total: 2]	no other dated material	
Inn - rm. 9	271.242	5	pre 89 BC	2 Campanian Ebusus TYPE 1 OR 2 [500, 573] [Total: 2]	no other dated material	
Inn - rm. 9	271.243	5	pre 89 BC	2 Massalia TYPE 2 unclass. [167, 324], 1 anomalous local TYPE 3B probable [379], 1 Ebusus import TYPE 2C [427], 1 Ebusus import TYPE 1 OR 2 [466]; 7 Ebusus TYPE 1 OR 2 [484, 488, 493, 506-07, 545, 549], 2 Campanian Ebusus TYPE 1 OR 2 [571, 589] 1 Campanian Ebusus TYPE 3 unclass. [721], 1 Ebusus import TYPE 4A [730] 1 Campanian Ebusus TYPE 8B [759], 2 Rep. *as* [832, 849], 1 Rep. *triens* [904], 6 illeg. [1209, 1262, 1316, 1319, 1390, 1488] [Total: 26]	cast glass	
Inn - rm. 9	271.250	5	pre 89 BC	1 Massalia import TYPE 2A [128]; 1 local TYPE 3A [374 – probable]; 1 Ebusus TYPE 1 OR 2 probably imports [464, 524, 526]; 1 Ebusus import TYPE 4A [731]; 1 Rep. *triens*, c. 206-144 BC [902] [Total: 7]	no other dated material	
Inn - rm. 9	271.259	5?	pre 89 BC	1 Cyrene, 220-140 BC [62], 2 Massalia TYPE 2 unclass. [250, 252], 1 anomalous local TYPE 1B [372], 1 Campanian Ebusus TYPE 1 OR 2 [592], 1 illeg. [1493] [Total: 6]	no other dated material	but may be phase 6
Inn Bar - rm. 1b	127.076	5	pre 89 BC	2 Ebusus coins, both probably Campanian Ebusus TYPE 1 OR 2 [481, 517] [Total: 2]	no other dated material	
Inn Bar - rm. 1b	127.078	5	pre 89 BC	1 Massalia import TYPE 1 [85]; 3 Massalia TYPE 2 unclass. [236, 305, 333]; deliberately cut Repub. quarter [1033]; 2 illeg. [1281, 1368] [Total: 7]	no other dated material	

Description	Context	Phase	Date	Coins [cat. nos.] [Totals]	Other dating evidence	Comments
Inn Bar - rm. 1b	127.089	5	pre 89 BC	1 Massalia import TYPE 2A [108] [Total: 1]	no other dated material	
Inn Bar - rm. 5b	166.063	5	pre 89 BC	1 Campanian Ebusus TYPE 3B [631] [Total: 1]	no other dated material	
Inn Bar - rms. 1b&3b	165.082	5 or 6	pre/post 89 BC	1 Ebusus import TYPE 2C [424], 1 probable Ebusus imports TYPE 1 OR 2 [534], 1 probable Campanian Ebusus TYPE 1 or 2 [546], 1 Rep. *as* 169-158 BC [786], 1 Rep. *sextans* [926], 1 illeg. [1212] [Total: 6]	no other dated material	probably phase 6 but could be late in phase 5

Phase 6 – mid to late 1st century BC

Description	Context	Phase	Date	Coins [cat. nos.] [Totals]	Other dating evidence	Comments
Inn Bar - rm. 1b	166.028	6	mid to late 1st c BC	1 Cyprus [71] [Total: 1]	blown glass c.4g (Augustus or later)	
Inn - rm. 1	123.038	6	mid to late 1st c BC	2 Campanian Ebusus TYPE 3C [646, 688], 1 Repub. *as* c. 206-144 BC [851] [Total: 3]	small amount of blown glass (c1g), 2 lead slingshot	
Inn - rm. 1	123.054	6	mid to late 1st c BC	1 Massalia import TYPE 2B [147; doubtful], a Repub. *triens*, c. 206-144 BC [910], 3 illeg. [1236, 1245, 1248] [Total: 5]	no other dated material	
Inn - rm. 1	123.056	6	mid to late 1st c BC	2 Massalia TYPE 2 unclass. [276, 335], 1 illeg. [1244] [Total: 3]	cast and blown glass	
Inn - rm. 1	123.061	6	mid to late 1st c BC	1 Massalia TYPE 2 unclass. [281], 1 Campanian Ebusus TYPE 3C [669] [Total: 2]	one lead slingshot	
Inn - rm. 3	161.016	6	mid to late 1st c BC	1 Campanian Ebusus TYPE 8B (but doubtful) [752], 1 *as*, c. 206-144 BC [873], 1 cut quarter [1029] [Total: 3]	one lead slingshot	
Inn - rm. 3	180.131	6	mid to late 1st c BC	1 Campanian Ebusus TYPE 1 OR 2 [513] [Total: 1]	no other dated material	
Inn - rm. 3	180.001	6	mid to late 1st c BC	2 Massalia TYPE 2 unclass. [214, 224], 1 Ebusus import TYPE 1 [391], 1 probable Campanian Ebusus TYPE 1 OR 2 [523], 1 halved *as*, c. 206-144 BC [992] [Total: 5]	one lead slingshot, one ballista ball	
Inn - rm. 3	180.003	6	mid to late 1st c BC	1 Campanian Ebusus TYPE 3 unclass. [705], 1 illeg. [1251] [Total: 2]	two lead slingshot	

Description	Context	Phase	Date	Coins [cat. nos./ Totals]	Other dating evidence	Comments
Im - rm. 3	180.008	6	mid to late 1st c BC	1 Massalia import TYPE 2A [137], 1 Ebusus import TYPE 1 OR 2 [497], 1 Campanian Ebusus TYPE 1 OR 2 [528], 1 illeg. [1315] [Total: 4]	two lead slingshot	
Im - rm. 3	180.020	6	mid to late 1st c BC	1 probable Campanian Ebusus TYPE 1 OR 2 [504], 2 illeg. [1352, 1444] [Total: 3]	no other dated material	
Im - rm. 3	180.021	6	mid to late 1st c BC	1 Campanian Ebusus TYPE 3 unclass. [704] [Total: 1]	no other dated material	
Im - rm. 3	161.014	6	mid to late 1st c BC	1 Megara [39], 1 Volcae Arecomici, c. 70-30 BC [49], 4 Rep. as, c. 206-144 BC [842, 846, 855, 869], 4 delib. halved as, c. 206-144 BC [936, 953, 968, 980], 1 deliberately cut ?1/8th [1039], 1 Aug., c. 15 BC [1058], 1 illeg. [1452] [Total: 13]	some blown glass	
Im - rm. 4	120.044	6	mid to late 1st c BC	1 Massalia TYPE 2 unclass. [280], 1 AE Rep. uncia, c.214-212 BC [777], 1 Rep. as, 169-158 BC [789; possibly], 1 Rep. triens [911], 1 illeg. [1201] [Total: 5]	10 lead slingshot	
Im - rm. 4	120.050	6	mid to late 1st c BC	1 Campanian Ebusus TYPE 1 OR 2 [595], 1 illeg. (but prob. Ebusus [1360]) [Total: 2]	no other dated material	
Im - rm. 4	120.037	6	mid to late 1st c BC	1 Rhegion, c260-215 BC? [25], 1 Ebusus import TYPE 1 OR 2 [495], 1 cut as [948], 1 illeg. [1464] [Total: 4]	Italian sigillata & Vesuvian red-slip ware (c3rd BC; 30 BC+)	
Im - rm. 6	121.028	6	mid to late 1st c BC	1 Epidamnos [38], 1 Hisp./Carth., 2nd c BC? [54], 1 Rep. denarius, late 3rd BC [782; possible] [Total: 3]	Itallian sigillata & Vesuvian red-slip ware (AD 25+); blown glass, one lead slingshot	
Im - rm. 6	121.033	6	mid to late 1st c BC	1 Massalia TYPE 2 unclass. [258], 1 Rep. semis [896] [Total: 2]	no other dated material	
Im - rm. 6	121.091	6	mid to late 1st c BC	1 Campanian Ebusus TYPE 3C [693] [Total: 1]	no other dated material	
Im - rm. 8	163.024	6	mid to late 1st c BC	1 probable Campanian Ebusus TYPE 1 OR 2 [543], 1 AR rep. quin. 90 BC [807], 1 illeg. [1349] [Total: 3]	no other dated material	
Im - rm. 9	181.179	6	mid to late 1st c BC	1 Ebusus TYPE 1 OR 2 [486], 1 Rep. triens [907], 1 illeg. [1394] [Total: 3]	no other dated material	

Description	Context	Phase	Date	Coins [cat. nos.] [Totals]	Other dating evidence	Comments
Inn - rm. 9	271.234	6	mid to late 1st c BC	1 Neapolis, c. 275-250 BC [3], 1 Massalia TYPE 2 VARIANT [165], 4 Massalia TYPE 1 OR 2 unclass. [230, 310, 320, 347], 1 anomalous local TYPE 3B [378], 1 anomalous local horse head uncertain [381], 1 Ebusus TYPE 1 OR 2 [470], 4 Campanian Ebusus TYPE 1 OR 2 [566, 578, 599, 612], 1 Campanian Ebusus TYPE 3A [623], 2 Campanian Ebusus TYPE 3C [677, 696], 1 Campanian Ebusus TYPE 3 unclass. [725], 1 Campanian Ebusus TYPE 4A [733 – but doubtful], 1 Campanian Ebusus TYPE 8B [760], 1 Rep. *triens* [913], 9 illeg. [1204, 1213, 1237, 1326, 1333, 1354, 1388, 1416, 1430] [Total: 29]	cast and blown glass, 9 lead slingshot	
Inn - rm. 9	271.235	6	mid to late 1st c BC	2 Massalia imports TYPE 2A [132, 143], 1 Campanian Massalia Type 2C [159], 2 Massalia unclass. TYPE 2 [199, 339], 1 Ebusus import TYPE 1 [387], 1 Ebusus import TYPE 1 OR 2 [451], 1 Campanian Ebusus TYPE 1 OR 2 [594], 1 AR rep. *quin.*, 89 BC [809], 1 Rep. quad. [923], 2 Rep. cut half [935, 963], 1 illeg. [1479] [Total: 13]	cast and blown glass (c7g), 2 lamps (1 Buccero, c 4th – 3rd c BC, and 1 c170-150 BC), 17 lead slingshot	
Inn - rm. 9	271.263	6	mid to late 1st c BC	1 Massalia TYPE 2 unclass. [247], 1 Ebusus import TYPE 1 [386] [Total: 2]	7 lead slingshot	
Inn - rm. 9	271.254	6	mid to late 1st c BC	1 Campanian Ebusus TYPE 1 OR 2 [597] [Total: 1]	no other dated material	
Inn - rm. 9	222.003	6	mid to late 1st c BC	1 Massalia TYPE 2 unclass. [361], 1 Campanian Ebusus 3A [618], 1 prob. Bes [767], 1 Rep. as 152 BC [794], 1 illeg. [1454] [Total: 5]	Italian sigillata, Vesuvian red-slip ware, blown glass (0.3g), 1 lead slingshot	
Inn - rm. 10	164.014	6	mid to late 1st c BC	1 Campanian Ebusus probable TYPE 1 OR 2 [547], 1 Campanian Ebusus TYPE 5 [744] [Total: 2]	c.0.7g blown glass	

Description	Context	Phase	Date	Coins [cat. nos./Totals]	Other dating evidence	Comments
Inn - rm. 12	182.016	6	mid to late 1st c BC	1 Massalia TYPE 2 unclass. [312], 2 Ebusus import TYPE 1 OR 2 [462], 1 Campanian Ebusus TYPE 1 OR 2 probable [510] [Total: 3]	c.2.7g blown glass, 3 lead slingshot	
Inn - rm. 12	182.030	6	mid to late 1st c BC	3 Campanian Ebusus TYPE 1 OR 2 [454, 458, 553], 1 Campanian Ebusus TYPE 3B [630], 2 Campanian Ebusus TYPE 3C [656, 667], 4 illeg. [1218, 1225, 1336, 1399] [Total: 10]	59 lead slingshot	
Inn - rm. 12	182.109	6	mid to late 1st c BC	1 Massalia (unclass.) [350], 1 Campanian Ebusus TYPE 1 OR 2 [461], 1 halved Rep. as [1022] [Total: 3]	no other dated material	
Inn - rm. 12	182.114	6	mid to late 1st c BC	1 Massalia TYPE 2 unclass. [235] [Total: 1]	5 lead slingshot	
Inn - rm. 12	182.011	6	mid to late 1st c BC	1 Massalia TYPE 2 variant [164] [Total: 1]	c7g cast and blown glass	
Inn bar - rm. 4b	225.035	6	mid to late 1st c BC	1 Ebusus import TYPE 2C [425], 1 halved Rep. as [981] [Total: 2]	Vesuvian red-slip ware, early 1st c AD	
Inn bar - rm. 6b	126.028	6	mid to late 1st c BC	1 Massalia TYPE 2 unclass. [202] [Total: 1]	no other dated material	
Inn bar - rm. 6b	126.052	6	mid to late 1st c BC	1 Massalia TYPE 2 unclass. [227] [Total: 1]	no other dated material	
Casa del Triclinio, ramp	270.032	6	mid to late 1st c BC	1 Ebusus TYPE 1 OR 2 [460] [Total: 1]	no other dated material	
Via Consolare	509.012	6	mid to late 1st c BC	1 probable Campanian Ebusus TYPE 1 OR 2 [535] [Total: 1]	blown glass (c 4g)	
Inn bar - rm. 1b	127.032	6 to 7	mid 1st c BC to mid 1st c AD	1 Cyrene [56], 1 Campanian Ebusus TYPE 1 OR 2 [607] [Total: 2]	no other dated material	
Inn bar - rm. 1b	127.050	6 to 7	mid 1st c BC to mid 1st c AD	1 Cyrene [67], 1 illeg. [1240] [Total: 2]	small quantity of blown glass	

Description	Context	Phase	Date	Coins [cat. nos./ Totals]	Other dating evidence	Comments
Phase 7 (late Augustus to mid 1st century AD)						
Inn – rm. 1	123.017	7	late Aug to mid c 1st AD	2 Campanian Ebusus TYPE 3C [642, 689], 1 Rep. cut *as* [969] [Total: 3]	Vesuvian red-slip ware (AD 41-68), small quantity of blown glass	
Inn – rm. 1	123.019	7	late Aug to mid c 1st AD	1 Massalia TYPE 2 unclass. [198], 1 Campanian Ebusus TYPE 3A [617], 1 Campanian Ebusus TYPE 3C [684], 1 probable Rep. *den.* 121 BC [804], 1 illeg. [1273] [Total: 5]	Vesuvian red-slip ware, c26g blown glass	equals 123.024
Inn – rm. 1	123.024	7	late Aug to mid c 1st AD	1 Siracusa, c. 275-215 BC [35], 1 Campanian Ebusus TYPE 3C [660], 1 Campanian Ebusus TYPE 3 unclass. [709], 1 Rep. cut half [976] [Total: 4]	Vesuvian red-slip ware, cast glass, 1 lead slingshot	
Inn – rm. 1	160.042	7	late Aug to mid c 1st AD	1 Cyrene, c. 220-140 BC [55], 1 Campanian Ebusus TYPE 1 OR 2 [568], 1 Rep. *quadrans* [920] [Total: 3]	blown glass (c5.5g)	
Inn – rm. 3	161.013	7	late Aug to mid c 1st AD	1 halved Repub. *as* [983], 1 Aug. 15 BC [1055] [Total: 2]	no other dated material	
Inn – rm. 3	180.135	7	late Aug to mid c 1st AD	1 Campanian Ebusus TYPE 2B OR 2C [440] [Total: 1]	no other dated material	
Inn – rm. 3	180.010	7	late Aug to mid c 1st AD	1 AR Repub. *den.*, 115-114 BC [805] [Total: 1]	no other dated material	
Inn – rm. 3	120.015	7	late Aug to mid c 1st AD	1 Aug. 15 BC [1053] [Total: 1]	Italian sigillata, Vesuvian red-slip ware (10 BC-AD 54), cast and blown glass (c21g), 2 lead slingshot	
Inn – rm. 6	121.051	7	late Aug to mid c 1st AD	1 Aug. AD 8-10 [1107] [Total: 1]	no other dated material	
Inn – rm. 4	120.016	7	late Aug to mid c 1st AD	1 probable Cyprus/Ptolemy [69], 2 Campanian Ebusus TYPE 3 unclass. [710, 717], 2 Rep. *as* [844, 847], 2 Rep. cut halves [938, 1000], 1 Rep. cut quarter [1035], 1 Tib. AD 22-23 [1123], 1 Claud. AD 50-54 imitation? [1179], 1 illeg. [1290] [Total: 11]	Vesuvian red-slip ware (prior 10 BC; prior 1-40 AD), cast and large quantity of blown glass (c21g)	

Description	Context	Phase	Date	Coins [cat. nos./Totals]	Other dating evidence	Comments
Inn - rm. 4	120.018	7	late Aug to mid c 1st AD	1 Massalia TYPE 2 unclass. [286], 1 Campanian Massalia TYPE 3 [369], 1 Campanian Ebusus TYPE 1 OR 2 [565], 2 illeg. [1206, 1414] [Total: 5]	Italian sigillata and Vesuvian red-slip ware (140-130 BC; AD 1-40; 20 BC-; AD 10-45), cast and blown glass (c18g), 32 lead slingshot	
Inn - rm. 9	181.132	7	late Aug to mid c 1st AD	1 Campanian Ebusus TYPE 3C [657], 1 illeg. [1460] [Total: 2]	1 lead slingshot	
Inn - rm. 9	222.004	7	late Aug to mid c 1st AD	1 halved Rep. fraction [1013] [Total: 1]	no other dated material	
Inn - rm. 9	222.011	7	late Aug to mid c 1st AD	2 Campanian Ebusus TYPE 1 OR 2 [574, 576], 1 Rep. as 153 BC [793], 2 Rep. as [852, 876], 1 Rep. semuncia, local imitation [931] [Total: 6]	Italian Sigillata, Vesuvian red-slip ware (prior to AD 1-40; 50 BC- early 1st c AD; AD 41-68; AD 1-50), blown glass (c 20g), 5 lead slingshot	
Inn - rm. 9	222.002	7	late Aug to mid c 1st AD	1 Paestum, late 2nd/early 1st BC? [11], 1 Massalia TYPE 2 unclass. [238], 1 illeg. [1297] [Total: 3]	Italian sigillata and Vesuvian red-slip ware (AD 41-68); blown glass (c 1.5g), 1 lead slingshot	
Inn - rm. 9	222.012	7	late Aug to mid c 1st AD	1 Campanian Ebusus probable TYPE 1 OR 2 [508], 1 Campanian Ebusus TYPE 3C [665], 1 Campanian Ebusus TYPE 3 unclass. [722], 2 halved Rep. asses [957, 996], 1 Octavian/Aug. 38 BC ?imitation [1043], 1 illeg. [1301] [Total: 7]	Vesuvian red-slip ware, prior to AD 1-40; blown glass (c3g)	
Inn - rm. 9	222.014	7	late Aug to mid c 1st AD	1 coin, Campanian Ebusus TYPE 3C [674] [Total: 1]	Italian sigillata	
Inn - rm. 9	223.007	7	late Aug to mid c 1st AD	1 Massalia import TYPE 2A [120], 1 Massalia TYPE 2 unclass. [307], 1 Campanian Ebusus TYPE 2 unclass. [572], 1 AR den. late 3rd BC [780], 1 Rep. AR undated [823], 1 halved Rep. as [989], 1 illeg. [1396] [Total: 7]	lamps, late 1st BC/early 1st AD, blown glass (c17g), one lead slingshot	
Inn Bar - rm. 1b	127.020	7	late Aug to mid c 1st AD	1 probable Ebusus import TYPE 1 OR 2 [482], 1 Campanian Ebusus TYPE 3C [695], 1 Aug. 9 BC [1070], 1 Gaius, AD 37-41 [1143] [Total: 4]	no other dated material	

Description	Context	Phase	Date	Coins [cat. nos.] [Totals]	Other dating evidence	Comments
Inn Bar - rm. 1b	127.057	7	late Aug to mid c 1st AD	2 Massalia TYPE 2 unclass. [268, 362], 1 Ebusus TYPE 1 OR 2 [485], 1 Ebusus import TYPE 1 OR 2 [490], 1 Ebusus unclass. [765], 1 Rep. cut half [977], 2 illeg. [1292, 1458] [Total: 8]	blown glass (c0.5g)	
Inn Bar - rm. 1b	127.059	7	late Aug to mid c 1st AD	1 Aug. 8 BC [1079], 1 illeg. [1320] [Total: 2]	some cast glass	equals 127.057
Inn Bar - rms. 1b&3b	165.017	7	late Aug to mid c 1st AD	1 Tib. AD 22-23 [1131] [Total: 1]	blown glass (c1.5g)	
Inn Bar - rms. 1b&3b	165.008	7	late Aug to mid c 1st AD	1 halved Repub. as [998], 1 Tib. AD 22-23 [1121], 1 Gaius [AD 37-38] [1147] [Total: 3]	cast and blown glass (c12g), 1 lead slingshot	equals 165.012
Inn Bar - rms. 1b&3b	165.012	7	late Aug to mid c 1st AD	1 possible Rhegion, 260-215 BC? [29], 1 Ebusus import TYPE 1 [392], 1 Ebusus import TYPE 1 OR 2 [489], 1 Rep. quadrans, c. 146-100 BC [929], 2 Rep. halved as [966, 1001], 1 probable Tib. AD 21-22 [1115], 4 illeg. [1252, 1286, 1362, 1364] [Total: 11]	blown glass (c35g)	equals 165.008
Inn Bar - rms. 1b&3b	126.022	7	late Aug to mid c 1st AD	1 Claudius, AD 41-50 [1174] [Total: 1]	small quantity of blown glass	
Inn Bar - rm. 4b	225.022	7	late Aug to mid c 1st AD	Campanian Ebusus TYPE 3A [624] [Total: 1]	no other dated material	
Casa del Triclinio - rm. 1	168.100	7	late Aug to mid c 1st AD	1 Rep. semis, c206-144 BC [895] [Total: 1]	some blown glass	
Casa del Triclinio - rm. 4	272.017	7	late Aug to mid c 1st AD	1 Massalia import TYPE 2A [118] [Total: 1]	small quantity of blown glass (c0.4g)	
Casa del Triclinio, ramp	270.018	7	late Aug to mid c 1st AD	1 Massalia TYPE 2 unclass. [166] [Total: 1]	no other dated material	
Casa del Triclinio, ramp	270.036	7	late Aug to mid c 1st AD	1 Neapolis c.275-250 BC [2] [Total: 1]	cast & blown glass (c22g)	

Description	Context	Phase	Date	Coins [cat. nos.] [Totals]	Other dating evidence	Comments
Via Consolare	513.029	7	late Aug to mid c 1st AD	1 Paestum, AD 14-37 [19] [Total: 1]	no other dated material	
Via Consolare	513.041	7	late Aug to mid c 1st AD	1 Massalia import TYPE 2A [112], 1 Repub. halved *as* [945] [Total: 2]	no other dated material, but a significant amount of iron slag, charcoal, ceramic, brick & tile, and a gaming piece	
Inn - rm. 1	123.042	8	AD 62+	1 Campanian Ebusus TYPE 3 unclass. [726], 2 illeg. [1296, 1511] [Total: 3]	no other dated material	
Inn - rm. 6	121.059	8	AD 62+	1 Claud. AD 41-50 [1172] [Total: 1]	no other dated material	
Inn - rm. 12	169.003	8	AD 62+	1 Massalia TYPE 2 unclass. [265], 1 illeg. [1263] [Total: 2]	cast and blown glass (c.1g)	
Inn - rm. 12	169.005	8	AD 62+	1 Aug., 8 BC [1080], 1 Tib. AD 21-22 [1119] [Total: 2]	cast glass	
Inn bar - rms. 1b&3b	165.006	8	AD 62+	1 Titus, AD 73 [1188]	no other dated material	
Inn bar - rms. 1b&3b	165.009	8	AD 62+	1 Tib., AD 21-22 [1116], 1 Claud. AD 41-50 [1171], 1 Claud. AD 50-54 [1176] [Total: 3]	blown glass (c.5.7g)	
Inn bar - rm. 5B	166.006	8	AD 62+	1 Nero, AD 66-67 [1185] [Total: 1]	blown glass (c.18g)	
Casa del Triclinio - ramp	185.008	8	AD 62+	1 Rep. *as*, 206-144 BC [831], 2 illeg. [1189, 1200] [Total: 3]	blown glass (c.17g)	
Casa del Triclinio - ramp	185.013	8	AD 62+	1 Rep. AR, undated [821], 3 illeg. [1190, 1191, 1220] [Total: 4]	very large quantity of blown glass (c286g)	
Casa del Triclinio - ramp	270.017	8	AD 62+	1 probable halved Aug., c 27 BC – AD 14 [1048], 1 possible Aug., 15 BC [1056] [Total: 2]	blown glass (c.3g)	
Via Consolare	226.013	8	AD 62+	1 Rhegion, 1st c BC? [30]	Italian sigillata and blown glass	

Table 18. Casa del Chirurgo (plots 5-6)

Description	Context	Phase	Date	Coins [cat. nos.]	Other dating evidence	Comments
Phase 3 (c200 BC – 150 BC)						
Casa del Chirurgo - rms. 3&4	277.036	3	c200 BC – 150 BC	1 Neapolis coin, c. 250-225 BC? [5] [Total: 1]	no other dated material	
Casa del Chirurgo - rms. 3&4	277.156	3	c200 BC – 150 BC	1 Republican *uncia* c. 214-212 BC [774] [Total: 1]	no other dated material	
Casa del Chirurgo - rm. 5	275.038	3	c200 BC – 150 BC	1 Campanian Ebusus TYPE 1 OR 2 [567] [Total: 1]	no other dated material	
Casa del Chirurgo - rms. 17&18	612.027	3	c200 BC – 150 BC	1 Massalia import TYPE 2A [114] [Total: 1]	Vesuvian red-slip ware, 2nd to 1st c BC	
Phase 4 (c100 BC)						
No coins.						
Phase 5 (late 1ˢᵗ c BC to early 1ˢᵗ c AD)						
Casa del Chirurgo rms. 3&4	277.065	5	late 1st c BC to early 1st c AD	1 Campanian Ebusus TYPE 3 unclass. [707] [Total: 1]	Vesuvian red-slip. ware c. 10 BC+	
Casa del Chirurgo rms. 3&4	277.085	5	late 1st c BC to early 1st c AD	1 Tiberius AD 22-23 [1132], 1 Claudius, AD 42 [1166] [Total: 2]	Italian sigillata	
Casa del Chirurgo rm. 6c	184.009	5	late 1st c BC to early 1st c AD	1 Campanian Massalia TYPE 2C [154], 1 Campanian Ebusus TYPE 3C [647] [Total: 2]	no other dated material	
Casa del Chirurgo rm. 11	265.085	5	late 1st c BC to early 1st c AD	1 uncertain bust/crab [36], 1 Massalia TYPE 2 unclass. [241] [Total: 2]	Italian sigiliata & Vesuvian red-slip ware to early 1st AD	
Casa del Chirurgo – rm. 12	610.026	5	late 1st cBC to early 1st c AD	1 Paestum, AD 14-37 [17] [Total: 1]	Vesuvian red-slip ware	
Casa del Chirurgo rm. 13	613.024	5	late 1st c BC to early 1st c AD	1Campanian Ebusus TYPE 1 OR 2 [531] [Total: 1]		

Description	Context	Phase	Date	Coins [cat. nos.]	Other dating evidence	Comments
Casa del Chirurgo rms. 17&18	612.019	5	late 1st c BC to early 1st c AD	1 Campanian Ebusus TYPE 1 OR 2 [560] [Total: 1]	blown glass	

Phase 6 (early to mid 1st century AD)

Description	Context	Phase	Date	Coins [cat. nos.]	Other dating evidence	Comments
Casa del Chirurgo – rms. 3-4	277.038	6	early to mid 1st c AD	1 Augustus, c. 10-5 BC [1062] [Total: 1]	small quantity of blown glass (c.0.6g)	
Casa del Chirurgo – rm. 5	260.012	6	early to mid 1st c AD	1 Rep. quadrans, c. 206-144 BC [918] [Total: 1]	Italian sigillata, Vesuvian red-slip c. 100 BC, cast & blown glass (c.0.5g)	
Casa del Chirurgo - rm. 6c	184.008	6	early to mid 1st c AD	1 Campanian Ebusus TYPE 3C [645] [Total: 1]	no other dated material	
Casa del Chirurgo – rms. 17&18	612.017	6	early to mid 1st c AD	2 Octavian, c. 9 BC [1066, 1069] [Total: 2]	Italian sigillata and Vesuvian red-slip ware, prior to 40 BC to c. AD 40, blown glass (c 6g)	
Casa del Chirurgo rms. 17&18	612.022	6	early to mid 1st c AD	1 Ebusus import TYPE 2C [426] [Total: 1]	no other dated material	
Casa del Chirurgo rms. 17&18	612.023	6	early to mid 1st c AD	1 Massalia TYPE 2 unclass. [176], 1 Campanian Ebusus TYPE 2B [423], 1 Campanian Ebusus TYPE 3 unclass. [724] [Total: 3]	Itallian sigillata, Vesuvian red-slip ware, cast & blown glass	
Casa del Chirurgo shop – rm. 2	507.032	6	early to mid 1st c AD	1 AE Aug. c. 9 BC [1074] [Total: 1]	no other dated material	
Casa del Chirurgo shop – rm. 2	507.072	6	early to mid 1st c AD	1 AE Claud. cAD 41-50 [1169] [Total: 1]	Italian sigillata and Vesuvian red-slip ware (AD 1-20), large quantity of blown glass (c14g)	
Casa del Chirurgo shop – rm. 2	507.078	6	early to mid 1st c AD	1 AE Claud. cAD 42 [1168] [Total: 1]	Italian sigillata, blown glass (c.1.5g)	
Casa del Chirurgo shop - rm. 2	507.080	6	early to mid 1st c AD	1 Campanian Ebusus TYPE 3C [686] [Total: 1]		

Description	Context	Phase	Date	Coins [cat. nos.]	Other dating evidence	Comments
Phase 7 (post AD 62)						
Casa del Chirurgo - rms. 5&8A	505.008	7	post AD 62	1 Cyrenaica, c220-140 BC [61] [Total: 1]	Italian sigillata & blown glass	
Casa del Chirurgo - rm. 6c	184.006	7	post AD 62	1 Campanian Ebusus TYPE 3B [633] [Total: 1]	no other dated material	
Casa del Chirurgo - rm. 11	265.004	7	post AD 62	1 Aug. 7 BC [1083] [Total: 1]	Italian sigillata & blown glass (c2g)	
Casa del Chirurgo - rm. 23	262.008	7	post AD 62	1 Campanian Ebusus TYPE 3B [635] [Total: 1]	blown glass (c0.8g)	
Casa del Chirurgo - rm. 23	262.009	7	post AD 62	1 Rep. *triens* c. 206-144 BC [900] [Total: 1]	Italian sigillata and Vesuvian red-slip ware (270 BC; prior to 10-1 BC; 27 BC-AD 1; 20 BC +; AD 1-40), cast and blown glass (c0.1g)	

Table 19. The Shrine (plot 4)

Context[1]	Phasing	Date range	Coins [cat. nos.] [Totals]	Other dating evidence	Context characteristics	Notes
Phases 2 to 3 – mid 2ⁿᵈ c BC to early 1ˢᵗ c BC						
320.050	2-3?	Mid 2ⁿᵈ BC to early 1ˢᵗ BC	1 illeg. [1329] [Total: 1]		Loose slightly rubbly fill, possibly of a robbery cut in Room B.	Before tanks, but very tenuous phase attribution.
Phase 3 – late 2ⁿᵈ c BC to early 1ˢᵗ c BC						
310.088	3	Late 2ⁿᵈ to early 1ˢᵗ BC	2 Massalia TYPE 2 unclass. [271, 336] [Total: 2]		A rough soil accumulation in Room B, south of wall 310.013, which dates to phase 3a. (See comments on 310.037).	
310.215	3?	Late 2ⁿᵈ to early 1ˢᵗ BC	1 Rep. *quad.*, c146-100 BC [930] [Total: 1]		Hard packed floor surface on the sidewalk which covers the tank 'extension' and also seems to underlay the samo blocks which are purported to be from the original frontage in this area – very uncertain.	
Phases 3-4 – late 2ⁿᵈ c BC to post Sulla						
510.016	3-4	Late 2ⁿᵈ to post Sulla	1 Campanian Ebusus TYPE 9 [762] [Total: 1]	vessel glass: end C1 BC+	Contained in room B in the east of the shrine (Room D) abutting SUs 510.005-010. Compacted silty sand.	Probably phase 4.
510.050	3-4	Late 2ⁿᵈ to post Sulla	2 illeg. [1459, 1482] [Total: 2]		The fill of the second amphora in Room B.	
320.025	3-4?	Late 2ⁿᵈ c BC to post Sulla	1 possible Ebusus import TYPE 1 or 2 [512]; 2 Aug. 6-4 BC [1091, 1098] [Total: 3]	vessel glass: AD 25+	Pale grey brown silty sand found in the Room A under 320.011. Deposit also contained high status glass and much metalwork. Probably a deliberate levelling deposit for set stone underfloor (320.002).	More likely to be Phase 3, but very tenuous, not much information to go on for this deposit

[1] All contexts come from Room 1 of the Shrine (see Figure 11).

Context	Phasing	Date range	Coins [cat. nos.] [Totals]	Other dating evidence	Context characteristics	Notes
320.074, 320.117	3-4?	Late 2nd c BC to post Sulla	1 Massalia import TYPE 2 [110]; 1 Massalia TYPE 2 unclass. [322]; 2 Campanian Ebusus TYPE 1 or 2 [537, 596]; 1 Campanian Ebusus TYPE 4B [741]; 1 Rep. as, 147 BC [802]; 1 Aug. 8-10 AD [1108]; 6 illeg. [1243, 1327, 1374, 1404, 1436, 1472] [Total: 13]		Fill deposit in plaster lined tank 320.095 in west side of Room B.	Very tenuous.
Phases 3 to 5 – late 2nd c BC to early imperial						
310.106	3-5	Late 2nd to early imperial	1 Massalia TYPE 2 unclass. [203]; 1 Aug. c. 9 BC [1072]; 1 illeg. [1429] [Total: 3]	vessel glass: 1st quarter of 1st c AD	One of a series of deposits excavated in the north back room (Rooms B/E), a dark grey floor surface in the SE area between walls 310.096 & 310.071. This area seems to have been a kind of corridor, with these two walls acting as a 'pedestrian funnel'. This is one of a number of such deposits which seem more like random dumps of material than formal floor surfaces. Back room suggested as some kind of service quarter.	Probably phase 4 but could have been present from after the decommissioning of tank E up until after the reorganisation of the space into the shrine.
310.116	3-5	Late 2nd c BC to early imperial	1 Tib. AD 22-23 [1128]; 1 Claud. AD 50-54 [1178]; 1 illeg. [1205] [Total: 3]		A dark greyish brown packed earth surface, the 'earliest decent floor surface in the south room' (Rooms B/E). Lies adjacent to 310.106 so is contemporary with it.	Probably phase 4, but could have been present from after the decommissioning of tank E up until the reorganisation of the space into the shrine.
310.117	3-5	Late 2nd c BC to early imperial	1 Judaea, 6 BC-AD 11 [74] [Total: 1]	vessel glass: end C1 BC+	Loose grey artefact rich soil deposit probably under 310.106 in NW corner of back room (Room E). Considered to be a dump of domestic/hearth debris, but the stratigraphy is problematic.	Probably phase 4

Context	Phasing	Date range	Coins [cat. nos,] [Totals]	Other dating evidence	Context characteristics	Notes
310.223	3-5	Late 2nd c BC to early imperial	1 Massalia TYPE 2 unclass. [237] [Total: 1]		Fill of 310.224, a vestigial cut between cisterns SU80 and SU75 (Room B).	Probably phase 4, probably the same deposit as 310.116.
510.023	3-5	Late 2nd c BC to early imperial	1 Massalia TYPE 2 unclass. [290]; 1 Campanian Ebusus TYPE 4B [740] [Total: 2]		A circular clod of hard packed earth with vertically set ceramics. Very similar material to 510.022. Room B.	Probably phase 5 (see above)
510.024	3-5	Late 2nd c BC to early imperial	1 Rhegion, 1st c BC [31]; 1 Massalia TYPE 2 unclass. [349]; 1 Ebusus import TYPE 2B [415]; 4 illeg. [1426, 1440, 1465-66] [Total: 7]		Underlies 510.022 & 510.023. Mixed rubble, ceramic and plaster, a loom weight, some carbonised seeds & shells (so an occupation deposit, no?). Room B	Probably Phase 5 (see above)
510.042	3-5	Late 2nd c BC to early imperial	1 Massalia TYPE 2 unclass. [267] [Total: 1]		A rubble and soil deposit in cut which follows the line of the sarno and black lava wall (510.017 – the main wall which 1st divides the space, on a NW/SE alignment, parallel to Via Consolare; seems to be of very early construction, if not the earliest; seems to overly the large rubble packing of the soakaway (510.047). Room B.	Probably phase 4
510.047, 510.051	3-5	Late 2nd c BC to early imperial	1 Massalia TYPE 2A [144];1 Campanian Ebusus TYPE 1 or 2 [605]; 1 Rep. *as* [856]; 3 illeg. [1325, 1405, 1413, 1439] [Total: 7]		A soakaway next to the wall (510.017), consisting of large rocks, pebbles and soil. Room B.	Probably phase 3 but very tenuous

Phase 4 – post Sulla

Context	Phasing	Date range	Coins [cat. nos,] [Totals]	Other dating evidence	Context characteristics	Notes
310.220	4	Post Sulla	1 ?Vibo Valentia [24]; 2 Massalia TYPE 2A [97, 106]; 9 Massalia TYPE 2 unclass. [190, 194, 200, 207, 213, 221, 245, 264, 301]; 2 Campanian Ebusus TYPE 1 or 2 [548, 606]; 1 Campanian Ebusus TYPE 8B [756]; 1 illeg. [1468] [Total: 16]		Light grey rubbly fill of the lime slaking tank 310.202. This layer overlies 310.082. This layer produced large pot sherds. Room E.	Fill of tank E, thus after its decommissioning

Context	Phasing	Date range	Coins [cat. nos.] [Totals]	Other dating evidence	Context characteristics	Notes
310.090	4	Post Sulla	3 Massalia TYPE 2A [100, 103, 129]; 4 Massalia TYPE 2 unclass. [173, 296, 299, 321]; 1 Ebusus TYPE 1 or 2 ?import [465]; 2 Campanian Ebusus TYPE 1 or 2 [603, 608]; 1 Campanian Ebusus TYPE 4B var. [742]; 1 Rep. *triens* [915] [Total: 12]		This is also another fill of the lime-slaking tank (310.202) in Room E, beneath 310.082, a brownish layer towards the base of the tank. Overlies 310.089, which did not produce any coins.	Fill of tank, thus after its decommissioning.
310.082	4	Post Sulla	3 Massalia TYPE 2A [124, 126, 140]; 6 Massalia TYPE 2 unclass. [172, 218, 223, 233, 246, 275]; 1 anomalous local TYPE 6 [384] [Total: 10]		Silty sand, loose soil, with lots of charcoal and pottery, bones brick and tile. One of the fills of the stone built lime-slaking tank in Room E (310.202) which had been cut into the natural gritty green sand (310.264).	Fill of tank, thus after its decommissioning.
310.087	4	Post Sulla	1 Cyrene [64]; 1 Massalia TYPE 2A [117]; 3 Massalia TYPE 2 unclass. [191, 192, 196]; 1 Campanian Ebusus TYPE 1 or 2 [579]; 1 cut Rep. quarter [1037]; 2 illeg. [1321, 1366] [Total: 9]		Fill of lime slaking tank (310.202) directly beneath 310.082 (effectively part of the same context). Room E.	Fill of tank, thus after its decommissioning.
310.197	4	Post Sulla	2 Massalia TYPE 2 unclass. [208, 226]; 2 Rep cut ½ *as* [946, 995] [Total: 4]		Underlies 310.155; a layer of grey sandy silt, probably a floor levelling layer on the inside of the tank (310.202) in Room E.	Seals tank E, thus after its decommissioning.
310.304	4	Post Sulla	1 Massalia TYPE 2 unclass. [234] [Total: 1]		Fill of 310.303 around vessel 310.302 in Room B. (The uppermost amphora of the soakaway).	Probably equal to SU 310.299.
320.009	4	Post Sulla	1 Campanian Ebusus TYPE 8B [758] [Total: 1]		A large deposit of grey brown fine sandy silt found backfilling a plaster-lined tank (320.018) in the north-west corner of the AA (Room A).	

Context	Phasing	Date range	Coins [cat. nos.] [Totals]	Context characteristics	Other dating evidence	Notes
320.076	4	Post Sulla	2 Massalia TYPE 2 unclass. [323, 363] [Total: 2]	Dark brown grey stony fill in north section of the plaster lined tank (320.095) in Room B, underlying 320.074. Considered to be backfill of the tank.		Fill of tank, therefore decommissioning of it.
320.081	4	Post Sulla	1 Ebusus uncertain [770]; 1 illeg. [1291] [Total: 2]	Fill of plaster lined tank (320.095) in Room B, below 320.076.		Fill of tank, therefore decommissioning of it.
320.088	4	Post Sulla	6 Massalia TYPE 2 unclass. [263, 331, 344, 351, 356, 367]; 3 illeg. [1341, 1503–04] [Total: 9]	Fill of plaster lined tank (320.095) in Room B, below 320.083 (no coins), which was in turn below 320.081.		Fill of tank, therefore decommissioning of it.
320.092	4	Post Sulla	1 Ebusus import TYPE 1 or 2 [448] [Total: 1]	Possible demolition debris in Room B.		Fill of tank, therefore decommissioning of it.
510.014	4	Post Sulla	2 Massalia TYPE 2 unclass. [204, 282]; 1 Campanian Ebusus TYPE 1 [403]; 1 illeg. [1322] [Total: 4]	Of little archaeological interest as only comprises the clear of an area between a wall (510.008/009/010) and the section baulk (Room B). High risk of contamination from previous season's of excavation.		
510.004, 510.028, 510.034	4	Post Sulla	1 Katane [32]; 3 Massalia TYPE 2 unclass. [269, 298, 352]; 1 Campanian Ebusus TYPE 3B [632]; 1 Campanian Ebusus TYPE 3C [651]; 1 Campanian Ebusus TYPE 3 unclass. [711]; 2 Rep. *as* [850, 888]; 1 Rep. *semis* [897]; 14 illeg. [1211, 1221, 1367, 1387, 1391, 1403, 1431, 1450, 1477, 1487, 1489–90, 1494–95] [Total: 24]	Fill of plaster-lined tank (510.002) in south west corner of Room B; also included ironwork and gaming pieces and a large volume of ceramics. Also lots of fish bone, bird shell, fish scales, more shell and charcoal. Possibly used for water storage.		This fill is likely to be associated with the decommissioning of the tank.

Phases 4 to 5 – post Sulla to early imperial

Context	Phasing	Date range	Coins [cat. nos.] [Totals]	Other dating evidence	Context characteristics	Notes
203.165	4-5	Post Sulla to early imperial	1 probable Ebusus import TYPE 1 or 2 [459]; 1 Campanian Ebusus TYPE 1 or 2 [540]; 1 x Rep. *as* [887] [Total: 3]		Loose brown rubble soil in sidewalk test pit.	Fill of the tank in the sidewalk, so likely to be phase 5 but could be a subphase of 4 up through to the end
310.092	4-5	Post Sulla to early imperial	1 Massalia TYPE 2 unclass. [184]; 1 Rep. AR uncertain [822]; 1 Rep. cut 1/2 [1015]; 1 Aug. 15-8 BC [1103]; 1 Claud. AD 41 [1159]; 1 illeg. [1284] [Total: 6]	sigillata stamp 10 BC+; vessel glass: AD 10-60	A grey floor surface in room A of compacted occupation debris which 'proved impossible to excavate… separately from the occupation surface which underlay it'. Directly below an extremely well preserved plaster floor 310.041.	Probably phase 5 but could be phase 4 – after the decommissioning of the tanks and the construction of wall 13-17.
310.128	4-5	Post Sulla to early imperial	1 Rep. cut 1/2 [1019] [Total: 1]	sigillata stamp, prior to 27 BC+	Hard floor surface of very firm sandy silt. This deposit is in room A and is characterised by a sequence of such surfaces' the deposit seals the last of the metal working debris pits.	Probably phase 5 if it 'seals' the metalworking deposits, which can probably be assigned to phase 4.
310.155	4-5	Post Sulla to early imperial	1 illeg. [1309] [Total: 1]	vessel glass: end C1 BC+	Greyish sandy silt layer in east half of Room E, underlies 310.117.	Probably phase 4 – immediately overlies tank E, but also immediately underlies 310.116
310.164	4-5	Post Sulla to early imperial	1 illeg. [1456] [Total: 1]	vessel glass: end C1 BC+	A rubbly layer which is part of the general robbing/ rubble dumping, overlies wall 310.096 which has been dated to phase 3b (Room E).	Probably phase 4

Context	Phasing	Date range	Coins [cat. nos.] [Totals]	Other dating evidence	Context characteristics	Notes
310.169	4-5	Post Sulla to early imperial	1 Massalia TYPE 2 unclass. [326];1 probable Ebusus import TYPE 1 or 2 [467]; 1 Rep. AR, 89 BC [810]; 1 Rep. cut 1/2 [1014] [Total: 4]	vessel glass: late C1 BC+	A grey-brown layer of soil beneath 310.128. An occupation layer with evidence of metal working? The layer filled the entirety of Room A – contained large amounts of slag, especially in the SW corner. During this time the room seems to have been host to metalworking after construction of the cistern, but this seems to have lasted only a short time; the use of the space for a specific project or a failed business are offered as explanations. Room E.	Probably phase 4 – similar elevation to 310.116/106
310.200	4-5	Post Sulla to early imperial	1 Cyprus, late 2nd to 1st BC [72] [Total: 1]		Hard layer of plaster debris located in east of room A to west of wall 310.154 (which has been placed in phase 5). Possibly a N-S wall fallen over. 310.169 is earlier.	Underlies 310.169
310.243	4-5	Post Sulla to early imperial	1 Rep. as 153 BC [791]; 1 Aug. 15 BC [1059] [Total: 2]	vessel glass: end C1 BC+	Fill of cut at back end of room A, below 310.169 (which has a coin of 89 BC). Loose rubbly sandy silt, rectangular feature which was interpreted as a 'borrow pit' dug to quarry volcanic natural sand and then backfilled with demolition material from subsequent activity.	Probably phase 4
310.263	4-5	Post Sulla to early imperial	1 Rep. den. 89 BC [813] [Total: 1]		Fill of feature 310.262, a small post hole, purpose unclear (Room B).	Probably phase 4 – cut into SU 310.088
310.268	4-5	Post Sulla to early imperial	1 Campanian Ebusus TYPE 3C [650]; 1 illeg. [1448] [Total: 2]		Fill of cut 310.267, a small scruffy pit used to dispose of slag in Room A. Contained c. 5-10% slag & iron including hearth bottoms; what you would expect from a 'litter bin' for metal working debris, slag, hammerscale etc.	Probably phase 4 – likely equal to SU 310.169.

Context	Phasing	Date range	Coins [cat. nos.] [Totals]	Other dating evidence	Context characteristics	Notes
320.062	4-5	Post Sulla to early imperial	1 Massalia import TYPE 2A [105]; 1 x Rep. 1/2 as [974] [Total: 2]	vessel glass: end C1 BC+	Firm greyish brown silty sand that formed a floor layer in Room B.	After tank decommissioning, but before shrine phase 1.
320.067	4-5	Post Sulla to early imperial	1 Massalia import TYPE 2A [109]; 1 Rep. as [829]; 1 illeg. [1228] [Total: 3]		No information. Room D.	Probably phase 5
320.068	4-5	Post Sulla to early imperial	1 Massalia TYPE 2 unclass. [303] [Total: 1]		A hard surface tamped down around the top of the soakaway amphora (320.063) (Room C).	Probably phase 5, overlies SU 320.084 which is a soakaway capping in room C
320.071	4-5	Post Sulla to early imperial	1 Rep. cut 1/2 as [955] [Total: 1]		Mortary rubble overlying the mortar floor in Room D.	Probably phase 5
320.073	4-5	Post Sulla to early imperial	1 Massalia import TYPE 2A [101]; 1 Mass. TYPE 2 unclass. [249]; 2 Rep. as [870, 877]; 2 Rep. cut 1/2 as [979, 993]; 1 illeg. [1502] [Total: 7]	vessel glass: end C1 BC+	Dark loose silty sand, fill of cistern 320.072 in Room D. Underneath wall 320.017, which was put in when rooms A&B were created.	Probably phase 5
320.107	4-5?	Post Sulla to early imperial	1 Massalia TYPE 2 unclass. [239] [Total: 1]		Fill of cut 320.106 in SW corner of Room B. The cut was made into the natural.	Very uncertain.
Phases 4 to 6 – post Sulla to AD 62+						
310.079	4-6	Post Sulla to AD 62+	1 illeg. [1476] [Total: 1]		Hard packed surface on top of plaster lined tank on sidewalk.	Must be after phase 4 as it fills or is 'on top' of a tank, but not possible to be more specific.

Context	Phasing	Date range	Coins [cat. nos.] [Totals]	Other dating evidence	Context characteristics	Notes
203.080	4-6?	Post Sulla to AD 62+	1 AR *quin.* 89 BC [811] [Total: 1]	sigillata stamp AD 20+	Grey/brown fill of wall 9 construction trench. Room D.	Phasing difficult to determine; there is very little information about form where the cut for this deposit was made. Phase 6 seems most likely since it cuts through the eastern extensions of the small rooms in the southern portion of the shrine, but this is tenuous.
310.135	4-6?	Post Sulla to AD 62+	1 Massalia TYPE 2 unclass. [260] [Total: 1]		Back-fill of construction trench for wall 310.206 (Room C), which has been dated to Phase 3b.	Same problem with the phasing as 203.008.
Phase 5 – late Republic to early imperial						
320.048	5	Late Republic to early imperial	1 Campanian Ebusus TYPE 1 or 2 [588]; 1 x illeg. [1355] [Total: 2]	vessel glass: end C1 BC+	Fill of 'cut' in SE corner of AA320, south of the altar pier (Room B). Backfill, or seal of backfill, of construction cut SU60 for wall SU9.	
510.022	5	Late Republic to early imperial	1 Campanian Massalia TYPE 2C [153]; 10 Massalia TYPE 2 unclass. [243, 259, 270, 302, 315-16, 328, 346, 355, 358]; 5 illeg. [1461, 1463, 1475, 1496, 1498] [Total: 16]	vessel glass: AD 50+	Broad packed earth of sandy silt between 510.021 (in plan) and the section baulk; so still near to wall 510.008/009/010 (room B). The deposit was filled with gravel. Possibly the base of a deep cut pit.	Probably phase 5.
320.064	5?	Late Republic to early imperial	2 Tib. AD 22-23 [1125, 1127]; 1 Tib. AD 36-37 [1135] [Total: 3]	vessel glass: mid C1 AD	Dark brown soil in cut 320.069 (a small pit dated to phase 5 in Room C) near the altar.	Probably phase 5 but no information available.
Phases 5 to 6 – late Republic to AD 62+						
203.091	5-6	Late Republic to AD 62+	1 illeg. [1389] [Total: 1]		Grey/brown soil in n. test pit containing brick, pottery, charcoal and bone; possible floor surface. Shrine.	Probably phase 6.

Context	Phasing	Date range	Coins [cat. nos.] [Totals]	Other dating evidence	Context characteristics	Notes
203.134	5-6	Late Republic to AD 62+	1 illeg. [1266] [Total: 1]		Loose sand silt with inclusions in n. test pit on sidewalk.	Probably phase 6.
310.032	5-6	Late Republic to AD 62+	1 Aug. 9 BC [1068]; 1 Tib. AD 21-22 [1113]; 1 illeg. [1250] [Total: 3]	vessel glass: end C1 BC+	Loose silty sand, a levelling fill in the northern 1/3rd of the sidewalk outside the plot.	
310.033	5-6	Late Republic to AD 62+	1 Claud. AD 41 [1154] [Total: 1]	vessel glass: end C1 BC+	Same stratigraphic level as 032, also a 'levelling' fill. Sidewalk.	
310.039	5-6	Late Republic to AD 62+	1 Rep 1/2 *as* [950] [Total: 1]		Hard packed surface under 310.032. Sidewalk.	
310.043	5-6	Late Republic to AD 62+	1 Paestum, early 1st BC [16] [Total: 1]	vessel glass: mid C1 AD	A compacted floor layer in the NW corner of room B. One of a number of deposits not particularly instructive as the function of Room B.	Probably phase 5.
310.044	5-6	Late Republic to AD 62+	1 Rep 1/2 *as* [985] [Total: 1]	vessel glass: AD 25+	A loose rubbly layer in the extreme SE corner of Room C, the fill of pit SU70, cut into gritty green soil. This material is below the set stone underfloor which marked the final phase of the shrine.	Probably phase 6 – levelling layer for set stone floor

Context	Phasing	Date range	Coins [cat. nos.] [Totals]	Other dating evidence	Context characteristics	Notes
320.061	5-6	Late Republic to AD 62+	1 ?Kese [53]; 1 uncertain ?import [81]; 3 Massalia TYPE 2A [96, 125, 136, 139]; 12 Massalia TYPE 2 unclass. [185, 254, 257, 272, 278-79, 283, 329-30, 340, 365]; 1 Ebusus import TYPE 1 [396]; 1 Ebusus import TYPE 2B [417]; 1 Ebusus import TYPE 2C [428]; 1 Campanian Ebusus TYPE 2D [436]; 6 Campanian Ebusus TYPE 1 or 2 [503, 551, 563-64, 575, 590], 1 Campanian Ebusus TYPE 7 [746]; 1 Campanian Ebusus TYPE 8A [748]; 1 Campanian Ebusus TYPE 8B [761]; 1 Campanian Ebusus TYPE 9 [763]; 1 Rep *as* 147 BC (probably) [800]; 5 Rep. *as* [862-63, 868, 880, 890]; 1 Rep. *triens* [912]; 2 Rep. cut 1/2 *as* [990-91]; 3 Rep. 1/2 fraction [1004, 1012, 1020]; 1 Aug. 1/2, 16BC [1052]; 2 Aug. 7 BC [1082, 1084]; 1 Aug. 4 BC [1101]; 1 Tib. AD 21-22 [1117]; 1 Tib. AD 22-23 [1129]; 1 Claud. AD 50-54 [1181]; 15 illeg. [1210, 1231, 1267, 1318, 1377, 1406, 1410-11, 1427, 1433, 1449, 1455, 1457, 1467, 1473] [Total: 65]	vessel glass: AD 25+ (50+)	Olive brown soil full of stone, mortar & plaster inclusions, artefact rich: overlies the south part of Room B. A thick deposit of compacted levelling layers and micro-laminated floor deposits. The layer overlies the plaster-lined tank (320.095) of phase 3A (creation and occupation of Rooms A&B).	
Phase 6 – mid 1st century AD to AD 62+						
203.006	6 (shrine phase 1)	mid 1st century AD to AD 62+	1 Campanian Ebusus TYPE 1 or 2 [501] [Total: 1]		Coarse stone surface, the floor of the shrine.	Given the date of construction the coin is likely to be intrusive.

Context	Phasing	Date range	Coins [cat. nos.] [Totals]	Other dating evidence	Context characteristics	Notes
203.055	6 (shrine phase 1)	mid 1st century AD to AD 62+	1 Aug 6 BC [1090] [Total: 1]		Loose brown levelling soil under 203.006. Room D.	
310.037	6	mid 1st century AD to AD 62+	1 Claud. AD 41 [1158] [Total: 1]	vessel glass: C1 AD	A grey mortary rubble layer to the north of a wall (310.013). Possibly a levelling or wall demolition deposit. The wall was built during phase 3a, when the Rooms A & B were created (310.013 is a later re-build of 310.278).	Levelling fills below the set stone floor that seals phase 6 for the entire area of the shrine.
310.040	6	mid 1st century AD to AD 62+	1 Aug, 8-5 BC [1102]; 1 Claud. AD 41 [1153] [Total: 2]		A layer of firm brown/grey soil with strong rubble running over the whole of the back room (Room E).	
320.020	6	mid 1st century AD to AD 62+	1 probable Campanian Ebusus type 1 or 2 [478]; 1 Claud. AD 41 [1157] [Total: 2]	vessel glass: 2nd quarter of C1AD	Layer of loose demolition rubble including cocciopesto, laid down as levelling for the shrine floor (320.002).	Levelling for Shrine phase 1. The Claudius coin provides a *tpq* for the building of the shrine and the final phase of the plot.
320.026	6	mid 1st century AD to AD 62+	1 Gaius, AD 39 [1150]; 1 illeg. [1199] [Total: 2]		Part of the levelling of the final shrine phase floors. Loose mortary rubbly material scattered over the threshold between Room B and the back room (Rooms C & D). Slightly ramped.	Levelling for Shrine Phase 1.
320.039	6	mid 1st century AD to AD 62+	1 Rep cut quarter [1036] [Total: 1]		A soil fill overlying a rubbish fill of SU33, a pit cut into the natural in Rooms B & C.	Levelling for Shrine phase 1.
320.049	6?	mid 1st century AD to AD 62+	1 illeg. [1371] [Total: 1]		Main fill of rubbish pit SU51 in Room D.	Potential fill of construction cut for eastern shrine property wall (cuts one of the walls of rooms C and D).

Phase 8 - modern

| 320.005 | 8 | modern | 1 Rep. *as* 150 BC [796] [Total: 1] | | Backfill, unstratified. | |

Context	Phasing	Date range	Coins [cat. nos.] [Totals]	Other dating evidence	Context characteristics	Notes
510.002	8	modern	1 Rep. *as* [861] [Total: 1]	vessel glass: end C1 BC+	Build of the tank on the south western edge of the trench (Room B). A stone wall build which contains SUs 510.004, 510.028, 510.034.	-
510.015, 510.043	8	modern	1 Campanian Massalia TYPE 2B [149]; 3 Massalia TYPE 2 unclass. [206, 232, 317]; 2 Campanian Ebusus TYPE 1 or 2 [457, 556]; 1 Campanian Ebusus TYPE 4B [737]; 1 Campanian Ebusus TYPE 5 [743]; 1 Rep. *as* 153 BC [790]; 1 Rep. *triens* [906]; 6 illeg. [1255, 1446, 1492, 1499, 1501, 1507] [Total: 16]		Packed earth between the baulk and the SE corner tank (510.002 from which 510.004 came) (Room B). A mixed deposit of lead, iron, lots of charcoal, worked bone, teeth, plaster and pottery.	Unstratified clean. Originally thought to date the late 3rd to 2nd c. BC because of high volume of black-gloss ware, now undated.
510.020	8	modern	2 Massalia TYPE 2 unclass. [215, 240]; 1 Campanian Ebusus TYPE 1 or 2 [580]; 1 Campanian Ebusus TYPE 4B [738]; 1 Campanian Ebusus TYPE 8B (doubtful) [757] [Total: 5]		The fill of a pit, 510.021, located along the mid south wall. Also contained a very high volume of plaster, mostly painted red. Room C.	Unstratified clean.
No phasing data						
310.062	No data	?	1 Rep. *as*, 147 BC [801] Total: 1]	vessel glass: end C1 BC+	No data available on this context.	Probably a mistake in the numbering.
320.011	-	?	1 Rep. *as* cut ½ [997]; 1 Aug c15-8 BC [1104] [Total: 2]	vessel glass: end C1 BC+	A levelling layer of firm green-brown silty sand found underneath the set stone underfloor (320.002) in Room B.	
510.001	-	?	1 Campanian Ebusus TYPE 4B [739] [Total: 1]	vessel glass: AD 50+]	Cleaning of section above tank, comprising silty sand filled with stones, mortar, rubble: backfill from previous season.	unstratified
310.239	?	?	1 probable Campanian Ebusus TYPE 1 or 2 [511] [Total: 1]		Fill of possible earlier tank or tank extension; next to wall 310.046. Sidewalk.	unclear

Context	Phasing	Date range	Coins [cat. nos.] [Totals]	Other dating evidence	Context characteristics	Notes
320.040	?	?	1 illeg. [1443] [Total: 1]		Rubbish fill of 320.035 (a pit, Room B), underlying 320.039. Consistent charcoal inclusions and high concentrations of bone and pottery.	The context is unclear as it appears to only be recorded in section.
320.046	?	?	1 illeg. [1234] [Total: 1]	vessel glass: early to mid C1 AD	The final floor surface in Room B when it was still a tripartite property.	The context is unclear as it appears to only be recorded in section.

APPENDIX 2 – THE BATHHOUSE HOARD[1]

The discovery of the hoard in 1950 in Regio VIII, 5, 36, is described by Maiuri (1950, 127):

> Nel lavoro di ripulimento di uno dei pozzetti della cunetta delle acque di scarico delle terme e precisamente nel pozzetto *q*, insieme con molte tracce di ossido di ferro e di bronzo, si raccolse un gruzzolo di monete di bronzo de medio e piccolo modulo, concrezionate le più dall'ossido, le quali, dopo un accurato lavoro di distacco e di ripulimento, risultarono del numero di 90 monete.[2]

The coins are part of the collections of the Medagliere of the Museo Archeologico Nazionale di Napoli. The Medagliere numbers are provided below.

List of coins in the Bathhouse hoard

For convenience, the coins are listed in the same order as in the catalogue, and in order to ensure no confusion with the AAPP coins are given the code 'BH' before their respective catalogue number.

'FOREIGN' IMPORTS

Neapolis (Campania)

AE unit. *obv.* head of Apollo, laureate, l.; *rev.* man-headed bull stg. r., above Nike. c. 275-250 BC. *HN* 590

BH1. 14mm 1.61g   Medagliere 38

AE unit. *obv.* head of Apollo, laureate, l.; *rev.* caduceus, lyre & omphalos. c. 250-225 BC. *HN* 592

BH2. 20mm 4.40g   Medagliere 40

Katane (Sicilia)

AE unit. *obv.* jugate heads of Serapis & Isis r.; *rev.* 2 corn ears, around 'καταναιωχ'. Third to second c. BC. *SNG* Copenhagen (4-5: Sicily) 188

BH3. 13mm 1.43g   Medagliere 86

---

[1] I am grateful to Dott.ssa. Teresa Giove and Dott.ssa. Teresa Elena Cinquantaquattro for allowing me permission to publish a list of the coins in the Bathhouse hoard and photographs of the casts which Dott.ssa. Giove allowed me to make during a study visit to the Medagliere in March 2009.

[2] Also reproduced in Stannard (2005a), 122.

Massalia imports/ Campanian Massalia

Type 2A

AE unit. *obv.* Head of Apollo r.; *rev.* bull butting r., above 'ΜΑΣΣΑ', below exergual line 'ΛΙΗΤΩΝ'. c 170-100 BC. Depeyrot (1999) 39/40; Stannard (2005a) Figure 11, no. 85; Py (2006) 405-92

BH4. 13mm 1.44g	Medagliere 36	above bull '[MA]ΣΣΑ'
BH5. 12mm 1.30g	Medagliere 35	above bull 'ΜΑΣΣΑ'
BH6. 12mm 1.10g	Medagliere 32	above bull 'ΜΑΣΣ[Α]'

Campanian Massalia (local imitations)

TYPE 2C

AE unit. *obv.* Head of Apollo r.; *rev.* bull bullting r., various garbled inscriptions, above and below bull. c. 125-90 BC? Stannard (2005a) 103-07

BH7. 12mm 0.98g	Medagliere 31	above bull 'ΑΜΣΣ'
BH8. 12mm 1.10g	Medagliere 24	above bull 'ΑΜΟΣ'
BH9. 13mm 1.50g	Medagliere 27	above bull 'ΑΟΜ[Σ]'
BH10. 13mm 1.17g	Medagliere 25	above bull 'ΑΟΜΣ'
BH11. 12mm 0.96g	Medagliere 28	above bull 'ΑΟΜΣ'
BH12. 11mm 0.96g	Medagliere 29	above bull 'ΑΟΜΣ'
BH13. 13mm 1.30g	Medagliere 26	above bull ']ΜΑ', inscription below'
BH14. 13mm 0.97g	Medagliere 30	above bull 'ΑΟΣΣ'; obv. Apollo head left

TYPE 2 (unclassifiable) – Massalia imports and Campanian Massalia

AE unit. *obv.* head of Apollo r.; *rev.* bull butting r. Sometimes traces of inscriptions above or below bull, but too worn or corroded to classify. Mid. second c. BC to early first c. BC?

BH15. 13mm 1.20g	Medagliere 34
BH16. 12mm 1.21g	Medagliere 37
BH17. 11mm 1.16g	Medagliere 33

Anomalous local type

AE unit. obv. head of Mars r.; rev. toad. Late 2nd to early 1st c BC? Stannard (2005a), Group IV, 1, no. 35; Stannard & Frey-Kupper (2008) 32

BH18. 15mm 2.40g	Medagliere 41

EBUSUS & CAMPANIAN EBUSUS

BES ON BOTH OBVERSE AND REVERSE

TYPE 1 (without symbols)

AE unit. *obv.* & *rev.* full figure of Bes facing, feet together, right arm raised holding hammer, a serpent in his left, no symbol visible in field, imitative style (head poorly rendered, body full but 'loose' style; smaller and lighter in weight). Late second to early first c. BC? Stannard (2005a) Group V

BH19. 16mm 1.48g	Medagliere 45	Campanian Ebusus

TYPE 2 (with symbols)

TYPE 2A [flower]

AE unit. *obv.* & *rev.* full figure of Bes facing, feet together, right arm raised holding hammer, a serpent in his left. On one or both sides four-petalled flower to right of figure in field. c. 214-150 BC. Campo (1976) Group XVIII, 53; Campo (1994) 130-34; Stannard (2005a) Figure 4, no. 8

BH20. 16mm 1.49g   Medagliere 53   probably an import

TYPE 2B [cornucopia]

AE unit. *obv.* & *rev.* full figure of Bes facing, feet together, right arm raised holding hammer, a serpent in his left. On one or both sides cornucopia to right of figure in field. c. 214-150 BC. Campo (1976) Group XVIII, 62; Campo (1994) 147-49

BH21. 14mm 1.32g   Medagliere 44   probably an imitation
BH22. 14mm 1.11g   Medagliere 52   probably an import

TYPE 1 OR 2

Ebusus imports or probable Campanian Ebusus (local imitations); arranged by diameter.

AE unit. *obv.* & *rev.* full figure of Bes facing, feet together, right arm raised holding hammer, a serpent in his left. On one or both sides symbol in field or no symbol, but too worn or corroded to identify. Second to early first c. BC? Campo (1976), various. Stannard (2005a), Group V, various

BH23. 16mm 2.50g   Medagliere 64   probably an imitation
BH24. 15mm 4.18g   Medagliere 59   import
BH25. 15mm 2.18g   Medagliere 73   uncertain symbol in field
BH26. 15mm 2.16g   Medagliere 61   probably an imitation
BH27. 15mm 2.15g   Medagliere 68   uncertain symbol in field
BH28. 15mm 1.81g   Medagliere 46   imitation
BH29. 15mm 1.50g   Medagliere 74   probably an imitation
BH30. 11mm 1.15g   Medagliere 50   imitation

Campanian Ebusus

TYPE 3C

AE unit. *obv.* & *rev.* rudimentary figure of Bes, left arm raised on **both** obverse and reverse: slanted 'T' symbol usually visible on both obverse and reverse to left of figure in field. c. 125-89 BC. Campo (1976) 71; Stannard (2005a), group VI, 7 (e.g. no. 57)

BH31. 17mm 3.02g   Medagliere 58
BH32. 17mm 2.95g   Medagliere 66   flower symbol below raised right arm;
                                                 die-linked to BH33
BH33. 17mm 2.25g   Medagliere 67
BH34. 17mm 2.01g   Medagliere 71
BH35. 16mm 2.58g   Medagliere 55   flower symbol below raised right arm;
                                                 die-linked to BH32
BH36. 16mm 2.30g   Medagliere 76
BH37. 16mm 2.06g   Medagliere 54
BH38. 16mm 1.74g   Medagliere 65
BH39. 16mm 1.72g   Medagliere 69

BH40. 16mm 1.68g	Medagliere 63
BH41. 16mm 1.52g[b]	Medagliere 62
BH42. 15mm 2.50g	Medagliere 75
BH43. 15mm 2.32g	Medagliere 60
BH44. 15mm 1.37g	Medagliere 90
BH45. 15mm 1.32g	Medagliere 70
BH46. 14mm 2.36g	Medagliere 82
BH47. 14mm 2.19g	Medagliere 88
BH48. 14mm 2.17g	Medagliere 72
BH49. 14mm 2.05g	Medagliere 57
BH50. 14mm 2.02g	Medagliere 56
BH51. 14mm 1.70g	Medagliere 81
BH52. 14mm 1.65g	Medagliere 87
BH53. 14mm 1.62g	Medagliere 78
BH54. 14mm 1.50g	Medagliere 83
BH55. 14mm 1.22g	Medagliere 85
BH56. 14mm 1.20g	Medagliere 84
BH57. 14mm 1.02g	Medagliere 77	probably this sub-type
BH58. 13mm 1.89g	Medagliere 49	probably this sub-type
BH59. 13mm 1.70g	Medagliere 51
BH60. 13mm 1.60g	Medagliere 79
BH61. 13mm 1.24g	Medagliere 47
BH62. 13mm 1.10g	Medagliere 80
BH63. 12mm 1.66g	Medagliere 48
BH64. 12mm 1.35g	Medagliere 89

Campanian Ebusus

TYPE 7

AE unit. *obv.* figure of Bes facing, right arm leaning on staff; *rev.* toad. Late second to early first c. BC? Stannard (2005a) Group IV, 2; Frey-Kupper & Stannard (2010) Figure 2, no. 26

BH65. 11mm 1.38g   Medagliere 42

TYPE 8B

AE unit. *obv.* full figure of Bes stg., right arm raised holding hammer, serpent in left; *rev.* bust of Apollo r. Mid to late second c. BC?. Stannard (2005a) Group II, 3-4

BH66. 13mm 1.30g   Medagliere 43

ROMAN REPUBLICAN - DATED

AE uncia. *obv.* helmeted head of Roma r.; *rev.* ship prow, above 'ROMA' & corn ear. Sicily, c. 214-212 BC. *RRC* 42/4

BH67. 20mm 4.77g   Medagliere 8

AE semis. *obv.* laureate head of Saturn r., behind 'S'; *rev.* prow r., above 'S'. Rome, after 211 BC. RRC 56/3

BH68. 27mm 32.47g   Medagliere 1
BH69. 26mm 20.36g   Medagliere 9

AE triens. *obv.* helmeted head of Minerva r.; *rev.* prow r., above 'ROMA'. Rome, after 211 BC. *RRC* 56/4

BH70. 26mm 11.27g   Medagliere 4
BH71. 26mm 6.55g   Medagliere 13
BH72. 24mm 12.83g   Medagliere 5

AE triens. *obv.* head of Mercury r.; *rev.* ship prow, above 'ROMA', below 2 dots, before 'C'. Sardinia, 211 BC. *RRC* 63/4

BH73. 23mm 10.80g   Medagliere 7

AE triens. *obv.* helmeted head of Minerva r.; *rev.* ship prow, above griffin and hare's head, below 'ROMA', Rome, 169-158 BC. *RRC* 182/4

BH74. 23mm 11.15g   Medagliere 3

AE as. *obv.* laureate head of Janus; *rev.* ship prow r., above ass, below 'ROMA'. Rome, 169-158 BC. *RRC* 195/1

BH75. 29mm 9.16g   Medagliere 10

AR denarius. *obv.* Helmeted head of Minerva, r., behind 'GRAG'; *rev.* Jupiter in quadriga r., below 'L. ANTES', in exergue ;ROMA'. Rome, 136 BC. *RRC* 238/1

BH76. 18mm 2.49g[b]   Medagliere 39   plated

AE quadrans. *obv.* head of Hercules r.; *rev.* prow r., above '[?] METE'. Rome, 130 BC. *RRC* 256/4a or 4b

BH77. 16mm 4.80g   Medagliere 15

AE quadrans. *obv.* head of Hercules r.; *rev.* prow r., above 'ROMA'. Rome, 91-90 BC. *cf. RRC* 339 etc.

BH78. 16mm 3.67g   Medagliere 18
BH79. 16mm 2.82g   Medagliere 22

AE triens. *obv.* helmeted head of Minerva, r.; *rev.* prow l., above 'ROMA'. Rome, 86 BC. RRC 350B/2a-c.

BH80. 23mm 5.00g   Medagliere 14

ROMAN REPUBLICAN - UNDATED

AE as. *obv.* Janus head; *rev.* ship prow, above fly or butterfly. Rome, c. 206-144 BC

BH81. 31mm 16.47g   Medagliere 2

AE semis. *obv.* head of Saturn r.; *rev.* prow r., below 'ROMA'. Rome, c. 206-144 BC

BH82. 22mm 5.10g   Medagliere 17   imitation, reversed 'S' in front of prow
BH83. 21mm 5.32g   Medagliere 16   an imitation

AE triens. *obv.* helmeted head of Minerva, r.; *rev.* prow r., above 'ROMA'. Rome, c. 206-144 BC

BH84. 25mm 10.63g   Medagliere 6   possibly an imitation
BH85. 25mm 8.55g   Medagliere 11
BH86. 24mm 8.15g   Medagliere 12

AE quadrans. *obv.* head of Hercules r.; *rev.* prow r., above 'ROMA'. Rome, c. 150-125 BC

BH87. 18mm 3.42g   Medagliere 19
BH88. 18mm 2.58g   Medagliere 23
BH89. 17mm 2.95g   Medagliere 20
BH90. 16mm 2.83g   Medagliere 21

CONCORDANCE

PLOTS 1-3   **Workshop (249 coins)**

Room	AA.SU	Cat nos.
Workshop - rm. 1	009.000	152
Workshop - rm. 1	009.002	289, 348, 1100, 1278, 1295, 1428
Workshop - rm. 1	009.013	987
Workshop - rm. 1	018.007	1486
Workshop - rm. 1	018.011	812, 816, 1007, 1016, 1214
Workshop - rm. 1	018.012	1227
Workshop - rm. 1	018.013	319
Workshop - rm. 1	018.014	121, 332
Workshop - rm. 1	018.017	522
Workshop - rm. 1	140.000	92, 113
Workshop - rm. 1	140.002	787
Workshop - rm. 1	140.027	20, 73, 93, 111, 115, 170, 212, 216, 219, 304, 582, 1021, 1049, 1134, 1438, 1447
Workshop - rm. 1	140.038	174, 1096, 1264, 1358, 1408
Workshop - rm. 1	140.043	1380
Workshop - rm. 1	140.046	95, 169, 747, 951
Workshop - rm. 1	140.056	1412
Workshop - rm. 1	140.066	954
Workshop - rm. 1	140.069	211, 406, 413, 422, 471, 544, 552, 559, 587, 841, 1151, 1372, 1384,1441
Workshop - rm. 1	140.072	964, 1042
Workshop - rm. 1	140.073	41, 131, 222, 244, 376, 555, 659, 1202
Workshop - rm. 1	140.083	505
Workshop - rm. 1	140.084	1435
Workshop - rm. 1	140.086	205, 536
Workshop - rm. 1	140.097	1257
Workshop - rm. 1	140.099	687
Workshop - rm. 1	140.103	527
Workshop - rm. 1	140.105	1249
Workshop - rm. 1	140.143	4
Workshop - rm. 1	140.144	1382
Workshop - rm. 1	140.147	12, 44, 48, 57, 76, 130, 158, 179, 248, 273, 313, 373, 394, 402, 437, 442, 620, 625, 691, 732, 745, 784, 937, 971, 1017, 1063, 1085, 1087, 1208, 1345, 1375, 1425, 1469
Workshop - rm. 1	140.151	961
Workshop - rm. 1	140.154	157
Workshop - rm. 1	140.155	371
Workshop - rm. 1	140.162	242, 550, 703, 944, 1023, 1111, 1287-88, 1337
Workshop - rm. 1	140.163	360
Workshop - rm. 1	140.164	1415
Workshop - rm. 1	140.166	23, 228, 294, 343, 600, 616, 872, 881, 1246, 1418
Workshop - rm. 1	140.172	58, 825, 982, 1011, 1253
Workshop - rm. 1	140.174	87, 293, 628
Workshop - rm. 1	140.175	839, 1294, 1338
Workshop - rm. 1	140.177	297, 1006

Workshop - rm. 1	140.192	90
Workshop - rm. 2	321.033	145, 162, 186, 217, 256, 736, 1328, 1402, 1491
Workshop - rm. 2	321.034	398
Workshop - rm. 2	321.042	727
Workshop - rm. 2	321.052	581
Workshop - rm. 2	503.003	978
Workshop - rm. 2	503.004	1305
Workshop - rm. 2	503.009	514
Workshop - rm. 2	503.014	584
Workshop - rm. 2	503.018	83, 1030, 1032
Workshop - rm. 2	503.020	70, 1393
Workshop - rm. 2	503.035	463
Workshop - rm. 2	503.037	452
Workshop - rm. 2	503.042	1060
Workshop - rm. 2	503.045	636
Workshop - rm. 2	503.054	325, 516, 795, 1008
Workshop - rm. 2	503.064	407, 638
Workshop - rm. 2	503.067	898
Workshop - rm. 2	503.070	33
Workshop - rm. 2	503.072	755
Workshop - rm. 2	503.073	390
Workshop - rm. 2	503.086	91, 1451
Workshop - rm. 2	600.002	412, 644, 1219, 1417
Workshop - rm. 2	600.005	859
Workshop - rm. 2	600.021	662
Workshop - rm. 2	600.026	368
Workshop - rm. 2	600.027	799
Workshop - rm. 2	600.033	865, 1484
Workshop - rm. 2	600.035	201
Workshop - rm. 2	600.036	377, 751, 1313
Workshop - rm. 2	600.039	1300
Workshop - rm. 2	600.044	1258
Workshop - rm. 2	600.052	502
Workshop - rm. 4	001.003	591
Workshop – back entrance to rm. 4	025.002	84, 133, 405
Workshop - rm. 4	311.009	598, 1359
Workshop - rm. 4	311.010	43
Workshop - rm. 4	311.027	1141
Workshop - rm. 4	311.031	499, 967
Workshop - rm. 4	311.038	1156
Workshop - rm. 4	311.048	750
Workshop - rm. 4	311.050	475-76, 1462
Workshop - rm. 4	311.069	520
Workshop - rm. 4	311.076	720
Workshop - rm. 4	311.077	715
Workshop - rm. 4	311.097	492
Workshop - rm. 4	311.229	306, 1497
Workshop - rm. 4	311.234	409, 593
Workshop - rm. 4	322.002	1088, 1142
Workshop - rm. 4	322.025	1118
Workshop - rm. 4	322.037	940
Workshop - rm. 4	322.043	1271

Workshop - rm. 4	322.050	27, 1285, 1306
Workshop - rm. 4	322.055	837
Workshop - rm. 4	322.058	1420
Workshop - rm. 4	322.063	251
Workshop - rm. 4	322.067	1010
Workshop - rms. 5&3	504.004	1081
Workshop - rms. 5&3	504.007	1215
Workshop - rms. 5&3	601.017	1094
Workshop - rms. 5&3	601.033	1173
Workshop - rms. 5&3	601.036	1481

Bar of Acisculus (126 coins)

Room	AA.SU	Cat nos.
Acisculus rm. 1 - behind counter	145.002	1114
Acisculus rm. 1- behind counter	145.004	569, 629, 649, 661, 892, 1086, 1092, 1112, 1133, 1148, 1232, 1282
Acisculus rm. 1- behind counter	145.005	59, 78, 949, 1067, 1155, 1269
Acisculus rm. 1- behind counter	145.008	388
Acisculus rm. 1- behind counter	145.009	1136
Acisculus rm. 1- behind counter	145.011	830
Acisculus rm. 1- behind counter	145.013	135, 183, 187, 288, 468, 474, 675, 702, 922, 943, 1261, 1342
Acisculus rm. 1- behind counter	145.017	418
Acisculus - rm. 1	323.002	220, 285, 342, 583, 621, 699, 1002, 1353, 1474
Acisculus - rm. 1	323.007	209
Acisculus - rm. 1	323.017	311
Acisculus - rm. 1	323.030	345
Acisculus - rm. 1	323.047	178, 338, 357, 778, 1432
Acisculus - rm. 1	323.048	783
Acisculus - rm. 1	323.055	538, 690, 713, 986
Acisculus - rm. 1	323.062	1138
Acisculus - rm. 1	323.070	22
Acisculus - rm. 1	502.006	400
Acisculus - rm. 1	502.011	719
Acisculus - rm. 1	502.018	150
Acisculus - rm. 1	502.029	383
Acisculus - rm. 1	502.036	353, 455, 610, 692, 708
Acisculus - rm. 1	502.037	160
Acisculus - rm. 1	502.038	1233
Acisculus - rm. 1	502.039	102
Acisculus - rm. 1	502.042	385
Acisculus - rm. 1	502.048	122, 141, 253, 284, 334, 341, 450, 663
Acisculus - rm. 1	502.050	672, 905, 1193
Acisculus - rm. 1	502.054	1500
Acisculus - rm. 1	502.058	697
Acisculus - rm. 1	502.070	673, 676
Acisculus - rm. 2	142.001	1089

Acisculus - rm. 2	142.002	50, 1050
Acisculus - rm. 2	142.007	1332
Acisculus - rm. 2	142.008	1304
Acisculus - rm. 2	142.010	456
Acisculus - rm. 2	142.011	473, 532, 666, 776, 1222, 1272, 1303, 1347
Acisculus - rm. 2	142.014	401, 509
Acisculus - rm. 2	142.020	525
Acisculus - rm. 2	142.025	1099
Acisculus - rm. 2	142.035	274
Acisculus - rm. 2	142.037	266, 287, 449, 857, 874, 1453
Acisculus - rm. 2	142.038	308
Acisculus - rm. 2	142.043	127, 446, 885
Acisculus - rm. 2	142.045	1, 151
Acisculus - rm. 2	142.047	639
Acisculus - rm. 2	142.048	229, 445, 903, 1277
Acisculus - rm. 2	142.051	775
Acisculus - rm. 3	141.019	231
Acisculus - rm. 3	141.034	318

Bar of Phoebus (47 coins)

Room	AA.SU	Cat nos.
Phoebus - rm. 1	324.004	1009, 1044, 1485
Phoebus - rm. 1	324.006	1018
Phoebus - rm. 1	324.014	104
Phoebus - rm. 1	324.019	698
Phoebus - rm. 1	324.023	68
Phoebus - rm. 1	324.024	773, 1192
Phoebus - rm. 1	324.025	277
Phoebus - rm. 1	324.047	714
Phoebus - rm. 1	324.059	643, 1197
Phoebus - rm. 1	500.005	37, 554, 833, 959, 1239, 1343
Phoebus - rm. 1	500.013	648, 701, 706, 893
Phoebus - rm. 1	500.014	814
Phoebus - rm. 1	500.017	1407
Phoebus - rm. 1	500.018	94, 494, 652
Phoebus - rm. 1	500.030	77, 984, 1508
Phoebus - rm. 1	500.031	1109
Phoebus - rm. 1	500.038	1505-06, 1509
Phoebus - rm. 1	500.039	1144
Phoebus - rm. 1	500.041	956
Phoebus - rm. 1	500.049	148, 193
Phoebus - rm. 3	602.012	433, 444
Phoebus - rm. 3	602.078	1256
Phoebus - rm. 4	603.005	1106, 1274
Phoebus - rm. 4	603.017	1400
Phoebus - rm. 4	603.024	735
Phoebus - rm. 4	603.000	626

PLOT 4   Shrine (340 coins)

Room	AA.SU	Cat nos.
Shrine - rm. 1	203.002	1095
Shrine - rm. 1	203.006	501
Shrine - rm. 1	203.055	1090
Shrine - rm. 1	203.080	811
Shrine - rm. 1	203.091	1389
Shrine - rm. 1	203.134	1266
Shrine - rm. 1	203.165	459, 540, 887
Shrine - rm. 1	310.000	1064
Shrine - rm. 1	310.032	1068, 1113, 1250
Shrine - rm. 1	310.033	1154
Shrine - rm. 1	310.037	1158
Shrine - rm. 1	310.039	950
Shrine - rm. 1	310.040	1102, 1153
Shrine - rm. 1	310.043	16
Shrine - rm. 1	310.044	985
Shrine - rm. 1	310.062	801
Shrine - rm. 1	310.079	1476
Shrine - rm. 1	310.082	124, 126, 140, 172, 218, 223, 233, 246, 275, 384
Shrine - rm. 1	310.087	64, 117, 191-92, 196, 579, 1037, 1321, 1366
Shrine - rm. 1	310.088	271, 336
Shrine - rm. 1	310.090	100, 103, 129, 173, 296, 299, 321, 465, 603, 608, 742, 915
Shrine - rm. 1	310.092	184, 822, 1015, 1103, 1159, 1284
Shrine - rm. 1	310.106	203, 1072, 1429
Shrine - rm. 1	310.116	1128, 1178, 1205
Shrine - rm. 1	310.117	74
Shrine - rm. 1	310.128	1019
Shrine - rm. 1	310.135	260
Shrine - rm. 1	310.155	1309
Shrine - rm. 1	310.164	1456
Shrine - rm. 1	310.169	326, 467, 810, 1014
Shrine - rm. 1	310.197	208, 226, 946, 995
Shrine - rm. 1	310.200	72
Shrine - rm. 1	310.215	930
Shrine - rm. 1	310.220	24, 97, 106, 190, 194, 200, 207, 213, 221, 245, 264, 301, 548, 606, 756, 1468
Shrine - rm. 1	310.223	237
Shrine - rm. 1	310.239	511
Shrine - rm. 1	310.243	791, 1059
Shrine - rm. 1	310.263	813
Shrine - rm. 1	310.268	650, 1448
Shrine - rm. 1	310.304	234
Shrine - rm. 1	320.000	1073, 1283
Shrine - rm. 1	320.005	796
Shrine - rm. 1	320.009	758
Shrine - rm. 1	320.011	997, 1104
Shrine - rm. 1	320.020	478, 1157
Shrine - rm. 1	320.021	975
Shrine - rm. 1	320.025	512, 1091, 1098
Shrine - rm. 1	320.026	1150, 1199
Shrine - rm. 1	320.039	1036

Shrine - rm. 1	320.040	1443
Shrine - rm. 1	320.046	1234
Shrine - rm. 1	320.048	588, 1355
Shrine - rm. 1	320.049	1371
Shrine - rm. 1	320.050	1329
Shrine - rm. 1	320.061	53, 81, 96, 125, 136, 139, 185, 254, 257, 272, 278-79, 283, 329-30, 340, 365, 396, 417, 428, 436, 503, 551, 563-64, 575, 590, 746, 748, 761, 763, 800, 862-63, 868, 880, 890, 912, 990-91, 1004, 1012, 1020, 1052, 1082, 1084, 1101, 1117, 1129, 1181, 1210, 1231, 1267, 1318, 1377, 1406, 1410-11, 1427, 1433, 1449, 1455, 1457, 1467, 1473
Shrine - rm. 1	320.062	105, 974
Shrine - rm. 1	320.064	1125, 1127, 1135
Shrine - rm. 1	320.067	109, 829, 1228
Shrine - rm. 1	320.068	303
Shrine - rm. 1	320.071	955
Shrine - rm. 1	320.073	101, 249, 870, 877, 979, 993, 1502
Shrine - rm. 1	320.074	110, 322, 802, 1108, 1243, 1404, 1436, 1472
Shrine - rm. 1	320.076	323, 363
Shrine - rm. 1	320.081	770, 1291
Shrine - rm. 1	320.088	263, 331, 344, 351, 356, 367, 1341, 1503-04
Shrine - rm. 1	320.092	448
Shrine - rm. 1	320.107	239
Shrine - rm. 1	320.117	537, 596, 741, 1327, 1374
Shrine - rm. 1	510.001	739
Shrine - rm. 1	510.002	861
Shrine - rm. 1	510.004	32, 298, 352, 632, 651, 711, 850, 888, 897, 1211, 1221, 1367, 1387, 1403, 1431, 1450, 1477, 1494
Shrine - rm. 1	510.014	204, 282, 403, 1322
Shrine - rm. 1	510.015	149, 206, 232, 457, 556, 737, 743, 790, 906, 1446, 1492, 1499
Shrine - rm. 1	510.016	762
Shrine - rm. 1	510.020	215, 240, 580, 738, 757
Shrine - rm. 1	510.022	153, 243, 259, 270, 302, 315-16, 328, 346, 355, 358, 1461, 1463, 1475, 1496, 1498
Shrine - rm. 1	510.023	290, 740
Shrine - rm. 1	510.024	31, 349, 415, 1426, 1440, 1465-66
Shrine - rm. 1	510.028	1391, 1487, 1489, 1495
Shrine - rm. 1	510.034	269, 1490
Shrine - rm. 1	510.042	267
Shrine - rm. 1	510.043	317, 1255, 1501, 1507
Shrine - rm. 1	510.047	144, 605, 856, 1325, 1413, 1439
Shrine - rm. 1	510.050	1459, 1482
Shrine - rm. 1	510.051	1405
Shrine - rm. 2	204.026	827
Shrine - rm. 2	204.034	640
Shrine - rm. 2	204.036	700
Shrine - rm. 2	204.072	441
Shrine - rm. 2	204.109	40, 171, 521, 1076
Shrine - rm. 2	312.030	694, 1397
Shrine - rm. 2	312.051	496
Shrine - rm. 2	312.082	399, 1317
Shrine - rm. 2	315.012	1130
Shrine - rm. 3	604.021	655

Shrine - rm. 3   604.042   771
Shrine - rm. 3   604.044   1145

Plots 5-6   **Casa del Chirurgo (49 coins)**

Room	AA.SU	Cat nos.
Chirurgo - rms.3&4	277.036	5
Chirurgo - rms.3&4	277.038	1062
Chirurgo - rms.3&4	277.065	707
Chirurgo - rms.3&4	277.085	1132, 1166
Chirurgo - rms.3&4	277.156	774
Chirurgo – rms.3&4	606.013	1162
Chirurgo - rms.3&4	606.043	1265
Chirurgo - rm. 5	260.012	918
Chirurgo - rm. 5	260.014	772
Chirurgo - rm. 5	260.120	1270
Chirurgo - rm. 5	275.004	80
Chirurgo - rm. 5	275.016	875
Chirurgo - rm. 5	275.038	567
Chirurgo - rm. 5	275.093	1268
Chirurgo - rm. 5&8A	505.008	61
Chirurgo - rm. 6C	184.003	472
Chirurgo - rm. 6C	184.006	633
Chirurgo - rm. 6C	184.008	645
Chirurgo - rm. 6C	184.009	154, 647
Chirurgo - rm. 10	261.043	835, 901, 1445
Chirurgo - rm. 11	265.001	1167
Chirurgo - rm. 11	265.004	1083
Chirurgo - rm. 11	265.085	36, 241
Chirurgo – rm. 11	614.029	295
Chirurgo - rm. 12	610.021	79
Chirurgo - rm. 12	610.026	17
Chirurgo – rm.13	613.024	531
Chirurgo - rms. 16&20	508.015	1005
Chirurgo - rms. 16&20	508.026	854
Chirurgo - rms. 16&20	508.053	1314
Chirurgo - rms. 17&18	612.009	1152
Chirurgo - rms. 17&18	612.017	1066, 1069
Chirurgo - rms. 17&18	612.019	560
Chirurgo - rms. 17&18	612.022	426
Chirurgo - rms. 17&18	612.023	176, 423, 724
Chirurgo - rms. 17&18	612.027	114
Chirurgo - rms. 17&18	612.053	530
Chirurgo - rm. 23	262.006	1229
Chirurgo - rm. 23	262.008	635
Chirurgo - rm. 23	262.009	900
Chirurgo – rm. 11, 13 or 17&18	612, 613 or 614	1242

Chirurgo shop (10 coins)

Room	AA.SU	Cat nos.
Chirurgo shop - rm. 2	507.028	13
Chirurgo shop - rm. 2	507.032	20
Chirurgo shop - rm. 2	507.072	1169
Chirurgo shop - rm. 2	507.078	1168
Chirurgo shop - rm. 2	507.080	686
Chirurgo shop - rm. 2	607.233	1361
Chirurgo shop - rm. 2	607.236	1419
Chirurgo shop - rm. 2	607.261	337
Chirurgo shop - rm. 2	607.299	1110
Chirurgo shop - rm. 2	607.314	882

Plots 7-8

Casa delle Vestali (98 coins)

Room	AA.SU	Cat nos.
Vestali - rm. 2	036.003	671
Vestali - rm. 5	037.007	375, 429, 728, 828
Vestali - rm. 5	037.008	925
Vestali - rm. 5	037.031	541
Vestali - rm. 5	037.037	1351
Vestali - rm. 5	037.050	380
Vestali - rm. 5	039.013	834
Vestali - rm. 7	101.016	447
Vestali - rm. 7	101.018	354
Vestali - rm. 7	101.015 or 017	919
Vestali - rm. 7	128.002	1259
Vestali - rm. 7	128.035	933
Vestali - rm. 8	035.005	1308
Vestali - rm. 8	035.006	1031
Vestali - rm. 8	035.009	962
Vestali - rm. 8	086.006	681
Vestali - rm. 8	086.008	891
Vestali - rm. 8	086.010	879
Vestali - rm. 8	086.014	792
Vestali - rm. 9	068.001	1137, 1164
Vestali - rm. 9	068.007	1140
Vestali - rm. 9	085.008	99
Vestali - rm. 9	085.013	609
Vestali - rm. 9	085.017	28, 806
Vestali - rm. 9	085.020	175
Vestali - rm. 10	069.001	819
Vestali - rm. 10	069.018	15
Vestali - rm. 11/4	003.022	7
Vestali - rm. 11/4	003.090	6, 577
Vestali - rm. 12	032.003	1170
Vestali - rm. 12	032.005	18, 65, 393, 443, 634, 749, 941
Vestali - rm. 12	032.006	366
Vestali - rm. 12	032.007	8, 382
Vestali - rm. 12	032.008	435

Vestali - rm. 12	032.011	683
Vestali - rm. 12	032.017	389
Vestali - rm. 12	032.020	766
Vestali - rm. 14	040.002	1061
Vestali - rm. 14	040.036	815, 947
Vestali - rm. 15/53	010.004	1478
Vestali - rm. 15/53	011.007	886
Vestali - rm. 15/53	011.011	1378
Vestali - rm. 15/53	011.020	21
Vestali - rm. 15/53	011.024	803
Vestali - rm. 19	050.030	1028
Vestali - rm. 19	050.041	1510
Vestali - rm. 19	050.068	262
Vestali - rm. 19	050.071	156
Vestali - rm. 19	074.001	1223
Vestali - rm. 20	053.011	1146
Vestali - rm. 20	067.019	1025, 1034, 1392, 1395
Vestali - rm. 20	067.034	404
Vestali - rm. 21	033.004	1483
Vestali - rm. 21	033.005	820
Vestali - rm. 22	043.004	1077
Vestali - rm. 26	045.034B	1194
Vestali - rm. 26	045.045	519
Vestali - rm. 27	049.064	641, 1335
Vestali - rm. 27	049.081	66
Vestali - rm. 27	065.017	498, 542, 615, 678, 685, 818, 1238
Vestali - rm. 27	065.038	397, 611, 716, 1442
Vestali - rm. 27	065.041	558
Vestali - rm. 27	065.058	562
Vestali - rm. 27	065.072	1385
Vestali - rm. 32	076.001	1183
Vestali - rm. 32	076.006	960
Vestali - rm. 33	075.011	1186
Vestali - rm. 42	096.017	927
Vestali - rm. 42	096.020	1357
Vestali - rm. 44	129.015	477
Vestali – rm. 46	105.000	1230

Casa delle Vestali, bar (73 coins)

Room	AA.SU	Cat nos.
Vestali Bar - rm.1	073.001	75, 999, 1097
Vestali Bar - rm.1	073.010	314
Vestali Bar - rm.1	073.014	658
Vestali Bar - rm.1	073.023	1289, 1422
Vestali Bar - rm.1	073.026	788
Vestali Bar - rm.1	073.027	958, 1057
Vestali Bar - rm.1	073.030	939
Vestali Bar - rm.1	073.034	189
Vestali Bar - rm.1	073.039	47
Vestali Bar - rm.1	073.042	1226
Vestali Bar - rm.1	088.006	163, 210, 619, 723, 797

Vestali Bar - rm.1	088.007	712, 838, 878
Vestali Bar - rm.1	088.009	653-54, 679, 808
Vestali Bar - rm.1	088.013	292
Vestali Bar - rm.1	088.015	255
Vestali Bar - rm.1	088.019	430, 533
Vestali Bar - rm.1	088.021	188, 682, 894, 1386, 1398, 1434
Vestali Bar - rm.1	088.024	408, 586
Vestali Bar - rm.1	088.026	866, 1356
Vestali Bar - rm.1	088.028	585, 668
Vestali Bar - rm.1	088.049	9, 1299
Vestali Bar - rm.1	088.052	889
Vestali Bar - rm.1	088.053	88
Vestali Bar - rm.1	088.076	491
Vestali Bar - rm. 2	071.013	1105, 1184
Vestali Bar - rm. 2	071.018	1075, 1177, 1203
Vestali Bar - rm. 2	071.020	921, 1093, 1163
Vestali Bar - rm. 2	071.037	602, 764, 1071, 1311
Vestali Bar - rm.3	072.006	60, 952
Vestali Bar - rm.3	072.021	421
Vestali Bar - rm.3	072.025	1196
Vestali Bar - rm.3	072.026	300
Vestali Bar - rm.3	072.029	1046
Vestali Bar - rm.4	087.010	932
Vestali Bar - rm.4	087.025	1312
Vestali Bar - rm.4	125.009	680, 769
Vestali Bar - rm.4	125.023	845
Vestali Bar - rm.4	125.030	1247
Vestali Bar - rm.4	125.075	432
Vestali Bar – rms. 5&6	091.025	197

Plot 9   **Inn (355 coins)**

Room	AA.SU	Cat nos.
Inn - rm. 1	123.005	622, 848
Inn - rm. 1	123.017	642, 689, 969
Inn - rm. 1	123.019	198, 617, 684, 804, 1273
Inn - rm. 1	123.024	35, 660, 709, 976
Inn - rm. 1	123.038	646, 688, 851
Inn - rm. 1	123.042	726, 1296, 1511
Inn - rm. 1	123.054	147, 910, 1236, 1245, 1248
Inn - rm. 1	123.056	276, 335, 1244
Inn - rm. 1	123.059	909
Inn - rm. 1	123.061	281, 669
Inn - rm. 1	123.091	142, 161
Inn - rm. 1	160.002	1195
Inn - rm. 1	160.015	479, 785
Inn - rm. 1	160.042	55, 568, 920
Inn - rm. 1	160.049	798
Inn - rm. 3	161.005	1424
Inn - rm. 3	161.006	965, 1003
Inn - rm. 3	161.013	983, 1055
Inn - rm. 3	161.014	39, 49, 842, 846, 855, 869, 936, 953, 968, 980, 1039, 1058, 1452

Inn - rm. 3	161.016	752, 873, 1029
Inn - rm. 3	161.042	134
Inn - rm. 3	180.001	214, 224, 391, 523, 992
Inn - rm. 3	180.003	705, 1251
Inn - rm. 3	180.008	137, 497, 528, 1315
Inn - rm. 3	180.009	1379
Inn - rm. 3	180.010	805
Inn - rm. 3	180.014	1370
Inn - rm. 3	180.015	10, 168, 416, 431, 439, 518, 601, 734, 843, 908, 924, 1333, 1381
Inn - rm. 3	180.020	504, 1352, 1444
Inn - rm. 3	180.021	704
Inn - rm. 3	180.080	1344
Inn - rm. 3	180.116	195, 557
Inn - rm. 3	180.120	529
Inn - rm. 3	180.131	513
Inn - rm. 3	180.135	440
Inn - rm. 3	180.146	453
Inn - rm. 3	186.002	1161, 1165
Inn - rm. 3	186.003	840, 858, 1078, 1122, 1149, 1401
Inn - rm. 3	186.146	860
Inn - rm. 4	120.010	753, 824, 864, 867, 1175, 1198
Inn - rm. 4	120.015	1053
Inn - rm. 4	120.016	69, 710, 717, 844, 847, 938, 1000, 1035, 1123, 1179, 1290
Inn - rm. 4	120.018	286, 369, 565, 1206, 1414
Inn - rm. 4	120.021	1065
Inn - rm. 4	120.037	25, 495, 948, 1464
Inn - rm. 4	120.039	614, 637
Inn - rm. 4	120.044	280, 777, 789, 911, 1201
Inn - rm. 4	120.050	595, 1360
Inn - rm. 4	120.051	419, 768, 1038, 1307
Inn - rm. 4	120.063	480
Inn - rm. 4	120.066	107, 483, 1323
Inn - rm. 4	120.067	487, 1365
Inn - rm. 4	120.068	414
Inn - rm. 6	121.028	38, 54, 782
Inn - rm. 6	121.033	258, 896
Inn - rm. 6	121.051	1107
Inn - rm. 6	121.059	1172
Inn - rm. 6	121.063	1235
Inn - rm. 6	121.084	1027
Inn - rm. 6	121.091	693
Inn - rm. 8	163.024	543, 807, 1349
Inn - rm. 8	163.063	1512
Inn - rm. 9	170.001	1045
Inn - rm. 9	181.017	836
Inn - rm. 9	181.067	1217
Inn - rm. 9	181.114	883
Inn - rm. 9	181.132	657, 1460
Inn - rm. 9	181.139	82
Inn - rm. 9	181.179	486, 907, 1394
Inn - rm. 9	181 or 182	664

Inn - rm. 9	222.001	34, 718, 884, 1187, 1346
Inn - rm. 9	222.002	11, 238, 1297
Inn - rm. 9	222.003	361, 618, 767, 794, 1454
Inn - rm. 9	222.004	1013
Inn - rm. 9	222.011	574, 576, 793, 852, 876, 931
Inn - rm. 9	222.012	508, 665, 722, 957, 996, 1043, 1301
Inn - rm. 9	222.014	674
Inn - rm. 9	222.042	973
Inn - rm. 9	222.061	138
Inn - rm. 9	222.116	942
Inn - rm. 9	223.004	1124, 1180
Inn - rm. 9	223.005	1339
Inn - rm. 9	223.007	120, 307, 572, 780, 823, 989, 1396
Inn - rm. 9	223.024	1423
Inn - rm. 9	223.028	1340
Inn - rm. 9	223.029	119
Inn - rm. 9	223.031	934, 970
Inn - rm. 9	223.108	52
Inn - rm. 9	271.000	539, 1369
Inn - rm. 9	271.234	3, 165, 230, 310, 320, 347, 378, 381, 470, 566, 578, 599, 612, 623, 677, 696, 725, 733, 760, 913, 1204, 1213, 1237, 1326, 1334, 1354, 1388, 1416, 1430
Inn - rm. 9	271.235	132, 143, 159, 199, 339, 387, 451, 594, 809, 923, 935, 963, 1479
Inn - rm. 9	271.242	500, 573
Inn - rm. 9	271.243	167, 324, 379, 427, 466, 484, 488, 493, 506-07, 545, 549, 571, 589, 721, 730, 759, 832, 849, 904, 1209, 1262, 1316, 1319, 1390, 1488
Inn - rm. 9	271.250	128, 374, 464, 524, 526, 731, 902
Inn - rm. 9	271.254	597
Inn - rm. 9	271.259	62, 250, 252, 372, 592, 1493
Inn - rm. 9	271.263	247, 386
Inn - rm. 10	164.002	1182, 1276
Inn - rm. 10	164.014	547, 744
Inn - rm. 10	164.024	1160
Inn - rm. 10	164.026	1350
Inn - rm. 12	169.003	265, 1263
Inn - rm. 12	169.005	1080, 1119
Inn - rm. 12	182.011	164
Inn - rm. 12	182.013	45, 994
Inn - rm. 12	182.016	312, 462, 510
Inn - rm. 12	182.028	871, 1241
Inn - rm. 12	182.030	454, 458, 553, 630, 656, 667, 1218, 1225, 1336, 1399
Inn - rm. 12	182.032	1024
Inn - rm. 12	182.049	1421
Inn - rm. 12	182.109	350, 461, 1022
Inn - rm. 12	182.110	1216
Inn - rm. 12	182.114	235
Inn - rm. 12	182.117	561
Inn - rm. 12	182.160	1254

Inn Bar (98 coins)

Room	AA.SU	Cat nos.
Inn Bar - rm. 1b	127.006	1040
Inn Bar - rm. 1b	127.020	482, 695, 1070, 1143
Inn Bar - rm. 1b	127.032	56, 607
Inn Bar - rm. 1b	127.039	779, 1207
Inn Bar - rm. 1b	127.050	67, 1240
Inn Bar - rm. 1b	127.055	1139
Inn Bar - rm. 1b	127.057	268, 362, 485, 490, 765, 977, 1292, 1458
Inn Bar - rm. 1b	127.059	1079, 1320
Inn Bar - rm. 1b	127.076	481, 517
Inn Bar - rm. 1b	127.077	899
Inn Bar - rm. 1B	127.078	85, 236, 305, 333, 1033, 1281, 1368
Inn Bar - rm. 1b	127.079	928
Inn Bar - rm. 1b	127.082	116, 123, 146, 182, 225, 261, 309, 410, 434, 754, 1302, 1363, 1376
Inn Bar - rm. 1b	127.089	108
Inn Bar - rm. 1b	127.091	86, 89, 181, 291
Inn Bar - rm. 1b&3b	165.005	469
Inn Bar - rm. 1b&3b	165.006	1188
Inn Bar - rm. 1b&3b	165.008	998, 1121, 1147
Inn Bar - rm. 1b&3b	165.009	1116, 1171, 1176
Inn Bar - rm. 1b&3b	165.012	29, 392, 489, 929, 966, 1001, 1115, 1252, 1286, 1362, 1364
Inn Bar - rm. 1b&3b	165.017	1131
Inn Bar - rm. 1b&3b	165.082	424, 534, 546, 786, 926, 1212
Inn Bar - rm. 1b&3b	165.083	1373
Inn Bar - rm. 1b&3b	165.094	917
Inn Bar - rm. 1b&3b	165.096	1348
Inn Bar - rm. 4b	225.022	624
Inn Bar - rm. 4b	225.035	425, 981
Inn Bar - rm. 4b	225.041	826, 853
Inn Bar - rm. 5b	166.003	570, 613, 1120, 1126
Inn Bar - rm. 5b	166.006	1185
Inn Bar - rm. 5b	166.028	71
Inn Bar - rm. 5b	166.063	631
Inn Bar - rm. 5b	166.064	1279, 1437
Inn Bar - rm. 6b	126.017	1330
Inn Bar - rm. 6b	126.022	1174
Inn Bar - rm. 6b	126.028	202
Inn Bar - rm. 6b	126.052	227

Plot 10   **Casa del Triclinio (24 coins)**

Room	AA.SU	Cat nos.
Triclinio - rm. 4	221.001	26
Triclinio - rm. 4	221.010	155
Triclinio - rm. 4	221.111	914
Triclinio - rm. 4	221.259	327
Triclinio - rm. 4	272.010	670
Triclinio - rm. 4	272.017	118
Triclinio - rm. 1, clean	168.004	14
Triclinio - rm. 1, clean	168.078	1224
Triclinio - rm. 1, clean	168.100	895
Triclinio - Ramp	185.002	1331

Triclinio - Ramp	185.008	831, 1189, 1200
Triclinio - Ramp	185.013	821, 1190-91, 1220
Triclinio - ramp	270.001	1047
Triclinio - ramp	270.006	46
Triclinio - ramp	270.017	1048, 1056
Triclinio - ramp	270.018	166
Triclinio - ramp	270.032	460
Triclinio - ramp	270.036	2

Well and Fountain (11 coins)

Room	AA.SU	Cat nos.
Well/ Fntn.- south	143.004	1260
Well/ Fntn. - south	143.035	420
Well/ Fntn. - south	143.058	63
Well/ Fntn. - south	143.115	916
Well/ Fntn. - north	144.006	781
Well/ Fntn. - north	144.009	1409
Well/ Fntn. - north	144.026	1051
Well/ Fntn. - north	144.071	51, 1275
Well/ Fntn. - north	144.139	1041
Well/ Fntn. - north	146.166	627

Streets

Via Consolare (15 coins)

Room	AA.SU	Cat nos.
Via Consolare - Vestali front	104.007	1383
Via Consolare - Inn area	513.018	1480
Via Consolare - Inn area	513.029	19
Via Consolare - Inn area	513.041	112, 945
Via Consolare - outside inn	617.097	98, 177, 180, 370, 411, 1324
Via Consolare - outside inn	617.099	1293
Via Consolare - Porta Erc.	226.005	1280
Via Consolare - Porta Erc.	226.013	30
Via Consolare - Porta Erc.	509.012	535

Vicolo di Narciso (13 coins)

V. di Narciso - outside door 25	066.003	1310
V. di Narciso - back of Chirurgo	090.016	359
V. di Narciso - back of Chirurgo	110.017	1298
V. di Narciso - back of Chirurgo	110.020	438
V. di Narciso - n. end	133.008	817, 1470
V. di Narciso - nr. well & fntn.	205.000	1471
V. di Narciso - nr. well & fntn.	205.011	395, 604, 988
V. di Narciso - back of workshop	316.006	42
V. di Narciso - back of Chirurgo	512.051	515
V. di Narciso - by city wall	605.004	972

Unstratified (4 coins)

Room	AA.SU	Cat nos.
n/a	000.000	364, 729, 1026, 1054

PLATES

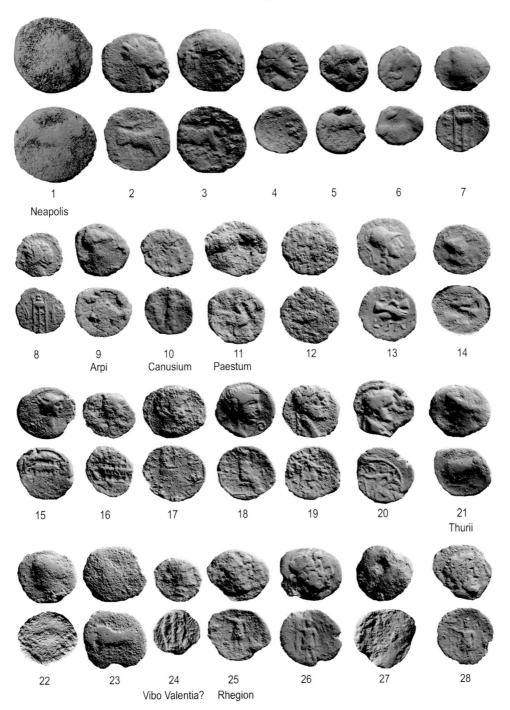

1
Neapolis

2

3

4

5

6

7

8

9
Arpi

10
Canusium

11
Paestum

12

13

14

15

16

17

18

19

20

21
Thurii

22

23

24
Vibo Valentia?

25
Rhegion

26

27

28

PLATE 1: imports, Italy (excl. Rome) [1-28]

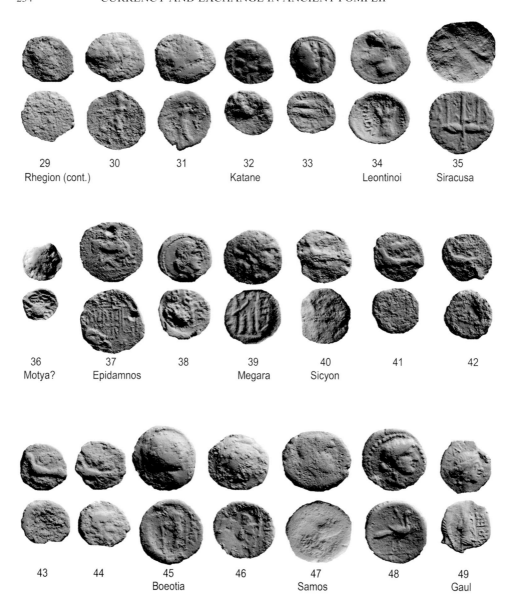

29 30 31 32 33 34 35
Rhegion (cont.) Katane Leontinoi Siracusa

36 37 38 39 40 41 42
Motya? Epidamnos Megara Sicyon

43 44 45 46 47 48 49
Boeotia Samos Gaul

PLATE 2: imports from Italy (cont.) & from outside Italy [29-49]

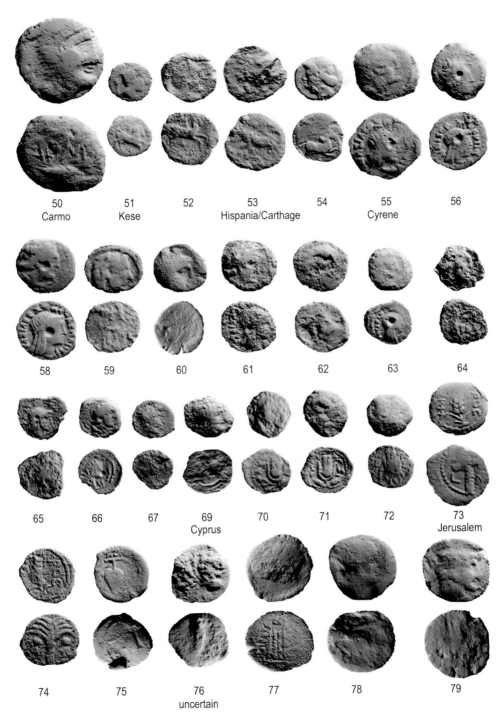

| 50 | 51 | 52 | 53 | 54 | 55 | 56 |
| Carmo | Kese | | Hispania/Carthage | | Cyrene | |

| 58 | 59 | 60 | 61 | 62 | 63 | 64 |

| 65 | 66 | 67 | 69 | 70 | 71 | 72 | 73 |
| | | | Cyprus | | | | Jerusalem |

| 74 | 75 | 76 | 77 | 78 | 79 |
| | | uncertain | | | |

PLATE 3: imports from outside Italy (cont.) to uncertain [50-79]

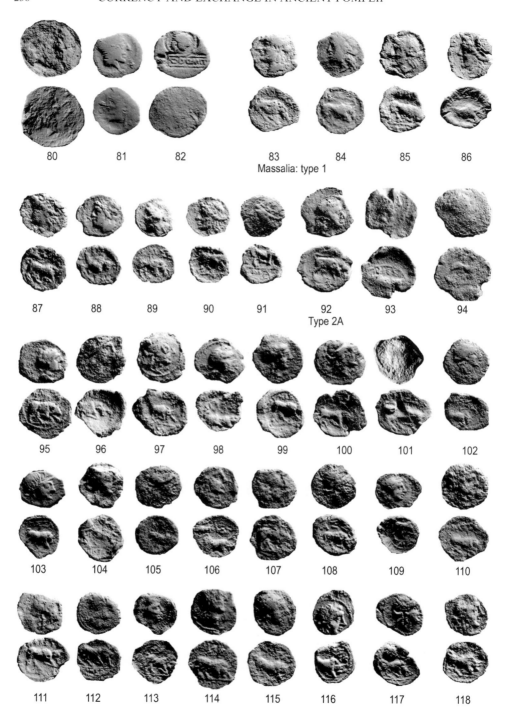

80 81 82 83 84 85 86

Massalia: type 1

87 88 89 90 91 92 93 94

Type 2A

95 96 97 98 99 100 101 102

103 104 105 106 107 108 109 110

111 112 113 114 115 116 117 118

PLATE 4: uncertain (cont.) to Massalia & Campanian Massalia [80-118]

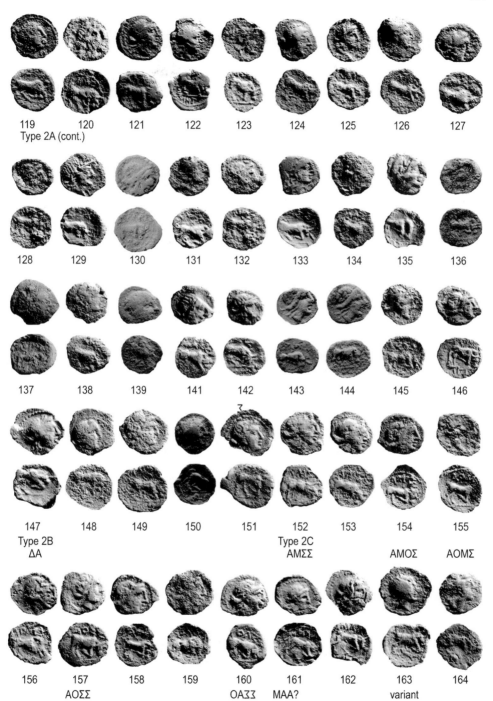

119 120 121 122 123 124 125 126 127
Type 2A (cont.)

128 129 130 131 132 133 134 135 136

137 138 139 141 142 143 144 145 146

147 148 149 150 151 152 153 154 155
Type 2B Type 2C
ΔΑ ΑΜΣΣ ΑΜΟΣ ΑΟΜΣ

156 157 158 159 160 161 162 163 164
ΑΟΣΣ ΟΑჳჳ ΜΑΑ? variant

PLATE 5: Massalia & Campanian Massalia (cont.) [119-164]

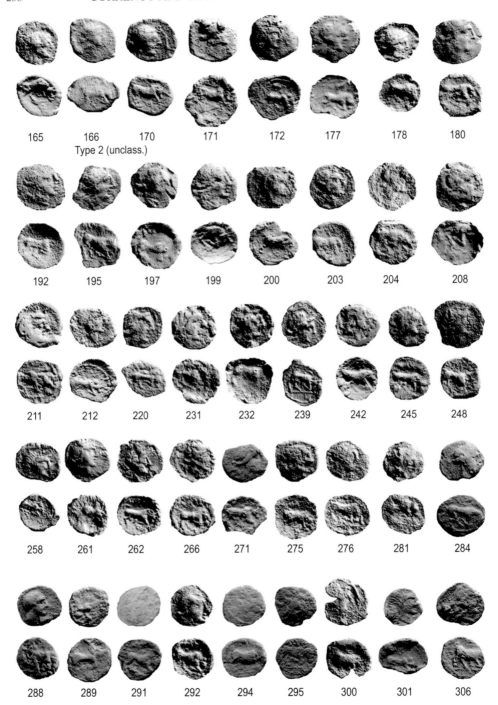

165   166   170   171   172   177   178   180

Type 2 (unclass.)

192   195   197   199   200   203   204   208

211   212   220   231   232   239   242   245   248

258   261   262   266   271   275   276   281   284

288   289   291   292   294   295   300   301   306

PLATE 6: Massalia & Campanian Massalia (cont.) [165-306]

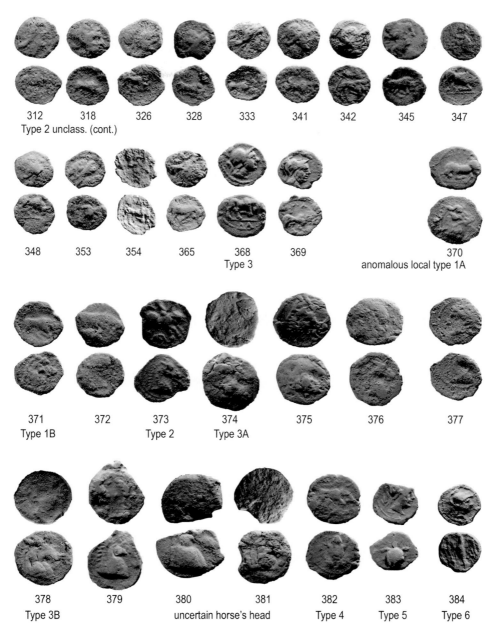

312 318 326 328 333 341 342 345 347
Type 2 unclass. (cont.)

348 353 354 365 368 369 370
Type 3 anomalous local type 1A

371 372 373 374 375 376 377
Type 1B Type 2 Type 3A

378 379 380 381 382 383 384
Type 3B uncertain horse's head Type 4 Type 5 Type 6

PLATE 7: Massalia & Campanian Massalia (cont.) to anomalous local types [312-384]

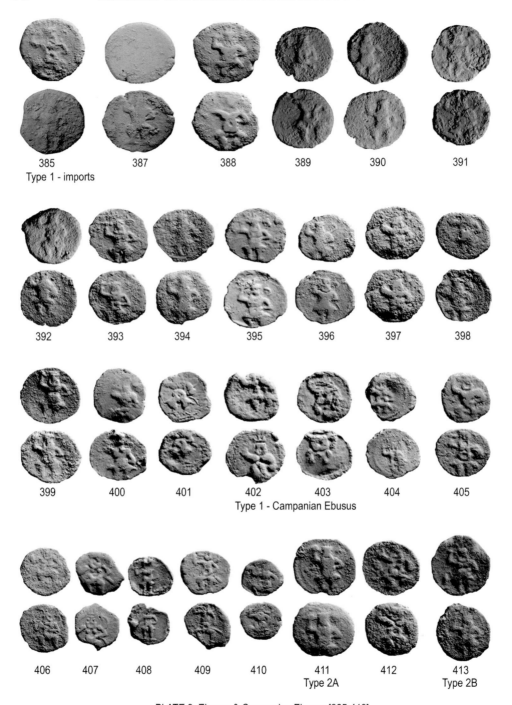

385   387   388   389   390   391

Type 1 - imports

392   393   394   395   396   397   398

399   400   401   402   403   404   405

Type 1 - Campanian Ebusus

406   407   408   409   410   411   412   413

Type 2A   Type 2B

PLATE 8: Ebusus & Campanian Ebusus [385-413]

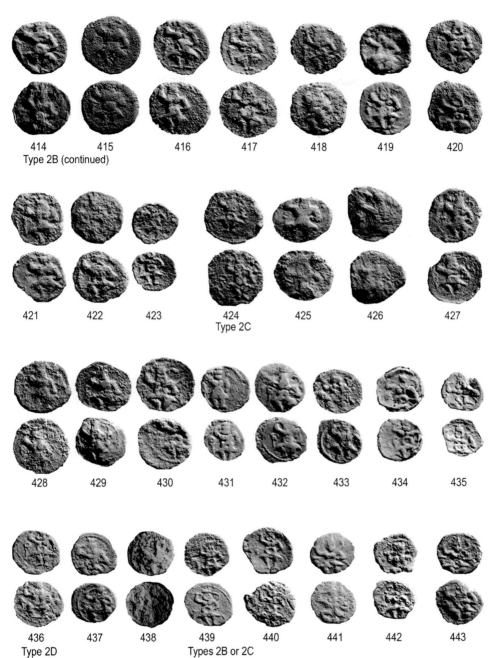

414   415   416   417   418   419   420
Type 2B (continued)

421   422   423   424   425   426   427
                                Type 2C

428   429   430   431   432   433   434   435

436   437   438   439   440   441   442   443
Type 2D   Types 2B or 2C

PLATE 9: Ebusus & Campanian Ebusus (cont.) [414-443]

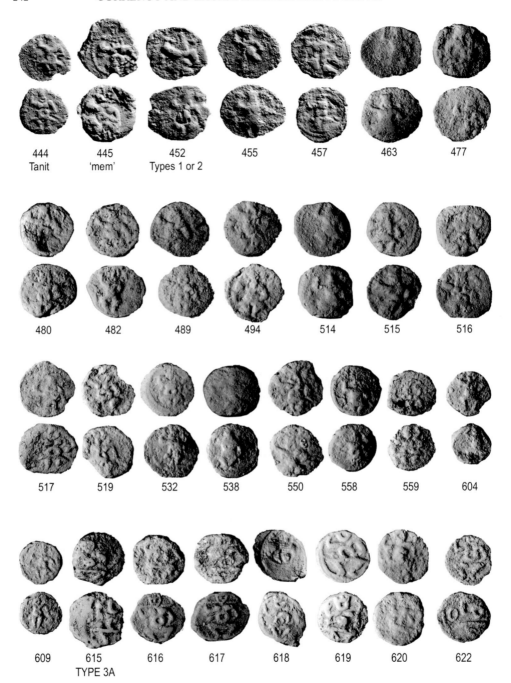

| 444 | 445 | 452 | 455 | 457 | 463 | 477 |
| Tanit | 'mem' | Types 1 or 2 | | | | |

| 480 | 482 | 489 | 494 | 514 | 515 | 516 |

| 517 | 519 | 532 | 538 | 550 | 558 | 559 | 604 |

| 609 | 615 | 616 | 617 | 618 | 619 | 620 | 622 |
| | TYPE 3A | | | | | | |

PLATE 10: Ebusus & Campanian Ebusus (cont.) [444-622]

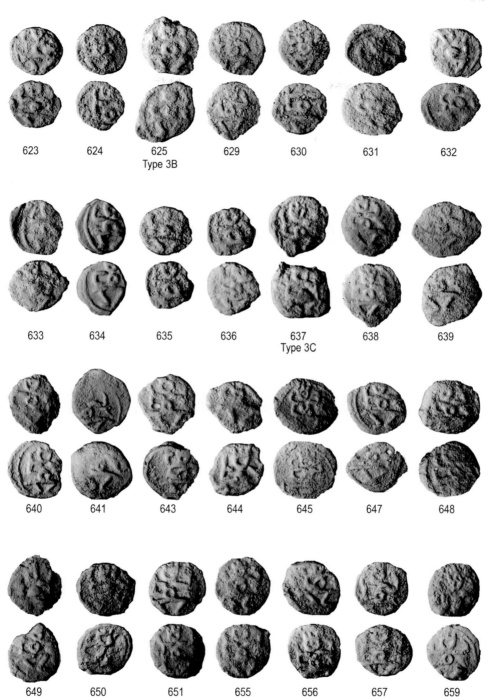

623   624   625   629   630   631   632
                     Type 3B

633   634   635   636   637   638   639
                                        Type 3C

640   641   643   644   645   647   648

649   650   651   655   656   657   659

PLATE 11: Campanian Ebusus (cont.) [623-659]

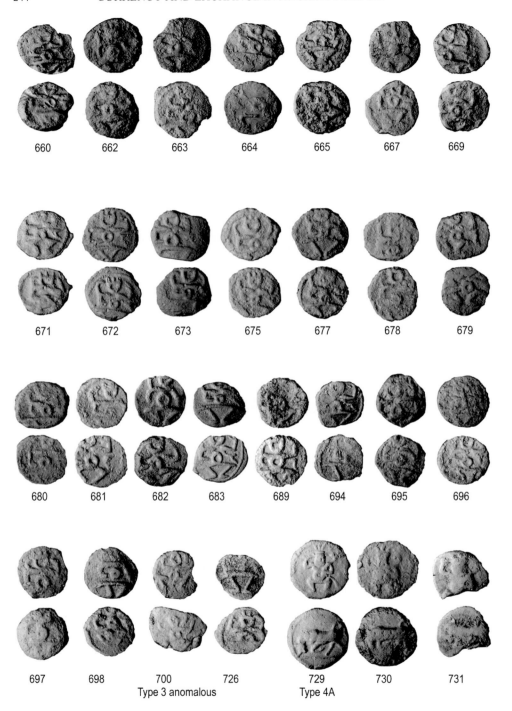

660 662 663 664 665 667 669

671 672 673 675 677 678 679

680 681 682 683 689 694 695 696

697 698 700 726 729 730 731
Type 3 anomalous Type 4A

PLATE 12: Ebusus & Campanian Ebusus (cont.) [660-731]

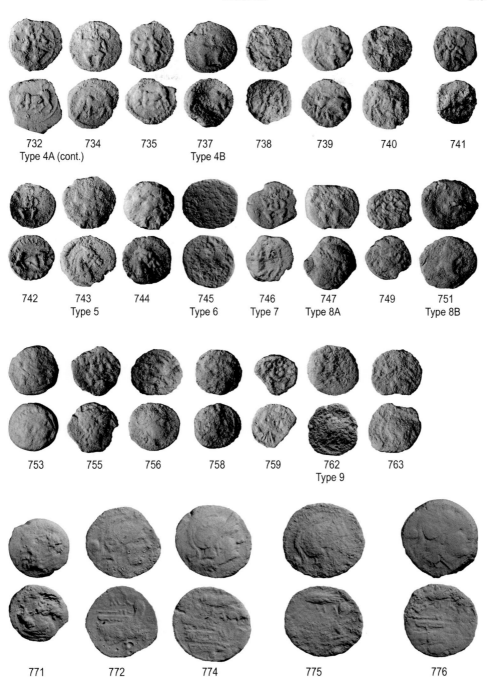

732   734   735   737   738   739   740   741
Type 4A (cont.)   Type 4B

742   743   744   745   746   747   749   751
Type 5   Type 6   Type 7   Type 8A   Type 8B

753   755   756   758   759   762   763
Type 9

771   772   774   775   776

PLATE 13: Ebusus & Campanian Ebusus (cont.) to Roman Republic [732-776]

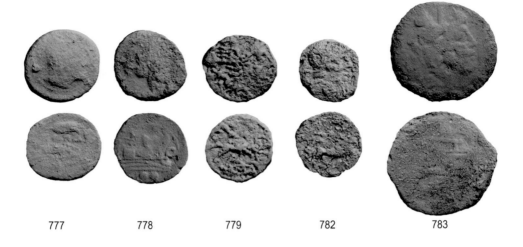

777 778 779 782 783

784 785 786

PLATE 14: Roman Republic (cont.) [777-786]

787   788   789

790   791   792

PLATE 15: Roman Republic (cont.) [787-792]

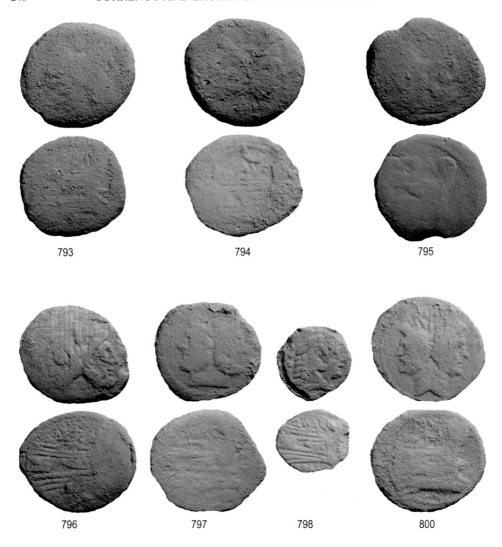

PLATE 16: Roman Republic (cont.) [793-800]

801 802 803 804

805 806 807 808 809 810 811

812 813 814 815 816 817 818

PLATE 17: Roman Republic (cont.) [801-818]

822   834   839   841

842   848   849

PLATE 18: Roman Republic (cont.) [822-849]

857   863   871

874   875   876

PLATE 19: Roman Republic (cont.) [857-876]

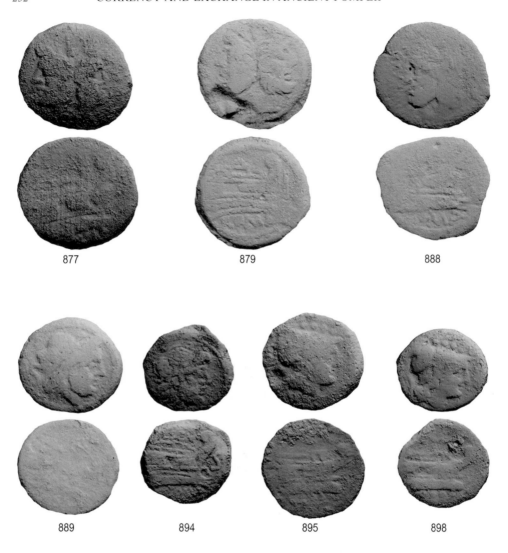

877

879

888

889

894

895

898

PLATE 20: Roman Republic (cont.) [877-898]

899   900   902   908

909   910   911   920   921

925   926   927   928   929   930

931   932

PLATE 21: Roman Republic (cont.) [899-932]

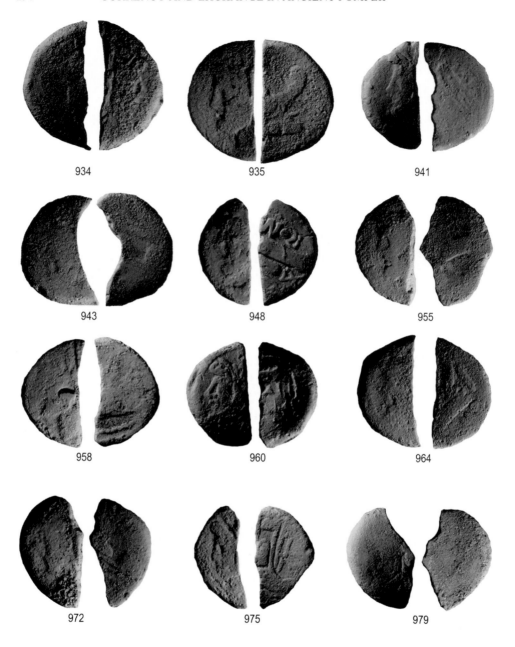

PLATE 22: Roman Republic (cont.) [934-979]

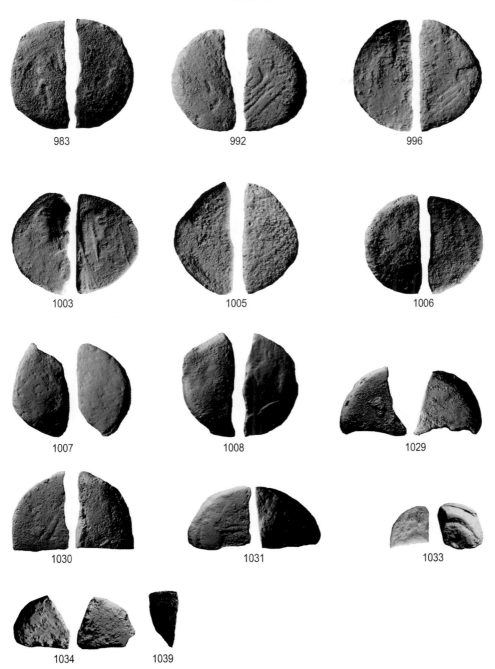

983 992 996

1003 1005 1006

1007 1008 1029

1030 1031 1033

1034 1039

PLATE 23: Roman Republic (cont.) [983-1039]

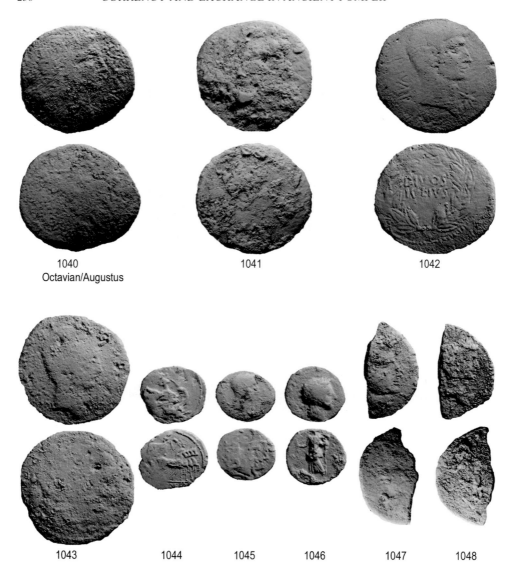

1040
Octavian/Augustus

1041

1042

1043

1044

1045

1046

1047

1048

PLATE 24: Roman imperial [1040-1048]

1049   1050   1051   1052

Octavian/Augustus (cont.)

1053   1054   1055   1056

PLATE 25: Roman imperial (cont.) [1049-1056]

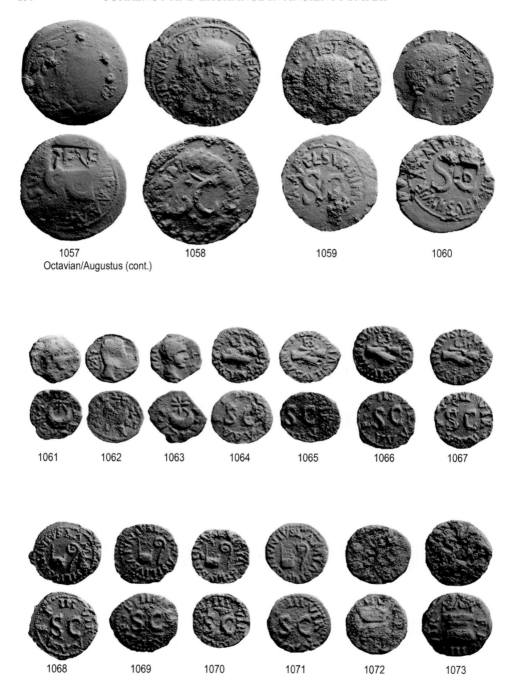

1057   1058   1059   1060
Octavian/Augustus (cont.)

1061   1062   1063   1064   1065   1066   1067

1068   1069   1070   1071   1072   1073

PLATE 26: Roman imperial (cont.) [1057-1073]

1074   1075   1076   1077   1078   1079

Octavian/Augustus (cont.)

1080   1081   1082   1083

1084   1085   1086   1087

PLATE 27: Roman imperial (cont.) [1074-1087]

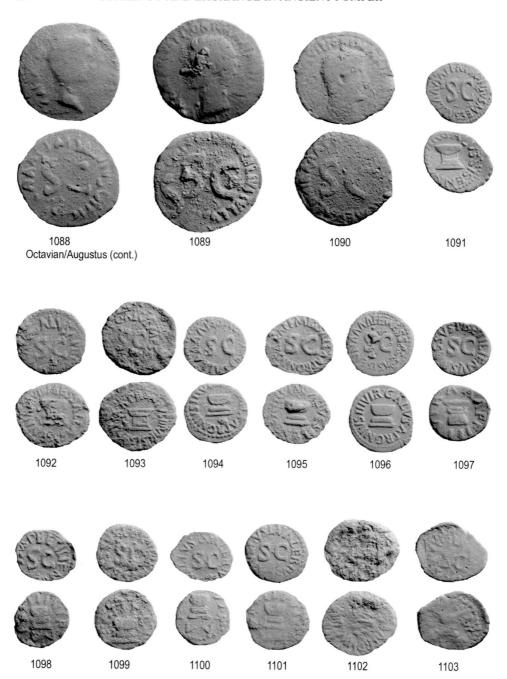

1088   1089   1090   1091

Octavian/Augustus (cont.)

1092   1093   1094   1095   1096   1097

1098   1099   1100   1101   1102   1103

PLATE 28: Roman imperial (cont.) [1088-1103]

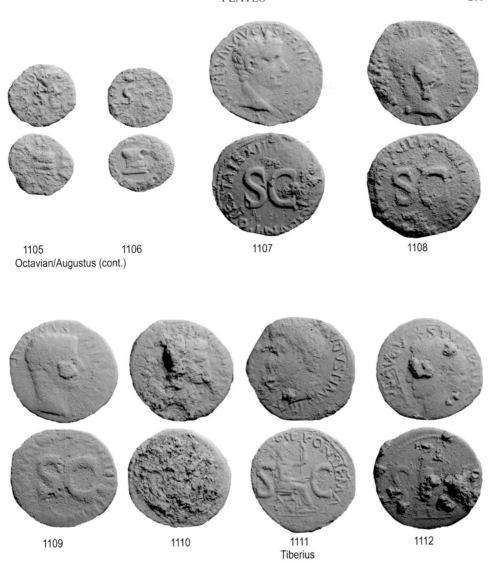

1105   1106   1107   1108
Octavian/Augustus (cont.)

1109   1110   1111   1112
                                   Tiberius

PLATE 29: Roman imperial (cont.) [1105-1112]

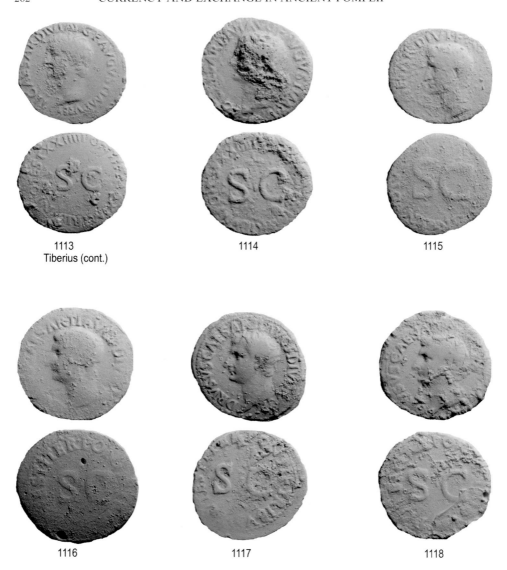

1113

Tiberius (cont.)

1114

1115

1116

1117

1118

PLATE 30: Roman imperial (cont.) [1113-1118]

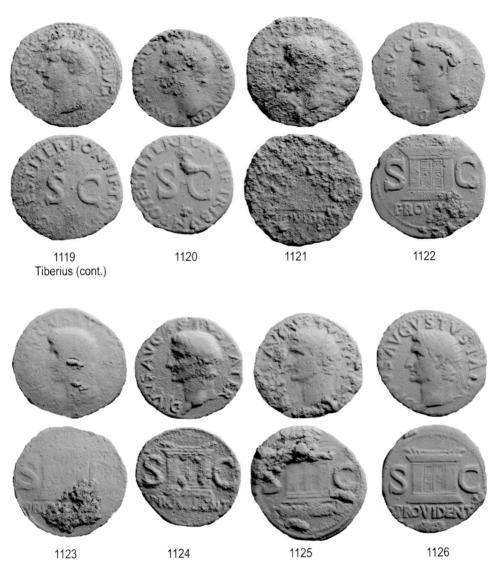

1119   1120   1121   1122

Tiberius (cont.)

1123   1124   1125   1126

PLATE 31: Roman imperial (cont.) [1119-1126]

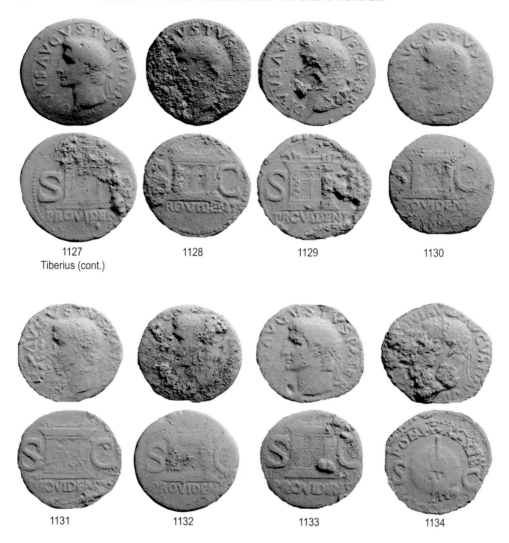

1127
Tiberius (cont.)

1128

1129

1130

1131

1132

1133

1134

PLATE 32: Roman imperial (cont.) [1127-1134]

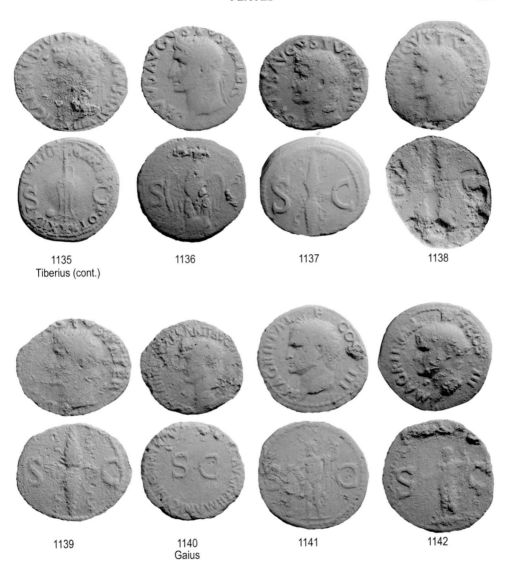

1135
Tiberius (cont.)

1136

1137

1138

1139

1140
Gaius

1141

1142

PLATE 33: Roman imperial (cont.) [1135-1142]

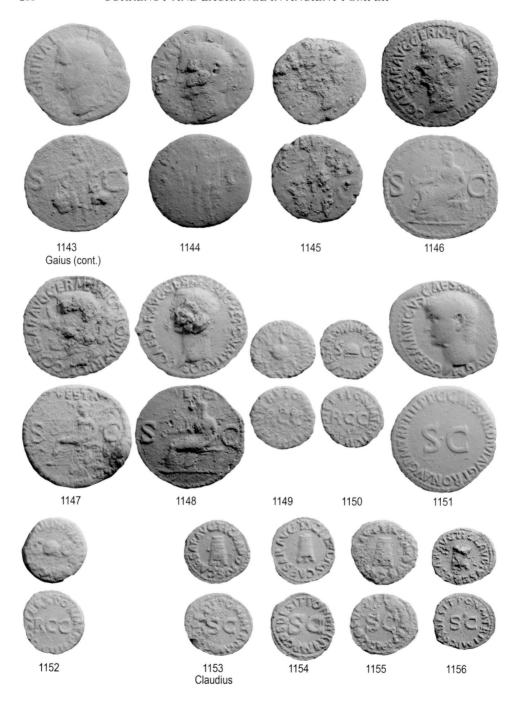

1143
Gaius (cont.)

1144

1145

1146

1147

1148

1149

1150

1151

1152

1153
Claudius

1154

1155

1156

PLATE 34: Roman imperial (cont.) [1143-1156]

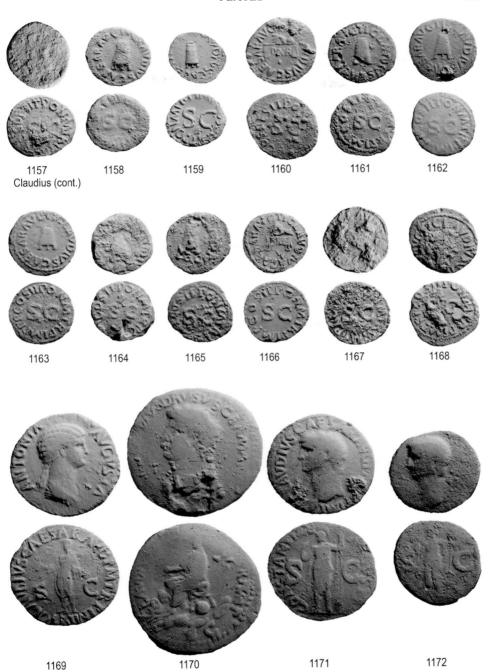

1157   1158   1159   1160   1161   1162
Claudius (cont.)

1163   1164   1165   1166   1167   1168

1169   1170   1171   1172

PLATE 35: Roman imperial (cont.) [1157-1172]

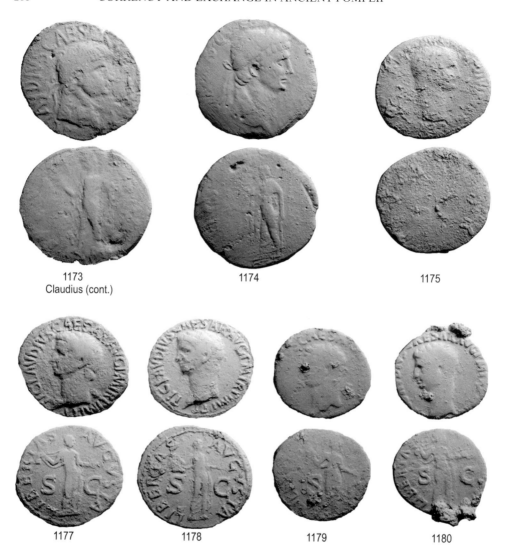

1173
Claudius (cont.)

1174

1175

1177

1178

1179

1180

PLATE 36: Roman imperial [1173-1180]

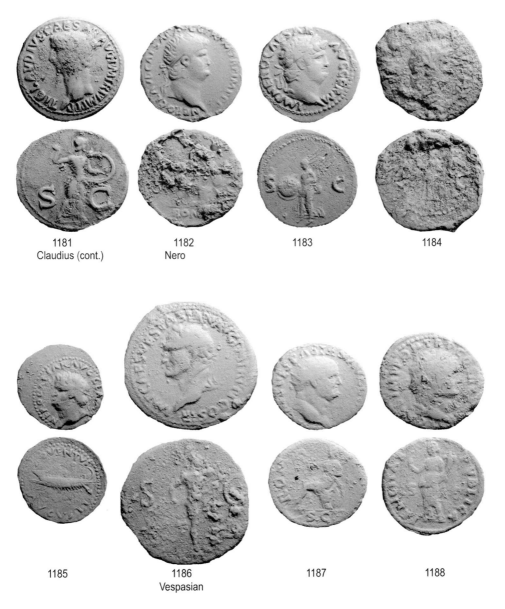

1181
Claudius (cont.)

1182
Nero

1183

1184

1185

1186
Vespasian

1187

1188

PLATE 37: Roman imperial (cont.) [1181-1188]

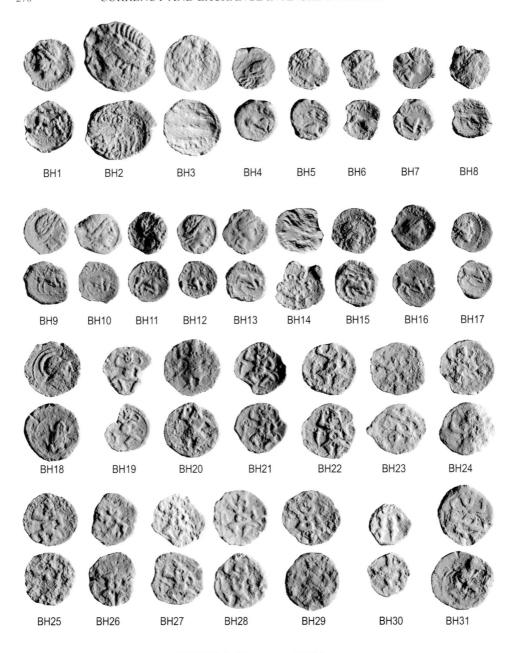

PLATE 38: Bathhouse hoard [1-31]

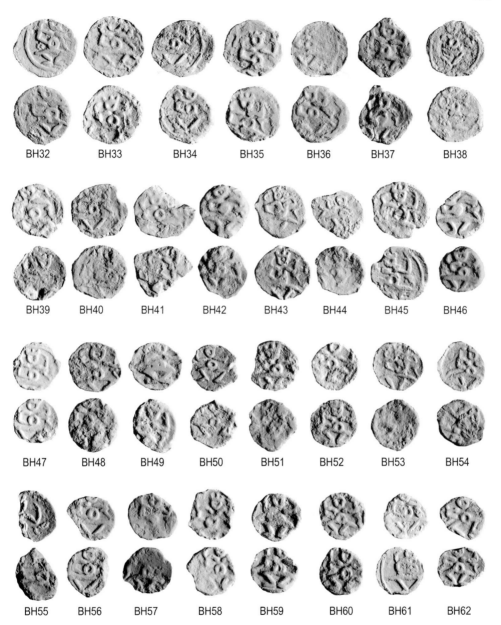

BH32   BH33   BH34   BH35   BH36   BH37   BH38

BH39   BH40   BH41   BH42   BH43   BH44   BH45   BH46

BH47   BH48   BH49   BH50   BH51   BH52   BH53   BH54

BH55   BH56   BH57   BH58   BH59   BH60   BH61   BH62

PLATE 39: Bathhouse hoard (cont.) [32-62]

PLATE 40: Bathhouse hoard [63-77]

BH78 BH79 BH80 BH81 BH82

BH83 BH84 BH85 BH86 BH87

BH88 BH89 BH90

PLATE 41: Bathhouse hoard [78-90]

INDEX

Note: catalogue numbers are preceded by 'c.', Bathhouse hoard coins (Appendix 2) by 'BH' and are presented in italics.